DIALOGUE BETWEEN ISLAM AND CHRISTIANITY

Discussion of Religious
Dogma between Intellectuals
from the Two Religions

Translated by
The Institute of Islamic and
Arabic Sciences in America (IIASA)

This book is translated and published by
Institute of Islamic and Arabic Sciences in America (IIASA)
affiliated with
Imam Muhammad Ibn Saud Islamic University
Kingdom of Saudi Arabia

Copyright © 1999 by IIASA
8500 Hilltop Road, Fairfax, Virginia 22031
United States of America
Tel: (703)641-4890 Fax: (703)641-4899

All rights reserved. No part of this publication may be printed or reproduced, stored in a retrieval, electronic, or mechanical system, or utilized in any means, now known or hereafter invented, including photocopying and recording, without the prior permission of IIASA.

Library of Congress Cataloging-in-Publication Data

Dialogue between Islam and Christianity : discussion of religious dogma between intellectuals from the two religions / translated by the Institute of Islamic and Arabic Sciences in America.
   p. cm.
   Includes bibliographical references and index.
   ISBN 1-56923-036-6
   1. Islam—Relations—Christianity. 2. Christianity and other religions—Islam. I. Institute of Islamic & Arabic Sciences in America.

BP172 .D537 2000
297.2'83—dc21

99-462198

ISBN 1-56923-036-6

Topics:
1. Contradictions in the Gospels
2. The Crucifixion
3. The Resurrection
4. Salvation
5. Paul
6. Jesus as prophet
7. Monotheism
8. Old Testament prophecies
9. The Church councils
10. The Qur'an

Muslim-Christian Dialogue

Table of Contents

PREFACE viii
NOTE FROM THE PUBLISHER 1
FOREWORD 3
   WHY THIS CONFERENCE WAS HELD 8
   DANGER OF THE INTELLECTUAL ASSAULT [ON MUSLIMS] 9
      A Convert's Advice to His People 9
      Returning to the Truth: an Excellent Virtue 10

OPENING STATEMENTS 17
   SHAYKH TAHIR AHMAD TALIBI RELIGIOUS ATTACHÉ, EMBASSY OF SAUDI ARABIA, KHARTOUM 17
   SHAYKH IWADULLAH SALIH PRESIDENT, ORGANIZATION OF THE REVIVAL OF ISLAMIC ACTIVITY IN THE SUDAN 18

PRELIMINARY REMARKS 21
   DR. MUHAMMAD JAMIL GHAZI 21
   STATEMENT OF THE CLERGY: MESSRS. JAMES BAKHEET AND TEEKHA RAMADAN 22
      Mr. James Bakheet: 22
      Mr. Teekha Ramadan: 22

QUESTIONS FORWARDED BY THE CHRISTIAN SIDE 25
      Mr. James Bakheet: 25

FINAL INTRODUCTORY WORD 29
   DR. MUHAMMAD JAMIL GHAZI 29

THE FIRST SESSION 33
   PROF. AHMAD ABDUL-WAHHAB 33
   DISCUSSION OF THE BOOKS OF THE NEW TESTAMENT 34
      The Legitimacy of the Gospels 34
      I. The Gospel of Mark 36
      The Gospel of Mark: Its Problems 37
      II. The Gospel of Matthew 38
      The Gospel of Matthew: Its Problems 38
      III. The Gospel of Luke 39
      A Scholar's Statement Regarding the Writings of Luke: 41
      The Gospel of Luke: Its Problems 41
      IV. The Gospel of John 42
      The Gospel of John: Its Problems 43
   A LOOK AT THE SCRIPTURES OF THE NEW TESTAMENT 48

    1. The Problem of Numerous Discrepancies 48
    Differences between Matthew and Luke Concerning Jesus'
    Genealogy 49
    Discrepancy in the Gospels Regarding the Names
    of the Apostles 52
    Discrepancies between Matthew and Mark Regarding the
    Story of the Purging of the Temple and the Fig Tree 53
    Dr. Ghazi: 55
    2. The Problem of Unfulfilled Prophecies 55
    A. Prophecy: The World Will End in the First Century C.E. 56
    B. Prophecy: Judas, the Traitor, Will Join
    Jesus in the Hereafter 57
    C. Prophecy: Jesus' Body Will Be Buried in the Earth for
    Three Days and Three Nights: 58
  THE CRUCIFIXION 60
  THE ISSUE OF THE CRUCIFIXION 62
    1. Rubbing Jesus' Body with Scent 62
    2. Preparations for the Last Supper 63
    3. The Time of the Last Supper and Its Effect on the Issue of the
    Crucifixion: 65
    4. The Last Supper and the Disciple Who Betrayed Jesus 66

SECOND SESSION 69
    Dr. Muhammad Jamil Ghazi 69
    Mr. James Bakheet 70
    Shaykh Ahmad Talibi, the Saudi Religious Attaché 71
    Dr. Muhammad Jamil Ghazi 71
    Mr. Ibrahim Khalil Ahmad 75
    Dr. Muhammad Jamil Ghazi 80
    Mr. Khalil: 80
    Dr. Ghazi: 81
    Mr. Khalil: 81
    Dr. Ghazi: 81
    Brig. General Ahmad 82
    5. Jesus' Sufferings 82
    6. The Arrest 85
    Where Is the Doubting of the Disciples? 87
    7. The Trial 90
    8. The Crucifixion 94
    Dr. Muhammad Jamil Ghazi: 100
    Some Comments on the Events of the Crucifixion 103
    The End of Judas Iscariot 103
    Jesus' Prophecies about His Suffering 106
    Jesus' Prophecy about his Deliverance 109
  TRUE SALVATION HAS NOTHING TO DO WITH THE CRUCIFIXION
  112

AFTERWORD BY DR. MUHAMMAD JAMIL GHAZI.................... 115
   The Conclusion on the Issue of Crucifixion: 115

THE THIRD SESSION 121
THE RESURRECTION AND THE APPEARANCE 121
THE RESURRECTION... 122
   The Women's Visit to the Tomb 123
   Discrepancies among the Gospels Regarding the Stories of the Visit... 126
THE APPEARANCE 130
   The Gospel of Mark Says Nothing.. 131
   The Narrations of the Other Gospels 132
   Some Observations about the Narrations of the Gospels......... 135
   The Disciples' Misgivings Concerning the Narratives of Jesus' Resurrection and His Subsequent Appearance 136
   Mr. Ibrahim Khalil Ahmad: 140
PAUL... 143
   Dr. Muhammad Jamil Ghazi: 150
   Mr. Ibrahim Khalil Ahmad: 151
   Brigadier General Ahmad Abdul-Wahhab 155
THE RELIGION OF JESUS WAS ISLAMIC MONOTHEISM 156
A WORD TO THE MISSIONARIES... 158

THE FOURTH SESSION 165
INTRODUCTION... 165
   Dr. Muhammad Jamil Ghazi 165
   Mr. Ibrahim Khalil Ahmad 170
THE BIRTH OF JESUS 175
   The "Son of God" 178
THE MESSIAH, A PROPHET OF ALLAH 180
   Bringing the Dead to Life.. 181
THE MESSIAH, A MESSENGER OF ALLAH................................. 184
   Fatherhood and Sonhood in the New Testament....................... 185
   Jesus Preached Monotheism 186
THE HOLY SPIRIT 189
THE MIRACLES OF JESUS 191
JESUS FACING THE PRIESTS 192
FORGIVENESS OF SINS 193
JESUS' ATTITUDE TOWARDS THE SABBATH............................ 196
   Dr. Muhammad Jamil Ghazi 199
   Brig. Gen. Ahmad Abdul-Wahhab 208

THE FIFTH SESSION 211
   Dr. Muhammad Jamil Ghazi 211
   Mr. Ibrahim Khalil Ahmad 213
OLD TESTAMENT PREDICTIONS OF THE FINAL MESSENGER .. 214
   The Mountains of Paran.. 216

Some of Paul's Alterations	219
Habakkuk's Prophecy	220
The Prophecy of David	221
Prophet Daniel's Explication of Nebuchadnezzar's Dream	223
THE PROPHECY OF ISAIAH	225
Madinah	226
Makkah	226
Brig. Gen. Ahmad Abdul-Wahhab	227
Mr. Ibrahim Khalil Ahmad	235
JESUS' PROPHECIES	235
The Helper	235
The Spirit of Truth	236
THE ECUMENICAL COUNCILS	240
AFTERWORD	241
Dr. Muhammad Jamil Ghazi	241
Professor Ibrahim Khalil Ahmad	245
DIVISIONS WITHIN THE CHURCH	246
The Council of Constantinople	246
The Deification of Mary	247
Birth of the Egyptian Orthodox Church	249
Allah Forgives Sins	250
Birth of the Maronite Church	251
Sanctification of Images	252
Birth of the Roman (Greek) Orthodox Church	252
The Pope and the Right of Forgiveness	253
Paul and His Bodily Sins	253
The Appearance of Martin Luther	254
THE SIXTH SESSION	**257**
Dr. Muhammad Jamil Ghazi	257
CHRIST AS A GOD	259
The Crucifixion and Vicarious Atonement	267
Racial Discrimination	270
THE TRUTH ABOUT THE BIBLE AND ITS AUTHENTICITY	274
ALLAH'S ATTRIBUTES IN THE BIBLE	276
DISTORTED AND FOOLISH IMAGES OF ALLAH'S PROPHETS AND MESSENGERS IN THE OLD TESTAMENT	279
Abraham	279
Lot	280
How They Address Allah	281
ISLAM	281
Islam Was the Religion of All the Prophets	283
Noah Brought the Message of Islam	283
Abraham Brought the Message of Islam	284
Jacob Brought the Message of Islam	285
Lot Brought the Message of Islam	285

Joseph Brought the Message of Islam 285
Moses Brought the Message of Islam 285
*Islam Was the Religion of the People of Moses (i.e.,
the Children of Israel)* 286
*Islam Was the Religion of the Sorcerers Who [Repented
and then] Believed in Moses:* 286
Islam Is the Religion of the Prophets of the Children of Israel. 287
Solomon Brought the Message of Islam 287
Islam Was the Religion of Jesus and His Disciples 287
Islam Is the Religion of the Rightly-Guided Jinns 288
Islam Is the Religion of the People of the Book 288
*Islam Is the religion of Muhammad, the Final Prophet (May
Allah's Peace and Blessings Be upon Him):* 288
THE FINAL PROPHET 290
THE MISSION OF CHRIST, A SPECIFIC MISSION 292
THE UNIVERSALITY OF THE MESSAGE OF MUHAMMAD ... 299
The Truthful, The Trustworthy 306
Physical Miracles 318
JIHAD IN ISLAM 328
WAR IN THE HOLY SCRIPTURES 337
The Documents Speak Out 347
Christians Under Fire of Persecution 348
The Balance of Power Shifts 350
The Language of Documents and Numbers 351
Christian Persecution of the Jews 354
POLYGAMY AND ITS WISDOM 356
The Wisdom of Polygamy 358
Europe and Polygamy 359
In the Muslim East 360
The Messenger's Many Wives 361
The Mothers of the Believers 365
Their Responsibility for Disseminating Good 374
A LOOK AT THE HOLY BOOK 375
Gideon 375
David 376
Solomon 380
ABROGATION 382
A. Divorce 383
B. Prohibitions 384
C. The Sabbath 384
D. Circumcision 385
Abrogation of the Laws of the Old Testament 387
The Qur'an and the Scriptures of the Past 389
The Qur'an Attests To The Truth 389
The Qur'an Preserves the Truth of Previous Scriptures 390
Previous Scriptures Support The Qur'an 391

 The Disciples 409
ALCOHOL 417
SWINE 425

THE HOLY SPIRIT IN THE QUR'AN AND THE BIBLE 431
 Confused Dreams 435
ARGUMENTS SUPPORTING HOW JESUS WAS SAVED (AND NOT
CRUCIFIED) 440
 Jesus Prepares His Disciples to be Filled with the Holy Spirit on
 Thursday 446
THE WORD OF ALLAH 447
 A Passage from the Gospel of John 449
THE PAGANS AND THE *MASJID AL-HARAM* 452
CONCLUSION 454
 1. The Wisdom of the Noble Qur'an 455
 The Wisdom of the Eminent Hadith 463
 The Building of a Muslim Personality 473

FINAL SESSION **481**
 CONCLUDING REMARKS 481
  A Word from Father James Bakheet Sulayman, Representing
  the Christian Side 481
  A Word from Shaykh Tahir Ahmad Talibi, Religious Attaché
  of the Embassy of Saudi Arabia (Khartoum) 482
  A Word from Rear Admiral Ibrahim Ahmad Umar, Secretary
  General, Organization for the Revival of Islamic Activity
  in Sudan 486
  A Word from Shaykh Muhammad Hashim Al-Hadiyyah, President,
  Association of Supporters of the Prophetic Way (Sudan) 489
  Concluding Comments by Professor Ibrahim Khalil Ahmad,
  on Behalf of His Colleagues 491

REFERENCES **495**
 Muslim References 495
 Non-Muslim References 496

Preface

Praise be to Allah (swt) Who sent His Prophet with the guidance of Islam to all mankind, though it may be to the dismay of the unbelievers. I bear witness that there is no deity but Allah (swt) and that Muhammad is His chosen messenger. May the peace and blessings of Allah (swt) be upon His prophet, his household, his companions, and those who follow in his footsteps.

When Allah (swt) sent Muhammad, the last of all prophets, with the message of Islam, He revealed to him that the messengers that had gone before him had been sent with the same truth revealed to him. Allah (swt) has said, "Say: We believe in Allah, the revelation presented to us, and to Abraham, Ishmael, Isaac, Jacob, and the tribes, and that given to Moses and Jesus, and that given to all prophets from their Lord; we make no difference between one and another of them; and to Allah we submit." The prophets of Allah are the guardians of His revelation whom He sent with the message of monotheism to straighten people's perceptions and faith so that they might worship Allah on a straight path. Allah (swt) has said, "Every messenger that We sent before you We sent with the revelation that there is no deity but I, and therefore worship none but me." Unfortunately, with the passage of time the followers of those messengers dismissed what Allah had revealed to them and engaged in fanatical pursuits, dissenting from the truth. They went to war with the Prophet of Allah, despite the signs in their holy books of his advent, thus deviating from the path of Allah.

It is because Islam is a faith based on science, reason, knowledge, and undisputed truths that it invited the People of the Book to the equitable pursuit of the truth without coercing them into the adoption of Islam. Islam delineated the proper manner of dealing with the People of the Book and how to engage in discussions with them. Allah (swt) has said, "Do not argue with the People of the Book except in an equitable manner." Consequently, the minds of the Muslims were enlightened and their scholars thoroughly studied the beliefs of the People of the Book, pointed out the misrepresentations that occurred, and uncovered the whimsical pursuits that these people infused into the truths these faiths came with. Muslim scholars debated the scholars and clerics of the People of the Book, and wrote valuable books on the beliefs of Muslims and those of the People of the Book, and as such they became uninhibited seekers of the truth. Their pursuit was prompted by the words of Allah (swt): "That is because Allah is the Truth, those they worship are not. For Allah is the sole Almighty." Dialogue between Muslims and the People of the Book has never stopped throughout the centuries; in fact the dialogue has intensified in recent times, the world having become the small place that it now is because of the technical revolution in communications. Another reason is the emergence of the spirit of forgiveness and tolerance between people of different faiths, the pursuit of dialogue by different religious organizations, and interrelated economic interests.

The Institute of Islamic and Arabic Sciences in America strives to initiate dialogues between Muslims, People of the Book, and those of other faiths. It is also a valuable source of scholarly materials needed by serious researchers. In its efforts to reach this goal, the Institute has responded to a noble request to translate and publish the valuable book, "Dialogue Between Islam and Christianity" into English. The book is based on a dialogue that was held between Muslim scholars and several priests in the city of Khartoum in the year 1401 A.H./1980 C.E. The book was published in Arabic by the Presidency of Islamic Research, Ifta, Call, and Guidance in the Kingdom of Saudi Arabia. It is worth noting that those priests converted to Islam at the end of this dialogue.

It is my hope that the English version will be well received by scholars and seekers of truth and that it will assist them in their noble endeavors.

On a final note, I would like to thank all those who contributed to the translation of the book, in particular, Brother Safi Khan, who translated most of the text. Thanks are also due to Dr. Mustafa Mould, Sheikh Jamaal al-Din Zarabozo, both of whom revised and edited the translated text. Thanks are also due to Ahmed Mirghani who followed up the project.

Sulaiman Al-Jarallah, Ph.D.
Director of the Institute

Word from the Publisher of the Arabic Edition

We thank Allah and praise Him for everything, and may His peace and blessings be showered upon the Prophet of Allah, his family and his companions.

The conflict between truth and falsehood, and between faith and unbelief, will remain for as long as the heavens and the earth exist. Their battles never subside nor their flames die out; their confrontations never cease. However, no matter how strong the forces of falsehood become and how potent its attacks, and despite its apparent powerful sway and majority, one thing is for sure: Allah willing, the final victory will always be for the God-fearing friends of Allah and those who sincerely impart the true message to others. It is sufficient for callers to truth that they draw their strength from the power of Allah and the evidences from the Book of Allah,[1] and the authentic Sunnah of His Prophet (may Allah's peace and blessings be upon him).

Not long ago, in Khartoum, a distinguished group of Muslim scholars answered an invitation from several Christian priests and missionaries. This meeting occurred between 1-23 and 1-29, 1401 A.H. (12-1 to 12-7, 1980 C.E.). The Muslims were represented by Shaykh Muhammad Jamil Ghazi, Ph.D., Professor Ibrahim Khalil Ahmad and Major Abdul-Wahhab.

The Christian delegation was represented by the president of the Christian Mission, James Bakheet Sulayman, and Professor Teekha Ramadan. Both gave a detailed account of the real essence of the Christian faith as documented in their scriptures and exegeses in light of their belief in the Trinity, the Crucifixion, the Blood Sacrifice, the Fatherhood and Sonship, and the sacredness of the Old and New Testaments. Eventually they disclosed many contradictions and inconsistencies inherent in the Gospels.

---

[1] i.e, the Qur'an.

Surely, such a discussion deserves close attention and study for it sheds light on the real nature of Christianity, of which many people are unaware. Even if no other benefit had come from such a dialogue, it would have been enough to know that the truth of Islam was clear and could not be ignored. No sooner had the long discussion with its convincing proofs ended, than the priests openly declared their embracing of Islam and their departure from Christian doctrines.

It is crucial for Muslims to carry out their responsibility seriously to invite people to Allah and spread the Islamic faith worldwide. Moreover, they should adhere strongly to their way of life (Islam) in methodology and in practice.

Finally, the General Directorship of the Department of Scholarly Research, Legal Decisions, Da'wah, and Guidance, being the leader in Islamic work in these five areas, has facilitated this project greatly. They helped publish this noble project at their own expense and distribute it free, hoping to do their share in combating paganism, disbelief and heresy, and providing wholesome literature for whomever Allah permits to be guided aright.

May Allah shower His peace and blessings upon Muhammad, his family and his companions.

Riyadh
22 Safar 1407 A.H.

FOREWORD

I seek Allah's protection from the accursed Satan. Allah, Most Exalted, says:

You who believe! Fear Allah as He should be feared and die not except in a state of Islam.[1]

Mankind! Fear Your Guardian Lord, Who created you from a single person, created out of it his mate, and from them both scattered (like seeds) countless men and women. Fear Allah, through Whom you demand your mutual (rights), and be heedful of the wombs (that bore you); for Allah ever watches you.[2]

You who believe! Fear Allah and make your utterance straightforward, that he may make your conduct whole and sound and forgive you your sins; he that obeys Allah and His Messenger, has already attained the great victory.[3]

People! Worship your Guardian Lord, Who created you and those who came before you that you may become righteous.[4]

Here is a plain statement to mankind, a guidance and instruction to those who fear Allah.[5]

And remember that Allah took a Covenant from the People of the Book, to make it known and clear to mankind and not to hide it...[6]

Mankind! the Messenger has come to you in truth from Allah: believe in Him; it is best for you. But if you reject the faith, to Allah belong all things in the heavens and on earth: and Allah is All-knowing, All-Wise.[7]

---

[1] Qur'an 3:102
[2] Qur'an 4:1
[3] Qur'an 33:70-71
[4] Qur'an 2:21
[5] Qur'an 3:138
[6] Qur'an 3:187
[7] Qur'an 4:170

Mankind! Verily there has come to you a convincing proof from your Lord for We have sent unto you a light (that is) manifest.[1]

Say: Mankind! Now truth has reached you from your Lord! Those who receive guidance do so for the good of their own souls; those who stray do so to their own loss; and I am not (set) over you to arrange your affairs.[2]

Yet there is among men such a one as disputes about Allah without knowledge and without a book of enlightenment.[3]

Say: 'People of the Book! Come to what is just between us and you that we worship none but Allah; that we associate no partners with Him; that we erect not, from among ourselves, lords partners other than Allah.' If then they turn back, say: 'Bear witness that we (at least) are Muslims (bowing to Allah's Will).'[4]

Certainly the most authentic speech is the Book of Allah,[5] and the best guide is the guidance of Muhammad (peace be upon him) and the worst matters are innovations, for such innovations in reality are heresy. Surely, all heresy is deviation. Undoubtedly, any such transgression only leads to Hellfire.

Clearly Islam is a way of life that readily opens its windows to light and genuine goodness. Its truths are undeniably clear, cogent, candid and unadulterated. Moreover, they provide guidance for the individual as well as the world and are eternal. Therefore, Islam and Muslims openly welcome any calm and objective dialogue between themselves and those who oppose them from any other religion or cult. As a matter of fact, Muslims consider such an occasion a golden opportunity to present their message to the sincere heart, the open mind and the clear conscience. They earnestly believe that wherever the message of Islam falls upon attentive ears, sincere hearts and informed minds, it always finds acceptance, belief and commitment to it.

---

[1] Qur'an 4:174
[2] Qur'an 10:108
[3] Qur'an 22:8
[4] Qur'an 3:64
[5] i.e., the Qur'an

This is what happened in the past, is happening today and will happen in every era. Countless intellectual discussions have taken place here and there, in the East and the West, past and present. They begin inevitably with an atmosphere of mystery, doubt and apprehension enveloping those who lack knowledge or understanding of Islam. Repeatedly, these discussions end with faith, appreciation and admiration once the clouds of mystery dissipate, ignorance disappears and the truth remains for all to see.

We openly invite every human being wherever they may be on God's earth to build new bridges of understanding between themselves and the authentic Islamic faith. No one, regardless of religion or cult, should fear or cower from sincere, scholarly discussions. After such scholarly discussions, nothing but the truth would be acknowledged as such.

Over the years, numerous meetings have occurred between Islam and Christianity. Frequent dialogues have occurred in the past and many more will take place in the future. We would like to mention some of these meetings which took place in the recent past.

A. Rajab, 1270 A.H. About a hundred thirty years ago in Calcutta, India, a dialogue took place between a group of Muslim scholars and Christian missionaries who had proceeded to discredit Islam and subtly misguide the ignorant masses. Five topics were chosen for discussion, namely, alteration (of the Bible), abrogation (of biblical passages), the Trinity, the truth of the Qur'an, and the prophethood of Muhammad (may Allah's peace and blessings be upon him). Divinely graced, the Muslim scholars successfully evinced the truth within the first two topics, i.e., alteration of the Bible and abrogation of biblical passages. Needless to say, the Christian scholars acknowledging their fiasco had no choice but to withdraw and conclude the discussions abruptly.

The news of this debate spread rapidly across the Muslim world, which had been reeling under the authoritarian rule of the Christian nations. Scores of Muslims sought to obtain all information about what exactly had transpired at that debate. This dialogue moved the leading Muslim scholar of the time, Rahmatullah Ibn Khalil Ar-Rahman Al-Hindi, to compose his invaluable book, *The Triumph of the Truth* (*Izhar al-Haqq*). To this day this book is still considered a unique resource in the field of Christian-Muslim dialogue.

B. At the request of some eminent European lawyers and intellectuals (via the Saudi Embassy in Paris) who expressed an interest in meeting scholars from Saudi Arabia to deepen their understanding of human rights in Islam, the Ministry of Justice of Saudi Arabia organized three sessions in Riyadh, starting on Wednesday, March 22, 1972 (7 Safar, 1392 A.H.)

Following these discussions, the various speakers of the European delegation, foremost of whom was Professor McBride of the University of Dublin, the former foreign minister of Ireland, the former president of the European Commonwealth, and the former general secretary of the International Law Commission, came forward one by one, and declared: "It is from here, and especially from this Muslim nation, and not from any other nation, human rights should be proclaimed. It is an absolute must for Muslim scholars to publicize these truths unknown to the rest of the world. Ignorance of these truths has ruined the reputation of Islam, Muslims and Islamic rule, and has kept Islam and Muslims from being supreme by the means of the enemies of Islam and Muslims."

C. In June, 1976 C.E., a conference was convened in Geneva, Switzerland, between Muslims and Christians at the invitation of the World Body of Churches. The topic of discussion was "The view of the Divinely Revealed Religions Concerning Humans and their Quest for Peace." During the conference, the World Body of Churches expressed its deep regret for the Christian treatment of Muslims. It was an established fact that it was the Christian missionaries delegated to Muslim countries who were solely responsible for undermining Christian-Muslim relations. It furthermore acknowledged that the main purpose of missionary activity was to serve the policies of European imperialism, and that they utilized education as a means to corrupt the Islamic creed. At this conference, the Christian delegation resolved to put an end to all educational and health facilities used to convert Muslims to Christianity.

D. In 1979 C.E., a second Christian-Muslim debate was held in Cordoba, Spain. Cardinal Trancone, Archbishop of Spain, gave the opening remarks where he declared,

> As a bishop, I would like to advise believing Christians to forget the past. This is what the office of the Pope also wishes. Also they should clearly declare their respect for the Prophet of Islam. This is extremely important for Christians. After all, how can one appreciate Islam and Muslims without appreciating their Prophet and the values he preached and is still preaching in the lives of his followers? I will not attempt to enumerate the major religious and human values taught by the Prophet of Islam for this is not my concern. Our Christian specialists and theologians will address these values. Regardless, I would like to shed light on two of his many positive attributes. They are his deep faith in maintaining the Unity of Allah and his preoccupation with justice.

During the conference, Dr. Yabheel Caruth presented a paper, titled "Social and Political Roots of the False Image Created by Christendom of Prophet Muhammad." Interestingly, he maintains that

> ...throughout history, not a single person can be found who, in carrying the divine message and inviting others to it, unjustly faced as much defamation, insult and abuse as Muhammad... I have already confirmed on an earlier occasion, though I feel as if I have declared this several times, the impossibility, on an historical and personal level, of the notion of the false prophet being attributed to Muhammad, as long we have refused it regarding Hebrew prophets such as Abraham, Moses and others who were considered prophets.
> Never did any of those prophets clearly and conclusively declare that the office of prophethood would end with them. As a matter of fact, according to the Jews, the office of prophethood is still open as they await the coming of the real Messiah. As for the Christian mission, there is nothing that

conclusively points to the termination of the office of prophethood.

Next comes the meeting in Khartoum (Sudan). It was a meeting of people who sincerely sought to return to Allah after searching for the truth for a long time far and wide. Perhaps this dialogue will serve as a lesson for missionaries to cease their attempts to corrupt the Muslim faith for, surely, truth always prevails.

Why this Conference was Held

Many of our Arab brethren spend the holidays in European capitals. Motivated before anything else to master the European languages, they enroll in night schools as soon as they arrive in the country of their choice. Interestingly, they discover that their libraries carry a lot of material about Islam, yet much of it is distorted and simply defamatory.

It must be remembered that many Arab Muslim countries were for a long time under the yoke of Christian imperialism. As a matter of fact, they still depend on them for many comforts and conveniences. They look up to them in awe and admiration. Without thinking, they proceed blindly towards them, being indifferent to the substance of their ways. Quite often they tend to imitate them and pay close attention to their views and opinions. All of this only prepares the way for Western literature and Western views to be spread among us.

Another very important matter is that the style and format of books about the life of Prophet Muhammad (may Allah's peace and blessings be upon him) and Arab history are still too difficult for students studying Islamic civilization. Rarely do we find one who can efficiently reference *Sirah Ibn Hisham* or *As-Sirat al-Halbiyah* or *Nihayat al-Arib* or *Tabaqat Ibn Sa'd*— not to speak of such invaluable works as *Tarikh At-Tabari* or *Tarikh Adh-Dhahabi* or *Tarikh-Ibn Al-Athir*.[1] Often many find that the

---

[1]Famous books of Islamic history.

writings of the Orientalists are much easier to read and more useful.

Contemporary writers have written many books about the brilliant life of Prophet Muhammad (may Allah's peace and blessings be upon him). However, the authors of many of these books concentrate only on systematically narrating and simplifying the various events of the Prophet's life. Of these, very few deal with the opinions of the Orientalists, and that also in only a few lines.

The most famous book written recently about the life of Prophet Muhammad (may Allah's peace and blessings be upon him) is the *Life of Muhammad* by Dr. Muhammad Hussayn Haykal. In this book, he deals with the view of some Orientalists in general terms. Later, he does specifically mention the French Orientalist, Emille Durmenjam. Unfortunately, from Dr. Haykal's writing one could be easily misled into thinking that Emille is an ally of Islam.

Danger of the Intellectual Assault [on Muslims]

Today, translation of Islamic literature has become widespread. Furthermore, what we feared most has already spread among Muslims. All of this points to one thing. It shows the dangerous intellectual assault carried out by a band of Orientalists, under the pretext of scientific research, and through missionary work under the title of "religious invitation" has became more intense. Not surprisingly, this has annoyed many of those sincerely concerned for Islam. They have subsequently banded together to turn back this assault and expose its fabrications about Islam. Unfortunately, they are few and overworked.

A Convert's Advice to His People

It would be good to cite what a French Muslim, Nasiruddin wrote in his profound book, *The East as Seen by the West*, where he says,

...Dr. Snook Hargharange was right when he said, 'The recent biography of Muhammad (may Allah's peace and blessings be upon him) shows that historical research would be completely sterile if made subjugated to any man-made theory or previous view.' Contemporary Orientalists and missionaries should rely on this fact, for it will cure them of their former misjudgments which are burdensome to them whereby they have reached certain incorrect conclusions which they might pull out to destroy some truths. Of course this is not easy. Subsequently, they could concoct items which would replace what they destroyed. This without a doubt is impossible.

Returning to the Truth: an Excellent Virtue

The twentieth century Orientalist-missionary needs to be familiar with many essential factors, i.e., the time and environment, the climate, the customs, the needs, the ambitions, the likes and dislikes, etc. More importantly he must be familiar with the subtle forces which cannot be measured intellectually yet they affect the actions of individuals and people.

At the end of the book written by Nasiruddin about Prophet Muhammad (may Allah's peace and blessings be upon him), he speaks about the Islamic Awakening:

> Sharfees, in his book *Bonaparte and Islam*, says, "When Allah raised the ingenious prophet of Islam from this world this established religion had already been completely organized with meticulous precision even in its minutest details.

The soldiers of Allah had conquered all of the Arab lands and now began their assault on the formidable imperialist empires of the North.

Quite naturally, a certain temporary uneasiness which gripped the Muslims soon after the death of their inspired leader caused some minor strife. Nonetheless, because Islam had solidified its structure and because of the high intensity of faith of its followers, it shocked the world with its amazing rise—which we believe has no equal in the annals of his-

Muslim-Christian Dialogue

tory.

In less than a hundred years, and in spite of their small numbers, the noble Arabs, for the first time in their history, ventured outside of the borders of their Peninsula to conquer the majority of the ancient civilized world from India to Spain.

This admirable story strongly preoccupied the mind of the greatest genius of our present time—i.e., Napoleon Bonaparte—who always used to look to Islam with interest and love. Once, in one of his famous speeches in Egypt he declared about himself, "I am a Muslim believer in one God."

Las Kazoos writes in his book, *The Memoirs of St. Helena* [vol. 3: p. 183]:

> He mentions Islam in his last days. He believes that if we were to put aside all the unexpected circumstances which produced wonders, there has to be some secret unknown to us which resulted in the rise of Islam. There has to be some hidden reason which enabled Islam to amazingly defeat Christianity. Perhaps that hidden reality was that these people who suddenly arose from the depths of the desert had already endured long and terrible internal warfare whereby they developed strong morals, unique talents and an indomitable spirit. Maybe, there was some other reason similar to the above.

On this basis, our session was held attended by some leading Christian and Muslim thinkers, between 1-23-1401 and 1-29-1401 A.H. (12-1 to 12-7-1980 C.E.). Our hope was for every Muslim and Christian to comprehend the forthcoming lessons so they might assess the position and impact of the Orientalists and missionaries.

As opposed to this we should not feign ignorance of any movements that are hostile to Islam, for under the guise of modern civilization they subtly affect us through the assaults of the media and notorious advertising. In view of the fact that we are more aware of the truths of our religion, it becomes obligatory upon us to respond to their specious arguments and clarify how they have deviated and the reasons for their attacks on Islam.

Muslim-Christian Dialogue

Dialogue in the light of the Noble Qur'an and the authentic Sunnah is one successful way to remove the defects of former testaments.

In this great and most important gathering, three respected Muslim scholars participated.

A. Dr. Muhammad Jamil Ghazi: Moderator and participant.
— born in January, 1936, at Kafr al-Jarayidah, Kafr ash-Shaykh
— Obtained the Degree of Scholarship from the illustrious University of Al-Azhar, College of Arabic Language.
— Doctorate in Literary Criticism
— President of the Islamic Center for Inviting People to *Tawhid*[1] and the Sunnah (Cairo, Egypt)
— General Vice President for the Organization of the Helpers of the Prophetic Way (Cairo, Egypt)
— author of many books in the field of exegesis and religious sciences, e.g.:

    1. *Qur'anic Vocabulary* (3 volumes)
    2. *The Most Truthful Speech* (also exegetical)
    3. *Sufism: The Other Side*
    4. *Ancient Tears*
    5. *The Names of the Qur'an Mentioned in the Qur'an*

— He has many works dealing with documenting and verifying Islamic literature, especially the works of Ibn Taymiyyah and Ibn Al-Qayyim
— He received a doctorate in the documentation of the old book, *The Firsts*, by Abu Hilal Al-Askari (2)
— He has also been very active in *da'wah* through lectures, seminars and discussions, in Egypt and elsewhere in the Muslim world.

B. Professor Ibrahim Khalil Ahmad.
Born on January 13, 1919 C.E. in Alexandria, Egypt, he was brought up a Christian, named Ibrahim Khalil Phillips. He was schooled in American missionary institutions where he graduated with a high school diploma from Asyut in 1942 C.E. Next

---

[1] *Tawhid*: maintaining the belief in the Oneness of Allah in His Lordship and Sovereignty, in His names and attributes, and in His Worship.

he obtained a diploma from the College of Biblical Theology in Cairo in 1948 C.E. Thereafter, he was appointed pastor at the Bafoor Biblical Church in Asyut. In 1952 C.E., along with his church work, he was appointed a priest at the Canadian College of Biblical Theology in Asyut. Soon after, he was promoted to missionary priest at the Swiss-German Missionary Office in Aswan. He held many positions at various centers, e.g., member of the Delegation of Christian Scholars of Asyut, member of Sidus al-Nil; a colleague of American missionaries and an expert in missionary strategy among Muslims along with American and European missionaries.

Professor Ibrahim Khalil Ahmad normally did not appear as a clergyman wearing clerical attire; rather, he used to wear normal Western garb, which would allow him to work unnoticed among Muslims and thereby successfully reap the fruits of his missionary work.

However, Allah, Whose wisdom is ever manifest, guided him to come upon the Qur'anic verse "...those who follow the Messenger, the unlettered Prophet, whom they find mentioned in their own (scriptures), Torah and the Injil[1]..."[2] after reading which he suddenly came to his senses.

He immediately embarked upon a comparative study of Islam and Christianity, which lasted from 1955 to December 25, 1959 C.E. Soon thereafter, he became convinced of the truth of Islam and declared his embracing of Islam. Ever since, he has worked hard for the sake of Allah. He has several publications in circulation, among which are:

— *Muhammad (Allah's peace and blessings be upon him) in the Torah, Injil and Qur'an*
— *Orientalists and Missionaries in the Arab and Islamic World*
— *Israel: the Problem of Generations (Ancient times)*
— *Israel: the Problem of Generations (Recent times)*
— *Israel and the Talmud (an Analytical Study)*
— *Orientalism and Missionary Work and their Relationship with World Imperialism.*

In addition to these, other works under publication are:
— *Jesus, the Messiah, the Word of God*

---

[1] i.e., the Five Books of Moses and the Gospel.
[2] Qur'an 7:157

— *Knowledge Leads to Faith*
— *The Islamic Response to the Challenge of Orientalism and Missionary Activity*
— *The Islamic Response to the Current Cultural and Intellectual Challenge*
— *Allah's Signs manifesting in the Age of Knowledge*
— *The Legal Statutes of Allah in the Torah, the Injil and the Qur'an*
— *Islam in the Torah, the Injil, and the Qur'an*
— *The Messiah in the Torah, the Injil, and the Qur'an.*

May Allah accept his work and usefulness to the Ummah of Muhammad (may Allah's peace and blessings be upon him).

C. Brigadier General Ahmad Abdul-Wahhab Ali,
— born in Tiaqous, Egypt, in Northern Province, in the first part of June 1930 C.E.
— obtained his Bachelor's degree in electrical engineering in the Branch of Communications at the University of Cairo, in 1954 C.E.
— joined the armed forces and advanced through the ranks until he became rear admiral
— deeply involved in the field of comparative religion for the last twenty-five years.
   — The following are some of his contributions
A. Series of Studies in Religions:
   1. *Revelation and Angels in Judaism, Christianity and Islam*
   2. *Prophets and Prophethood in Judaism, Christianity and Islam*
   3. *The Messiah in the Sources of Christian Belief*

B. Other publications:
   1. *Current Nuclear Science and its Place in the Islamic Legacy of Knowledge*
   2. *The Miraculous Organization of the Qur'an*
   3. *The Missionary Reality: Past and Present*

The meeting began with a sincere love and desire to ascertain the truth and acquire the proper guidance. It concluded with the truth prevailing and falsehood vanishing, for the entire panel of the Christian delegation embraced Islam, entering Islam with total faith and submission.

Their spokesman said, as 'Umar (may Allah be pleased with him) once said: "I swear by Allah, not a single gathering where I participated in disbelief shall remain without my participation therein with total faith." They have since served Islam well by playing their role in inviting people to Islam. As of this time, the number of people who have embraced Islam at their hands is five hundred! Scores are on the way to accepting Islam soon.

Surely, Allah has spoken the truth: "He is the One Who sent His Messenger with the Guidance and Religion of Truth to make him triumph over all other ways."[1]

"And proclaim: Truth has (now) arrived and falsehood perished: Surely falsehood (by its very nature) is bound to perish."[2]

---

[1] Qur'an 9:33; 61:9
[2] Qur'an 17:81

Opening Statements

Shaykh Tahir Ahmad Talibi

Religious Attaché,

Embassy of Saudi Arabia, Khartoum

We commence this meeting in the name of Allah, Ever Merciful, Ever Compassionate, and in praise of and thanks to Him. May Allah send peace and blessings to the best of His Creation, Muhammad, and upon his family, his companions and whoever invites to His way and is guided through His guidance until the Day of Judgment.

My respected brothers, distinguished audience, along with yourselves, it gives me great pleasure to be part of a Christian-Muslim meeting. This meeting was convened at the request of Pastor James Bakheet Sulayman. Invitations were sent to the president, the members of the Organization for Reviving Islamic Activity in the Sudan, and to the Religious Attaché of the Embassy of Saudi Arabia in Khartoum. What makes us all so happy about a meeting like this is that it was convened in an atmosphere of love and concern for each other so that we may know the truth and be able to differentiate between right and wrong. We ask Allah to permit us successfully to ascertain the truth wherever it may be. We ask Allah to enable us to follow it. Additionally, we wish that such meetings recur often, everywhere, and in all ages. We pray that our meeting will be fruitful and have a profound effect upon us, so that Allah will guide us to the path of truth, goodness, and peace.

In conclusion, it gives me great pleasure to begin this meeting with the honorable professor and esteemed Shaykh Iwadullah Salih, President of the Organization of the Revival of Islamic

Activity in Sudan. Formerly the Grand Mufti of the Republic of Sudan, he is currently a participating member of the Muslim World League in Makkah (Saudi Arabia). Without further ado, we invite you to come forward, and may Allah reward you for your service to Islam.

Shaykh Iwadullah Salih

President, Organization of the Revival of Islamic Activity in the Sudan

In the name of Allah, Ever Merciful, Ever Compassionate, I praise and thank Allah, Lord of the Universe. May His peace and blessings be upon our leader, Prophet Muhammad, and upon all of his brothers in prophethood.

On behalf of my brothers at the Organization for the Revival of Islamic Activity, I am very pleased to be a part of this meeting and welcome you to this forum.

About five years ago, I attended a dialogue similar to this one in Tripoli, Libya. What was so unique about that conference was that it stayed clear of any offensive or insulting words. Rather, whenever any prophet other than Muhammad (may Allah's peace and blessings be upon him) was mentioned by the Muslims, he was remembered with absolute respect and with the highest esteem. Likewise, whenever the Christians mentioned any prophet other than Jesus (may Allah's peace and blessings be upon him), they would do so with the utmost respect and honor. That conference was most certainly a conference to arrive sincerely at the truth.

The world today is fraught with error. Some misunderstandings about Islam are quite widespread. Certainly, these false notions should be corrected through objective and cool-headed discussions. It is true that there are some errors and deviations present even in the understanding and practice of those who associate themselves with Islam.

Muslim-Christian Dialogue

The objective student can discern that Islam is one thing and those associated with it are another. Islam, like any other system or religion, must be evaluated in terms of its authentic, acknowledged sources. Whatever is said about Islam must also be applicable to Christianity, which preceded Islam by many years.

An objective study, a sincere intention, and an ardent desire to arrive at the straight path are all factors which facilitate the correction of errors, the dispelling of specious arguments, the clarification of subtleties and the return of religion to its original purity and sanctity.

My words here are not part of the forthcoming dialogue; rather, they are merely welcoming words on my own behalf and on behalf of my brothers at the Organization of the Revival of Islamic Activity in Sudan. On this occasion I would be remiss in my introduction if I did not share with you at least a glimpse of the last conference, which greatly pleased me. I am confident that this conference will also be on the same level in terms of its objectivity, sincerity and discipline.

In the last one, both the Muslim and Christian discussants mutually agreed to stop their missionary activities in their areas, be they Christian or Muslim areas.

I really don't know what the Christians did following that agreement, which is now more than six years old. However, I assure you that in this area in particular, we have certainly lived up to our part of the agreement. We have worked only with Muslims and their children, safeguarding them and their understanding of Islam and thus ensuring that they are not suddenly swept away by some dubious and unsubstantiated words— something that would displease Islam and Christianity both. Likewise, I pray that, subsequent to the above-mentioned agreement, Christians will not visit Muslim areas to lure them. Often people most readily tempted by material gifts are the poor or the simple-minded. They can easily change from one faith to another.

I am afraid I have already spoken too long. Regardless, I welcome all of you and I sincerely hope that this discussion uncovers the truth regarding the most important issues pertaining to any human being's life, i.e., the right and authentically documented way to worship God.

May the peace, mercy and blessings of God be with all of you.

Preliminary Remarks

Dr. Muhammad Jamil Ghazi

I begin with the name of Allah, Ever Gracious, Ever Merciful, and say, "Praise be to Allah Who will soon show you His signs so that you shall know them. Surely your Lord is not unmindful of all that you do."[1] May the peace and blessings of Allah be upon Muhammad, his family and all his companions.

I will begin by first introducing to you brother,[2] James Bakheet. He will speak to you shortly. Before I introduce him to you, I must request a smile on all of your faces. I hope that every one of us is totally optimistic for we are about to embark— thank God— upon a truly noble and righteous task. We pray to Allah for its successful outcome. There is no hostility or antipathy between us. It is love that has brought us here together, and it is love that enables each one of us to converse comfortably with each other. So with a lot of love and honor, I would like to introduce to you Brother James Bakheet.

I hope that during his talk he will refer to the questions which he forwarded to our honorable and esteemed Shaykh Tahir Ahmad Talibi. These questions shall define the scope of the discussion in this forum, this Christian-Muslim gathering. Tonight is the beginning of this meeting and only Allah knows how many nights we will convene and how many hours we will spend with each other.

---

[1] Qur'an 27:93
[2] i.e., brother in humanity.

Statement of the Clergy:
Messrs. James Bakheet and Teekha Ramadan

Mr. James Bakheet:

Gentlemen, Good evening. Mr. Teekha Ramadan will speak on my behalf.

Mr. Teekha Ramadan:

Gentlemen, members of the Organization for the Revival of Islamic Activity, distinguished gentleman from the Saudi Religious Attaché in Khartoum, *as-salamu 'alaykum wa rahmatu Allah*.[1]

It is surely by the will of God that He has facilitated this spiritual meeting for us, not to criticize and denounce each other but to seek knowledge and elucidate certain religious issues in Islam and Christianity with facts and proofs. This is how God revealed the Message to the prophets. We hope to steer clear of any religious chauvinism. We pray that God will guide us all to what is good for our people.

Respected guests, we Christian leaders in the Triple Capital[2] and in the presence of the Nuba Mountains[3] were Muslims— born into Islam— yet we did not study Islam in depth. Then we learned a little about Christianity because of the heavy missionary activity conducted by many Christian groups in Sudan.

Gentlemen, needless to say, this caused confusion in understanding the two different areas and led to grave doubts in our minds, so we sought help from the missionary, Mr. James Bakheet, after his return from the United States of America and Canada where he had been invited by one of the Christian groups. We were hoping that he would help us out of this pre-

---

[1] May the peace and mercy of Allah be with you.
[2] i.e., the three cities of Omdurman, Khartoum and Khartoum North.
[3] Mountains in North Sudan

dicament, for we had decided that after ascertaining the truth we had to choose either Islam or Christianity.

What attracted us to seek help from the missionary, James, was his religious acumen and his belief in free worship. He had already been delegated to deal with all other Christian sects in the Sudan. Today he is involved in founding a Christian group managed and supervised by our Sudanese brothers.

The missionary James responded saying that, much as the revolution guaranteed freedom of worship for everyone, we must also help implement this basic principle whether we are Muslims or Christians. We must not show the slightest religious prejudice but give each individual a chance to choose the religion he wants. James further advised us not to join any religious group, even his denomination. As a matter of fact, he refused to let us join his denomination unless we were absolutely convinced of its truth. Later he selected the homes of some brothers to be centers for spiritual gatherings. His efforts and personal attention to this problem have made today's gathering possible.

Of course, we would be remiss if we forgot to thank Professor Juwayid An-Nufay'i, the Saudi Cultural Attaché (Khartoum), who worked very hard to arrange this meeting with our brothers from the Organization of the Revival of Islamic Activity and with the distinguished Shaykh Tahir Ahmad Talibi from the Saudi Religious Attaché (Khartoum).

In conclusion, we pray to God, Most Beneficent, to help us and guide us to the right way, and shower upon us His blessings, and strengthen us and endow us with the ability to fulfill His covenant through spiritual purity.

Wa as-salamu 'alaykum wa rahmatu Allahi wa barakatuh.[1]

---

[1] May Allah's peace, mercy and blessings be with you

Questions Forwarded by the Christian Side

These questions will formulate the subject matter for the Christian-Muslim discussion.

After the opening remarks by Mr. Teekha Ramadan, Mr. James Bakheet stood up to read the following questions, thus making them a part of the discussion. There were two types of questions. The first set of questions dealt with Christianity, while the second set dealt with Islam. These questions are given below.

Mr. James Bakheet:

A. Christianity

1. Does the Qur'an support the "Messiah" and the New Testament?
2. How did the abrogation and alteration of biblical passages occur, as the Muslims claim? Do the Muslims possess the original Bible?
3. Alcohol[1] is forbidden in the Qur'an but not in the Bible. How do you explain that? Is there a verse prohibiting alcohol?
4. Do Muslims believe in the disciples of Jesus, whom, as stated in the New Testament, he chose and commissioned with the responsibility of spreading the Gospel to all people?
5. Does the Noble Qur'an confirm the Holy Ghost?
6. According to the New Testament, Jesus (may Allah's peace and blessings be upon him) was crucified. He died and then was buried. Soon after, he rose from the dead on the third day. What does the Qur'an have to say about these matters?
7. The New Testament states that Jesus is the Son of God. What is the Qur'anic view?

---

[1] i.e., any alcoholic beverage.

8. Does the Qur'an support or confirm the Trinity, i.e., the Father, the Son and the Holy Ghost, as stated in the Bible?
9. What is the Muslim view of the Virgin Mary as the mother of Jesus (may Allah's peace and blessings be upon him)?

B. Islam
1. What was the life of Muhammad (may Allah's peace and blessings be upon him) like and how did the revelation of the Qur'an come to him?
2. How do we convince the skeptics that Muhammad (may Allah's peace and blessings be upon him) was the last prophet, based only on the Qur'an?
3. Was the sword used in the early days of Islam to compel nonbelievers to embrace Islam? Did that occur during the era of the Prophet (may Allah's peace and blessings be upon him) or during the era of the Rightly Guided Caliphs?
4. How do Muslims view those of their scholars who explained the Qur'an based on their own opinions, which later led to myriad sects. How did they fare?
5. A Muslim may marry more than one woman. Is there a Qur'anic verse supporting this? What were the reasons for the Prophet's (may Allah's peace and blessings be upon him) marrying more than four?
6. Why does the Qur'an prohibit pork? Is there a Qur'anic verse prohibiting it?
7. Does the Qur'an maintain that Jesus (may Allah's peace and blessings be upon him) was a messenger only to the Children of Israel?
8. We see that in the Qur'an there are some verses which contradict others. For example:
A. "Say: you that reject faith, I worship not that which you worship. Nor will you worship that which I worship. And I will not worship that which you have been wont to worship. Nor will you worship that which I worship. To you be your way and to me mine."[1]

---

[1] Qur'an 109: 1-6

B. "This day have I perfected your religion for you, completed my favor upon you and chosen for you Islam as your way.[1]

So what do the Muslims think about this contradiction?

9. How does a Muslim view a non-Muslim in terms of various social interactions?

10. Why do the Saudi authorities prohibit Christians from entering the sacred places in the Kingdom of Saudi Arabia?

---

[1] Qur'an: 5:3

Final Introductory Word

Dr. Muhammad Jamil Ghazi

If I must make a statement at the beginning of this meeting and as an introduction, then the best thing I could possibly say is to read you some verses from the Noble Qur'an:

At the outset I seek the protection of Allah from the accursed Satan! Allah, Most Exalted, Most High, says:

> And remember, Abraham and Ishmael raised the foundations of the House (with this prayer): "Our Lord! accept (this service) from us: for You are the All-Hearing, the All-Knowing.

> "Our Lord! make of us Muslims, bowing to Your (Will). and of our progeny a people Muslim, bowing to Your (Will); and show us our places for the celebration of (due) rites; and turn to us (in Mercy); for You are the Oft-Relenting, Most Merciful.

> "Our Lord! Send among them a Messenger of their own, who shall rehearse Your Signs to them and instruct them in Scripture and Wisdom, and purify them; for You are the Exalted in Might, the Wise."

> And who turns away from the religion of Abraham but such as debase their souls with folly? Him We chose and rendered pure in this world: and he will be in the Hereafter in the ranks of the Righteous.

> Behold! His Lord said to him: Submit (your will to Me). He said: "I submit (my will) to the Lord and Cherisher of the Universe."

> And Abraham enjoined upon his sons and so did Jacob: "My sons! Allah has chosen the Faith for you; then die not except in the state of submission."

Were you witnesses when Death appeared before Jacob? Behold, he said to his sons: "What will you worship after me?" They said: "We shall worship your God and the God of your father, of Abraham, Ishmael and Isaac, the one (True) God; to Him do we submit."

That was a people that has passed away. They shall reap the fruit of what they did, and you of what you do! You shall not be asked about what they did.

They say: "Become Jews or Christians if you would be guided (to salvation)." Say: "No! (I would rather) the Religion of Abraham the True, and he joined not gods with Allah."

Say: We believe in Allah, and the revelation given to us, and to Abraham, Ishmael, Isaac, Jacob, and the Tribes, and that given to Moses and Jesus, and that given to (all) Prophets from their Lord: we make no difference between one and another of them: and we submit to Allah.

So if they believe as you believe, they are indeed on the right path; but if they turn back, it is they who are in schism; but Allah will suffice you as against them, and He is the All-Hearing, the All-Knowing.

(Our religion) takes its hue from Allah, and who can give a better hue than Allah? It is He Whom we worship.

Say: Will you dispute with us about Allah, seeing that He is our Lord and your Lord; that we are responsible for our doings and you for yours; and that we are sincere (in our faith) in Him?

Or do you say that Abraham, Ishmael, Isaac, Jacob and the Tribes were Jews or Christians? Say: Do you know better than Allah? Ah, who is more unjust than those who conceal the testimony they have from Allah? But Allah is not unmindful of what you do!

That was a people that has passed away. They shall reap the fruit of what they did, and you of what you do! You shall not be asked about what they did. [2: 127-141]

I would like to direct my comments, not to these fine gentlemen, but to you Muslims. How will you respond to these fine statements that this respected brother has brought forth before you, whereby he highlighted some bitter realities? Have you thought that you are the ones really at fault? Have you thought about the fact that you will be questioned and held responsible before Allah for falling short in spreading Allah's message and never publicizing it or speaking up about it?

You have begun to relish this worldly life and its comforts and pleasures. You have begun to live in the lap of a calm, quiet and sedentary lifestyle. You have chosen the easy and peaceful way at a time when foreigners from the other side of the world have come vehemently knocking on the doors of your palaces to steal your children, your own blood.

Have you pondered these fine words, which have torn my heart to shreds, delivered by this honorable gentleman. I hope you understand that these words are directed at you. They should shake and disturb you to the extent that you cannot sleep comfortably, for the eyes of cowards never fall asleep. You must guard the house of Muhammad (may Allah's peace and blessings be upon him) and the message of all the prophets.

Regarding the questions presented by Professor James, I feel that we can organize them in a manner which will allow us to study many issues. We really do not need sermons or moving speeches. What we genuinely need is a calm, well-defined, objective and scholarly study where we can ascertain the truth and acknowledge the right way so we can tread it together as one body.

I decided to reorganize the schedule of sessions. I have distributed them to the scholars who will conduct the discussions with you, not only for tonight, but, with Allah's will, for the coming nights as well.

We ask for your patience throughout this conference. You must understand that centuries of ignorance have to be erased—a task not too enjoyable or comforting. This is a study of entire religions, and religions are not studied on a single trip somewhere or in just one sitting. Rather, they are studied carefully, using the sacred sources of both sides. Our schedule of events will be as follows:

Tonight, our brother, Professor Ahmad Abdul-Wahhab, will speak about the issue of the legitimacy of the Gospels. There were some questions posed concerning this topic, e.g., the questions asked about abrogation and alteration in the Gospels and how it took place as the Muslims claim, and if the Muslims possess the original Gospel.

Before I invite Professor Ahmad to come forward, I would like to draw your attention to two points. First, let us begin by answering the questions pertaining to Christianity, for the study of Christianity should precede the study of Islam. Second, I ask Professor Ahmad not to limit his answers to these two specific questions about abrogation and alteration. There are many other important and related topics that must also be dealt with, such as the story behind the actual recording of the Gospels. Why were only some of them accepted as legitimate, namely the four Gospels which later on became the Canon? How were the majority of the gospels rejected, and why? What are the points of agreement and disagreement among the four canonical Gospels? What is the status of the remaining scriptures of the New Testament and their value in terms of elucidating genuine beliefs? How were the four canonical Gospels put together?

There is this and so much more. I pray that we receive clear, well-defined answers to these queries from Professor Ahmad Abdul-Wahhab. I ask Allah to guide us to the truth. Surely no one but Allah guides people to the truth. I ask Allah to show us the truth clearly and to endow us with the ability to follow it and to show us falsehood clearly and to endow us with the strength to stay away from it.

And now I leave you with Professor Ahmad Abdul-Wahhab to begin his presentation.

The First Session

Prof. Ahmad Abdul-Wahhab

In the name of Allah, Ever Gracious, Ever Merciful.

I welcome you all to this gathering and especially all those who have come forward with their questions and queries about Christianity and Islam concerning matters of agreement and disagreement between them. Needless to say these matters are still points of contention between Christians and Muslims.

Perhaps the most obvious question in a meeting like this is: From where should people draw their beliefs?

It is commonly agreed upon that religious beliefs are usually drawn from sacred scriptures. Therefore, logic demands a thorough study of the sacred texts first, before we discuss any beliefs extrapolated from them. Undoubtedly, the most important studies pertaining to those sacred books are studies conducted by the scholars in that religion itself.

Accordingly, I would like to present a summary of some conclusions arrived at by some Christian scholars in their study of the sacred books entitled *A Statement about the Books of the New Testament*. This study clearly represents the conclusions reached by people concerned about the matter, in the form of a specialized committee organized to study a specific problem or issue. Moreover, it is quite appropriate for this meeting which we are now conducting, and one which usually does not last more than a short time, i.e., a few hours or a few days at most.

After this, I shall present a topic entitled "A Critical Look at the Books of the New Testament." This will allow any reader, regardless of his education, to see for himself with the truth of what is to be found in these "books". Moreover, he should become familiar with the reasons which have compelled many

Christian scholars to conclude what we hope to present when we talk about the "books" of the New Testament.

By this process any researcher will have a complete picture of the truth. Certainly he is entitled to this, for it seems as if every sincere individual is always saying to himself: I want to know, reflect, examine and verify, so I can satisfy my heart.

Consequently, respected gentlemen, all of the brief excerpts which I will read to you momentarily are not the words of a Muslim about Christianity; rather, they are merely a summary of statements by Christian scholars. As far as the Muslim viewpoint, we will leave that till the end, when it becomes necessary to comment on, clarify or relate different facts to one another. Here, it will be proper only to mention the Arabic titles of the most important Christian references cited[1] and their authors, along with a short biography of each. After this we need only to cite the name of the source and the page number.

Discussion of the Books of the New Testament

The Legitimacy of the Gospels

1. The early Christians never believed that their sacred books comprised a New Testament distinct from the Old Testament. As a matter of fact, both testaments were one joint testament. When the first Christian writings appeared, they were all viewed as authentic additions or footnotes to what was in the Books of Law and the Books of the Prophets. These were recited weekly in Jewish synagogues and Christian churches.

The New Testament is a non-homogeneous book which comprises many dissimilar accounts pieced together. It does not present one dominant view from beginning to end. Instead it really represents many different accounts of the same thing.[2]

---

[1]These references are listed under "Non-Muslim References" in the index at the end of the book.
[2]Frederick Grant, pp. 12, 17

2. In the last one hundred and fifty years, scholars have verified that the first three Gospels contradict the Gospel of John in substance and style.

The Gospel of John markedly differs from the other three (The Gospels of Matthew, Mark and Luke) which bear close resemblance to one another. For example, it does not narrate anything about the birth of Jesus... As for the accounts of the public activity of Jesus, there are noticeable differences in the exact time and place of the above when compared with similar accounts in the other three Gospels. Moreover, an accurate record of the period wherein the books of the New Testament were legitimized is uncertain.[1]

3. There is a very significant problem stemming from obvious contradictions in many respects between the fourth Gospel and the other three, which resemble each other.[2] The difference between them is so great that if the three similar Gospels are accepted as authentic and credible then the inevitable conclusion is that the Gospel of John is unmistakably false.[3]

4. We have no definite proof as to exactly on what grounds was the legitimacy of the four Gospels established, not to speak of exactly where such a decision was made.

5. Concerning the altering, adding or deleting words from the Biblical text, let us consider the following. The position of the Gospels is opposite to that portrayed in the Letters of Paul. Major distortions have occurred intentionally, such as insertion or addition of complete paragraphs.[4]

6. The texts of all the ancient manuscripts of the New Testament greatly differ from one another. It is impossible to believe that any one of them survived without errors... No matter how conscientious the writer was, he made mistakes. These errors remained in all the subsequent manuscripts copied from these originals. The majority of the available manuscripts, with

---

[1] Guntet Lanczkowski, *Sacred Writings*, pp. 32-38
[2] The three Gospels that are relatively similar to one another nd contrast so strongly with the fourth are more commonly referred to as the Synoptic Gospels (ed.).
[3] Encyclopedia Americana, vol. 13, p. 73
[4] Encyclopedia Britannica, vol. 2, pp. 519ff

different sizes, have been subject to numerous alterations at the hands of editors unskilled in correct reading.[1]

Let us proceed now and get a general overview of the Gospels. Whatever I am about to say is simply the words of the scholars of Christianity.

> The view that Matthew and Luke extensively used the Gospel of Mark has now become generally accepted. However, along with the Gospel of Mark, both of them (i.e., Matthew and Luke) must have used another document. This document is known today as Document Q, which is the code word for source as derived from the German word with this meaning.[2]

I. The Gospel of Mark

1. Papayas in 135 C.E. said:

> In reality, Mark, the scribe of Peter, recorded as accurately as he could whatever he remembered about what was narrated about the sayings and deeds of Jesus. But he did all this without being attentive to its organization. (And we observe that Mark was the writer of the Gospel on which Matthew and Luke relied.)
>
> This is what actually happened, for Mark never heard anything directly from Jesus and never personally followed him. Rather he came later on as I (Papayas) said before and he positively followed Peter.[3]

In accord with Papayas' statement, Eronis said,"...after the death of Peter and Paul, Mark, the student and scribe of Peter, left for us in writing whatever Peter told him."[4]

2. Secondly,

> There is no one with the name Mark who was known to have had a strong tie or a special relationship with Jesus, or

---

[1]George Caird, *Saint Luke*, p. 32
[2]Encyclopedia Britannica, vol . 2, p. 523
[3]Papayas.
[4]Grant, p. 73f

of any special note in the Early Church... Reports claiming that Mark was the supposed composer of the Gospel of Mark, referring in fact to John Mark, mentioned in the Acts [12:12, 25]; or to the Mark mentioned in the First Epistle of Peter [5:13]; or to the Mark mentioned in other letters of Paul: Colossians 4:10, II Timothy 4:11, Philemon 24, are all unconfirmed.

It was the custom of the early Church to assume that all events related to the name of an individual mentioned in the New Testament would be attributed to the person with that name. Yet, when we consider that Mark was the most commonly used Latin name in the Roman Empire, what becomes clear is the tremendous uncertainty of limiting this to a particular person in this situation.[1]

3. As far as the actual writing of the Gospel, "...it was most likely in the early period from 65-67 C.E., and in particular in 65 or 66 C.E. Many scholars strongly believe that what Mark wrote in Chapter 13 was written after 70 C.E."

As far as the place of writing of the Gospel:

...the earliest Christian sources are of no real help. Both Clement of Alexandria and Origen claim that it was Rome. Others maintain that it was written in Egypt. Due to the absence of a precise location of its writing in the above sources, scholars have looked into the Bible itself for answers. On this basis other suggestions, such as Antioch, were presented. However, Rome was to be the most widely accepted of all choices.[2]

From the above it becomes quite evident that no one truly knows who Mark, the writer of the Gospel of Mark, was. Moreover, no one really knows where this Gospel came from.

The Gospel of Mark: Its Problems

One of the major problems with the Gospel of Mark is its different versions with the passing of time. This has led Chris-

---

[1]Dennis Nineham,
[2]Ibid.

tian scholars to assert that "...alterations (in the biblical text) have continuously occurred and have been impossible to avoid. This happened intentionally and unintentionally. Among the hundreds of manuscripts— i.e., handwritten copies— of the Gospel of Mark, and especially those that have survived until today, we find no two versions in complete agreement with each other."

Another problem with the Gospel of Mark is its ending. Chapters nine to twenty, which talk about the resurrection of Jesus and his inviting the disciples to spread the Gospel worldwide, is considered an appendix. In other words, it was appended approximately 110 years later and did not appear for the first time until 180 C.E.[1]

II. The Gospel of Matthew

"To this day it remains clear that both Paul, the Greek, and Matthew, the Jewish missionary, had their own independent perspectives which completely differed from the other concerning the actions and teachings of Jesus."[2]

Historically, this Gospel can be said to have "...been written approximately between 85-105 C.E. All in all, one can say that it was probably written in the last quarter of the first century (C.E.) or the early years of the second century C.E."[3]

Regarding its place of authorship, "...strong evidence suggests Antioch, as it was his original homeland. Since it is very difficult to associate this Gospel with a certain area (such as Antioch), it is only appropriate to say that this Gospel comes from someplace in the area surrounding it or someplace north of Palestine."[4]

The Gospel of Matthew: Its Problems

1. Anticipation of a Quick End to the World.

---

[1]Op. cit., p. 11
[2]Grant, p. 141
[3]Fenton, *Saint Matthew*, p. 11
[4]Grant, p. 140

Even though this idea was generally pervasive in the thinking of the authors of the books of the New Testament, Matthew was the one most enthusiastic to verify this claim. He actually expected the world to end during the days of Jesus, i.e., even before his disciples would complete their missionary work to the cities of Israel [23:10], and before death would overtake some of Jesus' contemporaries who had listened to his teachings [28:16], and before the passing away of the generation that was considered the contemporaries of Jesus and his disciples [34:24].

Obviously, as John Fenton states on p. 21, "nothing of what Matthew was expecting ever happened..."

2. Scholars in general have major reservations about the ending of this Gospel, for they consider it mere spurious additions. It claims that Jesus once advised his disciples to "...go and teach all peoples and baptize them in the name of the Father, the Son and the Holy Ghost" [19:28]. These doubts are based, according to Adolf Hernck, one of the greatest scholars on the history of the Church, on the following:

a. "Not until the final phase of Christian teachings was any mention made of Jesus delivering sermons and teaching after rising from the dead, and that Paul knows nothing about this."[1]

b. "This issue of the Trinity is certainly very strange coming from Jesus. Such a concept never had any sway during the era of the prophets. Further, had this concept really come from Jesus himself, it would have been something worth mentioning by him."[2]

III. The Gospel of Luke

This Gospel begins with an introduction which sheds much light on what transpired at the beginning of Christianity, especially in reference to the authorship of the Gospel. He comments:

---

[1] Adolf Hernck.
[2] Op. cit., vol. 1, p. 79.

Forasmuch as many have taken in hand to set forth in order a declaration of those things which are most surely believed among us. Even as they delivered them unto us, which from the beginning were eyewitnesses, and ministers of the word; it seemed good to me also, having had perfect understanding of all things from the very first, to write unto thee in order, most excellent Theophilus, that thou mightest know the certainty of those things, wherein thou hast been instructed."[1]

From this preface, a few things become quite clear and as such must be acknowledged:

1. Luke is writing a personal letter to Theophilus. This information will be written "in order" depending on the availability of time and material to be recorded.

2. This endeavor was undertaken by Luke all on his own. He was hoping that what he knew would reach his friend. He never claimed in his letter that it was divinely inspired or that he was induced to write it by the Holy Ghost. Rather, he frankly declares that he acquired this knowledge due to his own "perfect understanding of all things," for he thoroughly followed up everything "...from the first."

3. Luke also declares that many people had set out to compose the Gospels.

4. Finally, Luke acknowledges that he never saw Jesus, nor was he one of his disciples. Instead, he wrote his letter based on information he received from those who were "...eyewitnesses and ministers of the word." i.e., at Jesus' service. It is commonly known that the Book of Acts, being the longest book of the New Testament, is the second part of Luke's letter to Theophilus.

Scholars have tried hard to identify Theophilus; however, their efforts have been in vain.

Frederick Grant comments:

> We never thought about who this Theophilus is. One could suppose that he was a Roman worker. Likewise, it never occurred to us who those "many" who had "...taken in hand to set forth in order..." to compose similar stories. Despite the fact that the entire scenario is nothing more than pure con-

---

[1] *The Holy Bible*, Luke I: 1-4

jecture, it is not inconceivable that the author of the Gospel of Luke had collected his material in Palestine or Syria early in the period between 70-80 C.E. He then combined with it the greater portion of the Gospel of Mark sometime in the 70s and subsequently proceeded to issue his Gospel around 80 C.E or 85 C.E. About five years later he appended this original manuscript with a second letter, which we now know as the Book of Acts. Then he disseminated his new manuscript around the year 95 C.E.

A Scholar's Statement Regarding the Writings of Luke:

There are many things in the Book of Acts which completely contradict the teachings narrated in the Epistles of Paul. Thus it is absolutely unthinkable that these (i.e., Book of Acts) were written by a person who had direct knowledge of Paul and his missionary trips, which the Book of Acts relates in detail. So much so that this Book is sometimes called the Book of Acts of Paul. Further, Luke is rarely mentioned as a towering personality in the annals of first century Christian history.[1]

The Gospel of Luke: Its Problems

1. "The text of the Gospel of Luke is plagued with alterations, much like the other books of the New Testament. As a matter of fact, the Western version of the Gospel of Luke and the Book of Acts suffer from many glaring differences because of additions or omissions of passages in comparison with other texts of the same Gospel, such as the Alexandrian or the Byzantine versions."[2]
2. "Then there is the grave problem stemming from the difference of opinion in the genealogy of Jesus as narrated in Luke

---

[1] George Cubbard, pp. 15ff
[2] Op. cit., p. 32f.

versus what was related in the Gospel of Matthew, or that related in the Books of the Old Testament."[1]

This is one of the problems of the Gospels which we shall discuss later.

IV. The Gospel of John

It was believed for a long time that John was well aware of the existence of the three other Gospels which were very similar to each other. It was also held that he had written his Gospel hoping to complete the other three and correct them in one or two places. For example, it was commonly known that John intentionally added the incident of purifying the Temple at the beginning of the message of Jesus. The earlier the incident occurred, according to John's recollections, the earlier it would be recorded historically.

Additionally, he corrected the history of the crucifixion. He recorded it on the evening of Easter, the day on which the Easter lambs were sacrificed. On the other hand, the title, "Son of Man" (which Jesus used for himself and preferred much more than other titles), was one which Paul never used, yet John recorded it.

John was certainly a Christian; he was also a Hellenist: he was probably not Jewish. However, he was from the East and was perhaps Greek.

It is very likely that the Gospel of John was written either in Antioch, Ephesus or Alexandria, or even Rome. Each one of these cities served as a major center for religious propaganda in the first and second centuries of the Christian Era. The people in those cities were in close communication with one another.[2]

John Marsh comments in his preface to the exegesis of the Gospel of John under the title, "The Impossibility of Confirmation":

---

[1]Op.cit, p. 45.
[2]Grant, pp. 156, 166, 174, 178.

When we come to discuss the many important and complicated problems connected with the Fourth Gospel— i.e., John's Gospel—we find it appropriate and helpful to acknowledge from the outset that there is not a single problem related to the identity of the Gospel or its composer for which a suitable answer can be found.

For example, who was this John about whom it is said that he was the author? Where did he live? For whom was he writing his Gospel? What source did he depend on? When did he write his Gospel? Concerning all of these questions and many others, there are explanatory rulings. Sometimes the rulings rest on strong confirmations. Yet, despite all of this, none of them can be elevated to a level of certainty.

Then Marsh concludes his introduction saying, "After emptying everything in our bag, we find it difficult, if not impossible, to authenticate anything beyond conjecture concerning the Gospel of John."

The writer of these lines (i.e., John Marsh) believes that it is not impossible to believe that during the last decade of the first century C.E., someone could have called himself John. John could be Mark. After all, he had gathered a lot of information about Jesus. It is quite possible that he was aware of one or more of similar Gospels (i.e., the Gospels of Mark, Matthew and Luke). He could have subsequently decided to compose a new version of the story of Jesus, being partial to his congregation, which considered itself universal and blessed with the presence of the students of John the Baptist.[1]

The Gospel of John: Its Problems

The *Encyclopedia Americana* states:
There are glaring contradictions between it and the other Gospels. The other three Gospels follow the historical chronology of events as narrated by Mark. Accordingly they claim that the main center of Jesus' message was the area of

---

[1] John Marsh, pp. 20, 80.

Galilee. In contrast, the Gospel of John declares the province of Judea as the main center.

Then there is the problem of its last chapter (Chapter 21). Even the casual reader can see that the Gospel concludes in an orderly manner with the end of chapter 20. Chapter 20 reads: But these are written that ye might believe that Jesus is the Christ, the Son of God..." This declaration clearly shows the purpose for which this book was written.

Thereafter, the twenty-first chapter informs us that Jesus as Lord rose from the dead in front of five disciples. He then tells Peter: "Feed my lambs." Then there is the dubious comment which reads: "This is the disciple." This "disciple" is part of a group which describes itself as "we". Realistically, these individuals in the group are unidentifiable.[1]

There appears to be some resemblance between the Gospels of Luke and John. As a matter of fact, there is a theory that John used the Gospel of Luke as one of his sources. However, this theory is problematic for there are clear difference between the texts of the two Gospels.

Both Gospels talk about Peter and the miracle of eating the fish. However, one (Luke) of the two places the story early in Jesus' ministry in Galilee. The other (John) places the story after his rising from the dead [Luke 5: 1-11, John 21: 1-14].

Both use similar words in narrating how Jesus used the "ointment" from a woman. According to Luke, she was an adulteress in the Pharisee's house. On the other hand, John states that this woman was a friend of Jesus and the whole incident took place at *her* house. [Luke 7: 36-38, John 12: 1-8][2]

In conclusion, as this brief overview of the findings of Christian scholars has already elucidated, one cannot realistically help but acknowledge that the canonical Gospels are no more than "composed" manuscripts, in every sense of the word.

---

[1] *Encyclopedia Americana*, vol. 16, p. 159.
[2] Cubbard, p. 20.

It only follows then that such "composed" manuscripts are open to truth and error. It is impossible to claim even for a moment that these Gospels were revealed writings.

Unknown authors have written Gospels at unknown places and at dates that cannot be confirmed. One thing for sure, which the casual as well as the thorough reader must notice, is that these Gospels are very dissimilar. As a matter of fact, they not only contradict themselves from within, but also contradict well-known truths of the world outside. For example, predictions of the end of the world have turned out to be untrue.

The above statement may upset a normal, everyday Christian; it may even shock him. However, as far as the Christian spheres of scholarship concerned with accuracy are concerned, such a statement about the existence of many errors in the chapters of the Bible is nothing short of an accepted truth.

The Catholic Church used to adhere very strongly to the belief in revelation, which, as Maurice Bucaille says, was confirmed by the meeting of the Vatican held in 1869-70 C.E. There it was declared "...that the Canonical Gospels of both the New and Old Testaments were writings inspired by the Holy Ghost and were given as is to the Church."

However, recently, after nearly a century, the Vatican has decided to reverse its stand and face the facts and acknowledge the truth. The Second Vatican Council (1962-65 C.E.) addressed the problem of the existence of errors in some of the chapters of the Old Testament. After three years of discussion and argument, it proposed five drafts. In the end there was one draft which received a majority vote of 2344 to 6 opposed. In the Conciliar Document no. 4 on Revelation, one complete paragraph dealing specifically with the Old Testament (Section 4, p. 53) was added. It says:

"In view of the human situation prevailing before Christ's foundation of salvation, the Books of the Old Testament enable everybody to know who is God and who is man... These books, even though they contain material which is imperfect and obsolete, nevertheless bear witness to truly divine teachings."[1]

---

[1] Bucaille, Maurice, *The Bible, the Qur'an and Science*, p. 41.

Muslim-Christian Dialogue

[Taken from the French doctor of Catholic origin, Maurice Bucaille, from his book, *The Bible, the Qur'an and Science*. Dar al-Ma'arif, a publishing house in Cairo, Egypt, published its Arabic translation under the title: *A Study of the Sacred Scriptures in Light of Modern Knowledge*. This paragraph was quoted from the first printing.]

The question which comes to mind now is how many of those who fully believe in the sanctity of these scriptures as divine teachings revealed by God are actually aware of what the Church has declared concerning the scriptures and the suspicious and false nature of its contents?

Actually we don't have to go far. In its preface to the Five Books of Moses, i.e., the Torah or Old Testament [sic.], we find the Holy Bible, i.e., the 1960 Catholic version, saying:

> ...many signs of improvement appear in the stories and laws of this book. As a matter of fact, this has pushed Catholic exegetes and others to search for the literary origin of these scriptures. No Catholic scholar today believes that Moses himself wrote the entire Pentateuch (i.e., the First Five Books of the Old Testament) from the story of creation to his death. Likewise, it cannot be said that Moses ever supervised the inspired writing of these scriptures. In essence, they were compiled by numerous writers over the course of forty years.

Moreover, in its preface to the Book of Ruth, this Holy Bible says:

> ...it is quite possible that in the beginning (i.e., of this Book) the author used traditional memoir whose context is unclear. Subsequently, he added numerous details thus endowing the narrative with more life and giving it literary value.

Today, missionary literature distributed among Muslims acknowledges that grave errors have crept into the books of the New Testament. In a book entitled, *Is the Holy Bible Really the Word of God?*, on p. 160, we find the following:

> By carefully comparing a large number of old manuscripts, scholars have been able to root out any errors that could have crept in. An example of this is the fallacious insertion in the First Epistle of John (Chapter Five). According to the

Arabic Protestant version (i.e., the American Printing in Beirut), the last para of verse 7 and the first part of verse 8 read, "For there are three that bear record in Heaven, the Father, the Word, and the Holy Ghost: and three are one. And there are three that bear witness on earth, the spirit, the water, and the blood, and these three agree in one. "

However, throughout the first centuries of the Christian era, not a single Greek manuscript included these words. The Harisa Arabic translation of the Bible deletes these words from the text completely. The Protestant Arabic version puts these words between parentheses, explaining in the introduction that these words do not exist in the oldest and most authentic manuscripts.

I think that the simplest comment on the above is that we should clearly understand that the significant passage, which was first inserted in the third century and from which comes the doctrine of the Trinity, did not exist throughout the previous centuries. This is something that cannot possibly be considered a simple distortion. Rather it is a grave distortion which touches the very foundation of the creed. In this manner, we find passages and ideas that have slipped into the writings which have been considered sacred for centuries. Thus, everything related to the doctrine of the Trinity is undoubtedly an insertion to the real religion of Jesus. Needless to say, some remnants of the original message of Jesus can still be found in the books of the present day Bible.

When scholars explain the last prayer of Jesus in the Book of John [17:3], which says, "And this is life eternal, that they might know thee the only true God, and Jesus Christ, whom thou has sent," they point out that no doubt this is the concept of the oneness of God.

Of course their contention, when expressed in another way, means: *La ilaha illa Allah; 'Isa Rasulu Allah,* i.e., 'No one is to be worshipped but Allah and Jesus is the Messenger of Allah.'

In light of these observations, it becomes possible for Christianity to meet Islam.

Elsewhere, in other scriptural passages and in other meetings with the Israelites, Jesus said "...Hear, O Israel, the Lord our God is one Lord." [Mark 12:29]. This passage resembles what appears in the books of the Old Testament [Deuteronomy 6:4]. When an Israelite came forward asking him, "...Good Master, what shall I do to inherit eternal life?" [Luke 18:18], how did Jesus respond? He did not tell him to do this or do that. Instead, he first objected to the word "good" about himself, saying "...Why callest thou me good? None is good, save one, that is, God" [Luke 18:19]. Then Jesus began to teach him what came in the Old Testament and its message; namely, to maintain the oneness of God in creed, adhere to the Law of Moses and to safeguard it.

I think this concludes our introductory look at the books of the New Testament. Now we should begin a more detailed discussion under the title "A Look at the Scriptures of the New Testament." This will enable everyone, regardless of his knowledge, to ascertain the truth of this discourse.

A Look at the Scriptures of the New Testament

1. The Problem of Numerous Discrepancies

There are numerous discrepancies among the Gospels, either between one Gospel and another, or within the contents of each one. Naturally, in any general or religious study, especially one concerned with revelation and the Holy Books, we must follow one basic rule that all of us should approve:

> Had it been from other than Allah, They would surely have found therein much discrepancy.[1]

---

[1] Qur'an 4: 82.

Differences between Matthew and Luke Concerning Jesus' Genealogy

Christian tradition holds that Joseph the Carpenter, the suitor of Mary, was the father of Jesus.[1] Luke says:
> Now Jesus Himself began his ministry at about thirty years of age, being (as was supposed) *the son* of Joseph, *the son* of Heli...[2]

Matthew's account of Jesus' genealogy differs from Luke's account. Matthew claimed that Jesus was the descendent of Solomon, the son of David, whereas Luke claimed that he was the descendent of another son of David, namely Nathan. The above can be illustrated by the following table which shows the genealogies listed by both Matthew and Luke. These can further be compared with the genealogies given in the Old Testament, especially in I Chronicles:

Matthew	1 Chronicles	Luke
1. David	David	David
2. Solomon	Solomon – Nathan	Nathan
3. Rehoboam	Rehoboam	Mattatha
4. Abijah	Abijah	Menna

---

[1] This is a shameful accusation. They have linked Joseph the Carpenter to this noble prophet who has nothing to do with him at all. Likewise, it is a great insult to the virtuous Virgin Mary. Allah, Most Exalted, has related the true story of Maryam (Mary) and in Surat Maryam of the Holy Qur'an, Allah says: "(Relate in the Book (the story of) Mary, when she withdrew from her family to a place in the East. She placed a screen (to screen herself) from them: then we sent to her Our angel, and he appeared before her as a man in all respects. She said: 'I seek refuge from you in (Allah) Most Gracious: (come not near) if you fear Allah.' He said: 'Nay, I am only a messenger from your Lord, (to announce) to you the gift of a holy son.' She said: 'How shall I have a son, seeing that no man has touched me, and I am not unchaste?' He said: 'So (it will be.) Your Lord said, "That is easy for Me: and (We wish) to appoint him as a sign unto men and a mercy from Us: it is a matter (so) decreed."'" In *Surat Tahrim* Allah says: "And Mary, the daughter of Imran, who guarded her chastity; and We breathed into (her body) of Our Spirit; and she testified the truth of the words of her Lord and of His revelations, and was one of the devout (servants)."

[2] Luke 3:23.

Muslim-Christian Dialogue

5. Asa	Asa	Melea
6. Jehoshaphat	Jehoshaphat	Eliakim
7. Joram	Joram	Jonam
8. Uzziah	Ahaziah	Joseph
9. ---	Jotham	Judah
10. ---	Ahaz	Simeon
11. ---	Azariah	Levi
12. Jotham	Jotham	Mattahat
13. Ahaz	Ahaz	Jorim
14. Hezekiah	Hezekiah	Eliezer
15. Manasseh	Manasseh	Joshua
16. Amos	Amos	Er
17. Josiah	Josiah	Elmadam
18. ---	Jehoiakim	Cosam
19. Jechoniah	Jechoniah	Addi
20. Shealtiel	Shaeltiel	Melchi
21. ---	Pedaiah	Neri
22. Zerubbabel	Zerubbabel	Shealtiel
23. Abiud	Hananiah	Zerubbabel
24. Eliakim	Rhesa	
25. Azor	Joanan	
26. Zadok	Joda	
27. Achim	Josech	
28. Eliud	Semein	
29. Eleazar	Mattathias	
30. Matthan	Maath	
31. Jacob	Naggai	
32. Joseph, the Carpenter	Esli	
33.	Nahum	
34.	Amos	
35.	Mattathias	
36.	Joseph	
37.	Jannai	
38.	Melchi	
39.	Levi	
40.	Matthat	
41.	Heli	
42.	Joseph, the Carpenter	

For the sake of simplicity, we have only treated the descendants of Solomon, the son of David, down to the twenty-third generation, as mentioned in I Chronicles of the Old Testament. Further, we did not pursue the chain of Nathan, son of David. The missing names replaced by (-) in the Gospel of Matthew were dropped by mistake from the listing prepared by Matthew.

The above table brings to light a number of observations. Many Bible exegetes have already talked about this. For example, John C. Fenton says:

> Matthew has probably continued to draw upon I Chronicles [3:5, 10-16], but he has omitted three generations between Joram and Jotham, and omitted Jehoiakim after Josiah. Luke's genealogy is traced through another son of David, namely Nathan [Luke 3:31; I Chronicles 3:5]
>
> Matthew was able to take the first three names, Jechoniah, Shealtiel, and Zerubbabel, from I Chronicles 3:16ff.; but for the remainder of the list Matthew had, as far as we know, no written source. Luke also has Shealtiel and Zerubbabel in his genealogy, but none of the others [Luke 3:27].
>
> Matthew now looks back over the genealogy, and points out that in each of the three ages there were fourteen generations (though in fact he has only thirteen names in the last period [Matthew 1:12-16].[1]

George Bradford Caird says:

> In the middle of this list (of Luke) occur the three names 'Joanan, the son of Rhesa, the son of Zerubbabel'. But Joanan is only another form of the name Hananiah, and Hananiah was the son of Zerubbabel; there never was such a person as Rhesa [I Chronicles. 3:19]. Rhesa is the Aramaic word for prince, and in the original list it must have been appended as a title to the name of Zerubbabel, the only man who could conceivably have been so designated after 586 B.C. The error which has crept into the Lucan list could

---

[1]Fenton, p. 39f.

have occurred only if the original list was compiled in the reverse order, Zerubbabel the prince begot Joanan.[1]

In short, if we take the Book of I Chronicles as the major reference for Jesus' genealogy, we can point out the following:

1. Matthew was mistaken in Jesus' genealogy when he dropped five names from it (nos. 9, 10, 11, 18, and 21).
2. Luke was mistaken when he added "Rhesa" (no. 24) between "Zerubbabel" and "Joanan".
3. A major discrepancy between Matthew and Luke appears when Luke considers Joseph the Carpenter as one of the descendents of Nathan, the son of David; whereas Matthew records him as a descendent of Solomon, the son of David.

For centuries, several defenders of the Gospels— which they consider to be divine revelation— have exerted great efforts to reconcile the Gospels of Matthew and Luke by using Israelite traditions. Naturally, their efforts have all been in vain.

Obviously, there is a great error in Matthew's version of the genealogy when compared with the version of I Chronicles. Matthew has omitted Joash, Amaziah, Azariah, and Jehoiakim from the lineage. So clear is this issue that it needs no further discussion. Likewise, it is obvious that Luke's version also differs from Matthew's version. Not surprisingly, this is exactly what Christian scholars affirm.

Discrepancy in the Gospels Regarding the Names of the Apostles

In his Gospel, Matthew says:

> Now the names of the twelve Apostles are these: first, Simon, who is called Peter, and Andrew his brother; James the son of Zebedee, and John his brother; Philip and Bartholomew; Thomas and Matthew the tax collector; James the son of Alphaeus, and Lebbaeus, whose surname was Thaddaeus; Simon the Canaanite, and Judas Iscariot, who also betrayed Him.[2]

---

[1]Caird, G. B., *Saint Luke*, p. 19.
[2]Matthew 10:2-4.

On the other hand, Luke states:

> And when it was day, He called His disciples to Himself; and from them He chose twelve who He also named apostles; Simon, whom He also named Peter, and Andrew his brother; James and John; Philip and Bartholomew; Matthew and Thomas; James the son of Alphaeus and Simon called the Zealot; Judas, the son of James, and Judas Iscariot who also became a traitor.[1]

John mentions the names of some apostles. Among them is another Judas, not the betrayer. He is the one whom John calls "...Judas (not Iscariot)".[2]

Clearly, discrepancies exist between what Matthew and Mark say on one hand, and what Luke and John say on the other. Accordingly, George Caird comments:

> When the Gospels were written, the names of the apostles were not verified. Judah, the son of Jacob, did not appear in the lists of both Matthew and Mark. Instead, Lebbaeus, whose surname was Thaddaeus, took his place.

Here, we draw attention to the fact that Prophet Muhammad (may Allah's peace and blessings be upon him) had more than one hundred thousand companions. Their names and biographies are well known. How could the authors of the Gospels have failed to verify the names of twelve apostles?!

Discrepancies between Matthew and Mark Regarding the Story of the Purging of the Temple and the Fig Tree

The Gospel of Matthew narrates:

> Then Jesus went into the temple of God and drove out all those who bought and sold in the temple... And He said to them, "It is written, 'My house shall be called a house of prayer,' but you have made it a 'den of thieves.'" Then He left them and went out of the city to Bethany, and he lodged there.

---

[1] Luke 6:13-16.
[2] John 14:22.

Now in the morning, as He returned to the city, He was hungry. And seeing a fig tree by the road, He came to it and found nothing on it but leaves, and said to it, "Let no fruit grow on you ever again." Immediately the fig tree withered away.

And when the disciples saw it, they marveled, saying, "How did the fig tree wither away so soon?"

So Jesus answered and said to them, "Assuredly, I say to you, if you have faith and do not doubt, if you say to this mountain, 'Be removed and be cast into the sea,' it will be done."[1]

However, concerning this incident, the Gospel of Mark says:

Now the next day, when they had come out from Bethany, He was hungry. And seeing from afar a big tree having leaves, He went to see if perhaps He would find something on it. When He came to it He found nothing but leaves, for it was not the season for figs. In response Jesus said to it, "Let no one eat fruit from you ever again." And His disciples heard it.

So they came to Jerusalem. Then Jesus went into the temple and began to drive out those who bought and sold in the temples, and overturned the tables of the money changers and the seats of those who sold doves... Then He taught, saying to them, "Is it not written, 'My house shall be called a house of prayer for all nations'? But you have made it a 'den of thieves.'" And the scribes and chief priests heard it and sought how they might destroy Him: for they feared Him, because all the people were astonished at His teaching.

When evening had come, He went out of the city. Now in the morning, as they passed by, they saw the fig tree dried up from the roots. And Peter, remembering, said to Him, "Rabbi, look! The fig tree which You cursed has withered away." So Jesus answered and said to them, "Have faith in God. For assuredly, I say to you, whoever says to this mountain, 'Be removed and be cast into the sea,' and does not

---

[1] Matthew 21: 12-21.

doubt in his heart, but believes and those things he says will be done, he will have whatever he says."[1]

Clearly, discrepancies exist between the two narrations. these differences can be summarized as follows:

1. Whereas the Gospel of Matthew mentions that Jesus purged the Temple of its sellers and money changers before he saw the fig tree and cursed it, we find the sequence reversed in the Gospel of Mark. Mark narrates the fig tree incidents happening before the purging of the Temple.

2. Between the two accounts, there are some discrepancies in the details of the fig tree incident. J. Fenton discusses the discrepancies between the two, saying:

> In Mark, Jesus looks for fruit on the tree, and 'curses' it, on one day; then on the next day Peter draws Jesus' attention to it [Mark 11: 912]. The result of Matthew's rearrangement here is that the whole incident takes place on the same day.[2]

Dr. Ghazi:

One of the narrations said that the time was not a time of figs. This means that the knowledge of Jesus, who is claimed by many to be a god, or the son of God, was not even up to par with the knowledge of a simple farmer who knows if the season for figs is here or not. Moreover, He could not figure out whether or not the tree, obviously seen with bare eyes, was carrying figs. Amazingly, both stories relate that this hungry god went to the tree. Unable to find any figs on the tree, he cursed it.

2. The Problem of Unfulfilled Prophecies

Now we come to a very serious issue, namely the problem of unfulfilled prophecies. There is general agreement among the scholars of religion, especially scholars of religions having holy books, that one of the definitions of a prophet is "one who is sent by God, or one who speaks from revelation that he receives

---
[1] Mark 11:12-23.
[2] Fenton, p. 336.

from his Creator." Also his message should be free of discrepancies.

Surely, the prophet who tells you truthfully about what is happening in this life should also tell you the truth about what is promised in the Hereafter. However, when one or more prophecies attributed to a prophet claim that the life we live has come to an end, then how will the prophecies about the Hereafter fare? Obviously, what he promised about the Hereafter will also be fulfilled. I believe that this principle is agreeable to all.

Regarding prophecies in the Gospels we find the following :

A. Prophecy: The World Will End in the First Century C.E.

The Gospels relate that Jesus

> ...called His twelve disciples to Him, He gave them power over unclean spirits, to cast them out, and to heal all kinds of sickness ...and commended them, saying, "Behold, I send you out as sheep in the midst of wolves. Therefore be wise as serpents and harmless as doves... When they persecute you in this city, flee to another. For assuredly, I say to you, you will not have gone through the cities of Israel before the Son of Man (i.e., Jesus) comes."[1]

This means that Jesus would come back to the world before his disciples would have had time to preach in all the towns of Israel. Also, Jesus' return would be before some of his contemporaries, who lived during the first half of the first century C.E., had died. "For the Son of Man shall in the glory of his Father come with his angels, and then he will reward every man according to his works. Verily, I say unto you, there be some standing here which shall not taste of death till they see the Son of Man coming in his kingdom."[2]

In other words, the end of the world and Jesus' return to the world must take place before the generation which lived in the first century C.E. had passed away.

---

[1]Matthew 10:1-23.
[2]Matthew 16:27-28.

Immediately after the tribulation of those days the sun will be darkened, and the moon will not give its light; the stars will fall from heaven, and the powers of the heavens will be shaken. Then the sign of the Son of Man will appear in heaven, ...and they will see the Son of Man coming on the clouds of heaven with power and great glory... "Assuredly, I say to you, this generation will by no means pass away till all these things take place."[1]

Both the Gospels of Mark[2] and Luke[3] agree with the serious statement made by Matthew.

Obviously, as John Fenton says, it did not happen as Matthew expected.[4] As seen above, prophecies attributed by the Gospels to Jesus about the end of the world during the first century C.E. were never fulfilled, thus making it impossible for anyone to defend them.

B. Prophecy: Judas, the Traitor, Will Join Jesus in the Hereafter

During a conversation between Jesus and his disciples about who will be saved in the Hereafter, Peter asked his teacher about the reward of those who believe in him. He says:

> ...See, we have left all and follow You. Therefore what shall we have? So Jesus said to them, "Assuredly, I say to you, that in the regeneration when the Son of Man sits on the throne of His Glory, you who have followed Me will also sit on twelve thrones, judging the twelve tribes of Israel. And everyone who has left houses or brothers or sisters or father or mother or wife or children or lands, for My name's sake, shall receive an hundred fold, and inherit eternal life."[5]

Judas Iscariot was one of the twelve disciples who listened to this prophecy. After his betrayal he was known as the damned one because he was removed from the company of Jesus in this

---

[1] Matthew 24:29-34.
[2] Mark 13:24-30.
[3] Luke 21:25-32.
[4] Fenton, p. 21.
[5] Matthew 19:27-29.

life and in the Hereafter. As such it becomes impossible to fulfill this prophecy.

When we refer to the narrative corresponding to the above narrative given in the Gospel of Luke, we find, as Fenton says, "...that Luke's version omits the number twelve here, possibly because Luke was thinking of Judas Iscariot."[1]

C. Prophecy: Jesus' Body Will Be Buried in the Earth for Three Days and Three Nights:

> Some Jews tried to challenge Jesus, saying: "Teacher, we want to see a sign from You." But He answered and said to them, "An evil and adulterous generation seeks after a sign, and no sign will be given to it except the sign of the prophet Jonah. For as Jonah was three days and three nights in the belly of the great fish, so will the Son of Man be three days and three nights in the heart of the earth."[2]

This is a common statement in the Gospels. It has been repeated in most of the Gospels and in more than one place. It has been mentioned in the Gospel of Mark. It has also been mentioned in the Gospel of Luke, though with an important difference which anyone would notice. Jesus says: "This is an evil generation. It seeks a sign, and no sign will be given to it except the sign of Jonah the prophet. For as Jonah became a sign to the Ninevites, so also the Son of Man will be to this generation."[3]

The three days were also mentioned in the Gospel of John.[4] In the Old Testament we read what happened to Jonah. The Book of Jonah relates: "Now the Lord had prepared a great fish to swallow Jonah. And Jonah was in the belly of the fish three days and three nights.[5] Then Jonah prayed to the Lord his God from the fish's belly... so the Lord spoke to the fish, and it vomited Jonah onto dry land."[6]

---

[1] Fenton, p. 317.
[2] Matthew 12: 38-40.
[3] Luke 11:29-30.
[4] John 2:19.
[5] Jonah 1:17.
[6] Jonah 2:1-10.

Thus, in order to fulfill this prophecy, the crucified body must stay in "the heart of the earth" for three days and three nights. However, when we go back to what the Gospels say about the crucifixion, we find that the crucified body was taken off the cross Friday evening (the Day of Crucifixion):

Now when evening had come, because it was the Preparation Day, that is, the day before the Sabbath, Joseph of Arimathea, ...went in to Pilate and asked for the body of Jesus. Pilate marveled that He was already dead; and summoning the centurion, he asked him if He had been dead for some time. So when he found out from the centurion, he granted the body to Joseph. Then he bought fine linen, took Him down, and wrapped Him in the linen. And he laid Him in a tomb which had been hewn out of the rock, and rolled a stone against the door of the tomb.[1]

In the early morning hours of Sunday, Jesus' disciples and followers discovered that the tomb was empty. In this context the Gospel of Matthew narrates:

> Now after the Sabbath, as the first day of the week began to dawn, Mary Magdalene and the other Mary came to see the tomb... the angel answered and said to the women... He is not here; He is risen, as He said.[2]

Similarly the Gospel of John says:

> Now on the first day of the week Mary Magdalene went to the tomb early, while it was still dark, and saw that the stone had been taken away from the tomb.[3]

By a simple calculation we can figure out that:

a. The number of days in which the body stayed in the "heart of the earth" (in the tomb) = one day (i.e., Saturday)

b. The number of nights in which the body stayed in the "heart of the earth" (in the tomb) = two nights (i.e., Friday night and a part of Saturday night at best). Thus the prophecy of the body remaining buried in the earth for three days and three nights could not possibly have been fulfilled.

---

[1] Mark 15: 42-46.
[2] Matthew 28:1-6.
[3] John 20:1.

The Crucifixion

Let us move on to discuss an important and crucial issue, namely, that of the crucifixion. Let me say sincerely that one of the greatest miracles of the Qur'an is its absolute rejection of the story of the crucifixion of Jesus (may Allah's peace and blessings be upon him). It states the issue in a single verse: "That they said (in boast), 'We killed Christ Jesus, the son of Mary, the messenger of Allah.' But they killed him not, nor crucified him, but so it was made to appear to them."[1]

As for other issues, such as their claim that God is Jesus, or Jesus is the son of God, the Qur'an discusses them in several places, refuting their claims as outright disbelief. As a matter of fact, *tawhid*[2] and related issues are discussed in about a third of the Holy Qur'an. As is well known among Muslims, the message of Surat Al-Ikhlas[3] is equivalent to the message of one third of the whole Qur'an. It reads, "Say, He is Allah, the one and only. Allah, the Eternal, Absolute; He begetteth not, nor is He begotten; and there is none like unto Him."[4]

Now we must ask: Had the Qur'an come from someone other than Allah (or God), i.e., had some human being made it up and claimed that it was revealed to him, wouldn't it have been more appropriate and more convenient for him, in preaching his message, to simply acknowledge the crucifixion of Jesus? After all, this belief was widespread among the people at that time. As a matter of fact, he would have attracted Christians and would have minimized any problems or obstacles that would have kept them from accepting Islam.

Recent evidence indicates that a Christian can change from one sect to another without much of an outcry. This is due to the fact that all these sects share many fundamental beliefs. Similarly, evidence from the past shows that the conversion of the people with idolatrous beliefs (in pagan Rome) to Christianity was due mostly to the similarity of beliefs between paganism

---

[1] Qur'an, 4:157.
[2] *Tawhid*— belief in the Oneness of God in His Lordship, His Names and Attributes, and as the only One Who deserves to be worshipped.
[3] Chapter 112 of the Holy Qur'an.
[4] Qur'an 112:1-4.

and Christianity. Both shared the idea of an incarnate god, along with other ideas and customs which we will discuss later in detail. In contrast, the conversion of a Christian to Islam is considered a revolution in his life and beliefs. This is so because s/he has to change a lot of concepts and beliefs already entrenched in his or her mind and heart.

However, the Holy Qur'an, the book of Islam, never concurred with the Christians in their beliefs or customs. It dealt with all issues very clearly. For example, it declared that statements such as "God is the Christ," or "Christ is the Son of God," are plain unbelief, unforgivable. In the story of Jesus' assassination— and remember how many prophets the Jews had killed before him— we find that the Qur'an unequivocally rejects Jesus' assassination and his crucifixion. It holds this position for no other reason but to declare boldly that this never really happened.

The Qur'an speaks nothing but the truth. It does so regardless of whether that truth conforms to what people accept as basic truths or whether that truth contradicts what they have inherited for centuries.

Since the crucifixion, as well as the other issues, are all topics of discussion, let us agree to a simple rule which will govern peoples' decisions concerning various issues. This rule is that whatever is open to the possibility (of doubt) cannot be used to prove something else. Thus, when two witnesses give conflicting statements before a judge in court, their testimonies cannot be considered unless and until a third witness corroborates the testimony of one of them. Otherwise, a just ruling cannot be issued.

Let us proceed to the discussion of the crucifixion issue as narrated by the Gospels. They start with a number of incidents where attempts were made to kill Jesus, and end with hanging a person crying desperately on the cross, and his subsequent shrouding and burial.

Muslim-Christian Dialogue

The Issue of the Crucifixion

1. Rubbing Jesus' Body with Scent

The Gospels differ even in this simple incident, which is considered a precursor to the events leading to the crucifixion. The Gospel of Mark says:

> After two days it was the Passover and the Feast of Unleavened Bread. And the chief priests and the scribes sought how they might take Him by trickery and put Him to death... And being in Bethany at the house of Simon the leper, as He sat at the table. A woman came having an alabaster flask of very costly oil of spikenard. Then she broke the flask and poured it on His head. But there were some who were indignant among themselves, and said, "Why was this fragrant oil wasted? For it might have been sold for more than three hundred denarii and given to the poor." And they criticized her sharply.[1]

Matthew mentions this incident in 26:6-9, Luke in 7:36-39, and John in 12:1-6. Needless to say, they differ with respect to the time of occurrence of the events and other major points. Regarding this incident Nineham says:

> ...we find that St. John narrated the story as a few days earlier than St. Mark did. St. Luke puts it in an entirely different period of Jesus' life. Whereas in the Gospel of Mark we find that this incident occurred in the house of Simon the Leper in Bethany, the Gospel of John says it took place in the house of Mary, Martha and Lazarus.[2]

The discrepancies between the Gospels relative to this incident may be summarized as follows:

The location of the incident:
In the house of Simon the Leper (Mark and Matthew)
In the house of a Pharisee (Luke)

---

[1] Mark 14:1-5.
[2] Nineham, p. 370.

In the house of Lazarus, Mary and Martha (John)

The identity of the woman:
unknown (Mark and Matthew)
a sinner (Luke)
Mary, the sister of Lazarus (John)

What she did:
rubbed Jesus' head with the scent (Mark and Matthew)
rubbed Jesus' feet with the scent (Luke and John).

The reaction of the attendees:
some were indignant (Mark)
the disciples were indignant (Matthew)
the Pharisee asked himself if Jesus knew the woman (Luke)
Judas Iscariot was indignant over her extravagance (John)

2. Preparations for the Last Supper

Mark relates:

Now on the first day of Unleavened Bread, when they killed the Passover lamb, His disciples said to Him, "Where do You want us to go and prepare, that You may eat the Passover?" And He sent out two of His disciples and said to them, "Go into the city, and a man will meet you carrying a pitcher of water; follow him. Wherever he goes in, say to the master of the house, 'the Teacher says, "Where is the guest room in which I may eat the Passover with My disciples?"' Then he will show you a large upper room, furnished and prepared; there make ready for us." So His disciples went out, and came into the city, and found it just as He had said to them; and they prepared the Passover. In the evening He came with the twelve.[1]

Nineham comments:

The majority of biblical exegetes believe that this passage with its verses [12-17] is actually a late addition to the narra-

---
[1] Mark 14:12-17.

tive St. Mark is following in this part of his Gospel. Among the reasons are:

(a) The day on which the story is said to have occurred is described in a way in which no ordinary Jew of the time would have described it.[1]

(b) Jesus' followers are described throughout this section as 'disciples', whereas in the surrounding passages (which seem to reproduce a relatively early strand of tradition, they are consistently referred to as 'the twelve'.[2]

(c) The writer of verse 17 knows nothing of the mission of the two disciples in v.13; the work of preparation referred to in v.16 would have been enough to keep them fully occupied right up to the last minute, and v.17, if it had known of the contents of this section, would have to refer to 'the Ten'.[3,4]

Matthew's version of the preparations for the Last Supper differs from Mark's version. Matthew, as John Fenton states in his exegesis,[5] puts all the disciples coming together for the

---

[1] While the day when people sacrificed the Passover lamb (v.12), Nissan 14, was occasionally included in the feast and so counted as the first day of Passover, this usage was confined to learned technical discussions, and the experts in such matters very much doubt if it was ever common parlance. Thus, it would seem to be either a mistranslation from an Aramaic original or the faulty expression of a non-Jewish author. The words *when they sacrificed the Passover lamb* make it quite clear that St. Mark was thinking of Nissan 14; the question is whether an early tradition would have referred to that day as the first day of Passover.

[2] Contrast vv. 12, 13, 14 and 16, and 10, 17 and 20. This at least suggests that this section is a late-comer to its present context.

[3] i.e., the writer of v. 17 ("In the evening He came with the twelve...") knew nothing of the two disciples mentioned in v. 13 being missing. It follows, then, that had the author of v. 17 known the contents of v. 13, he should have said "the ten", not the "the twelve".

[4] Nineham, p. 375f.

[5] Fenton, p. 414. Jesus' prediction at the beginning of the chapter mentions (a) Passover, (b) the delivering up of the Son of Man to be crucified. Matthew, in his characteristic way, has dealt with (b) first and now he comes to (a), the Passover, The day is probably Thursday, Nissan 14; on that day the Passover lambs were killed in Jerusalem, and the feast had to be eaten that evening, in the city. The disciples therefore

preparation. He says that Jesus "...said, 'Go into the city to such a one and say to him, "The Teacher says, My time is at hand. I will keep the Passover at your house with my disciples."'" And the disciples did as Jesus had directed them and they prepared the Passover.[1]

3. The Time of the Last Supper and Its Effect on the Issue of the Crucifixion:

"Matthew (Like Mark) thought," says John Fenton, "that the Last Supper was the Passover meal. In the fourth Gospel, on the other hand, the Passover is to be eaten on the evening after the death of Jesus [John 18:28]. The majority of scholars currently think that the Markan and Matthewan date is right, and that John changed it for theological reasons."[2]

This is because John feels that the Lord's Supper which Jesus and his disciples came to was before the Feast of the Passover. He says:

> Now before the Feast of the Passover... And supper being ended... Jesus... rose from supper and laid aside His garments, took a towel and girded Himself. After that, He poured water into a basin and began to wash the disciples' feet...[3]

John also maintains that they arrested Jesus on the evening before Passover. He says:

> [T]hey led Jesus from Caiaphas to the Praetorum, and it was early morning. But they themselves did not go into the Praetorum, lest they should be defiled, but that they might eat the Passover.[4]

---

ask Jesus where he wants them to prepare the meal, and Jesus sends them to Jerusalem with a message to a particular man who has a house there. The message includes the further prediction of Jesus: "My time is at hand," which Matthew has added in order to show that Jesus is aware of the plans and arrangements of the Sanhedrin and Judas Iscariot.

[1] Matthew 26:18-19.
[2] Fenton, p. 415.
[3] John 13:1-5.
[4] John 18:28.

The discrepancies between the Gospels on the Last Supper and its timing have led to differences between them on a very crucial point related to the crucifixion, namely, determination of the exact day of the crucifixion.

If we accept the story of Mark, Matthew and Luke, then Jesus would have eaten the Passover meal with his disciples Thursday night. Shortly thereafter, he was arrested— the same night i.e., Thursday night. As a result, the crucifixion would have taken place on Friday.

However, if we take John's story, then the arrest took place Wednesday night, and the crucifixion on Thursday.

Did the crucifixion take place on Thursday or on Friday?!

4. The Last Supper and the Disciple Who Betrayed Jesus

Mark relates:
> In the evening He came with the twelve. Now as they sat and ate, Jesus said, "Assuredly I say to you, one of you who eats with Me will betray Me." And they began to be sorrowful, and to say to Him one by one, "Is it I?" And another said, "Is it I?" He answered and said to them, "It is one of the twelve, who dip with Me in the dish. The Son of Man indeed goes just as it is written of Him, but woe to that man by whom the Son of Man is betrayed, It would have been good for that man if he had never been born."[1]

Matthew has made some alterations to the story of Mark. Luke says:
> Then Satan entered Judas, surnamed Iscariot, who was numbered among the twelve. So he went his way and conferred with the chief priests and captains, how he might betray Him to them... so he promised and sought opportunity to betray Him to them... When the hour had come, He sat down, and the twelve apostles with Him. Then He said to them, "With fervent desire I have desired to eat this Passover with you. ...But behold, the hand of My betrayer is with Me on the ta-

---

[1] Mark 14:17-21.

ble." ...Then they began to question among themselves, which of them it was who would do this thing.[1]

The story narrated by John differs noticeably from that narrated in the other three Gospels. John says:

> When Jesus had these things, He was troubled in spirit, and testified and said, "Most assuredly, I say to you, one of you will betray Me." Then the disciples looked at one another, perplexed about whom He spoke ...Jesus answered, "It is he to whom I shall give a piece of bread when I have dipped it." And having dipped the bread, He gave it to Judas Iscariot, the son of Simon. Now after the piece of bread, Satan entered him. Then, Jesus said to him, "What you do, do quickly."...Having received the piece of bread, he then went out immediately, and it was night.[2]

The discrepancies in the Gospel concerning Jesus' response to his disciples about who the betrayer would be are clear. While Mark claims that he is the one "...who dipped with me in the dish,"[3] John asserts that he is the one "...whom I shall give a piece of bread when I have dipped it."[4]

Even if we ignore the above discrepancies, what is important about Judas' betrayal is the conflicting version in the Gospels concerning the incident of Satan entering Judas' body. Luke maintains that Satan entered Judas body at least one day before the Last Supper.[5]

In contrast, John says that Satan entered Judas' body after Jesus gave him "the piece of bread" during the Last s supper.

At this point, we will close our discussion for today. Among the factors related to the issue of the crucifixion and discussed today were the following: rubbing Jesus' body with scent, then the preparation for the Last Supper, the timing of the Last Supper and its effect on the issue of the crucifixion, and finally what was said about the Last Supper and the disciple who betrayed Jesus.

---

[1] Luke 22:3-23.
[2] John 13: 21-30.
[3] Mark 14:20.
[4] John 13:26.
[5] Luke 22:3-7.

God willing, we shall resume our discussion of the issue of the crucifixion tomorrow.

Second Session

Dr. Muhammad Jamil Ghazi

Glory to your Lord, the Lord of Honor and Power! (He is free) from what they ascribe (to Him)! And Peace be on the Messengers! And Praise be to Allah, the Lord and Cherisher of the Worlds.[1]

> Say: Praise be to Allah, who begets no son, and has no partner in (His) dominion; nor (needs) He any to protect Him from humiliation. Yea, magnify Him for His greatness and glory![2]

Also, may Allah send his blessings upon our Prophet Muhammad, and on his family and all of his Companions.

Allah (swt)[3] says:

> When the anger of Moses was appeased, he took up the tablets: in the writing thereon was guidance and mercy for such as fear their Lord. And Moses chose seventy of his people for Our place of meeting: when they were seized with violent quaking, he prayed: "My Lord! If it had been Your will You could have destroyed, long before, both them and me: would You destroy us for the deeds of the foolish ones among us? This is no more than Your trial: by it You cause whom You will to stray, and You lead whom You will unto the right path. You are our Protector: so forgive us and give us Your mercy; for You are the best of those who forgive. And ordain for us that which is good, in this life and in the Hereafter, for we have turned unto You."

---

[1] Qur'an 37:180-182.
[2] Qur'an 17:111.
[3] i.e., *Subhanahu wa Ta'ala*: an Arabic phrase which Muslims repeat after speaking the name of Allah. It means, 'How Perfect is Allah, most Exalted'.

He (Allah) said: With My punishment I visit whom I will; but My mercy extends to all things. That (mercy) I shall ordain for those who do right, and practice regular charity, and those who believe in Our signs; those who follow the Messenger, the unlettered Prophet, whom they find mentioned in their own (scriptures)— in the Torah and the Gospel— for he commands them what is just and forbids them what is evil; he allows them as lawful what is good (and pure) and prohibits them from what is bad (and impure); he releases them from their heavy burdens and from the yokes that are upon them. So it is those who believe in him, honor him, help him and follow the light which is sent down with him; it is they who will prosper.

Mankind! I am sent unto you all as the Messenger of Allah, to Whom belongs the dominion of the heavens and the earth: there is no god but He: it is He That gives both life and death. So believe in Allah and His Messenger, the unlettered Prophet, who believes in Allah and His words: follow him that (so) you may be guided.[1]

With these eminent verses we begin the second session of this discussion between Islam and Christianity. This meeting was organized not only to discuss Christian beliefs and ideas but also to address some misgivings and specious arguments about Islam in people's minds. However, first I would like to introduce Mr. James Bakheet to you. He will talk to you about his way of running the discussion with his brothers. Mr. James...

Mr. James Bakheet

Respected gentlemen, we thank God for helping us to continue what we started as a spiritual and objective discussion concerning Christian and Islamic issues. We are aware undoubtedly, you must be expecting a response to our previous discussion; however, due to circumstances beyond our control, we haven't prepared any response. Our brother, the honorable shaykh

---

[1]Qur'an 7:154-158.

and Saudi Religious Attaché in Khartoum, will explain the situation. Thank you.

Shaykh Ahmad Talibi, the Saudi Religious Attaché

I begin in the name of Allah, Ever Beneficent, Ever Merciful. We seek His aid, and May His peace and blessings be upon His prophets and messengers, and upon His final prophet, Muhammad, may Allah's peace and blessings be upon him.

We had planned for James and his colleagues to study last night's discussion and then tonight present their views regarding the discussion. However, due to uncontrollable circumstances, we have agreed with him to continue our daily discussion until we finish responding to all the questions mentioned in his letter. They have also been taped on cassettes. After this they will all have a chance to study all our sessions and respond at their convenience.

This is what we have agreed upon. We ask Allah (swt) to grant us success and to guide us to the right way. Surely, He is capable of that. May His Peace and blessings be upon our Prophet Muhammad.

Dr. Muhammad Jamil Ghazi

In the first session, Brigadier General Engineer Ahmad Abdul-Wahhab talked about "the Legitimacy of the Gospels." Although the Brigadier has adequately dealt with the topic, some questions still remain. Let us reconsider these questions. One of these questions is: is it possible for the academic researcher to decide absolutely that there exists today a gospel ascribed directly to Jesus?

He proceeded to reply, saying: "The apparent contradictions in the Gospels are very small. Look, this is the size of all the Gospels (holding up the books of the New Testament in his hand)!" So, if it is established that the Gospels contain some discrepancies— even one, not a hundred[1]— then this invalidates it as a revelation from God, Most Perfect, Most Exalted. Why? Because Allah, Most Perfect, Most Exalted, said in the Qur'an, revealed to an illiterate prophet and to an illiterate nation that did not read or write: "Had it been from other than Allah, they would surely have found therein much discrepancy."[2]

In other words, if the Qur'an had come from any other than Allah, they would have found therein much discrepancy. That is why every Muslim frankly declares: Show us if there is one contradiction in 6,236 verses of the Holy Qur'an. No one can dare claim that there is even a single contradiction in the Qur'an. We are in front of you, ready to face any charge, doubt or misgiving that even a single contradiction exists in the Qur'an. In contrast, as you have seen, the Gospels, in spite of their small size, are contradictory. As a matter of fact, discrepancies exist on a single page. Let me give you an example of this.

In the Gospel of Matthew we find scores of such discrepancies. Without any bias we can refer to some of them. For example, Jesus tells Peter:

> And I also say to you that you are Peter, and on this rock I will build My church, and the gates of Hades shall not prevail against it. And I will give you the keys of the kingdom of heaven, and whatever you bind on earth will be bound in heaven, and whatever you loose on earth will be loosed in heaven.[3]

In other words, Jesus informs Peter: You are the bedrock and you are strong. Satan will not prevail against you. With you, I'll build my church. Then Jesus gives him a strange promise: "...and whatever you find on earth will be found in heaven, and whatever you loose on earth will be loosed in heaven,"[4] i.e., whatever you desire is what I desire and whatever you do, I'll also do the same. In other words, God's will follows the will of Peter.

---

[1] Cf. *Izhar al-Haqq* (Triumph of the Truth), by Rahmatullah Al-Hindi for details on the discrepancies between the New and Old Testaments.
[2] Qur'an 4:82.
[3] Matthew 16:18-19.
[4] Matthew 16:19.

Interestingly, this has been discussed in the Holy Qur'an. Allah, Most Exalted, Most Perfect, says:

> The Jews call Ezra a son of God, and the Christians call Christ the son of God. That is a saying from their mouth; (in this) they but imitate what the unbelievers of old used to say. God's curse be on them: how they are deluded away from the Truth! They take their priests and their anchorites to be their lords in derogation of God, and (they take as their Lord) Christ the son of Mary; yet they were commanded to worship but one God: there is no god but He. Praise and glory to Him: (Far is He) from having the partners they associate (with Him).[1]

Referring to the above, 'Adiy Ibn Hatim At-Ta'i, who was Christian and embraced Islam, said: "Prophet of Allah, we were not worshipping them." His comment was based on the understanding that worship means bowing and praying to them. To this the Prophet of Allah (may Allah's peace and blessings be upon him) said: "Weren't they making things lawful and unlawful for you and you followed what they said?" "Yes," he said. "That," responded the Prophet (may Allah's peace and blessings be upon him), "is worshipping them besides Allah."[2]

In other words, if the right to make things lawful and unlawful is given to someone other than Allah (swt), that is paganism (*shirk*). Accordingly, we find that Islam refuses to give anyone the authority to make things lawful and unlawful except Allah— even His Prophet Muhammad (may Allah's peace and blessings be upon him) did not have such authority unless Allah revealed said ruling to him. Allah even reproached Muhammad (may Allah's peace and blessings be upon him) when he prohibited something:

---

[1] Qur'an 9:30-31.
[2] This is part of long *hadith* narrated by At-Tirmidhi in the book *Exegeses* 4:243, also in *Tafsir At-Tabari,* 14:209-210. Ibn Kathir refers to it in his *Tafsir* 2:349 as narrated by Ahmad Ibn Hanbal in his *Musnad*. At-Tirmidhi said, "This hadith is not known except through 'Abdullah Ibn Sallam, and Ghutayf Ibn A'yan is not known as a narrator." (Editor)

O Prophet! Why do you hold to be forbidden that which Allah has made lawful to you? You seek to please your wives? But Allah is Oft-Forgiving, Most Merciful.[1]

In the previous text taken from the Gospel of Matthew we find that Peter has a very high status. Now look at the end of the same page and notice what he says.

At the top of the page, Peter, as the Gospel of Matthew says on Jesus' tongue, is the rock that Jesus would build his message on and he is the firm rock that even the gates of Hell shall not prevail against. Moreover, he has the keys to the kingdom of Heaven. One hardly begins to revere this great description of Peter when suddenly he is shocked by another portrait of Peter in complete contrast with the first one. So different is this second description of Peter that it essentially transforms him from a divine being to a rebellious devil. What a surprise! And where do we find this? In the Gospel of Matthew itself, in the same chapter, i.e., Chapter 16, after only a few lines. Again, Jesus is seen speaking to Peter. Matthew says:

> From that time Jesus began to show to His disciples that He must go to Jerusalem, and suffer many things from the elders and chief priests and scribes, and be killed, and be raised the third day. Then Peter took Him aside and began to rebuke Him saying, "Far be it from You, Lord: this shall not happen to You!" But he turned and said to Peter, "Get thee behind Me, Satan! You are an offense to Me, for you are not mindful of the things of God, but the things of men."[2]

Look how Peter was at the top of the page. Jesus tells him: "Whatever you loose on earth will be loosed in heaven."[3] Then, at the end of the same page, Jesus says to him, "Get behind me! Satan."[4] Indeed, in the Gospels there are too many contradictions.

Now, I'd like to introduce Mr. Ibrahim Khalil Ahmad to talk to us for a few minutes about other contradictions.

---

[1] Qur'an 66:1.
[2] Matthew 16:21-23.
[3] Matthew 16:19.
[4] Matthew 16:23.

Mr. Ibrahim Khalil Ahmad

Professor James, I would like to take this opportunity to talk as a priest and a professor of theology in the College of Theology; I used to be both.

In fact, our profession as missionaries was based on a quotation in the Second Epistle of Peter, as we could confirm that the Torah and the Injil are both revealed scriptures from Allah (swt). We used to say: "...for prophesy never came by the will of man, but holy men of God spoke as they were moved by the Holy Spirit."[1]

Of course, this passage is the words of Peter as recorded in his Second Epistle. Unfortunately, it gives us the erroneous impression that the Holy Book (i.e., Bible) in our hands today is a revealed Book from Allah (swt).

In their work among Muslims, the priest also uses one of the Qur'anic verses in Surat Ali-'Imran. It says: "It is He Who sent down to you (step by step), in truth, the Book, confirming what went before it; and He sent down the Torah (Law of Moses) and the Gospel (of Jesus) before this, as a guide to mankind."

The Qur'an is very accurate. It does not mention the Old or the New Testaments. Instead, it mentions the Torah and the Injil (i.e., revelation to Jesus). When the Qur'an does refer to the Old and the New Testaments, it refers to them as "the Book." The Qur'an says: "People of the Book! Come to common terms as between us and you."[2] Thus, when the Book is mentioned as a whole, the Qur'an begins to provide sound guidance and direction for all. Accordingly, in Surat An-Nisa', Allah, Most Perfect, Most Exalted, says:

> People of the Book! Commit no excesses in your religion: Nor say of Allah aught but the truth. Christ Jesus the son of Mary was (no more than) a Messenger of Allah, and His Word, which He bestowed on Mary, and a spirit proceeding from Him: so believe in Allah and His Messengers. Say not "Trinity". Desist: it will be better for you: for Allah is one. Allah: Glory be to Him: (far exalted is He) above having a

---
[1] II Peter 1:21.
[2] Qur'an 3:64.

son. To Him belong all things in the heavens and on earth. And enough is Allah as a Disposer of affairs.[1]

In Surat Al-Ma'idah, Allah, Most Perfect, Most Exalted, says: "People of the Book! There has come to you our Messenger, revealing to you much that you used to hide in the Book, and passing over much (that is now unnecessary): there has come to you from Allah a (new) light and a perspicuous Book..."

Notice that when the term used is "the Book", the verse draws attention to the fact that something should be corrected. However, when the term used is the Torah and the Injil (i.e., what was revealed to Jesus) attention is drawn to confirmation of what was revealed previously without any mention of the Old nor the New Testaments.

Let us now move to the Gospels themselves. Let us look at the Gospel of Luke. Was it a revelation from Allah (swt), or was its writing affected by the revelation of Allah, Most Perfect, Most Exalted? Luke says:

> Inasmuch as many have taken in hand to set in order a narrative of those things which have been fulfilled among us, just as those who from the beginning were eyewitnesses and ministers of the word delivered them to us, it seemed good to me also, having had perfect understanding of all things from the very first, to write to you an orderly account, most excellent Theophilus.[2]

Speaking about the scriptures, Luke says, "those who from the beginning were eyewitnesses and ministers of the world delivered them to us." He never said that they were revealed to us by the Holy Spirit. Luke was not one of the twelve disciples who were with Jesus. This is a significant factor when evaluating the whole situation.

When we come to Saul, who was known as Paul afterwards, we find him saying, "But I say to the unmarried and to the widows: It is good for them if they remain even as I am."[3]

These are the words of Paul. He wanted people to remain, like himself, unmarried. Later he says, "Now to the married I

---

[1] Qur'an 4:171.
[2] Luke 1:1-3.
[3] I Corinthians 7:8.

command, yet not I but the Lord: A wife is not to depart from her husband."[1] This means separation without divorce. Still, a little further in his discourse, we find him saying, "...but to the rest I, not the Lord, say..."[2] Thus one time he says: "the Lord says," while in the another instance he says: "I, not the Lord, say". It seems as if he is on the same level as God, Most Perfect, Most Exalted in the Book (i.e., Bible).

What is more disturbing is that he has no objection to a believing woman marrying a pagan. Needless to say, such a marriage, i.e., between a believing woman and a pagan husband, opens itself to a lot of trouble. He advises, "And a woman who has a husband who does not believe, if he is willing to live with her, let her not divorce him."[3]

These are Paul's words. Was he actually awake and alert when he came to correct what was wrong? However, when he comes back to his senses we find him saying,

> Do not be unequally yoked together with unbelievers. For what fellowship has righteousness with lawlessness? And what communion has light with darkness? And what accord has Christ with Belial? Or what part has a believer with an unbeliever? And what agreement has the temple of God with idols? For you are the temple of the living God. As God has said: "I will dwell in them and walk among them, I will be their God, and they shall be My people." Therefore come out from among them and be separate, says the Lord.[4]

Hence, in the First Epistle, he says, "...the woman who has a husband who does not believe, if he is willing to live with her, let her not divorce him,"[5] whereas in the Second Epistle he says: "Be separate."[6]

Undoubtedly, this leaves a lot of uncertainty (as to which version is right)— in a holy Book which is supposed to be absolutely true and credible.

---

[1] I Corinthians 7:10.
[2] I Corinthians 7:12.
[3] I Corinthians 7:13.
[4] II Corinthians 6:114-17.
[5] I Corinthians 7:13.
[6] II Corinthians 6:17.

Next, let us move to Paul and the virgins. In the First Epistle to the Corinthians, he says:

> Now concerning virgins I have no commandment from the Lord; yet I give judgment as one whom the Lord in His mercy has made trustworthy. I suppose, therefore, that this is good because of the present distress— that it is good for a man to remain as he is.[1]

I think that mere assumption or supposition in holy books is something very dreadful. As such, no one can rely on them. Moreover, marriage in Christianity cannot be annulled unless the death of one of the spouses occurs. If it so happens that a woman marries a man and then later dislikes him and wants to end their relationship honorably, would you say that when he dies she can marry again? In other words, she should keep waiting for his death so she can be free of a miserable man who was nothing more than a nightmare in her life!

So what does Paul say about this? He says, "a wife is bound by law as long as her husband lives, but if her husband dies, she is at liberty to be married to whom she wishes, only in the Lord; but she is happier if she remains as she is, according to my judgment— and I think I also have the spirit of God."[2]

In other words, he is unsure whether he has the spirit of God or not. When such a statement comes from a man like Paul, it puts grave doubts in our minds about the credibility of what is written in the New Testament.

Having seen the pranks played out in the New Testament, let us take a look at the Old Testament. In the Torah, as represented by the first five Books, which Moses (may Allah's peace and blessings be upon him) delivered to the Levites, we find it narrated:

> So it was, when Moses had completed writing the words of this law in a book, when they were finished, that Moses commanded the Levites who bore the ark of the covenant of the LORD, saying: "Take this Book of the Law, and put it beside the ark of the covenant of the LORD your God, that it

---

[1] I Corinthians 7:25-26.
[2] I Corinthians 7:39-40.

may be there as a witness against you. For I know your rebellion and your stiff neck. If today, while I am yet alive with you, you have been rebellious against the LORD, then how much more after my death?"[1]

Here we have Prophet Moses (may Allah's peace and blessings be upon him) attesting to the coming generations that the Jews are a rebellious people, not only against Moses (may Allah's peace and blessings be upon him), but also against Allah, the Creator of the people of Israel.

In the Old Testament, we find very strange statements. It says, "So Moses the servant of the LORD died there in the land of Moab..."[2]

Can a dead person write? If Moses (May Allah's peace and blessings be upon him) died, how could he write these chapters saying, "I died and then such and such happened"? Obviously this passage was written later. Once more, the Torah was not written in the days of Moses, thus, exposing it to error and alteration.

Furthermore, if we study the Old and New Testaments from a historical perspective, we can confidently say that in reality the Torah (i.e., the original revelation to Moses) has disappeared. The history of the Israelites tells us that Nebuchadnezzar entered the temple with his army. After confiscating its property inside, which included the holy books and some utensils, he destroyed the temple and took the confiscated items back to Babylon. Thus, history affirms that the Torah written by Moses has been lost completely. When Cyrus, the King of Persia, allowed the Israelites to return to Palestine, Ezra and Nehemiah began to recompose the Torah from their memories.

Moreover, because of various human concepts existing in these Books, we cannot believe everything in the Old and New Testaments. On the other hand, we cannot discount everything in these scriptures, either. Despite the above, Allah guided me to Islam. I used to be a priest so it was not easy for me to convert. Surely, I needed to have strong proof. Indeed, I did. All Books from Moses (may Allah's peace and blessings be upon him) to

---

[1] Deuteronomy 31:24-27.
[2] Deuteronomy 34:5-6.

Jesus (may Allah's peace and blessings be upon him) predicted the coming of Prophet Muhammad (may Allah's peace and blessings be upon him). Allah, Most Perfect, Most Exalted says, "Do they not consider the Qur'an with care. Had it been from other than Allah they would surely have found therein much discrepancy."[1]

It is not necessary for everyone to be a scholar, or to devote their time to study and compare the details. Rather, I do believe that what I have presented to you, i.e., Paul's epistles to the Corinthians, clearly proves the existence of human input in the New Testament.

Prophet Muhammad (May Allah's peace and blessings be upon him) was commanded by Allah to say that he was only a human being. He never said that he was God. The Qur'an says: "...say: 'I am but a man like yourselves, (but) the inspiration has come to me, that your God is one God.'"[2] Moreover, the Qur'an challenges all creation, saying, "...say: If the whole of mankind and jinns were to gather together to produce the like of this Qur'an they could not produce the like thereof, even if they backed up each other with help and support.[3]

Dr. Muhammad Jamil Ghazi

So, can we say for sure that Jesus' Injil (i.e., original revelation to Jesus) does not exist?

Mr. Khalil:

Certainly.

---

[1] Qur'an 4:82.
[2] Qur'an 18:110.
[3] Qur'an 17:88.

Dr. Ghazi:

How do you explain when the Qur'an says: "Let the People of the Injil judge by what Allah had revealed therein."[1] "It was We Who revealed the Torah (to Moses): therein was guidance and light. By its standard have the Jews been judged by the prophets who bowed (as in Islam) to Allah's Will."[2] "Say: Bring the Torah and study it, If you be men of truth."[3] Which Torah and which Injil are the verses referring to?

Mr. Khalil:

The existing Torah has some statements ascribable to Moses (may Allah's peace and blessings be upon him). However, not all its contents can be attributed to Moses. Similarly, the Gospels carry statements ascribable to Jesus, but not all of its contents are the words of Jesus.

Dr. Ghazi:

So in summary we can say that when Allah Most Exalted says: "It was We Who revealed the Torah, therein was guidance and light"[4], and when He says: "Let the People of the Gospel judge by what Allah had revealed therein,"[5] He, Most Exalted, explains that to His Prophet (may Allah's peace and blessings be upon him), saying, "To you We sent the Scripture in truth, confirming the scripture that came before it, and guarding it in safety."[6]

So, the only real source of reference and proof to what is right in the New and Old Testaments, and what pleases Allah (swt), is the Holy Qur'an. Thus, whatever the Qur'an states and

---

[1] Qur'an 5:47.
[2] Qur'an 5:44.
[3] Qur'an 3:93.
[4] Qur'an 5:44.
[5] Qur'an 5:47.
[6] Qur'an 5:48.

affirms is the truth; conversely, whatever it abrogates is considered invalid for all. Also, whatever it refutes is considered false.

Let us now introduce Brigadier General Ahmad Abdul-Wahhab. He will talk to us about the Crucifixion, the Resurrection and the Sacrifice. These are by far the most fundamental and crucial issues in the Christian religion.

Brig. Gen. Ahmad

In the name of Allah, Ever Beneficent, Ever Compassionate.

We resume this session with a discussion of the problem of the Crucifixion. Yesterday we finished our discussion with the charge of betrayal. We learned that Satan entered Judas before the Last Supper, according to Luke, but according to John, Satan entered Judas after Jesus gave him a piece of bread during the Last Supper, and afterwards Judas went out to betray Jesus.

We will now, talk about a subject known as "The Suffering in the Garden," or "Jesus' Pain and Hardship in the Garden."

As usual we will refer to the text. As always, I prefer to start with Mark's Gospel, it being the oldest one. I would like us to concentrate, when listening to the text that describes this important and definitive period of Jesus' life, on one thing: Does the scenario, as portrayed by the writers of the Gospels, indicate that Jesus came to sacrifice his blood with his crucifixion for all of creation and that sacrificing his blood would become the principal objective of his message, as many claim? Or was Jesus suddenly confronted with an oppressive force that wanted to kill him, such that he would feel his life constantly threatened and feel so afraid moment to moment that he would try to save himself at any cost from death?

5. Jesus' Sufferings[1]

Mark says:
Then they came to a place which was named Gethsemane and He said to His disciples, "Sit here while I pray." And He

---

[1] No. 5 follows the first four topics discussed in the previous session.

took Peter, James and John with Him and He began to be troubled and deeply distressed. Then he said to them, "My soul is exceedingly sorrowful, even to death. Stay here and watch." He went a little farther, and fell on the ground, and prayed that if it were possible the hour might pass from Him. And He said: "Abba, Father, all things are possible for You. Take this cup away from Me; nevertheless, not what I will, but what You will." Then He came and found them sleeping, and said to Peter, "Simon, are you sleeping! Could you not watch one hour? Watch and pray, lest you enter into temptation the spirit indeed is willing, but the flesh is weak." Again he went away and prayed, and spoke the same words. And when He returned, He found them asleep again, for their eyes were heavy: and they did not know what to answer Him. Then He came the third time and said to, them, "Are you still sleeping and resting? It is enough, The hour has come; behold, the Son of Man is being betrayed into the hands of sinners. Rise, let us be going. See, My betrayer is at hand."[1]

The simplest comment on the above passage is that it is quite obvious that Jesus was not expecting this sudden, shocking news about his being hunted by his enemies. Of course, he knew that if they captured him they would kill him. Therefore he was praying all the time so that "the hour" or this hardship or "this cup" would go away and he would be saved.

Henceforth, we can firmly resolve that any claim stating that he came to sacrifice himself to redeem others, or the spilling of Jesus' blood was necessary to expiate Adam's sin or for the salvation of mankind is unacceptable.

Once more, If Adam's disobedience had to be expiated by killing the "Son of God" against the will of the "Son of God" "himself" then this becomes an even greater disaster. In this way the sin multiplies many times. Let us survey the different opinions of the scholars and exegetes of the Gospels.

Dennis Nineham says:

---

[1] Mark 14:32-42.

Muslim-Christian Dialogue

Opinions are sharply divided about the historical value of this section, and even as to whether it formed part of St. Mark's narrative source. Others emphasize that there could not possibly have been any witness for a good deal of what is here described and that no one could have known what Jesus prayed in private (v. 35). They regard the model prayer (v. 36) and the threefold structure of the incident as artificial, similar to Peter's threefold denial. A confident decision on what happened in the Garden is impossible.[1]

In Luke's version of Jesus' suffering, we find him saying of Jesus:

> Coming out, He went to the Mount of Olives as He was accustomed, and His disciples also followed Him. When He came to the place He said to them, "Pray that you may not enter into temptation." And He was withdrawn from them about a stone's throw, and He knelt down and prayed, saying, "Father, if it is Your will, take this cup away from Me; nevertheless not My will, but Yours be done." Then an angel appeared to Him from heaven, strengthening Him. And, being in agony, He prayed more earnestly. Then His sweat became like great drops of blood falling down to the ground. When He rose up from prayer, and had come to His disciples, He found them sleeping from sorrow. Then He said to them, "Why do you sleep? Rise and pray, lest you enter into temptation."[2]

Explaining the above passages, George Caird says:

> According to Mark—Luke's source of information—we find Jesus consumed talking to his disciples about his sadness. Unable to join his best friends, he spent the night praying. But Luke's briefer version in comparison to Mark gives us a more dire impression about the state of horror consuming Jesus. It says that Jesus was the one who himself withdrew from his disciples, He was suffering very much and his sweat became like great drops of blood.

---

[1] Nineham, p. 389f.
[2] Luke 22:39-46.

Muslim-Christian Dialogue

When we remember the courage and steadfastness with which other men, courageous in every respect in facing the most painful tortures, have faced death, we cannot help but ask what type of cup was it that Jesus prayed to God to take away from him?

The prayers of Jesus show us that his feeling of doubt was one element of his complicated hardship. How many times he predicted his suffering, but now, when it was about to happen, we find him extremely worried. He is unable to afford. These verses "...Then an angel appeared to Him from heaven, strengthening Him. And being in agony, He prayed more earnestly. Then His sweat became like great drops of blood falling down to the ground."[1] are missing from *Codex Vaticanus* and a few other manuscripts, and some scholars regard them as a scribal "improvement". But the passage was known to Justin Martyr, Irenaeus, Tatian, and Hippolytus in the second century, and is found in the majority of manuscripts, including *Codex Sinaiticus* and *Codex Bezae*. Its omission is best explained as the work of a scribe who felt that this picture of Jesus overwhelmed with human weakness was incompatible with his own belief in the Divine Son who shared the omnipotence of his Father.[2]

If we accept that this is what actually happened to Jesus in the Garden, then this clearly means that Jesus was not expecting to be killed. As for the feeling of doubt that he faced, let us recount what happened. It seems that he was very sure that his enemies would never be able to catch him.[3] However, when he noticed that his enemies were about to catch him, he began to have doubts whether he would really be saved or they would finish him off.

6. The Arrest

Mark says:

---

[1] Luke 22:43-44.
[2] Caird, *Saint Luke*, p. 243.
[3] We will discuss this topic later in greater detail under the heading "Jesus' Prophecies about His Escaping the Crucifixion."

> And immediately, while He was still speaking, Judas, one of the twelve, with a great multitude with swords and clubs, came from the chief priests and scribes and the elders. Now his betrayer had given them a signal, saying, "Whomever I kiss, He is the One; seize Him and lead Him away safely." As soon as He had come, immediately he went up to Him and said to Him, "Rabbi, Rabbi!" and kissed Him. Then they laid their hands on Him and took Him. And one of those who stood by drew his sword and struck the servant of the high priest, and cut of his ear. Then Jesus answered and said to them, "Have you come out, as against a robber, with swords and clubs to take Me? I was daily with you in the temple teaching, and you did not seize Me. But the Scriptures must be fulfilled." Then they all forsook Him and fled. Now a certain young man followed Him, having a linen cloth thrown around his naked body. And the young men laid hold of him, and he left the linen cloth and fled from them naked.[1]

The kiss was the beginning of the operation to arrest Jesus. Matthew and Luke agree with Mark's version of the story with minor discrepancies. But in the Gospel of John, there is no place for the kiss. His version differs completely from the other three Gospels, which are similar in content. John says:

> Then Judas, having received a detachment of troops and officers from the chief priests and Pharisees, came there with lanterns, torches, and weapons. Jesus therefore, knowing all things that would come upon Him, went forward and said to them, "Whom are you seeking?" They answered Him, "Jesus of Nazareth." Jesus said to them, "I am He." And Judas, who betrayed Him, also stood with them. Now when He said to them, "I am He," they drew back and fell to the ground. Then He asked them again, "Whom are you seeking?" And they said, "Jesus of Nazareth." Jesus answered, "I have told you that I am He. Therefore, if you seek Me, let these go their way."[2]

---

[1] Mark 14:43-52.
[2] John 18:3-8.

The four Gospels all agree that his disciples left him and fled during the darkness of the night. (It must have been dark for the people carried torches and lamps.)

Where is the Doubting of the Disciples?

The Gospels mention Jesus as saying to his disciples: "All of you suspect me tonight." We have here two possibilities:

First, Jesus, speaking to his disciples, predicted that a conspiracy would take place against him. In spite of causing a lot of pain and suffering, it would fail, and Allah (swt) would save him from an impending assassination at the hands of the conspirators.

Second, Jesus predicted to his disciples that a conspiracy would cause him much pain and suffering. This hardship would end in his being killed. If we assume that the first possibility is true, then the disciples, as the Gospels clearly relate, saw Jesus being arrested that night and defeated by the power of oppression. Here the students must have some doubts in their teacher's prediction that he would be saved. Of course, ensuing events before their very eyes proved that this didn't happen. Such situations often give rise to doubts and misgivings, and even turns people away from the faith.

It is known that doubt is something different from denial. The thief, when arrested, may deny the crime of robbery. At the same time, he knows for certain that he committed the robbery; he has no doubt about the crime although he denies it.

All the Gospels showed that the disciples did not suspect Jesus on that night. Instead they talked about the denial of Peter that he was one of Jesus' disciples. This obviously means that events went on according to the first assumption and ended in Jesus' being saved from the arrest and the killing.

However, if the second assumption is true, i.e., Jesus predicted to his disciples his arrest and killing, then what the disciples saw, as also narrated by the Gospels, is exactly what happened.

In this case, there is no room for doubt; a denial of the fact that the disciples had any doubts that night cannot lead to accusing Jesus of false prophecy. This is something impossible for Jesus to have done. We deny it and we detest such a thought.

From the above we can conclude that the four Gospels have discrepancies in the story of the arrest and its circumstances. Mark and Matthew narrate that Judas kissed Jesus. Luke relates that Judas was about to kiss him. In contrast, John does not know anything about a kiss.

Mark and Matthew mention that Judas and Jesus greeted and talked to each other. Luke keeps silent about the exchange of greetings between them. In contrast, John does not mention anything about Judas except complete silence after he led the people to arrest Jesus in the Garden.

Even if we ignore the stories of the twelve armies of angels and the young man who escaped naked, there are three basic issues which must be thoroughly understood. They are:

1. The kiss was the only means for members of the arresting force to recognize Jesus, according to Mark, Matthew and Luke. In the Gospel of John the arrest was completed only when Jesus himself came forward in front of them, showing his defiance and steadfastness as men of great missions and noble messages normally do.
2. An unusual incident happened at that moment, shocking the members of the arresting force and making them retreat and fall down.
3. The disciples, according to Gospel writers, never doubted Jesus, even for a moment, on the night of the arrest.

The story of Jesus with all its details always goes back to the prophecies of the Old Testament, especially the book of Psalms. So let us look at Psalm 91, which is widely used as a reference. It says:

> Because you have made the LORD, Who is my refuge, even the Most High, your dwelling place, no evil shall befall you, nor shall any plague come near your dwelling. For He shall give His angels charge over you, to keep you in all your ways. In their hands they shall bear you up, lest you dash your foot against a stone. You shall tread upon the lion and the cobra. The young lion and the serpent you shall trample underfoot. Because he has set his love upon Me; therefore I

will deliver him; I will set him on high, because he has known My name. He shall call upon Me, and I will answer him; I will be with him in trouble; I will deliver him and honor him. With long life I will satisfy him. And show him my salvation.[1]

Isn't it true that someone can say that Allah's angels carried Jesus in their hands, at that moment when the hearts of believers began to have misgivings and after seeing that this oppressive force was about to destroy them? If someone wonders where Jesus went after that, we would ask: Where did Elijah (Ilyas) go when he was lifted to heaven?

Regarding this the Old Testament says:

Then it happened, as they[2] continued on and talked that suddenly a chariot of fire appeared with horses on fire, and separated the two of them; and Elijah went up by a whirlwind into heaven. And Elisha saw it, and he cried out, "My father, my father, the chariot of Israel and its horsemen!" So he saw him and no more.[3]

Also, where did Enoch (Idris) go when he was raised into heaven? The Old Testament says: "...Enoch walked with God, and he was not, for God took him."[4]

By the Mercy of Allah, Most Perfect, Most Exalted, all the miracles carried out by Jesus were also performed by other prophets before him. For example, when he gave life to the dead, by Allah's Will, there were no more than three that he revived, according to the Gospels. In contrast, one prophet before him (Ezekiel) had given life to an army, by Allah's Will, after they had died. Likewise, others gave life, by Allah's Will, to individuals who had died recently or a long time before.

In terms of other miracles performed by Jesus, other prophets also carried out similar miracles before him. The same applies to curing the sick; it was also performed by previous prophets. All of this was Allah's mercy upon His creation so

---

[1] Psalms 91:9-16.
[2] Prophet Elijah and his disciple, Elisha.
[3] II Kings 2:11-12.
[4] Genesis 5:24.

they should not be led astray by being so infatuated with Jesus that they would consider him to be God.

7. The Trial

The Gospels do not agree on the number of trials that took place. Due to a lack of time limitation we will only talk about two trials:

1. The First Trial, before the Council (Sanhedrin) of the Jews: Mark says:

> And they led Jesus away to the high priest; and with him were assembled all the chiefs, priests, the elders and the scribes. But Peter followed Him at a distance right into the courtyard of the high priest. And he sat with the servants and warmed himself at the fire. Now the chief priests and all the council sought testimony against Jesus to put Him to death, but found none. For many bore false witness against Him, but their testimonies did not agree. Then some rose up and bore false witness against Him, saying, "We heard Him say, 'I will destroy this temple made with hands, and within three days I will build another made without hands.'" But not even then did their testimony agree. And the high priest stood up in the midst and asked Jesus, saying, "Do You answer nothing? What is it these men testify against You?" But He kept silent and answered nothing. Again the high priest asked Him, saying to Him, "Are You the Christ, the Son of the Blessed?" Jesus said, "I am. And you will see the Son of Man sitting at the right hand of the Power, and coming with clouds of heaven." Then the high priest tore his clothes and said, "What further need do we have of witnesses? You have heard the blasphemy! What do you think?" And they all condemned Him to be deserving of death. Then some began to spit on Him, and to blindfold Him, and to beat Him, and to say to Him, "Prophesy!" And the officers struck Him with the palms of their hands.[1]

---

[1] Mark 14:53-65.

Nineham says:

How this section grew up it is not easy to say. If the significance in the Gospel of Mark, i.e., 14:53-72, is thus clear, the question of its historicity has been, and still is, the subject of lively debate. The main reason for doubting its historicity must be briefly set out and discussed.

1. St. Mark describes the trial as taking place before "the council" (Sanhedrin, v. 55), i.e., the Sanhedrin, an official body of seventy-one members, under the presidency of the high priest, which was the supreme judicial authority in Israel. The Tractate Sanhedrin in the Mishnah sets out fully the procedure adopted in trials before this body, and a comparison of what it says with St. Mark's account of the trial of Jesus reveals numerous discrepancies, many of them very considerable.

2. But would members of the Sanhedrin have met, even for such informal proceedings, in the middle of Passover night or, for that matter, if St. Mark's chronology of the Passion week is inaccurate, in the middle of a night just before the Passover? Certainly, despite the arguments of Jeremiah, a formal trial at such a time seems unthinkable... and most scholars are very doubtful about the holding of even an informal investigation at such a time.[1]

2. The Second Trial: Before Pilate:
Mark says:

Immediately, in the morning, the chief priests held a consultation with the elders and scribes and the whole council; and they bound Jesus, led Him away, and delivered Him to Pilate. Then Pilate asked Him, "Are you the King of the Jews?" He answered and said to him, "It is as you say." And the chief priests accused Him of many things, but He answered nothing. Then Pilate asked Him again, saying, "Do You answer nothing? See how many things they testify against You!" But Jesus still answered nothing, so that Pilate marveled. Now at the feast he was accustomed to releasing

---

[1] Nineham, p. 398-401.

one prisoner to them, whomever they requested. And there was one named Barabbas, who was chained with his fellow rebels; they had committed murder in the rebellion. Then the multitude, crying aloud, began to ask him to do just as he had always done for them. But Pilate answered them, saying, "Do you want me to release to you the King of the Jews?" For he knew that the chief priests had handed Him over because of envy. But the chief priests stirred up the crowd, so that he should rather release Barabbas to them. Pilate answered and said to them again, "What then do you want me to do with Him whom you call the King of the Jews?" So they cried out again, "Crucify Him!" Then Pilate said to them, "Why, what evil has He done?" But they cried out all the more, "Crucify Him!" So Pilate, wanting to gratify the crowd, released Barabbas to them, and he delivered Jesus, after he had scourged Him, to be crucified.[1]

Commenting on this Nieneham says that,

> although the trial before Pilate is represented as taking place out of doors, St. Mark's account of it is by no means an eyewitness report; indeed it is not a report at all, so much as a series of traditions, each making some apologetic point about the trial. This explains why we are not told how Pilate learned of the charge (in v. 2 he already knows it), and why there is no mention of a formal verdict or passing of sentence. Luke narrates an account completely opposite to the above. He says, "...And Pilate gave sentence that it should be as they required."[2]

As far as what was narrated about the custom of releasing a prisoner, most of the scholars did not know about it as described here. The claim that it was a practice of the Roman rulers to release one prisoner on Easter, and that it was the people who had the right to choose him regardless of his crime, has no evidence at all. In fact, it contradicts what we know about the spirit of Roman rule in Palestine and its way of dealing with its people.

---

[1] Mark 15:1-15.
[2] Luke 23:24.

All in all, the contents of the dialogue between Pilate and the crowd are also problematic. It seems that Pilate had already been directed to choose between the prisoners, such that if he released one he would have to execute the other. At the end of the passage we find that Jesus was not yet convicted. According to what was narrated by the story, we find no reason preventing Pilate from discharging Jesus, if he believed that Jesus was innocent, and at the same time freeing Barabbas. We find that in St. Matthew's version of the story, the name of that prisoner is mentioned twice. In most of the scriptures it used to read "Jesus Barabbas". The prevailing belief is that the name Jesus Barabbas was the original text.

Removal of the word "Jesus" from the commonly circulated copies of the Bible can be explained simply. Although the name "Jesus" was widely used at the time of the Messiah, the Christians felt that it was a sacred and holy name that shouldn't be used by everybody. In particular, if any criminal was named Jesus, it was insulting.[1]

Matthew adds two more incidents to Mark's narrative. The first is about Judas' end. We will deal with this issue at its proper time. The second talks about the dream of Pilate's wife. In addition, Matthew explains how Pilate completely absolves himself of any responsibility for the one crucified. He says:

Then the governor said, "Why, what evil has He done?" But they cried out all the more, saying, "Let Him be crucified!" When Pilate saw that he could not prevail at all, but rather that a tumult was rising, he took water and washed his hands before the multitude saying, "I am innocent of the blood of this just Person. You see it." And all the people answered and said, "His blood be on us and on our children." Then he released Barabbas to them, and when he had scourged Jesus, he delivered Him to be crucified.[2]

Still, scholars doubt that the incident of Pilate's washing his hands ever occurred. Commenting on this John Fenton notes that "...the action of washing hands as a sign of innocence is Jewish

---

[1] Nineham, pp. 411-416.
[2] Matthew 27:23-26.

rather than Roman; see Deut. 21:1-9: ...and note all the elders of that city nearest to the slain man shall wash their hands... and they shall testify, 'Our hands did not shed his blood...' It is very unlikely that Pilate would have done this."[1]

I think this is enough said about the trials and the problems associated with them to let us now move on and study some elements of the Crucifixion issue. For this issue, we don't need to cite the comments of the scholars so much, since the discrepancies between the Gospels themselves are so clear that there is no need for any comment.

8. The Crucifixion

A. The Cross Bearer:

Mark says:

> And when they had mocked Him, they took the purple off Him, put His own clothes on Him, and led Him out to crucify Him. Then they compelled a certain man, Simon of Cyrene, the father of Alexander and Rufus, as he was coming out of the country and passing by, to bear His cross. And they brought Him to the place Golgotha, which is translated, Place of the Skull.[2]

Matthew and Luke agree with Mark that the cross bearer was Simon the Cyrenian, but John says something else:

> Then he delivered Him to them to he crucified. So they took Jesus, and led Him away. And He, bearing His cross, went out to a place called the Place of the Skull, which is called in Hebrew, Golgotha.[3]

Nineham comments:

> Those condemned to be crucified were normally made to carry their own crosses. John 19:17 states that the usual procedure was followed in Jesus' case, but according to Mark[4]

---
[1] Fenton, p. 436.
[2] Mark 15:20-22.
[3] John 19: 16-17.
[4] Also Matthew and Luke.

an otherwise unknown figure, Simon of Cyrene, was "impressed" by the Romans to carry it for Jesus.[1]

> As far as the location of Golgotha... [t]he tradition which locates the place within the Church of the Holy Sepulcher cannot be traced back beyond the fourth century and is open to considerable question; other sites have been suggested in modern times, but certainty is unattainable.[2]

In other words, all this talk about the Holy Sepulcher— where Jesus is supposedly buried, as the Christians claim, and which sparked the Crusades, where the Crusaders claimed that they were trying to save that "holy tomb" from the hands of the "infidels" in a war that lasted for 280 years, where tens of thousands of Christians and Muslims were killed, where many cities were destroyed, and where the blood of innocent people was spilled— has no basis at all!

B. The Drink of the One Crucified:

Mark says, "Then they gave Him wine mingled with myrrh to drink, but He did not take it."[3]

Matthew says, "...they gave Him sour wine mingled with gall to drink. But when He had tasted it, He would not drink."[4]

C. Charge against the One Crucified:

Mark says, "And the inscription of His accusation was written above: THE KING OF THE JEWS."[5]

Matthew says, "And they put up over His head the accusation written against Him: THIS IS JESUS, THE KING OF THE JEWS."[6]

John says, "Now Pilate wrote a title and put it on the cross. And the writing was: JESUS OF NAZARETH, THE KING OF THE JEWS."[7]

Nineham comments:

---

[1] Nineham, p. 422.
[2] Nineham, p. 422.
[3] Mark 15:23.
[4] Matthew 27:34.
[5] Mark 15:26.
[6] Matthew 27:33.
[7] John 19:19.

As to its authenticity, opinions are very divided, some scholars thinking the precise formula was known through eyewitnesses and was in fact the Christians' only certain indication of the charge on which Jesus was condemned, others holding that the Romans are unlikely to have used such a bald form of words and that St. Mark's particular formulation of the charge is due once again to his desire to show that it was as Messiah that Jesus was executed.[1]

The discrepancy between the Gospels concerning the inscription of the accusation of the crucified, which is no more than a few simple words written on a board seen by people, gives us an indication of how accurate the Gospels are. Thus, as long as there is a discrepancy, even in appearance as in this case, it becomes absolutely impossible to achieve complete accuracy. Based on the above, we can clearly see the degree of accuracy of the Gospels when they narrate Jesus' titles. One of the Gospels calls him "righteous"; another one calls him the son of God; a third one narrates that his disciples called him the "Teacher"; another Gospel calls him "the Master", while one refers to him as "the Lord".

The truth here always remains subject to discrepancies.

D. The Two Thieves and the Crucified:

Mark says, "With Him they also crucified two robbers, one on His right and the other on His left. ...those who were crucified with Him reviled Him."[2] Matthew agrees with Mark that the two thieves mocked and blasphemed him. However, Luke says:

> ...then one of the criminals who were hanged blasphemed Him, saying, "If You are the Christ save Yourself and us." But the other, answering, rebuked him, saying, "Do you not even fear God, seeing you are under the same condemnation? And we indeed justly, for we receive the due reward of our deeds, but this Man has done nothing wrong." Then he said to Jesus, "Lord, remember me when You come into

---

[1] Nineham, p. 424.
[2] Mark 15:27-32.

Your kingdom." And Jesus said to him, "Assuredly, I say to you, today you will be with me in Paradise."[1]

As you can clearly see, the Gospels differ markedly concerning the attitude of the two thieves towards the Crucified.

E. The Time of the Crucifixion:

Mark says: "Now it was the third hour, and they crucified Him."[2] But John says that it happened after the sixth hour. He says:

> Now it was the Preparation Day of the Passover, and about the sixth hour. And he[3] said to the Jews, "Behold your King!" But they cried out, "Away with *Him*, away with *Him*! Crucify *Him*!" ...Then he delivered Him to them to be crucified.[4]

Asserting the above, Nineham says:

> From the point in St. Mark's narrative where Jesus is finally disowned by men, the time is carefully marked off in three-hour intervals as in 15:25, 33, 34. In this instance at least, the reckoning seems artificial, for it is hardly possible that everything[5] recounted in vv. 1-24[6] could have taken place in the course of a single three-hour period, and John 19:14 clearly implies that it did not.[7]

F. The Prayer of the Crucified:

Luke says, "And when they had come to the place called Calvary there they crucified Him, and the criminals, one on the right hand and the other on the left. Then Jesus said, 'Father, forgive them, for they do not know what they do.'"[8] Only Luke recounts this prayer, which is absent from the other Gospels.

---

[1] Luke 23:39-43.
[2] Mark 15:25.
[3] i.e., Pilate.
[4] John 19:14-16.
[5] i.e., from the beginning of the gathering in the morning to the time of the Crucifixion.
[6] i.e., Mark 15:1-24.
[7] Nineham, p. 424.
[8] Luke 23:33-34.

Interestingly, even some copies of the Gospel of Luke did not mention it.

George Caird comments:

> It was said that this prayer[1] was probably removed from one of the earlier scriptures of the Gospel of Luke by one of the clerks in the second century, who thought it unbelievable that God could forgive the Jews. Taking into consideration the double destruction of Jerusalem in the years 70 and 135, it was certain that God would not forgive them.[2]

G. The Desperate Cry on the Cross:

Mark says:

> Now when the sixth hour had come, there was darkness over the whole land until the ninth hour. And at the ninth hour Jesus cried out with a loud voice, saying, "Eli, Eli, lama sabachthani?" which is translated, "My God, My God, why have You forsaken me?[3]

But Luke says, "And when Jesus had cried out with a loud voice, He said, 'Father, into Your hands I commit My spirit.'"[4]

In contrast, John says, "So when Jesus had received the sour wine, He said, 'It is finished!' And bowing His head, He gave up His spirit."[5]

The cry of despair on the cross raised a number of problems which were and still are debated among scholars. One said:

> St. Luke and St. John appear to have found the words mysterious and liable to misinterpretation; both have omitted them and substituted, the one: "Father into thy hands I commit my spirit," [Luke 23:46], the other: "It is finished."

> On the other hand, such a view assumes a narrator who, interested primarily in historical fact, reports faithfully for posterity a terrible and inexplicable utterance.

---

[1] Luke 23:34, i.e., "And Jesus said, 'Father, forgive them; for they know not what they do.'"
[2] Caird, p. 250.
[3] 15:33-34.
[4] Luke 23:46.
[5] John 19:30.

Consequently many modern scholars adopt a quite different interpretation, which rests on the fact that the words are a quotation from Psalms 22:1. Taken as a whole, this psalm is anything but a cry of despair; it is the prayer of a righteous sufferer who yet trusts fully in the love and protection of God and is confident of being vindicated by him.[1]

H. After the Crucifixion:

Mark says:

> Then the veil of the temple was torn in two from top to bottom, so when the centurion, who stood opposite Him, saw that He cried out like this and breathed His last, he said, "Truly this Man was the Son of God!"[2]

Matthew says:

> Then, behold, the veil of the temple was torn in two from top to bottom; and the earth quaked, and the rocks were split, and the graves were opened; and many bodies of the saints who had fallen asleep were raised; and coming out of the graves after His resurrection, they went into the holy city and appeared to many.[3]

Luke says:

> Then the sun was darkened, and the veil of the temple was torn in two...So when the centurion saw what had happened, he glorified God, saying, "Certainly this was a righteous Man!"[4]

In contrast, John has nothing to say about the above. George Caird says:

> An eclipse of the sun[5] while the moon is full is an astronomical impossibility, but this would only enhance the value of the story for its earliest readers. It was a widespread belief in antiquity that events of great and tragic moment were ac-

---

[1] Nineham, p. 427f.
[2] 15:38-39.
[3] Matthew 27:51-53.
[4] 23:45-47.
[5] i.e., acording to Luke.

companied by portents, nature showing its sympathy with the distress of man.[1]

Meanwhile, Nineham says that "Similar portents are said to have marked the deaths of some of the great rabbis and also the death of some great figures of pagan antiquity, most notably Julius Caesar."[2]

Finally, John Fenton says that "Matthew adds further signs: an earthquake, the opening of the tombs, the resurrection of the saints and their appearing to many in Jerusalem after the resurrection of Jesus. These legendary events are included by Matthew to show that the death of Jesus was an act of God."[3]

The plain truth is that the sun and the moon are two of Allah's signs. They don't eclipse for the death of anyone.

Dr. Muhammad Jamil Ghazi:

We have already seen more than thirty contradictions concerning the crucifixion. Here is a copy of *The Dictionary of the Bible*, published by the Council of Churches of the Near East. Oddly enough there is a discrepancy in the shape of the cross used. This dictionary says that there is the cross (X), the cross (T) and the cross (†). The cross which is used as a symbol for Christianity is (†). However, it says that the cross used for Jesus took the shape (T). This is exactly what the dictionary says: "There are three patterns for a cross. First the cross of St. Andrew takes the shape of (X). The second takes the shape of (T), while the third takes the shape of a sword (†) and is known as the Latin Cross.

"The Cross of Jesus was probably like the third one (†), in the opinion of the specialists. This shape made it easy to put the name and the charge of the victim on its upper part."

If there is a difference of opinion even in the shape of the cross, then Allah's statement about this scenario is clear. Allah, Most Exalted, says, "But it was made obscure to them."[4] This

---

[1] Caird, p. 253.
[2] Nineham, p. 427.
[3] Fenton, p. 444.
[4] Qur'an 4:157.

clearly shows us that everything related to the crucifixion is a confused and unknown matter. Even today, they still disagree with each other concerning any details of the issue of the crucifixion, whether it is the cross-bearer or the charge against the crucified or the two thieves and the crucified or the time of crucifixion or the prayer of the crucified or the desperate cry of the crucified or what happened after the crucifixion.

Brigadier General Abdul-Wahhab concluded with a sentence concerning Ibrahim, the son of Prophet Muhammad (may Allah's peace and blessings be upon him): It proves to every sane individual the truthfulness of the Prophet (may Allah's peace and blessings be upon him). He never entertained any superstitions or erroneous beliefs. He only wanted the truth to prevail.

What happened was that when his son, Ibrahim, passed away there was an eclipse of the sun. This is something that happens naturally. However, some people said that the solar eclipse was due to the death of Ibrahim. It just happened that Ibrahim passed away on the same day that a solar eclipse occurred. The common people linked the two events as if they were related. Now, had Prophet Muhammad (may Allah's peace and blessings be upon him) wanted their support, even through falsehood, he could have remained silent. Instead, the Prophet (may Allah's peace and blessings be upon him), refusing to yield to any type of falsehood to gain support, angrily ascended the pulpit and declared, "People! The sun and the moon are two signs of Allah. They do not eclipse because of the birth or death of someone. So when you witness this (i.e., a solar or lunar eclipse), stand up and pray."[1]

I. Those Who Witnessed the Crucifixion:

This is perhaps one of the most important elements of the crucifixion issue. It reveals that the witnesses were women standing far away watching the one crucified. They really had no chance to ascertain from close up what they saw.

Mark says:

---

[1] Narrated by Al-Bukhari, the chapters on eclipses.

> There were also women looking on from afar, among whom were Mary Magdalene, Mary the mother of James the Less and of Joses, and Salome, who also followed Him when He was in Galilee, and many other women who came up with Him to Jerusalem.[1]

Matthew says the same in 27: 55-56. Luke related, "But all His acquaintances, and the women who followed Him from Galilee, stood at a distance, watching these things."[2] Finally, John says, "Now there stood by the cross of Jesus His mother, and His mother's sister, Mary the wife of Cleopas, and Mary Magdalene."[3]

Reviewing the above, John Fenton says:

> ...The disciples had fled when Jesus was arrested, and though Peter had followed as far as the high priest's courtyard, we do not hear any more of him after his denials of Jesus. Mark, Matthew and Luke tell us that the witnesses of the crucifixion were women who had come with Jesus from Galilee to Jerusalem. They see his burial, they find the tomb empty on the Sunday morning, and they meet Jesus.[4]

Regarding what John said about the presence of Mary, the mother of Jesus, near the cross, the scholars comment, "It is intrinsically improbable that friends and relations of Jesus would be allowed to stand near the cross."[5]

Likewise, the *Encyclopedia Britannica*, commenting on the discrepancies in the Gospels regarding the witnesses of the crucifixion, says:

> We find in the three Gospels[6] resembling each other that only women followed Jesus, and the list which was carefully and comprehensively written did not include his mother, and that they were "looking on from afar" [Mark 15:40] But in the Gospel of John we find that Mary, his mother, was standing with two other Marys and with the beloved disciple

---
[1] Mark 15:40-41.
[2] 23:49.
[3] John 19:25.
[4] Fenton, p. 455.
[5] Nineham, p. 431.
[6] i.e., the Gospels of Mark, Matthew and Luke.

by the cross. And from that hour that disciple took her to his own home.

His mother didn't appear in Jerusalem, as narrated by the old references, until before the feast accompanied by his brothers [Acts 1:14].[1]

From the above, we can clearly see that the witnesses of the principal events upon which the Christian creed is based— such as the crucifixion, the resurrection and the appearance of the Christ— were women watching from afar. Subsequently, they narrated whatever they saw.

Some Comments on the Events of the Crucifixion

Now it is upon us to comment on some of the events related to the crucifixion.

If the writers of one Gospel rely on what another has narrated, then there should be harmony among the Gospels; any discrepancies and contradictions should disappear. But the reality is completely different. If we believe in what the Gospels tell us about the crucifixion and its related events, we will find that they differ with one another from A to Z.

It is quite enough for the reader to review what the Gospels narrate about the arrest, the trials, the time of the crucifixion (date and hour), the desperate cry, and the witnesses to the crucifixion. After this it will be obvious that the Gospels differ markedly from one another. If we accept one Gospel version, we must reject another. This is the dilemma: which one do we accept; which one do we reject?

It may very well happen that one who used to believe blindly in what the Gospels narrate, will have no other response but to say, "Only God knows!"

The End of Judas Iscariot

Of the four Gospels, only the Gospel of Matthew talks about the end of Judas. Likewise, the Book of Acts, written by Luke,

---

[1] *Encyclopedia Britannica*, 1960, vol. 13, p. 99.

relates Judas' end. Let us go back to these two sources and see how the end of Judas came, and whether or not both narrate the same story about this crucial part. Do both agree that this event was directly related to the issue of the crucifixion, or do they disagree, as usual?

Matthew says:

> Then Judas, His betrayer, seeing that he had been condemned, was remorseful and brought back the thirty pieces of silver to the chief priest and elders, saying, "I have sinned by betraying innocent blood." And they said "What is *that* to us? You see to *it*!" Then he threw down the pieces of silver in the temple and departed, and went and hanged himself. But the chief priests took the silver pieces and said, "It is not lawful to put them into the treasury, because they are the price of blood." And they consulted together and bought with them the potter's field, to bury strangers in. Therefore, that field has been called the Field of Blood to this day. Then was fulfilled what was spoken by Jeremiah the prophet, saying, "And they took the thirty pieces of silver, the value of Him who valued, whom they of the children of Israel did value, and gave them for the potter's field, as the LORD directed me."[1]

In reference to this John Fenton says:

> Matthew uses the period between the decisions of the Sanhedrin and the trial before Pilate to tell his readers about the end of Judas. At this point we find that Matthew doesn't follow Mark, who did not mention anything about Judas after the Jesus arrest. He tells us that Judas changed his mind after he found out that Jesus had been condemned. He returned the money back to the members of the Sanhedrin and confessed to them about his crime. Then he put the money in the treasury of the temple and went to hang himself.

The chief priests said that the money, being a price for a human life, could not be put in the treasury of the temple. As a result they utilized it to buy a piece of land as a graveyard for strangers. This fulfilled a prophecy that Matthew mistakenly

---

[1]Matthew 27:3-10.

traces back to the Book of Jeremiah. In reality it is of Zachariah, who earlier played an important role in Matthew's version. Luke has written the story of Judas in Acts 1:18. His version only agrees partially with Matthew's, and differs from it in other parts.[1]

Before we see what Luke says about the death of Judas in the Book of Acts, John Fenton tells us that Luke agrees with Matthew in part of the story and differs with him in another. Moreover, Matthew associates the story of the "Field of Blood" to a prophesy that he mistakenly thought was from the Book of Jeremiah. In fact a similar prophecy is related in the Book of Zachariah.

Luke's version of the story as mentioned above appears in the Book. It says:

> And in those days Peter stood up in the midst of the disciples (altogether the number of names was about a hundred and twenty), and said, "Men *and* brethren, this Scripture had to be fulfilled, which the Holy Spirit spoke before by the mouth of David concerning Judas... Now this man purchased a field with the wages of iniquity; and falling headlong, he burst open in the middle and all his entrails gushed out. And it became known to all those dwelling in Jerusalem: so that field is called in their own language, Akel Dama, that is, Field of Blood. For it is written in the Book of Psalms: Let his dwelling place be desolate, And let no one live in it,' and, 'Let another take his office.'[2]

According to Luke's version, Judas himself bought the field. Then he dies there. For this reason, the field was called the "Field of Blood". In other words, either Matthew and Luke both had an independent source to the story of Judas, or Luke condensed Matthew's version and made some changes to it.[3]

Regardless of whether it is this version or that, once again this is just one of hundreds of conclusive proofs that we are dealing with books that were composed in every sense of the word. They have nothing to do with the revelation of Allah.

---

[1] Fenton, p. 431.
[2] Acts 1:15-20.
[3] Fenton, p. 431.

What Matthew and Luke agreed upon, as opposed to Mark and John, who have kept silent on the issue, is that Judas, the betrayer, died under suspicious circumstances. Their stories, however, differ in three places.

First, the way he died: Matthew narrates that Judas committed suicide, as he "hanged himself".[1] On the other hand, Luke says Judas died in a bloody way, where "he burst open in the middle and all his entrails gushed out."[2]

Next is the buyer of the field: While Matthew relates that the chief priests bought the field,[3] Luke says that Judas was the buyer.[4]

Finally, both the version of Matthew and that of Luke differ as to the reason for calling the field "the Field of Blood". Matthew claims that it was so named because the money used to buy the field was "the price of blood"[5] of an innocent life. In contrast, Luke says that it was named so because of the bloody way in which Judas died.

What Matthew and Luke narrate about the death of Judas means only one thing: that Judas disappeared during the period of disturbance which followed the events of the Crucifixion.

Jesus' Prophecies about His Suffering

The Gospels, the oldest of which (i.e., Mark's) was written more than fifteen years after Paul's Epistles, were influenced by the theory of Jesus shedding his blood as a sacrifice for others. This is the idea that Paul preached. He made this the central theme of the Gospel he preached. In his first Epistle to the Corinthians, he says, "For I determined not to know anything among you except Jesus Christ and Him crucified."[6]

It was expected that Jesus would talk about his sufferings, and how people would refuse to believe in him, as manifesta-

---

[1] Matthew 27:5.
[2] Acts 1:18.
[3] Matthew 27:7.
[4] Acts 1:18.
[5] Matthew 27:6.
[6] I Corinthians 2:2.

tions always linked with the responsibility of disseminating the divine message. However, we find the Gospel of Mark using whatever was possible as a basis for prophecy about the anticipated suffering. Mark narrates the words of Jesus to his disciples, saying, "And how is it written concerning the Son of Man, that he must suffer many things and be treated with contempt?"[1]

Matthew develops this a little further, and makes it a prophecy about the crucifixion of Jesus. He relates Jesus as saying, "Behold, we are going up to Jerusalem, and the Son of Man will be betrayed to the chief priests and to the scribes; and they will condemn Him to death, and deliver Him to the Gentiles to mock and to scourge and crucify."[2]

It is well known that the Gospel of Mark was a major source of reference for Matthew. It is also known that the Gospel of Matthew is the only Gospel that attributes the prophecy of the crucifixion to Jesus.

We have already seen how Matthew developed what was said about the sign of Jonah. For example, Mark begins by saying, "Then the Pharisees came out and began to dispute with Him, seeking from Him a sign from Heaven, testing Him. But He sighed in His Spirit, and said, 'Why does this generation seek a sign? Assuredly, I say to you, no sign shall be given to this generation.'"[3]

Luke developed it more, saying, "And while the crowds were thickly gathered together, He began to say, 'This is an evil generation. It seeks a sign and no sign will be given to it except the sign of Jonah the prophet. For as Jonah became a sign to the Ninevites, so also the Son of Man will be to this generation.'"[4]

Matthew, basing his Gospel on the Gospel of Mark and composing it after Luke's, processes the above even more. He transforms the statements ascribed to Jesus along with other details that he adds into a false prophecy. He says, "Then some of the scribes and Pharisees answered, saying, 'Teacher, we want to see a sign from You.' But he answered and said to them, 'An

---

[1] Mark 9:12.
[2] Matthew 20:18-19.
[3] Mark 8:11-12.
[4] 11:29-30.

evil and adulterous generation seeks after a sign, and no sign will be given to it except the sign of the prophet Jonah. For as Jonah was three days and three nights in the belly of the great fish, so will the Son of Man be three days and three nights in the heart of the earth.'"[1]

We have already explained the error of the prophecy when we discussed other unfulfilled prophecies. What remains is a further look at some statements ascribed to Jesus. This concerns his saying that the Son of Man would suffer greatly and be rejected by his generation. What does a statement like this mean? Charles Dodd addresses this. He says:

> There are written statements saying that Jesus prophesied about his anticipated sufferings and his followers. Generally, the best thing that can be said about the belief concerning his warning about his death—a claim repeatedly attributed to Jesus by the Gospels—is that it is a prophecy contrary to what actually happened. In reality, Jesus' sudden disappearance occurred while his generation was living. Moreover, his disciples were unable to come near the person killed on the crucifix. Church authorities could not believe that their Lord was ignorant of what was going to happen to him. Frankly speaking, the accuracy of some of these prophecies is commonly based on facts the church learned afterwards.
>
> Realistically, the impression that we have after reading the Gospels, as a whole, is that Jesus led his followers to the town with the clear understanding that some hardship awaited him there. This might very well cause him and his followers a lot of pain and grief.
>
> The most notable verse in this respect is Mark's statement:
>
> 35 Then James and John, the sons of Zebedee, came to Him, saying, "Teacher, we want You to do for us whatever we ask." And He said to them, "What do you want me to do for you?" They said to Him, "Grant us that we may sit one on Your right hand and the other on Your left, in Your glory." But Jesus said to them, "You do not know what you ask. Are you able to drink the cup that I drink, and be baptized

---

[1] Matthew 12:38-40.

> with the baptism that I am baptized with?" They said to him, "We are able." So Jesus said to them, "You will indeed drink the cup that I drink, and with the baptism I am baptized with you will be baptized; but to sit on My right and on My left hand is not Mine to give, but it *is for those* for whom it is prepared."[1]

Here, the sons of Zebedee affirmed that they would drink the cup that he would drink and be baptized with the baptism that he would be baptized with. This is quite clear. As far as the prophecy about the brothers (i.e., the sons of Zebedee) coming to the same end as their Master, it was just one of the many unfulfilled prophecies.

Since crucifixion was the only means of execution known to the Romans, the above passage gives us the impression that Jesus wanted to prepare them to face any hardship, even death. All in all, it is possible to accept the idea that what we find in the Gospels in terms of prophecies is nothing more than a reflection of the initial experiences of the church wherein Christian teachings were formulated. Certainly, at least some of these prophecies stem from those experiences. Moreover, there are written records of unfulfilled prophecies attributed to Jesus.[2]

Jesus' Prophecy about his Deliverance

Jesus refuses any attempt to kill him:

From the time that Jesus started his mission till the last day, the Gospels remind us from time to time of his rejection and absolute denial of the idea of being killed. He also did his best to foil any attempt planned by the Jews to kill him. The Gospel of John says:

> Jesus answered them and said, "My doctrine is not Mine, but His who sent Me...Why do you seek to kill me?[3] ...But now you seek to kill Me, a Man who has told you the truth which I heard from God."[4]

---

[1] Mark 10:35-40.
[2] Dodd, The Parables of the Kingdom, pp. 41-47.
[3] John 7:16-19.
[4] John 8:40.

As Jesus was human, he did not know what the future held. Naturally, he took the necessary precautions to avoid falling into the traps of his enemies like the Jews. If he knew that they would arrest him on a certain day, why did he take such precautions? The Gospel of John says:

> After these things Jesus walked in Galilee; for he did not want to walk in Judea, because the Jews sought to kill Him.[1]
> Then, from that day on, they plotted to put Him to death. Therefore Jesus no longer walked openly among the Jews, but went from there into the country near the wilderness...[2]

Let us restrict ourselves to a number of clear prophecies which Jesus prophesied concerning his escaping execution. These prophecies coincide with those precautions taken by him to secure his life.

1. Once, in an attempt to arrest Jesus, "...the Pharisees and the chief priests sent officers to take Him. Then Jesus said to them, 'I shall be with you a little while longer, and *then* I go to Him who sent Me. You will seek Me and not find *Me*, and where I am you cannot come.'"[3]

We don't think that anyone will argue about the clear statements above. In other words, when the Jews would go after Jesus to kill him, they wouldn't find him because he would "go to Him who sent Me."[4] This means that Allah would raise him up unto himself, as He did earlier with Elijah (Elyas) whose disciple Elisha (Alyasa') watched as he ascended into the heavens.

2. In another provocative situation between Jesus and the Jews, Jesus reiterated his previous prophecy to the Jews and how their plots against him would lead to his being raised up into heaven:

> Then Jesus said to them again, "I am going away, and you will seek Me, and will die in your sin. Where I go you cannot come." So the Jews said, "Will He kill Himself, because He says, 'Where I go you cannot come'? ...Then Jesus said to them, "When you lift up the Son of Man, then you will

---
[1] John 7:1.
[2] 11:53-54.
[3] 7:32-34.
[4] John 7:33.

know that I am *He,* and *that* I do nothing of Myself; but as My Father taught Me, I speak these things. And He who sent Me is with Me. The Father has not left Me alone, for I always do those things that please Him.[1]

Interestingly, the person crucified on the cross cried out in despair, "My Lord, My Lord, why hast thou forsaken me?"

3. In his last words to his disciples, moments before his arrest, Jesus reassured them that Allah was always with him and would not forsake him:

Indeed the hour is coming, yes, has now come, that you will be scattered, each to his own, and will leave Me alone. And yet I am not alone because the Father is with Me.... But be of good cheer, I have overcome the world.[2]

Certainly, the person crucified was left to himself as he cried out in despair. Certainly the one crucified was defeated by his enemies and conquered by death.

4. In the final, stormy confrontation between Jesus and the Jewish clergy, he said, "For I say to you, you shall see Me no more till you say, *'Blessed is He who comes in the name of the Lord!'* Then Jesus went out and departed from the temple."[3]

The threat in the above verse is very clear. Jesus warned his enemies that they would not see him again until he came at the end of the world "with power and glory". But the person crucified was seen by the Jewish clergy as a prisoner during the trial. Afterwards, they saw him hanging on the cross. Nothing was left of him except a dead body! Permit me to use the language of Jesus in the Bible, when he says, "Whoever has two ears for hearing let him listen, and whoever listens let him comprehend."

Before we listen to what the Psalms say, I'd like everyone to know that the translations of the Old and the New Testament change from time to time with respect to studies conducted by Bible scholars. They do this in order to render the translations more accurate and to get rid of contradictions and discrepancies.

For example, in one of the Catholic editions of the New Testament, when talking about the end of Judas the betrayer (i.e., in

---

[1] John 8:21-29.
[2] John 16:32-33.
[3] Matthew 23:39, 24:1.

the first chapter of the Book of Acts), it relates that he choked himself to death. This was done to match what the Gospel of Matthew says. In contrast, the Protestant edition still narrates the end of Judas as "...falling headlong, he burst open in the middle and all his entrails gushed out."[1] Needless to say, this is completely different from committing suicide by hanging oneself. Similarly, new editions of the Psalms have also come out which differ substantially from previous versions. Although David is the name normally associated with most of the Psalms, scholars differ about the identity of the author of each Psalm, its history and the circumstances related to its author. There is also a dispute about their numbering. We have already explained this. For example, the current translation of Psalm 69 says in one of its paragraphs, "...then I restored that which I took not away."[2] or "They also gave me gall for my food."[3] As opposed to this, recent translations of the same two verses read, "How do I restore what I have never stolen?" and "They gave me poison for my food." The difference between the two versions is evident in content or when it happened.

True Salvation Has Nothing to Do with the Crucifixion

True salvation has nothing to do with the Crucifixion or with the shedding of blood. This is purely Pauline theory. It was Paul who implanted these ideas into the pure message of Jesus. This is something which we can glean from the Gospels.

1. Once, while Jesus was walking outside,

> ...one came and said to Him, "Good Teacher, what good thing shall I do that I may have eternal life?" So He said to him, "Why do you call Me good? No one is good but One, that is, God. But if you want to enter into life, keep the commandments." He said to Him, "Which ones?" Jesus said,

---

[1] Acts 1:18.
[2] Psalms 69:4.
[3] Psalms 69:21.

"'You shall not murder; you shall not commit adultery; you shall not steal; you shall not bear false witness; honor your father and your mother; and you shall love your neighbor as yourself.'" The young man said to Him, "All these things I have kept from my youth. What do I still lack?" Jesus said to him, "If you want to be perfect, go, sell what you have and give to the poor, and you will have treasure in heaven: and come, follow Me."[1]

Here we can see that Jesus, before responding to the man's inquiry, corrected the way the question was asked. He refused the quality of "good" for himself, as goodness is only for Allah. In essence, Jesus was loudly proclaiming, "To Him belongs the loftiest similitude (we can think of) in the heavens and the earth."[2] Thus any attempt to merge Allah, Most Exalted, and Jesus is absolutely rejected and downright disbelief.

Obviously, true salvation is based on a strong belief in Allah the One, and then on good deeds. Regarding Allah, the notions of crucifixion or the cross never arise, for these are all terms imported by Paul and his disciples, without any authority from Allah.

2. On the Day of Judgment, salvation will be granted on the basis of [Allah's Mercy and] good deeds. It has nothing to do with crucifixion and its theories, not even its name. There,

"...the King will say to those on His right hand, 'Come, you blessed of My Father, inherit the kingdom prepared for you from the foundation of the world: for I was hungry and you gave Me food; I was thirsty and you gave Me drink; I was a stranger and you took Me in: I was naked and you clothed Me; I was sick and you visited Me; I was in prison and you came to Me.' Then the righteous will answer Him, saying, 'Lord, when did we see You hungry and feed You, or thirsty and give You drink? When did we see You a stranger and take You in, or naked and clothe You?' Or, 'When did we see You sick, or in prison, and come to You?'

---

[1] Matthew 19:16-21.
[2] Qur'an 30:27.

> And the King will answer and say to them, 'Assuredly, I say to you, inasmuch as you did it to one of the least of these My brethren, you did it to Me.'
>
> Then He will also say to those on the left hand, 'Depart from Me, you cursed, into the everlasting fire prepared for the devil and his angels: for I was hungry and you gave Me no food; I was thirsty and you gave Me no drink; I was a stranger and you did not take Me in, naked and you did not clothe Me, sick and in prison and you did not visit Me.'
>
> Then they also will answer Him, saying, 'Lord, when did we see You hungry or thirst or a stranger or naked or sick or in prison, and did not minister to You?'
>
> Then He will answer them, saying, 'Assuredly, I say to you, inasmuch as you did not do it to one of the least of these, you did not do it to Me,' and these will go away into everlasting punishment, but the righteous into eternal life."[1]

This is the way people will be judged: the people practicing righteousness and good deeds shall go to an eternal life of happiness, and the people practicing evil and niggardliness shall be consigned to eternal damnation.

Once more, the philosophy of crucifixion and blood sacrifice will not save the people of evil. It will not avail them in the least.

3. James says in his general epistle that the religion which promises eternal life for a person is based on two elements: Belief in one God along with good deeds. Without them, there is no hope. Both elements have nothing to do with the Crucifixion or the Blood Sacrifice. In other words, "You believe that there is one God. You do well. Even the demons believe—and tremble! But do you want to know, O foolish man, that faith without works is dead?...You see then that a man is justified by works, and not by faith only.[2] Pure and undefiled religion before God and the Father is this: to visit orphans and widows in their trouble, and to keep oneself unspotted from the world."[3]

---

[1] Matthew 25:34-46
[2] James 2:19-24.
[3] James 1:27.

From the above passage—and many more like them—we can clearly see that true salvation has absolutely nothing to do with the Crucifixion. With this we conclude our discussion on the issue of the Crucifixion and its related details. What remains is the issue of the Day of Judgment and the Second Coming of Jesus. We will deal with these topics in the next session.

Afterword by Dr. Muhammad Jamil Ghazi

The Conclusion on the Issue of Crucifixion:

Let us put forward a number of questions to the Christians pertaining to the Crucifixion and the Blood Sacrifice. Hopefully we will answer these questions if time permits in another session. These questions are:

1. Christians claim that the Crucifixion of Jesus was for the sake of justice and mercy. What kind of justice and mercy was there in torturing and crucifying an innocent man? They may say that Jesus was the one who accepted that. However, we would remind them that the one who cuts his own hand or tortures his body or commits suicide is a sinner, even if he wants to hurt himself.
2. If Jesus is the Son of God, where was the affection of fatherhood and the feeling of mercy and compassion when His only son, who was innocent, was facing torture and scorn and then crucifixion with the hammering of nails into his hand?
3. What is the Christian concept of God, Most Exalted, Who is not content unless He humiliates people, in view of the promise of God—whom they call Father and say that God is Love and God is mercy—that He is very forgiving and very Compassionate?
4. Who compelled Allah to adhere specifically to justice and mercy? Who forced Allah to bring these attributes together by bringing down His only son in human form only to have him crucified as redemption for Adam's error?

5   Christians claim that Adam's descendants are all subject to punishment (i.e., in the hellfire) because of Adam's sin. What type of divine law would make the descendants responsible for their forefather's sins, especially when the Bible clearly says, "Fathers shall not be put to death for their children, nor shall children be put to death for their fathers; a person shall be put to death for his own sin."[1]

6. If the Crucifixion of Jesus was supposed to be an exemplary action, then why do Christians hate Jews and consider them inveterate sinners who illegally assaulted Jesus?

In reality, from a Christian understanding of Crucifixion, the Jews, particularly Judas Iscariot, should be considered the most devoted to God. After all, they were the ones who implemented God's will by crucifying His son.

7. Was it really necessary to crucify the Son of God in order to expiate the sins of mankind, or were there other possible means for Allah to forgive the sins of mankind?

How do Christians respond to a question like this? Paul Sabat, a Christian writer and priest, writes that

> ...it was unnecessary for God or the Son of God to come in human form for the salvation of mankind. Such an idea is inconceivable when one thinks about God's extraordinary might and power." Thereafter, the writer continues and mentions the reason for choosing Jesus to redeem the sins of mankind. He says, "In spite of the many options available to Him to redeem mankind of its sins and save it from total doom as a result of disobedience to divine commandments, God, Most Exalted, chose to redeem mankind by sacrificing the dearest thing to Him (i.e., His son). This would be the strongest and quickest way to achieve the desired goal." Thus, if we use the logic of the priest, we could say that the simplest option available to Allah, Most Exalted, was for Allah to say: "Adam, I forgive you." This is what the Qur'an says: "Then learned Adam from his Lord words of inspiration, and his Lord turned toward him; for He is Oft-Returning, Most Merciful.[2]

---

[1] Deuteronomy 24:16.
[2] Qur'an 2:37.

We must confront this writer and say that it is absolutely unwise to sacrifice or spend a dollar where one can spend a penny. There is one more answer to the question above. Let us quote another Christian writer, Father Paul Al-Yafi. He says, "Undoubtedly, Jesus could have sacrificed mankind and then reconciled that with his

Father (i.e., God) by saying one word or by doing one simple prostration, on behalf of all mankind, to his Father in Heaven. But Jesus refused and instead chose to suffer, not because he loved pain, or that His Father was a tyrant Who liked the sight of blood, especially the blood of his only son. The real reason for the suffering was that the God-Son together with the God-Father wanted to give the people an eternal example of love that would last forever. Moreover, it would motivate them to repent of their sins and to exchange love with God."

Once again we must confront this writer and say that he was accurate in describing the illness when he talked about blood and cruelty. However, when he starts to give the solution and describes the medicine, he stumbles and falls flat on his face. He says nothing but empty words devoid of any real meaning.

8. Let us come back to the priest, Paul Sabat, to ask him: If Jesus was put into human form to redeem mankind of original sin, then what about the coming sins? His answer is: "If people return to commit sins, they are responsible and accountable for their sins. After all, they have forgotten the light and preferred darkness by their own will."

This means that one sin was forgiven. As far as the millions of other sins they would stay and multiply afterwards. People will be held accountable for what they commit, some of which are much more serious than the disobedience of Adam. For example, some people deny the existence of Allah. Others attack His message and mock His Paradise and Hell. Hence, why did all this take place for one single sin. Why where countless more serious sins left?

9. Where was Allah's justice and mercy from the time of Adam's sin to the time of Jesus' crucifixion? Does this mean that Allah—and He is beyond such a thought—was unable to choose between justice and mercy for thousands of years, until

Jesus came only two thousand years ago and accepted the idea of crucifixion to expiate Adam's sin?

10. In all religions, punishment should be according to the sin. Accordingly, is the crucifixion of Jesus equivalent to the sin of Adam?

11. The sin of Adam was that he ate from the tree that Allah had forbidden him to eat from. It was nothing more. Surely, Allah, according to Christians and Muslims, punished him by expelling him from Paradise. This punishment was quite enough. Being expelled from Paradise to a life of hard work and exertion is no simple punishment. Allah chose this punishment Himself. He could have done more to Adam but he chose to stop there. How can one think that He kept this inside Him and remained angry for thousands of years, until the time of crucifying Jesus?

12. From the time of Adam to the time of Jesus, many events took place. Many tyrants perished, especially in the time of Noah (may Allah's peace and blessings be upon him) where no one was saved unless he believed in Noah, followed him and rode with him on the Ark. These were people with whom Allah was pleased. How can there still be so much rancor and hatred that it would require Jesus to sacrifice himself to redeem all of humanity?

13. Abdul-Ahad Dawud, a Christian writer who embraced Islam and who used to be the archbishop of Mosul, critiques the story of expiation in a profound way, saying, "What is so strange about this whole issue is that Christians believe that this divine secret of Adam's sin and God's anger with the human race for it, remained hidden from all previous prophets until the Church discovered it after the incident of Crucifixion."

14. Abdul-Ahad Dawud also said that it was exactly this issue and its falsehood which drove him to leave Christianity. The Church demanded that he believe in concepts which he could not justify. For example,

    A. The human race is sinful and deserves eternal damnation.

    B. God will not save any of the sinners from eternal Hell-fire which they deserve without an intercessor.

C. The intercessor must be a perfect God and perfect human being.

This writer has debated at length with Christian scholars about these things he was ordered to believe. They claim that the intercessor must be free of Adam's sin. Furthermore, they think that for this reason, Jesus was born without a father so as to avoid inheriting the sin from his father. The writer asks: Doesn't Jesus receive part of the sin through his mother? Their response is that God purified Mary of that sin before the son entered her womb.

The writer asks again: If God can so easily purify some of his creatures, then why didn't He purify all His creatures of this sin with the same ease, without bringing His son down to earth and without the whole series of events related to his birth and crucifixion?

In addition to Abdul-Ahad Dawud's discussion, we would also like to shed light on some issues. First, Adam's sin—secondarily this means that Jesus had to be born without a father or that Mary was purified before Jesus entered her womb—entails a long and complicated process. It would be much easier for the son of God to descend directly to earth in human form, without going through the womb or the birth process.

Furthermore, this Christian belief contradicts another Christian belief. In other words, the belief is that the Son of God entered Mary's womb to take on human form and apparently suffer some of Adam's sin. Of course, the Son of God appears as one of Adam's descendants. Interestingly, then the Son of God will be crucified to expiate the sins of all mankind with whom he had become one and the same.

There are still some unanswered questions concerning this topic. Were all the prophets, Noah, Abraham, Moses, etc., defiled because of their father's sin? Was Allah angry with them also? In view of the above, could He choose them to guide mankind? We are putting these questions before the Christians hoping that they will try to respond to them.

THE THIRD SESSION

The Resurrection and the Appearance

We have finished our discussion of the Crucifixion issue. It is one of the most crucial Christian issues, being a major pillar of the beliefs adopted by Paul and which gained sway later. These beliefs, however, were never part of Jesus' teachings nor his message. So what do we think about all this?

We have seen that the Christian sources, i.e., the Gospels, were completely different in each detail of the issue of the Crucifixion. Earlier we stated that in legal cases, in any of our countries, we reject contradictory testimonies immediately. There is really only one common factor or denominator among these Christian sources. They are similar in that everything written therein is based on conjecture and contradiction. They repeatedly differ with one another. The Qur'an describes this situation in one of its verses. Indeed, such a precise description only bespeaks its miraculous nature. It says:

> That they said (in boast), "We killed Christ Jesus the son of Mary, the Messenger of Allah," but they killed him not, nor crucified him, but so it was made to appear to them, and those who differ therein are full of doubts, with no (certain) knowledge, but only conjecture to follow, for of a surety they killed him not.[1]

We find that everything written by the authors of the Gospels, especially beginning with and related to issues such as Jesus' rising from the dead and appearing to some people, is subject to discrepancies from A to Z.

Let us start our discussion on the issue of Jesus' resurrection, which says, according to Christian teachings, Jesus was

---
[1] Qur'an 4:157.

crucified; he died and was then buried; thereafter, he rose from the dead on the third day and was seen alive by some people.

We have already established—as stated by the Gospels—that he was not buried in the heart of the earth for three days and three nights. Instead the one crucified was buried in the ground for one day and two nights at best.

The Resurrection

Reports of Jesus rising from the grave and his live appearance after death began circulating very slowly among the first Christian generation. This was due to the denial of such stories by his disciples and companions, especially Peter, who was foremost in rejecting them. They were skeptical about such stories; moreover, they did not believe that Jesus' true mission, which they had received from their teacher, would have anything to do with the idea of resurrection from the dead. Unfortunately, this later became one of the crucial beliefs of Christianity.

For that reason, the announcement of Jesus' resurrection and his appearance was delayed for seven weeks. This news was not told to the Christian public for fifty days, according to the Book of Acts. Luke composed this scripture more than sixty years after Jesus departed.

If this is all the Gospels have to say about Jesus' resurrection, then we must keep one thing in mind, as George Caird says:

> The earliest evidence for the resurrection is provided, not by the Gospels, but by the Epistles of Paul, and particularly by I Corinthians 15, written at least ten years before the earliest Gospel. In this chapter Paul quotes a tradition which he had received from those who were Christians before him, perhaps at the time of his conversion, twenty years or more earlier, which a list of the eyewitnesses to the resurrection.[1]

---

[1] Caird, p. 255.

We have already seen that whatever the Gospels relate about the crucifixion of Jesus is full of discrepancies and contradictions. This is sufficient proof for its rejection. Therefore, whatever is based on the crucifixion story, i.e., Jesus' resurrection and appearance, should also categorically be rejected. Regardless, let us discuss the subject of resurrection as narrated by the Gospels through its major narratives.

The Women's Visit to the Tomb

Mark says:

Now, when the Sabbath was past, Mary Magdalene, Mary the mother of James, and Salome bought spices, that they might come and anoint Him. Very early in the morning, on the first day of the week, they came to the tomb when the sun had risen. And they said among themselves, "Who will roll away the stone from the door of the tomb for us?" But when they looked up they saw that the stone had been rolled away, for it was very large. And entering the tomb, they saw a young man clothed in a long white robe sitting on the right side; and they were alarmed. But he said to them, "Do not be alarmed. You seek Jesus of Nazareth, who was crucified. He is Risen! He is not here. See the place where they laid Him. But go, tell His disciples, and Peter, that He is going before you into Galilee: there you will see Him, as He said to you." So they went out quickly and fled from the tomb, for they trembled and were amazed. And they said nothing to anyone, for they were afraid.[1]

Nineham says:

The motive suggested for the visit, however, is surprising. Quite apart from the question raised in v. 3, it is hard to credit the women with the intention of going to anoint a body a day and two nights after death, and most commentators echo the comment of Monteffori [1, 401]: "The cause assigned for their visit to the grave is very unlikely." According to St. Mark, the body of Jesus was in fact never

---

[1] Mark 16:1-8.

anointed after death. Contrast John, who says, "Then they (Joseph and Nicodemus) took the body of Jesus, and bound it in strips of linen with spices, as the custom of the Jews is to bury."[1] Many readers will probably sympathize with the conclusion of Vincent Taylor that "[i]t is probable that Mark's description is pure imagination. He tells us what he thinks happened."[2]

Matthew is the only one who talks about the request of the Jews to Pilate, the Roman governor, to send guards to secure the tomb, which he did: "So they went and made the tomb secure, sealing the stone and setting the guard."[3]

After this he talks about the women's visit to the tomb in a different way:

> Now after the Sabbath, as the first day of the week began to dawn, Mary Magdalene and the other Mary came to see the tomb. And behold, there was a great earthquake; for an angel of the Lord descended from heaven, and came and rolled the stone from the door, and sat on it. His countenance was like the lightning, and his clothing was white as snow. ...But the angel answered and said to the women, "Do not be afraid... and go quickly and tell His disciples that He is risen from the dead... So they went out quickly from the tomb with fear and great joy, and ran to bring His disciples word.[4]

Commenting on the above, John Fenton says the

> ...earthquake, the angels descending from heaven and rolling back the stone, and fear of the guards (vv. 2-4) are all Matthean additions.

In Mark the women do not obey the message, but in Matthew they do (telling the disciples about the resurrection).[5]

Luke says:

> Now on the first day of the week, very early in the morning, they, and certain other women with them, came to the tomb

---

[1] John 19:40.
[2] Nineham, pp. 443ff.
[3] Matthew 27:66.
[4] 28:1-8.
[5] Fenton, p. 449f.

bringing the spices which they had prepared. But they found the stone rolled away from the tomb. Then they went in and did not find the body of the Lord Jesus. And it happened, as they were greatly perplexed about this, that behold, two men stood by them in shining garments. Then, as they were afraid and bowed their faces to the earth, they said to them, "...He is not here but is risen! Remember how He spoke to you as He was still in Galilee," ...and they remembered His words. Then they returned from the tomb and told all these things to the eleven and to all the rest. It was Mary Magdalene, Joanna, Mary the mother of James, and the other women with them, who told these things to the apostles.[1]

George Caird explains:

Luke's story of the empty tomb runs parallel to Mark's, but differs from it at four points. Where Mark mentions one young man at the tomb, Luke has two; and the identical phrase (behold, two men) is found in the stories of the transfiguration and the ascension [Luke 9:30, Acts 1:10], perhaps as a form of cross-reference linking the three events. According to Mark [16:7], the women were told: "Go, tell his disciples and Peter that he is going before you to Galilee; there you will see him, as he told you." In place of this Luke has a reference to teaching given formerly in Galilee; for according to Luke's special source the resurrection appearances occurred not in Galilee but only in and around Jerusalem. Again, according to Mark, the women, having been entrusted with a message, failed to deliver it because they were afraid; but Luke tells us that they made a full report to the other disciples of what they had seen and heard. Finally, the list of the names is different, Luke giving Joanna in the place of Mark's Salome.[2]

But John's story of the Resurrection differs—in its basic elements—from what the other three Gospels narrate. John says:

Now on the first day of the week Mary Magdalene went to the tomb early, while it was still dark, and saw that the stone

---

[1] Luke 24:1-10.
[2] Caird, p. 256.

had been taken away from the tomb. Then she ran and came to Simon Peter, and to the other disciple, whom Jesus loved, and said to them, "They have taken away the Lord out of the tomb, and we do not know where they have laid Him." Peter therefore went out, and the other disciple, and were going to the tomb. So they both ran together, and the other disciple outran Peter and came to the tomb first. And he, stooping down and looking in, saw the linen clothes lying there; yet he did not go in. Then Simon Peter came, following him, and went into the tomb; and he saw the linen clothes lying there, and the handkerchief that had been around His head, not lying with the linen cloths but folded together in a place by itself. Then the other disciple, who came to the tomb first, went in also; and he saw and believed. For as yet they did not know the Scripture, that He must rise again from the dead. ...But Mary stood outside by the tomb weeping, ...And she saw two angels in white sitting, one at the head and the other at the feet, where the body of Jesus had lain.[1]

Discrepancies among the Gospels Regarding the Stories of the Visit

From the above, it is clear that the Gospels differ in what they narrate about the visit of the women to the tomb. In addition, we also note the following:
1. Mark says that the time of the women's visit to the tomb was after sunrise. In contrast, the others state that the visit was before sunrise. According to Matthew and Luke, the visit was at dawn, while according to John it was still dark.[2]
2 Mark says that the visitors were three women. Matthew says there were only two. Luke says there was a group of women. John makes Mary Magdalene the sole visitor, who went to bring with her Peter and John, the beloved disciple.

The authors of the four Gospels do not agree on anything pertaining to even the basic elements of the story of the visit.

---

[1] John 20:1-12.
[2] 20:1.

But they do agree to make Mary Magdalene the most important visitor, so much so that John makes her the only visitor. For this reason, Mary Magdalene, from whom Jesus exorcised seven demons, became the major source of all that was said about the Resurrection of Jesus from the dead.

3. At the tomb, the women saw "a young man, clothed in a long white robe, sitting on the right side," according to Mark. In Matthew he was "an angel of the Lord, ...his clothing as white as snow." In Luke, it was "two men...in shining garments", in John, "two angels in white, sitting, one at the head and the other at the feet."

In fact, the accounts given in the four Gospels vary so much that it is only appropriate to summarily dismiss all of them.

Besides, Mr. Ibrahim Khalil Ahmad adds to what was discussed earlier concerning the issue of resurrection. He says that Matthew was the only one who narrates:

> On the next day, which followed the day of Preparation, the chief priests and Pharisees gathered together to Pilate, saying, "Sir, we remember, while He was still alive, how that deceiver said, 'After three days I will rise.' Therefore command that the tomb be made secure until the third day, lest His disciples come by night and steal Him away, and say to the people, 'He has risen from the dead.' So the last deception will be worse than the first." Pilate said to them, "You have a guard; go your way, make it as secure as you know how." So they went and made the tomb secure, sealing the stone and setting the guard.[1]

So, the procedures taken were the guarding of the tomb and the sealing of the stone. Even if we disregard how the stone was rolled away and how the Gospels differ about it, we can still read after all of the above, the following in Matthew's Gospel:

> Now while they (Magdalene and the other Mary) were going, behold, some of the guard came into the city and reported to the chief priests all the things that had happened. When they had assembled with the elders and consulted together, they gave a large sum of money to the soldiers, say-

---

[1] Matthew 27:62-66.

ing, "Tell them, 'His disciples came at night and stole Him away while we slept,' and if this comes to the governor's ears, we will appease him and make you secure." So they took the money and did as they were instructed; and this saying is commonly reported among the Jews until this day.[1]

From the above, it is clear that the enemies of Jesus, i.e., the chief priests, the elders and the guards, did not see the resurrection of Jesus, nor did they see him after the resurrection. However, the one thing that they all agreed upon was that the tomb, wherein he was said to be buried, was empty.

If we go back to the story of Daniel, when he was a prisoner in Babylon, we find a story similar to the story of the tomb wherein there were guards who also sealed off the entrance (to the den of lions where Daniel was thrown) with a sealed boulder. The enemies of Daniel conspired against him and disclosed to the king that he was not worshipping him; rather he was worshipping one God, the Creator of the universe. At this, the king got angry and ordered that Daniel be put in the den of lions which was to be sealed shut with a sealed stone.

Regarding this story the Book of Daniel narrates:

> So they answered and said before the king, "That Daniel, who is one of the captives from Judah, does not show due regard for you, O king, or for the decree that you have signed, but makes his petition three times a day." And the king, when he heard these words, was greatly displeased with himself... So the king gave the command, and they brought Daniel and cast him into the den of lions. But the king spoke, saying to Daniel, "Your God, whom you serve continually, He will deliver you." Then a stone was brought and laid on the mouth of the den, and the king sealed it with his own signet ring and with the signets of his lords.
>
> ...[T]he king arose very early in the morning and went in haste to the den of lions. And when he came to the den, he cried out with a lamenting voice to Daniel. The king spoke, saying to Daniel, "Daniel, servant of the living God, has your God, whom you serve continually, been able to deliver

---

[1] Matthew 28:11-15.

you from the lions?" Then Daniel said to the king, "O king, live forever! My God sent His angel and shut the lions' mouths, so they have not hurt me, because I was found innocent before Him; and also, O king, I have done no wrong before you."

Now the king was exceedingly glad for him, and commanded that they should take Daniel up out of the den. So Daniel was taken up out of the den and no injury whatever was found on him, because he believed in his God. And the king gave the command, and they brought those men who had accused Daniel and they cast them into the den of lions—them, their children, and their wives; and the lions overpowered them, and broke all their bones in pieces before they ever came to the bottom of the den.[1]

Here is a real miracle. The seals were removed before witnesses who saw Daniel standing alive among them. He had overcome what was awaiting him at the jaws of the lions. As a matter of fact, Daniel's enemies as well as his friends all witnessed this.

Thus if Jesus was the man they crucified, and then put in the tomb, assigning guards to the tomb and sealing the stone, then it is only fitting that his rising from the dead—as they claim—should have happened in the presence of his enemies—before his friends. As such, the miracle would have occurred before witnesses, especially, since Jesus executed all of his miracles in front of the people, were they believers or disbelievers.

As for the empty tomb, it is claimed that Jesus, who was buried therein, rose from it and that no one saw him rise. This claim is baseless due to the contradictions evident in the narratives of the Gospels pertaining to the resurrection. Later, this became one of the central doctrines of Christian belief. Needless to say, this issue surpasses in importance the story of Daniel's deliverance from the lions' den a thousandfold.

Commenting on this, John Fenton says:

> ...Daniel's escape from the den of lions was a type of parable of Jesus' resurrection, in the early Church. Matthew has

---

[1] Daniel 16:23-34.

changed Mark's statement that the women bought spices so that they might go and anoint him to see the sepulchre. Presumably, since Matthew has introduced the sealing of the stone [27:66], he had to make this adjustment here.[1]

If the Church considers Daniel's escape from the lions' den to be similar to Jesus' rising from the dead, doesn't it become necessary, in order to validate this supposed resemblance, that there be some substantial evidence verifying the "incident"? In other words, shouldn't there be eye-witness accounts of friends and foes alike? This factor was present in Daniel's story but completely missing from Jesus' story. In light of the above, we can now fully appreciate the concise words of Adolf Hernack. He says: "...there are some points which are historically confirmed. One of them is that none of Jesus' enemies saw him after his death."[2]

Indeed, the testimony of enemies, rather than friends, is important proof, yet it is missing. For anyone believing in Jesus' rise from the dead, such evidence is an absolute must. Suffice it to say that such proof is unavailable, and as a matter of fact it will be missing forever.

The Appearance

In all of our previous discussions, the course which we have adopted in citing evidence is that we first cite the Gospel of Mark concerning the various topics under study. Then we follow that by citations from the remaining Gospels concerning the same topic. This is because Mark's Gospel, as agreed upon, is considered the oldest of the canonical Gospels reaching us. Moreover, it was the basic source which Matthew and Luke referred to. Thus, if we apply the same rule which we have adopted in our study and begin by first referring to the Gospel of Mark regarding Jesus' appearance after his rise from the dead, we observe the following:

---

[1] Fenton, p. 443.
[2] Harnack, *The History of Dogma*, vol. 1, p. 85.

The Gospel of Mark Says Nothing

Really, the Gospel of Mark says nothing about Jesus' appearance. Naturally, some readers will rush to the copies of the Gospel that they have, looking to verify the truth of this serious allegation. Upon checking, they will find that the end of this Gospel, i.e., Chapter 16, verses 9-20, talks about Jesus appearing in front of some people after the trials of the crucifixion and the events of the resurrection.

Here some confusion can occur; however, the following facts clarify the matter. The end of the Gospel of Mark, which talks about Jesus' appearance, i.e., verses 19-20, is not the work of Mark, the supposed writer of the Gospel. Instead, they were additions appended to the Gospel around 180 C.E. In other words, they were added a hundred twenty years after Mark had written his Gospel. Furthermore, they were not recognized officially until after 325 C.E.

We already pointed to this when we talked about the problems with the Gospel of Mark. Now let us add what Nineham says in this context. He declares that

> ...Although these verses appear in most of the extant MSS.[1] of Mark, R.S.V.[2] is certainly right in treating them as spurious and relegating them to the margin. The great Roman Catholic scholar, Lagrange, is quite clear that, though "canonically authentic" (i.e., part of the canon of Holy Scripture), they are not authentic in a literary sense (i.e., not the work of St. Mark). The reason for this view—in which all other scholars concur—are basically three.
>
> (i) Some of our best MSS. of Mark end at 16:8; other MSS. agree with them in omitting vv. 9-20, but have the alternative ending.
>
> (ii) The great fourth-century scholars, Eusebius and Jerome, testify that the verses were wanting in all the best Greek MSS. known to them, and they are quoted only once (or

---

[1] i.e., manuscripts.
[2] i.e., the Revised Standard Version of the Bible.

possibly twice) in the whole of Christian literature down to A.D. 325.

(iii) Most decisively of all, the style and vocabulary of the verses, which smack of the second century, are completely different from those of St. Mark.

The passage cannot be dated exactly; it had become accepted as part of Mark's Gospel by about A.D. 180.[1]

Likewise, John Fenton comments, saying:

...As far as we know, the Gospel according to Mark, as Matthew had it, ended at Mark 16:8; so the appearance of Jesus to the women in Matthew 28:9f has been added by Matthew...Mark's Gospel, as far as we know, contained no account of the appearance of the risen Lord.[2]

The Narrations of the Other Gospels

Nevertheless, let us explore Mark's Gospel to see what it says about Jesus' appearance. It says:

Now when He rose early on the first day of the week, He appeared first to Mary Magdalene, out of whom he had cast some demons. She went and told those who had been with Him, as they mourned and wept, and when they heard that He was alive and had been seen by her, they did not believe. After that, He appeared in another form to two of them as they walked and went into the country. And they went and told it to the rest, but they did not believe them either. Later He appeared to the eleven as they sat at the table; and He rebuked their unbelief and hardness of heart, because they did not believe those who had seen Him after He had risen.[3]

We have seen, according to Matthew's version of the women's visit to the tomb, that Mary Magdalene and the other Mary were commissioned by the Lord's Angel to carry a message saying:

---

[1] Nineham, p. 449f.
[2] Fenton, p. 449f.
[3] Mark 16:9-14.

> ...And go quickly and tell His disciples that He is risen from the dead, and indeed He is going before you into Galilee; there you will see Him, I have told you. So they went out quickly from the Tomb with fear and great joy, and ran to bring His disciples word.[1]

Matthew continues, saying:

> ...And as they went to tell His disciples, behold, Jesus met them, saying, "Rejoice!" So they came and held Him by the feet and worshipped Him. Then Jesus said to them, "Do not be afraid. Go and tell My brethren to go to Galilee, and there they will see Me." ...Then the eleven disciples went away into Galilee, to the mountain which Jesus had appointed for them. When they saw Him, they worshipped Him; but some doubted.[2]

Luke, after narrating what the women had said about Jesus' resurrection to the disciples, talks about Jesus' appearance. He says:

> ...Now behold, two of them were traveling that same day to a village called Emmaus, which was seven miles from Jerusalem. And they talked together of all those things which had happened. So it was, while they conversed and reasoned, that Jesus Himself drew near and went with them. But their eyes were restrained, so that they did not know Him. And He said to them, "What kind of conversation is this that you have with one another...? "...So they said to Him, "The things concerning Jesus of Nazareth, who was a prophet mighty in deed and word before God and all the people..." Then they drew near to the village where they were going, and He indicated that He would have gone farther... So they rose up that very hour and returned to Jerusalem, and found the eleven and those who were with them gathered together, saying, "The Lord is risen indeed, and has appeared to Simon!" ...Now as they said these things, Jesus Himself stood in the midst of them, and said to them, "Peace to you."

---

[1] Matthew 28:7-8.
[2] Matthew 28:9,10,16,17.

But they were terrified and frightened, and supposed they had seen a spirit. And He said to them, "Why are you troubled? And why do doubts arise in your hearts? Behold My hands and My feet, that it is I Myself. Handle Me and see, for a spirit does not have flesh and bones as you see I have." When He had said this, He showed them His hands and His feet... So they gave Him a piece of a broiled fish and some honeycomb. And He took it and ate in their presence.[1]

John says that Mary Magdalene was crying at the tomb, so the two angels

> ... said to her, "Woman, why are you weeping?" She said to them, "Because they have taken away my Lord, and I do not know where they have laid Him." Now when she had said this, she turned around and saw Jesus standing there, and did not know that it was Jesus. Jesus said to her, "Woman, why are you weeping? Whom are you seeking?" She, supposing him to be the gardener, said to Him, "Sir, if You have carried Him away, tell me where You have laid Him, and I will take Him away." Jesus said to her, "Mary!" She turned and said to Him, "Rabboni!" (which is to say, Teacher). Jesus said to her, "Do not cling to Me, for I have not yet ascended to My Father: but go to My brethren and say to them, 'I am ascending to My Father and your Father, and to My God and your God.'" Mary Magdalene came and told the disciple that she had seen the Lord, and that He had spoken these things to her. Then, the same day at evening, being the first day of the week, when the doors were shut where the disciples were assembled, for fear of the Jews, Jesus came and stood in their midst, and said to them, "Peace be with you." When He had said this, He showed them His hands and His side. Then the disciples were glad when they saw the Lord. ...Now Thomas, called the Twin, one of the twelve, was not with them when Jesus came. The other disciples therefore said to him, "We have seen the Lord." So he said to them, "Unless I see in His hands the print of the nails, and put my finger into the print of the nails and put my hand into His side, I will

---

[1] Luke 24:13, 15-17, 19, 28, 33-34, 36-40, 42-43.

not believe." And after eight days His disciples were again inside, and Thomas with them. Jesus came, the doors being shut, and stood in their midst, and said, "Peace to you!"[1]

After these things Jesus showed Himself again to the disciples at the Sea of Tiberias, and in this way He showed *Himself*: ...But when the morning had now come, Jesus stood on the shore; yet the disciples did not know that it was Jesus. ...Jesus then came and took the bread and gave it to them, and likewise the fish. This is now the third time Jesus showed Himself to His disciples after He was raised from the dead.[2]

Some Observations about the Narrations of the Gospels

Having surveyed what the Gospels say about Jesus' appearance, we can see that these narratives bring to light the following observations.

1. Mark, Matthew and John agree that Jesus' first appearance was in the presence of Mary Magdalene, who did not recognize Jesus and thought he was the gardener. In contrast, Luke deletes this story entirely and places his first appearance in the presence of the two people traveling to a village called Emmaus.

2. The appearance occurred only once in the presence of the disciples, according to Mark, Matthew and Luke; whereas John talks about it being three times, each time with a different vision.

3. Mark and Matthew agree that Jesus' appearance in the presence of eleven disciples occurred in Galilee, whereas Luke and John maintain that it was in Jerusalem.

4. More significant than all of the above is the agreement of all four Gospels on one point regarding this issue, namely that the person who appeared to Mary Magdalene and the disciples was a stranger to them. They really didn't recognize him and they doubted him. Yet they were the ones who lived with Jesus and knew him intimately. In view of the above, how can it be

---

[1] John 20:13-20, 24-26.
[2] John 21:1,4,13,14.

claimed that Jesus rose in the presence of his disciples and acquaintances?

The Disciples' Misgivings Concerning the Narratives of Jesus' Resurrection and His Subsequent Appearance

The stories in the Gospels about Jesus' resurrection and his subsequent appearance are full of discrepancies. Any casual reader can notice this simply by reading and comparing the same stories in the different Gospels. In reality, such discrepancies are enough to dismiss everything that the stories tell about Jesus' resurrection and appearance. In fact, how is it possible not to reject them totally?! After all, the original writer of the Gospel of Mark himself discards these stories. As discussed earlier, he omits them from his version by ending his Gospel at Chapter 16:8. Similarly, the disciples of Jesus also refused to accept it and had strong doubts about it. All the disciples were skeptical about the story of Mary Magdalene and the woman with her about Jesus' resurrection. Luke narrates that

> ...they returned from the tomb and told all these things to the eleven and to all the rest. It was Mary Magdalene, Joanna, Mary the mother of James, and the other women with them, who told these things to the apostles. And their words seemed to them like idle tales, and they did not believe them. But Peter arose and ran to the tomb; and stooping down, he saw the linen cloths lying by themselves; and he departed, marveling to himself at what had happened.[1]

This was the position of Jesus' disciples regarding the stories about Jesus' resurrection. They were the ones who adhered to him closely from the time he chose them till his departure. Peter was the leader among them, and John was one of them. They were the ones who received and comprehended his teachings before or after Mary Magdalene would appear. However, the Gospels of Mark, Matthew and Luke tell us about a conversation that took place between Jesus and his disciples, where he

---

[1] Luke 24:9-12.

predicted his killing and then his resurrection. The Gospels narrated:

> ...He began to teach them that the son of Man must suffer many things, and be rejected by the elders and chief priests and scribes, and be killed, and after three days rise again. He spoke this word openly. Then Peter took Him aside and began to rebuke Him. But when He had turned around and looked at His disciples, He rebuked Peter, saying, "Get behind Me, Satan! For you are not mindful of the things of God, but the things of men."[1]

Matthew[2] and Luke[3] give similar accounts.

The way this dialogue was narrated gives the impression that Jesus' resurrection was an inevitable reality, similar to his killing. The Gospels say that Jesus "spoke these words openly."[4]

Now, if we find that the stories narrated by Mary Magdalene about Jesus were considered by Peter, the leader of the disciples who discussed this issue earlier, and his companions, to be incredible nonsense, then the inescapable conclusion can only be as follows, namely the dialogue that supposedly took place between Jesus and his disciples, where he predicted his killing and subsequent resurrection, never happened. Moreover, what we read in the Gospels about this conversation is nothing more than statements added afterwards.

This is exactly what the Gospel of John says. It reports that the idea of Jesus' resurrection was a totally strange idea to the disciples. Mary Magdalene's narration took them by complete surprise. Thus, when she went and told Peter and John, they raced to the tomb and there "...the other disciple, who came to

---

[1] Mark 8:31-33.
[2] Matthew 16:21-23: "From that time Jesus began to show to His disciples that He must go to Jerusalem, and suffer many things from the elders and chief priests and scribes, and be killed, and be raised the third day. Then Peter took Him aside and began to rebuke Him saying, 'Far be it from You, Lord: this shall not happen to You!' But he turned and said to Peter, 'Get behind Me, Satan! You are an offense to Me, for you are not mindful of the things of God, but the things of men.'"
[3] Luke 9:22: "The Son of Man must suffer many things, and be rejected by the elders and chief priests and scribes, and be killed, and be raised the third day."
[4] Mark 8:32.

the tomb first, went in also; and he saw and believed. For as yet they did not know the scripture, that He must rise again from the dead. Then the disciples went away again to their own homes."[1]

How can John's statement, "[f]or as yet they did not know the scripture, that He must rise again from the dead,"[2] be in agreement with the long conversation between Jesus and his disciples, when he told them about his resurrection, as narrated by Mark, Matthew and Luke?

Furthermore, the disciples doubted what Mary Magdalene and others narrated about Jesus' appearance. "She went and told those who had been with Him...and when they heard that He was alive and had been seen by her, they did not believe."[3] Likewise, the two people to whom Jesus supposedly appeared "...went and told it to the rest, but they did not believe them either."[4]

Matthew has recorded the disciples' doubts about the one said to be Jesus whom they had accompanied earlier. Matthew says that "...the eleven disciples went away into Galilee, to the mountain which Jesus had appointed for them. When they saw Him, they worshipped Him; but some doubted."[5]

Similarly, Luke says about the disciples that "...they were terrified and frightened, and supposed they had seen a spirit."[6]

Finally, in recording Thomas' doubt, John proves conclusively that the concept of Jesus' resurrection had nothing whatever to do with Jesus' teachings and mission. He says that "...Thomas...one of the twelve, was not with them when Jesus came. The other disciples therefore said to him, 'We have seen the Lord.' So he said to them, 'Unless I see in His hands the print of the nails, and put my hand into His side, I will not believe.'"[7]

Traditional Christianity—i.e., Pauline Christianity—has dedicated itself to the claim that it is based on historical events, such as the claims of Jesus being killed on the Cross and his res-

---

[1] John 20:8-10.
[2] John 20:9.
[3] Mark 16:10-11.
[4] Mark 16:23.
[5] Matthew 28:16-17.
[6] Luke 24:37.
[7] John 20:24-25.

urrection on the third day. Thus, if these events cannot be verified, then Christianity has no real evidence to support it. Similarly, if it is proven that these events never took place, then the whole traditional Christian creed will fall from its foundation. Nothing will remain.

On this issue its scholars confirm that

> ...Christianity is considered a historical religion in a unique sense. It is unparalleled in this respect by any other religion; namely, it could either stay in existence or disappear depending on the credibility of certain events, in particular, events that are said to have taken place during a certain period of time, approximately forty-eight hours, in Palestine, about two thousand years ago.
>
> Naturally questions arise. What are some of the points which could spell doom for the Christian creed? How can the Christian religion, then, be subject to historical collapse? But, looking carefully at these questions, we have to confess that it is impossible to verify beliefs based on historical events as real facts. More precisely stated, these beliefs represent nothing more than a very high level of probability.[1]

Surely, whoever sees the real Christianity of Jesus (may Allah's peace and blessings be upon him) as nothing more than the Crucifixion and Resurrection has put his Christianity at the mercy of history.

If we refer to what history has provided us about the stories of the Crucifixion, his resurrection and appearance, we would not find it in favor of a cardinal pillar of the Christian creed, that is, the belief in the Crucifixion. In fact, Paul saw nothing else as real Christianity, and traveled all over inviting people to it until it gained sway.

Regardless, scholars decided that such beliefs based on history cannot be considered confirmed facts. I ask the audience, is it possible to build belief upon doubt, possibility and likelihood?

---

[1] D. M. Mackinnon, *Objections to Christian Beliefs*, London, Constable, 1936, pp. 58, 64, 65.

Mr. Ibrahim Khalil Ahmad:

The most significant issue in Christianity is the issue of forgiveness. It claims that, due to the inherited sin of Adam, the whole of humanity is absolutely doomed. Consequently, Jesus came to sacrifice himself for its sake. His murder on the Cross, as the only son of God, was the price which Paul claimed was paid to reconcile with God. In other words, according to Paul "...we were reconciled to God through the death of His Son."[1]

But if we suppose that what was said about the inherited sin is true—although it is absolutely untrue and inconsistent with Allah's Justice and divinely revealed law of which the Law of Moses was a part—then was it necessary to entertain a tragic story as portrayed by Christianity, wherein Jesus was crucified on the cross despite his desperate cries in the face of such a bloody death? Wasn't forgiveness possible without spilling innocent blood? Let us go back to the Gospel of Matthew. He says:

> So He got into a boat, crossed over, and came to His own city. Then, behold, they brought to Him a paralytic lying on a bed. When Jesus saw their faith, He said to the paralytic, "Son, be of good cheer; your sins are forgiven you." And at once some of the scribes said within themselves, "This Man blasphemes!" But Jesus, knowing their thoughts said, "Why do you think evil in your hearts? For which is easier, to say, '*Your* sins are forgiven you, or to say, 'Arise and walk'? But that you may know that the Son of Man has power on earth to forgive sins."—Then He said to the paralytic, "Arise, take up your bed, and go to your house." And he arose and departed to his house. Now when the multitude saw it, they marveled and glorified God, who had given such power to men.[2]

Jesus said to the paralytic: "your sins are forgiven you," meaning that Allah (swt) will forgive his sins, since his creation cannot forgive sins. Similarly, when one says about someone

---

[1] Romans 5:10.
[2] Matthew 9:1-8.

who has passed away, "May he be forgiven," what is meant is, "may Allah forgive him."

As a matter of fact, Matthew narrates Jesus as saying, "But that you may know that the Son of Man has power on earth to forgive sins."[1]

From the above, it appears as if Allah (swt) granted Jesus the power to forgive sins by a command from Him. Accordingly, forgiveness of human sins does not require the crucifixion and murder of Jesus. All that dramatic action only helped to multiply the sins—if it happened as they claim—rather than erase them. More significantly, Jesus gave Peter, whom he described as Satan, and who, as the Gospels report, withdrew from his master at the time of hardship and denied him before the Jews, the power to forgive sins, saying to him, "And I will give you the keys of the kingdom of heaven, and whatever you bind on earth will be bound in heaven, and whatever you loose on earth will be loosed in heaven."[2]

Can a human being forgive by using one word, whereas the Lord of mankind cannot?

Where are the minds that people think with? As you know, the Gospels were written decades after Jesus departed. Subsequently, they were subjected to many additions and omissions. Jesus had known those who surrounded him and those who claimed to be associated with his name and his message and claimed to be his apostles and disciples, but who in reality were disciples of the Devil, who would help them with miracles and illusions that would misguide people.

Accordingly, the author of Matthew's Gospel says:

> ...Not everyone who says to me, "Lord, Lord," shall enter the kingdom of heaven, but he who does the will of My Father in heaven. Many will say to Me in that day, "Lord, Lord, have we not prophesied in Your name, cast out demons in Your name, and done many wonders in Your name?" And then I will declare to them, "I never knew you; depart from Me, you who practice lawlessness!"[3]

---

[1] Matthew 9:6.
[2] Matthew 16:19.
[3] Matthew 7:21-23.

Muslim-Christian Dialogue

The Holy Spirit played a big role in preaching in the name of Jesus. So popular was this term that if someone was found to be talking irrationally, people would say he was full of the Holy Spirit. Undoubtedly, a criminal is the one most able to show us ways of committing crimes. Thereafter, when we need to decrease the number of crimes, we can get a group of criminals and ask them to show us their ways. This will help us develop the necessary strategy to fight crime.

Now we come to Saul, i.e., Paul. In his second epistle to the Corinthians, we find him saying:

> ...But what I do, I will also continue to do, that I may cut off the opportunity from those who desire an opportunity to be regarded just as we are in things of which they boast. For such are false apostles, deceitful workers, transforming themselves into apostles of Christ. And no wonder! For Satan himself transforms himself into an angel of light. Therefore it is no great thing if his ministers also transform themselves into ministers of righteousness, whose end will be according to their works. I say again, let no one think me a fool. If otherwise, at least receive me as a fool, that I also may boast a little. What I speak, I speak not according to the Lord, but as it were foolishly, in this confidence of boasting.[1]

When we come to Paul's idea about the Crucifixion—with us having an absolute belief that Jesus was never crucified nor hanged on the Cross—we find Paul saying, "...Christ has redeemed us from the curse of the law, having become a curse for us, for it is written, 'Cursed is everyone who hangs on a tree.'"[2]

I ask the audience, how can this be possible? How can Jesus be a curse? It looks as if Jesus was taking precautions against Paul, his ideas and his followers when he said in the Gospel of John:

---

[1] II Corinthians 11:12-17.
[2] Galatians 3:13.

Indeed the hour is coming, yes, has now come, that you will be scattered, each to his own, and will leave Me alone, and yet I am not alone, because the Father is with Me.[1]

This is completely opposite to the sayings of the person whom they hanged on the Cross. He had desperately cried out, "My God, my God, why hast thou forsaken me?"[2]

This by itself is sufficient proof that Jesus was never crucified. These are our comments on the issue of the Crucifixion, and related issues such as the stories of Jesus rising from the dead and his appearance.

My next topic will be "The Prophecy of the Coming of Prophet Muhammad (may Allah's peace and blessings be upon him) in the Old and the New Testaments."

Paul

Our discussion now will center mainly around Paul. Earlier, we were introduced briefly to some of Paul's thought and philosophy concerning the Crucifixion and the Sacrifice. In essence, this becomes his own brand of Christianity that he preached. It was in direct contrast to the true Christianity of Jesus, which was characterized by love and tolerance. On the other hand, Pauline Christianity, i.e., the Christianity of the Crucifixion that Paul espoused, was full of blood and violence. We will see how Paul entered Christianity and what was the product of his philosophy. Here we must recall a famous proverb which says you cannot pick grapes out of thorns.

Paul, i.e., Saul, was originally Jewish. He was known for his harshness to his opponents and for his extreme hostility towards Jesus' followers. He never had the opportunity—not even once—to see Jesus in his lifetime. The Chapter of Acts states that

---

[1] John 16:32.
[2] Matthew 27:46.

> ...as for Saul, he made havoc of the church, entering every house, and dragging off men and women, committing them to prison.[1]

> And the witnesses laid down their clothes at the feet of a young man named Saul. And they stoned Stephen as he was calling on God. ...he knelt down and cried out with a loud voice, "Lord, do not charge them with this sin." And when he had said this, he fell asleep.[2]

> Now Saul was consenting to his death.[3]

After this, Paul suddenly announced his abrupt change to Christianity. The history of religion bears witness to many people who were once the most inveterate enemies of a given religion and its prophet or messenger who called to its message, and then eventually embraced the religion and became its best missionaries. But regarding Paul, there is one thing that separates him from the above. Paul never adhered to the teachings of the new faith, Christianity, which he had embraced. Instead he preached his own, self-concocted teachings. Using his talent and skills, he was able to push aside the disciples and, after uprooting all of them, Paul began to preside over all Christian missionary activity.

Let us now see what the Book of Acts says about Paul's abrupt move to Christianity. Chapter 9 states:

> Then Saul, still breathing threats and murder against the disciples of the Lord, went to the high priest and asked letters from him to the synagogues of Damascus, so that if he found any who were of the Way, whether men or women, he might bring them bound to Jerusalem. As he journeyed he came near Damascus, and suddenly a light shone around him from heaven. Then he fell to the ground, and heard a voice saying to him, "Saul, Saul, why are you persecuting Me?" And he said, "Who are You, Lord?" Then the Lord said, "I am Jesus, whom you are persecuting. ...So he, trembling and astonished, said, "Lord, what do you want me to do?" Then

---
[1] Acts 8:3.
[2] Acts 7:58-60.
[3] Acts 8:1.

the Lord said to him, "Arise and go into the city, and you will be told what you must do." And the men who journeyed with him stood speechless, hearing a voice but seeing no one.[1]

Allah, Most Perfect, Most Exalted, being merciful to mankind, always brings out the truth. Accordingly, we find that the story of Paul's conversion to Christianity, narrated in Acts 22, is related by Paul himself in his own words. He says:

> Now it happened, as I journeyed and came near Damascus at about noon, suddenly a great light from heaven shone around me. And I fell to the ground and heard a voice saying to me, "Saul, Saul, why are you persecuting Me?" So I answered, "Who are You, Lord?" And He said to me, "I am Jesus of Nazareth, whom you are persecuting." And those who were with me indeed saw the light and were afraid, but they did not hear the voice of Him who spoke to me.[2]

From the above we can conclude that the travelers heard the voice but did not see the light, according to Acts 9:7; whereas Act 22:9 claims the complete opposite, saying that they "...saw the light...but they did not hear the voice of Him who spoke to me." This is the beginning of Paul's entrance into Christianity—and I might add, it is an extremely dubious story, to say the least.

After embracing Christianity—according to a clearly false story—Paul began to propagate his own teachings, declaring that he had no need for the teachings of the Master (i.e., Jesus) compiled by his disciples. Instead, he claims that he received his teachings directly from Jesus through that alleged vision. He says:

> ...but when it pleased God, who separated me from my mother's womb and called *me* through His grace, to reveal His Son in me, that I might preach Him among the Gentiles, I did not immediately confer with flesh and blood, nor did I go up to Jerusalem to those *who* were apostles before me; but I went to Arabia, and returned again to Damascus. Then

---
[1] Acts 9:1-7.
[2] Acts 22:6-9.

after three years I went up to Jerusalem to see Peter, and remained with him fifteen days. But I saw none of the other apostles except James, the Lord's brother. (Now *concerning* the things which I write to you, indeed, before God, I do not lie.)[1]

In this story, Paul started preaching Christianity according his own understanding for three years before he met Jesus' disciples. Afterwards, they were the ones who established the main Church in Jerusalem. Moreover, they were the main source of reference for any matter pertaining to Christianity and its missionary activity.

Later, Paul says:

...after fourteen years I went up again to Jerusalem with Barnabas, and also took Titus with *me*. And I went up by revelation, and communicated to them that gospel which I preach among the Gentiles, but privately to those who were of reputation, lest by any means I might run, or had run, in vain...for those who seemed to be *something* added nothing to me. But on the contrary, when they saw that the gospel for the uncircumcised had been committed to me, as the gospel for the circumcised was to Peter.[2]

From the above, it is clear that:

1. The story of Paul's entrance into Christianity is highly dubious. At the same time, it is impossible to rely on it due to its glaring contradictions.

2. Paul did not concentrate on any Christian issue except the Crucifixion and the shedding of blood. He specialized in such issues. As for the other teachings of Jesus, he completely neglected them. He says:

But I make known to you, brethren, that the gospel which was preached by me is not according to man. For I neither received it from man, nor was I taught *it*, but *it came* through the revelation of Jesus Christ.[3]

---

[1] Galatians 1:15-20.
[2] Galatians 21:1,2.,6,7.
[3] Galatians 1:11-12.

> For I determined not to know anything among you except Jesus Christ and Him crucified.[1]

The scholars studied Paul's thought and the trends affecting it. Charles Dodd said:

> We have explained before how the idea of world commonwealth was widespread in the pagan world. Rome had fallen under the influence of stoic ideals.[2] During the time of Paul, people espousing such ideals had elected one of their own as the chief minister of the Roman empire. In the following century, one of these stoics became the Emperor of the Roman Empire. Soon after his ascent to the throne, he attempted to establish this commonwealth. Paul, as a Roman citizen, was influenced by such ideas.[3]

Paul had been thinking of establishing a Christian commonwealth based on one name and one symbol: the Christ and the Cross. He had no objection to accepting other ideas and religions within the projected commonwealth. And why not? After all, he himself admitted in his epistles that he would spare no means to procure the largest number of followers. He says:

> For though I am free from all men, I have made myself a servant to all, that I might win the more; and to the Jews I became a Jew, that I might win Jews; to those who are under the law, as under the law, that I might win those who are under the law; to those who are without law, as without law (not being without law toward God, but under law toward Christ), that I might win those who are without law; to the weak I became as weak, that I might win the weak. I have become all things to all men, that I might by all means save some. Now this I do for the gospel's sake, that I may be partaker of it with you.[4]

In this way, we find that Paul presented Christianity to the adherents of the various religions in a manner pleasing to them. The result of this behavior was that they embraced the new re-

---

[1] I Corinthians 2:2.
[2] The ideals were from a philosophy formulated by Zeno of Citium in about 300 B.C.E.
[3] Dodd, What Paul Means to Us Today, p. 49.
[4] I Corinthians 9:19-23.

ligion (i.e., Christianity) while still adhering to their old beliefs and ideas. Needless to say, this trend had—and still has today—a very significant effect on Christianity.

We know that Barnabas was the one who introduced Paul to the disciples. However, Paul later removed Barnabas from heading any Christian missionary activities.

The Book of Acts relates, "Then the contention became so sharp that they parted from one another. And so Barnabas took Mark and sailed to Cyprus."[1] Thereafter, Paul quarreled with Peter, the chief disciple, and drove him out, too. Paul says boldly, "Now when Peter had come to Antioch, I withstood him to his face, because he was to be blamed."[2]

Certainly, Paul did not understand the status of Peter, whom Jesus gave authority to do whatever he wished, and whom he appointed in charge of his disciples. There is no need to go through Paul's epistles; they are just personal letters. As a matter of fact, in one of them he says, "I have no mandate from the Lord; yet I give judgment."[3] He also says, "...I think I also have the spirit of God."[4] On another occasion he says, "...I say this as a concession, not as a commandment."[5] Such presumptive statements are absolutely inappropriate in establishing a creed.

Paul's epistles end with him encouraging others to greet each other and spread holy kisses to all men and women. He says, "Greet Tryphena and Tryphosa, who have labored in the Lord. Greet the beloved Persis, who labored much in the Lord."[6] "Greet one another with a holy kiss."[7]

Pauline Christianity is fundamentally based on the idea of a god who would be killed for Salvation. The most common religions in the Roman world at that time, such as the faiths of Isis, Mithra and Sybil, were based on the same idea. Quite naturally, religious historians point out that the similarity between Christianity and these pagan religions is very obvious.

---

[1] Acts 15:39.
[2] Galatians 2:11.
[3] I Cornithians 7:25.
[4] I Cornithians 7:40.
[5] I Cornithians 7:6.
[6] Romans 16:12.
[7] Romans 16:16.

Herbert Fisher, in his book *History of Europe*, says:

The Roman world with great fondness turned to oriental worship such as the worship of Isis, Serabaeus and Mithra. The worshippers of the Egyptian Isis, the Phrygean Sybil and the Persian Mithra shared many beliefs. These beliefs were later found in the Christian faith.

They believed in a secret holy communion with the divine being either by a connection through rituals or by a simpler way through eating the flesh of God in a ritual ceremony.

The belief that the God who would die in the midst of a lot of wailing and lament and then would rise again in the midst of cries of joy and happiness was one of the main features of those mysterious oriental rituals. The way that the worship of Isis was organized completely resembles what we find in the Catholic Church. For example, the hierarchy of the clergy was identical, i.e., being composed of the Pope along with the priests, the monks, the singers and the church servants. A picture of a lady was adorned with genuine and false jewels and she was decorated daily. Moreover, the morning prayers and the evening hymns were performed in its main temples. The clergy used to don shaved heads and wore white priestly garb made of linen. The change from paganism to Christianity did not entail the embracing of a totally strange practice, nor did it mean a revolution in one's beliefs. This transformation was being done gently. The new religious rituals were merely a rehash of ancient mysteries.

The idea of an intercessor was common in the Persian beliefs and among the followers of Neoplatonism. The idea of the Trinity was a prevailing religious belief based on a common concept that the number three is a perfect number.[1]

Ernest Killet in his book, *A Brief History of Religions*, says:

The amazing similarity between the Christian ritual of baptism, for example, and the rituals of purification in the religions of Atis and Adonis, would shock any researcher. Chris-

---

[1] Fisher, H., *History of Europe*, pp. 102-115.

tianity has shown a marked ability, in all eras, to take for itself whatever is suitable from other religions.

Let me give you a summary of Atis' fable and the ritual of his worship, not just because of its deep effect on Christianity, but also because it was widespread in most of the Roman empire. Atis' rise form the dead occurred on the twenty-fifth of March, which was also the beginning of spring season. This happens to be the exact same day that Jesus rose from the dead, according to the belief of many Christians. Also, the similarity between the mysterious rituals of the Mithran faith and Christianity is amazing. Mithra has its own rituals associated with the "Lord's Supper". It is difficult to differentiate between it and our Christian beliefs. Moreover, it has ceremonies identical to the celebration of Jesus' birthday. It also celebrates Easter...[1]

Dr. Muhammad Jamil Ghazi:

Based on the preceding discourse, we must clearly admit that the Christian religion should be called Pauline Christianity. It can only be ascribed to Paul and not Jesus (may Allah's peace and blessings be upon him). Likewise, it is worth noting that the Vatican acknowledges Paul's position toward Christianity and his awareness of it. In a book titled *Christianity: Belief and Action*, published by the Vatican in 1968, we read the following statement on page 50. It says that "...Saint Paul, from the beginning of Christianity, was advising the new believers to keep on following what they were doing before their belief in Jesus." This serious confession confirms everything that Brigadier General Abdul-Wahhab has said about Paul and Christianity.

Now let me introduce Mr. Ibrahim Khalil Ahmad. He will talk to us about the Passover and the Lord's Supper, both of which were practiced by the ancient pagan religions.

---

[1] Killet, E., A Brief History of Religions, pp. 130-262.

Mr. Ibrahim Khalil Ahmad:

In Chapter 22 of the Gospel of Luke, as well as in the other Gospels, we read:

> When the hour had come, He sat down, and the twelve apostles with Him. Then He said to them, "With fervent desire I have desired to eat this Passover with you before I suffer;
>
> 16 "for I say to you, I will no longer eat of it until it is fulfilled in the kingdom of God." Then He took the cup, and gave thanks and said, "Take this and divide it among yourselves; for I say to you, I will not drink of the fruit of the vine until the kingdom of God comes."
>
> 19 And He took bread, gave thanks and broke it, and gave it to them, saying, "This is My body which is given for you; do this in remembrance of Me." Likewise He also took the cup after supper, saying, "This cup is the new covenant in my blood, which is shed for you. But behold, the hand of My betrayer is with Me on the table. And truly the Son of Man goes as it has been determined, but woe to that man by whom He is betrayed!"[1]

It is obvious that the last days of Jesus were full of anxiety and fear. Yet Jesus was really undismayed by all the hardships and faced them steadfastly. Jesus had full faith in Allah (swt) and knew that He would save him.

But when we come to explain the above text, I must ask with complete candor: who was the real source of that text? Interestingly, there is another text in the Book of Acts prohibiting blood. It reads, "but that we write them to abstain from things polluted by idols, from sexual immorality, from things strangled, and from blood."[2]

Thus, if he asks people to "...abstain...from blood",[3] then how can it be claimed that he encouraged them to drink "...my blood"?[4]

---

[1] Luke 22:14:22.
[2] Acts 15:20.
[3] Acts 15:20.
[4] Luke 22:20.

Undoubtedly, this is clear paganism carried over from the pagan ritual widespread in the Roman Empire at that time. The source of the above text—or its inspiration—is the Persian faith of Mithraism. Among its rituals were the Lord's Supper, a birthday on the twenty-fifth of December, and Sunday as a day of rest. All of the above was vintage Persian paganism, i.e., it was all devoted to worshipping Mithra. Later, the symbol was changed from Mithra to Christ. Jesus challenges the Jews, saying: "...you will look for me but you will not find me and where I will be, you cannot come." He further tells them about their inability to reach him when he says:

> "...When you lift up the Son of Man, then you will know that I am He, and that I do nothing of Myself; but as My Father taught Me, I speak these things. And He Who sent me is with me. The Father has not left Me alone, for I always do those things that please Him."[1]

The story of the Crucifixion is completely baseless. Likewise, the one who was crucified resembled Jesus. The Gospel of John quotes Jesus as saying, "And as Moses lifted up the serpent in the wilderness, even so must the Son of Man be lifted up."[2]

The serpent lifted by Moses resembled a real serpent. Similarly, we can say that just as Moses lifted up the resemblance of a serpent in the wilderness, even so must the resemblance of the Son of Man be lifted up.

Accordingly, the text talking about eating Jesus' body and drinking his blood is a text borrowed from the prevalent pagan sources in the Roman empire at that time. Jesus (may Allah's peace and blessings be upon him) was safe and secure, i.e., his body and his blood were unharmed.

As a former priest, I cannot imagine that a broken piece of bread given to a brother in faith, who puts it between his teeth, can transform into the body of Jesus and that he feels flesh between his teeth! What I really want to focus on is to show how Paul was able to corrupt Christianity. Jesus said: "I did not come to abrogate the Laws of Moses." We read in Genesis:

---

[1] John 8:28-29.
[2] John 3:14.

...God said to Abraham: "As for you, you shall keep My covenant, you and your descendants after you throughout their generations. This is My covenant which you shall keep, between Me and you and your descendants after you. Every male child among you shall be circumcised; and you shall be circumcised in the flesh of your foreskins, and it shall be a sign of the covenant between Me and you. He who is eight days old among you shall be circumcised, every male child in your generations, ...and the uncircumcised male child, who is not circumcised in the flesh of his foreskin, that person shall be cut off from his people; he has broken My covenant."[1]

We find that Abraham (may Allah's peace and blessings be upon him) was approximately one hundred years old when he was circumcised. His first son, Ishmael, (may Allah's peace and blessings be upon him) was fourteen at the time of his circumcision. Thus Abraham, a great prophet, his son Ishmael, along with the rest of their servants and slaves were all circumcised. So how can Paul come along afterwards and abolish circumcision? Paul was an awfully dubious character in the eyes of the disciples and the apostles. Even after Barnabas introduced Paul to them, they remained very fearful of him. Paul was an ambitious man who yearned to reach the top, even if that meant disposing of anyone beneath him. Paul wanted to take the message beyond the Jews to other peoples. He knew very well that Jesus had not ordered this, for the message was restricted to the Children of Israel.

Since other people at that time were not circumcised, he attacked the practice of circumcision during the first synod, saying that circumcision should be in the heart. This is similar to one saying to a Muslim that you can pray without purification (*wudu'*). Obviously this nullifies the prayer, for the very basis upon which it must be established is compromised (i.e., purification).

Undoubtedly, he was able to influence others attending the meeting. Accordingly, we read the following verses in Acts:

---

[1] Genesis 17:9-14.

Then it pleased the apostles and elders, with the whole church, to send chosen men of their own company to Antioch with Paul and Barnabas, namely, Judas who was also named Barsabas, and Silas, leading men among the brethren.

They wrote this letter by them:

"The apostles, the elders and the brethren,
To the brethren who are of the Gentiles
in Antioch, Syria, and Cilicia:
Greetings.

Since we have heard that some who went from us have troubled you with words, unsettling your souls, saying 'You *must be* circumcised and keep the law'—to whom we gave no *such* commandment—it seemed good to us, being assembled with one accord, to send chosen men to you with our beloved Barnabas and Paul, men who have risked their lives for the name of our Lord Jesus Christ. We have therefore sent Judas and Silas, who will also report the same things by word of mouth. For it seemed good to the Holy Spirit, and to us, to lay upon you no greater burden than these necessary things: that you abstain from things offered to idols, from blood, from things strangled, and from sexual immorality. If you keep yourselves from these, you will do well.

Farewell."[1]

Consequently, the Holy Spirit became a puppet for their mouths, for it ordered them not to get circumcised. In this way, Paul destroyed the Law of Moses.

Regarding divorce, the Law of Moses allowed it, according to the Old Testament's Book of Deuteronomy. However, Paul was working to spread adultery among people. Thus, if a woman had problems with her husband, Paul would not allow her to seek divorce. This only helped to spread evil in the society, for now the woman was compelled to behave in a secret and dishonorable way.

---

[1] Acts 15:22-29.

Now I would like to ask another question. Why did the Church reject the Gospel of Barnabas? Could it be because Barnabas in his Gospel explained very clearly and cogently how Paul corrupted Christianity and transformed it into a Greek Christianity, and changed it from a religion believing in one God to a religion worshipping the son of God, much like Osiris, Isis and Horas were worshipped?

I think I have said enough for now. I'd like now to give a chance to the speaker to complete his presentation.

Brig. Gen. Ahmad Abdul-Wahhab

Finally, let us conclude our talk about Paul by relating Paul's own confessions regarding his physical sins, which he was unable to get rid of, and which made him one of the slaves of sin. By his own admissions he unknowingly proves that his claim regarding Jesus' crucifixion and assassination, for which he spent his life preaching and propagating, was sheer nonsense. Paul was after all, still, by his own confession, a slave of sin, and the price for that, according to his confession, is his eternal death. He says:

> For we know that the law is spiritual, but I am carnal, sold under sin.

> For what I am doing, I do not understand. For what I will to do, that I do not practice; but what I hate that I do. If, then, I do what I will not to do, I agree with the law that it is good. But now, it is no longer I who do it, but sin that dwells in me. For I know that in me (that is, in my flesh) nothing good dwells; for to will is present with me, but how to perform what is good I do not find. For the good that I will to do, I do not do; but the evil I will not to do, that I practice. Now if I do what I will not to do, it is no longer I who do it, but sin that dwells in me. I find then a law, that evil is present with me, when I will to do good. For I delight in the law of God according to the inward man. But I see another law in my members, warring against the law of my mind, and bringing me into captivity to the law of sin which is in my members.

O wretched man that I am! Who will deliver me from this body of death?[1]

The Religion of Jesus Was Islamic Monotheism[2]

After finishing our study of the sources of Christian belief, i.e., the Gospels and other scriptures, seeing how they became holy books, and what Christian scholars have said about them and their contents regarding unfulfilled prophecies, contradictions and discrepancies, especially regarding the Crucifixion and the Resurrection, we come to one final question: what was the real religion of the Messiah, Jesus the Christ?

Authenticated Christian sources say only that the mission of Jesus was that of *tawhid*. Soon after, various pagan beliefs crept into Christianity. Then, in the fourth century of the Christian era, the Christian belief in the Trinity appeared as a direct result of the Holy Christian Synods. The *Encyclopedia Americana* describes the situation as follows:

Unitarianism as a theological movement began much earlier in history; indeed it antedated trinitarianism by many decades. Christianity derived from Judaism and Judaism was strictly unitarian. The road which led from Jerusalem to Nicea was scarcely a straight one. Fourth century trinitarianism did not reflect accurately early Christian teaching regarding the nature of God; it was, on the contrary, a deviation from this teaching. It therefore developed against constant unitarian, or at least anti-trinitarianism opposition, and it was never wholly victorious.[3]

The religion of Jesus Christ was a pure unitarianism. Then other religions, especially pagan religions from the Roman world, were mixed with Christianity and gave it the idea of the Trinity. Thus, the prevailing traditional Christianity became the Christianity of the Trinity. Regardless, to this very day, there remains among the myriad sects of Christianity, a strong and

---

[1] Romans 7:14-24.
[2] i.e., *tawhid*— belief in the Oneness of God in his Lordship, Names, and Attributes.
[3] *Encylopedia Americana,* 1959, vol. 27, p. 294.

Muslim-Christian Dialogue

vibrant demonstration known as the Unitarians. They are spread all over the United States. Their basic belief is that there is no one worthy of worship but Allah, and Jesus is a Messenger of Allah, i.e., he was a mortal human being. Here is a summary of their basic beliefs:

1. The Unitarian Church considers the Bible a valuable record of human experience, but it maintains that its writers were subject to error. For much the same reason, the major parts of the Christian creeds are rejected.

2. The historical difference between Unitarianism and Trinitarianism derives from the fact that Unitarians, insofar as they were theists, believed that God possessed one rather than three persons. [As early as 1819, Channing urged that three persons would necessitate three essences, and hence three Gods. He added that Scripture gave no warrant to support a belief in the doctrine of the Trinity. Moreover, to Unitarians, theists and humanists alike—to the extent at least to which the latter use the term—the concept God has served for purposes of explaining the orderly procedure of cosmic happenings. The cosmos (order) requires one principle of explanation, not three. Therefore, the dogma of the Trinity has neither religious nor scientific value.]

3. Strong objections are presented against the dogma of the deity of Jesus Christ. The Bible does not warrant it. Jesus thought of himself as a religious leader (Messiah), not as a god. The disciples equally believed Jesus to be a man. If either Peter or Judas had been of the opinion that Jesus was a god, the denial by Peter and the betrayal by Judas could not be explained. One does not deny or betray an all-powerful divine being; that would be too dangerous.

4. The alleged fact that Jesus died for our sins, and thus guarded us against the effects of the wrath of God, is categorically denied. To believe that Jesus' death did have this result would be to cast aspersions on God's character. God should be defined not in terms of wrath, but of patience, wisdom, and love. [A wise and loving father does not destroy an erring and sinful child, but educates it and leads it in the direction of virtue and wisdom. A bloody death upon the cross to appease a wrathful God is inconsistent with the idea of divine patience and endless

affection. On the contrary, it represents the notion of vengeance. Moreover, man should not, Unitarians believe, accept such an offer on the part of Jesus, granted that the offer was made. To allow someone else to suffer for our own shortcomings is wrong.]

5. Unitarianism looks upon Jesus as one of the moral leaders of mankind. He was not infallible, either in thought or deed, but this increases his importance to us. If he were a god, his example of virtuous living would lack every vestige of value; since he would possess powers we do not share; a man cannot follow in the footsteps of a God.[1]

A Word to the Missionaries

Before I conclude, I would like to address the missionaries, especially the foreigners who work in Muslim countries.

Missionaries, keep your hands off the Muslims. It would be better for you to take your belongings and paraphernalia and go back home. Your ideas are not marketable and are unfit for distribution among Muslims. You know, better than others, what has happened to Christianity in terms of its beliefs, ethics and overall appearance. There is almost nothing left of it except its name.

It is only proper for the one whose house has collapsed to try first to rebuild it before going out into the world and inviting it—as you claim—to salvation and faith.

It is only proper for you that you agree on one Christian creed based on the belief in one God, Who revealed to Moses in His final revelation, saying of Himself, "...I live forever."[2]

Jesus commanded you to follow the Law of Moses as he did. This was recorded by the authors of the Gospels. There is no way to remove the differences among your sects and denominations unless you adopt the following beliefs:

You must believe in one God, the Ever-Living, Who dies not. Further, you must stop mixing God with Jesus, as some of

---

[1]Op. cit, p. 300f.
[2]Deuteronomy 32:40.

your own scholars advise and as mentioned in the beginning of this discourse. Only then can Christianity be considered a faith that believes in one God. But if you stay as you are, declaring each other to be disbelievers and cursing one another for years to come, your efforts among Muslims to take them away from worshipping the one and only Allah, and to invite them to adopt different rituals mixed with the pure Christianity of Jesus Christ (may Allah's peace and blessings be upon him), are all in vain. As a matter of fact, this reminds me of what Jesus (may Allah's peace and blessings be upon him) said in the Bible. He said, "Woe to you, scribes and Pharisees, hypocrites! For you travel land and sea to win one proselyte, and when he is won, you make him twice as much a son of hell as yourselves."[1]

Your preaching Christianity among Muslims reminds me of the story of a segment of Pharaoh's people and the believer among them who had concealed his belief (in one God). He silenced all of them with his strong argument. He said:

> "My people! How (strange) it is for me to call you to Salvation while you call me to the Fire! You do call upon me to blaspheme against Allah, and to join with Him partners of whom I have no knowledge; and I call you to the Exalted in Power, Who forgives again and again! Without doubt you do call me to one who is not fit to be called to, whether in this world, or in the Hereafter. Our return will be to Allah; and the transgressors will be companions of the Fire! Soon will you remember what I say to you (now). My (own) affair I commit to Allah: for Allah (ever) watches over His servants." Then Allah saved him from (every) evil that they plotted (against him). But the brunt of the penalty encompassed on all sides the people of the Pharaoh.[2]

Preachers and missionaries, your plans to Christianize Muslims have been exposed, and your ways of preaching among them are public knowledge. If enslavement of the body is a heinous sin, then the enslavement of the spirit is even more hateful and evil. You practice the slavery of the spirit when you materially help the Muslim poor—giving out a of handful of rice as

---

[1] Matthew 23:15.
[2] Qur'an 40:41-45.

you do in Indonesia. All of this is possible only on the condition that they accept Christianity, which you force upon them. My God! By doing this, you've usurped the most basic human right—the freedom to make a choice! What type of slavery can be more cruel than this? Such machinations drove some of you to say more than seventy years ago when the colonialists had subjugated the entire Muslim world, that missionary organizations must Christianize all Muslims within a period of twenty-five years.

We thank God that three times that estimated period has passed and Islam is still here, strong and firm. As a matter of fact, recent years have witnessed, by the grace of Allah alone, many Europeans and Americans embracing Islam with full conviction and satisfaction. This happened once they interacted with the Muslim world and learned of Islam the truth that you, missionaries, were so keen to distort.

Yes, your sole concern was, as George Bernard Shaw observed, to train Christians to hate Muhammad (may Allah's peace and blessings be upon him), the Qur'an and Islam.

You took advantage of any mistake or foolish act by certain individuals or groups in the Muslim world to announce that that was Islam, though you knew very well how wrong your statements were. You knew that Islam is one thing and the Muslims, their behavior and their current weak predicament are another thing which has nothing to do with Islam.

You surely know that there was an Islamic civilization based on the Qur'an, the Prophet's teachings, and the spirit of Islam, which calls for knowledge, freedom of thought, and a study of the universe. Schools and teaching circles were widespread. Scholars in diverse fields of knowledge reached the top of their fields, such as medicine, astronomy, mathematics, physics, chemistry and pharmacology.

The addition of the zero to mathematics and the discovery of logarithms—where the word logarithm stills refers to its Islamic source, Al-Khwarizmi—are still considered the greatest advance in the world of mathematics. This is acknowledged by European and American scholars. On the other hand, modern Western civilization could never have prospered until it rid itself of the authority of the Church, which burned scholars like Bruno, for no other reason but that he stated that the Earth was spherical. Then it adopted the knowledge of the Muslims and embraced their methodology in research and experiments until it gave rise to the European Renaissance.

I don't have to remind you that while Islamic civilization was shining at the time of Harun Ar-Rashid, Charlemagne, his contemporary, the Master of Europe, was busy christianizing the pagans of Europe by the use of the sword. It is quite enough here to mention that, according to your own official documents, Charlemagne in one day killed 4500 pagans who refused to be christianized and baptized. The agreements between him and them were either christianization or death.

After Charlemagne, the Church withdrew some of its Crusaders from Palestine—during the time of Crusades—to help christianize the peoples of the Baltic Sea areas by use of the sword. They were to continue their mission there for thirty years. In return, they were to receive a certain compensation determined by the Church. The compensation of the Church turned out to be the seizure of the lands of the pagans—in return for giving them Christianity.

In addition to this, you must know that the fundamentals of modern-day nuclear science has come to you from the Islamic world. Haven't you read what John O'Neil has said in his book *The Giant Atom*, published in 1945 C.E? He says:

> One of the brilliant advances of the Middle Ages came from the Islamic world where we find that Ali, father of Hassan and the son-in-law of Muhammad [may Allah's peace and blessings be upon him] said: "If you split the atom—any atom—you find at its core a sun." This clearly shows that his keen insight was able to behold the real nature of the solar system within the atom!

It should be mentioned here that Ali once stated that any knowledge he had was "knowledge taught by Allah (swt) to His Prophet (may Allah's peace and blessings be upon him). Then he taught it to me and asked Allah (swt) to help my heart comprehend it."

The idea of a system recapitulating the solar system within the atom is rooted in the Islamic legacy. Five centuries after Ali's statement, Fariduddin Al-'Attar said, "...there is a sun inside the atom...and if you were to split the atom you would find a new world inside. Moreover, all atoms of the world are working without the slightest interruption in their motion."

Modern nuclear science and its applications in war and peace were based on the idea that "the atom is a solar system." When did Europe learn this idea?

In answer to this, the physicist, Heisenberg, says:

> ...[T]he atom, as Democritus believed, was still of a size similar to that of the dust particles seen dancing in a ray of light, or even much smaller. Moreover, information about the shape of atoms and the energy present among atoms was very limited. What was known about the structure of the atom was very little or even nonexistent. Further, any inquiries into its shape were even more remote. In fact, the answer to this inquiry was stored away till the twentieth century.

Rutherford is considered to be the one who took the important step to build the first model of the atom in 1911 C.E. He thought that the atom was composed of a nucleus having a mass of positive charge, around which electrons rotate at various distances relatively. Furthermore, the number of electrons equals the number of the positive charges in the nucleus. Thus the atom is electrically neutral in terms of its structure.

The atom as such is similar to the solar system. Its nucleus is like the sun, while the electrons moving around the nucleus resemble the planets orbiting the sun. In fact, Otto Hahn, the German scientist who is credited with the splitting of the nucleus of the uranium atom, pointed out that "...for sure, some writers had thought about this issue before. Besides, many truths of the modern nuclear theory have been mentioned here or there."

As the ancient Greeks who talked about the atom had no idea about an organized system within the atom resembling the solar system, we are left with no other option but to corroborate that the origins of this theory are rooted in the Islamic legacy.

Finally, I find no better way to conclude my talk but to remind those among you who have heavily concentrated on destroying the Muslim creed by taking the Muslims away from the light of Monotheism and into the darkness of polytheism, of what the Qur'an says about them. It says:

> The Unbelievers spend their wealth to hinder (man) from the path of Allah, and so will they continue to spend; but in the end they will have (only) regrets and sighs; at length they will be overcome: and the Unbelievers will be gathered together to Hell—in order that God may separate the impure from the pure, put the impure one on another, heap them together, and cast them into Hell. They will be the ones to have lost.[1]

And let me repeat, preachers and missionaries, keep your hands off the Muslims. He whose house is made of glass should not throw stones at others, otherwise the prediction of Jesus mentioned in the Bible will come true. He said:

> You surely hear but do not comprehend. You see but you do not contemplate. This is because the hearts of the people have become hard, their hearing has become poor and they have shut their eyes so that they do not have to see with their eyes, nor hear with their ears, nor understand in their hearts. Then they will come back and I shall cure them.

We end our presentation with the best of all words: "Glory to your Lord, the Lord of Honor and Power! (He is free) from what they ascribe (to Him)! And peace on the messengers and Praise to Allah, the Lord and Cherisher of the Worlds.[2]

---

[1] Qur'an 8:36-37.
[2] Qur'an 37:180-182.

THE FOURTH SESSION

Introduction

Dr. Muhammad Jamil Ghazi

In the name of Allah, Ever Beneficent, Ever Merciful. Praise be to Allah, Lord of the Universe, and Peace and prayers be upon His final Prophet and Messenger, and upon all of his Companions. I seek Allah's protection from the accursed Satan. Allah says:

> Relate in the Book (the story of) Mary, when she withdrew from her family to a place in the East. She placed a screen (to screen herself) from them; then We sent her our angel, and he appeared before her as a man in all respects. She said: "I seek refuge from you to (God) Most Gracious: (come not near) if you fear God." He said: "Nay, I am only a messenger from your Lord, (to announce) to you the gift of a holy son." She said: "How shall I have a son, seeing that no man has touched me, and I am not unchaste?" He said: "So (it will be): Your Lord says, 'That is easy for Me: and (We wish) to appoint him as a Sign unto men and a Mercy from Us.' It is a matter (so) decreed."
>
> So she conceived him, and she retired with him to a remote place. And the pains of childbirth drove her to the trunk of a palm-tree: She cried (in her anguish): "Ah! Would that I had died before this! Would that I had been a thing forgotten and out of sight!" But (a voice) cried to her from beneath the (palm-tree): "Grieve not, for your Lord has provided a rivulet beneath you; And shake towards yourself the trunk of the palm-tree: It will let fall fresh ripe dates upon you. So eat

and drink and cool (your) eye. And if you see any man, say, 'I have vowed a fast to (God) Most Gracious, and this day will I enter into no talk with any human being.'"

At length she brought the (babe) to her people, carrying him (in her arms). They said: "Mary, truly an amazing thing have you brought, sister of Aaron! Your father was not a man of evil, nor your mother a woman unchaste!" But she pointed to the babe. They said: "How can we talk to one who is a child in the cradle?" "I am indeed a servant of God: He has given me revelation and made me a prophet; and He has made me blessed wheresoever I be, and has enjoined on me prayer and charity as long as I live; (He) has made me kind to my mother, and not overbearing or miserable. So peace is on me the day I was born, the day that I die, and the day that I shall be raised up to life (again)."

Such (was) Jesus the son of Mary: (it is) a statement of truth, about which they (vainly) dispute. It is not befitting to (the majesty of) God that He should beget a son. Glory be to Him! when He determines a matter, He only says to it, "Be," and it is. Verily God is my Lord and your Lord: Him therefore serve: this is a Way that is straight.[1]

Later in the same *surah*, Allah (swt) says:

They say: "(God) Most Gracious has begotten a son!" Indeed you have put forth a thing most monstrous! At it the skies are ready to burst, the earth to split asunder, and the mountains to fall down in utter ruin, that they should invoke a son for (God) Most Gracious. For it is not consonant with the majesty of (God) Most Gracious that He should beget a son. Not one of the beings in the heavens and the earth but must come to (God) Most Gracious as a servant. He does take an account of them (all), and has numbered them (all) exactly. And every one of them will come to Him singly on the Day of Judgment.[2]

Before I reintroduce Shaykh Ibrahim Khalil Ahmad to you, I would like to share a few words with you about a miraculous

---

[1]Qur'an 19:16-36.
[2]Qur'an 19:88-95.

statement made by Prophet Muhammad (may Allah's peace and blessings be upon him), when he said: "Do not exaggerate in praising me, as the Christians have exaggerated in praising Jesus the son of Mary, for I am only human. So refer to me as the Slave of Allah and His Messenger.[1]

Here the Prophet (may Allah's peace and blessings be upon him) points to a basic truth. He refers to the root of a grave error when people exaggerate their love or hatred. Sometimes the same person is viewed in two completely different ways. Some people elevate him to be a god while others denigrate him to a lowly devil. Jesus, the son of Mary, is a perfect example of this. Some of his people loved him a lot and they became excessive in their reverence of him. Eventually, they elevated him to be a god. Not surprisingly, Allah addresses these people in the Qur'an when He says:

> People of the Book! Commit no excesses in your religion: nor say of Allah aught but the truth. Christ Jesus the son of Mary was (no more than) a Messenger of Allah, and His Word, which He bestowed on Mary, and a Spirit proceeding from Him: so believe in Allah and His Messengers. Say not "Trinity": desist: it will be better for you: for Allah is one God: Glory be to Him: (far exalted is He) above having a son. To Him belong all things in the heavens and on earth. And enough is Allah as a Disposer of affairs.[2]

At another place in the Qur'an, Allah, Most Exalted, said:

> People of the Book! Exceed not in your religion the bounds (of what is proper), trespassing beyond the truth, nor follow the vain desires of people who went wrong in times gone by, who misled many, and strayed (themselves) from the even way.[3]

Thus, there were people who exaggerated their love of Jesus and raised him up to the level of divinity. For example, "...Thomas answered and said to Him, 'My Lord and my God.'"[4]

---

[1] Narrated by Al-Bukhari, *The Book of the Prophets*, 4:127; and Muslim 7:343.
[2] Qur'an 4:171.
[3] Qur'an 5:77.
[4] John 20:28.

At the same time, we find others who accused him of being Satan. Such were the Jews:

> Now when the Pharisees said, "This fellow does not cast out demons except by Beelzebub, the ruler of the demons." But Jesus knew their thoughts, and said to them: "Every kingdom divided against itself is brought to desolation, and every city or house divided against itself will not stand. If Satan casts out Satan, he is divided against himself. How then will his kingdom stand?"[1]

The Islamic view is always balanced, stating the truth and the facts. When we talk about Jesus (may Allah's peace and blessings be upon him), we should remember that he was not the only personality in history for whom people were excessive in their love or hatred. As a matter of fact, there have been many historical figures for whom people have gone overboard. Some have been raised to be superhuman while others have had their reputations run into the ground.

For example, consider 'Ali Ibn Abi Talib. Some people exaggerated in praising him to the extent that they claimed he was a god. They even prostrated themselves to him. Of course, 'Ali had them burned in the fire. On the other hand, there were others who cursed him, called him an unbeliever and rose up against him. The truth and the facts about 'Ali are not as they claimed. This phenomenon is not restricted to men of religion like Jesus or 'Ali Ibn Abi Talib. In fact, we find a similar trend for non-religious personalities where people have elevated them to superhuman status. Some poets have falsely praised certain tyrant kings in a very excessive manner; they have given their kings the attributes of God. For example, one poet addressed his king saying, "Whatever you wish, not whatever divine fate wishes. Go ahead and rule, you are the One, and the Subduer." And another says, "You have frightened the pagans so much that even the sperm that has not been created yet fears you."

Such exaggerated praise is not restricted to olden times alone. Even today, people excessively praise certain tyrant personalities, elevating them to superhuman status. You may recall

---

[1] Matthew 12:24-26.

that a newspaper extolled a modern dictator saying "...he is superhuman." In fact, one poet said in his eulogy, "We are the ones who killed you, you are the last of the prophets." At the same time, many others hated and cursed him.

As seen above, it is catastrophic to excessively praise or censure anyone. That is why our Prophet (may Allah's peace and blessings be upon him) warned us against praising him in an exaggerated way when he said, "Do not exaggerate in praising me as the Christians have exaggerated in praising Jesus, the son of Mary."

The Christians were guilty of paganism and unbelief through their exaggeration in praising Jesus. Eventually, they even claimed that he was the first light which came forth from God. Later their glorification of Jesus led them to declare that he was the Son of God. Actually, many went forward declaring him to be God. These and many other differences in creed find their root in the many Christian councils which were convened to discuss these matters, beginning with the Council of Nicea in 325 C.E. While a lot more can be said about this topic of excessive praise, we would like to caution Muslims against lavishly praising anyone, for this could expose them to the same evil that befell other peoples before them.

Prophet Muhammad (may Allah's peace and blessings be upon him) criticized the Jews and the Christians for adopting the tombs of their prophets and saints as places of worship. As one of his final pieces of advice to our righteous mother,[1] 'A'isha, may Allah be pleased with her, she relates:

> ...as death began to approach, he began to put a sheet over his face and when he felt hot, he would remove it from his face. Then he said, "May Allah's curse be on the Jews and the Christians for taking the graves of their prophets as places of worship." He was warning (the Muslims) to avoid doing what they (i.e., Jews and Christians) had done.[2]

---

[1] i.e., one of the "Mothers of the Believers". This title is used to refer to the wives of Prophet Muhammad (pbuh).
[2] Narrated by Al-Bukhari vol. 1, p. 422, vol. 6, p. 386; Muslim, vol. 1, p. 377; An-Nasa'i vol. 1, p. 115; Ad-Darimi vol. 1, p. 326; Ahmad in *Al-*

Upon her return from Abyssinia, Umm Habibah (may Allah be pleased her) narrated to the Prophet (may Allah's peace and blessings be upon him) what she had observed there. She told him about the pictures and tombs inside the churches. Hearing this, he said to her, "When a pious man among them dies, they build a place of worship over his grave. To Allah they are the worst creation."[1]

So all Muslims should be forewarned not to exaggerate in praising the Prophet, because much evil is caused by excessive and lavish praise of a human being.

Now let me leave you with Professor Ibrahim Khalil Ahmad. He will survey topics relating to the three elements of the Trinity, prophethood as related in their own texts, and how the concept of Trinity found its way into the Christian creed. Then, if time permits, he will talk about the holy councils and how the Christian belief system evolved through them. I ask Allah to make his presentation effective and replete with knowledge and wisdom.

Mr. Ibrahim Khalil Ahmad

In the name of Allah, the Compassionate, the Merciful, Praise be to Allah, Lord of the Worlds, and may His peace and blessings be upon Prophet Muhammad, his family and all his Companions.

Having been a priest whom Allah guided to Islam, I feel compelled to approach this topic with a brief introduction.

Dear young men, brothers and friends, I see a very good sign in our gathering. I see a sincere desire on everyone's part to see the truth exactly as Prophet Jesus commanded. He once said, "...you shall know the truth, and the truth shall make you free."[2]

Musnad vol. 1, p. 218; Abdur-Razzaq in *Al-Mussanif* vol. 1, p. 406; and Abu-Awanah, vol. 1, p. 339.
[1] Narrated by Al-Bukhari, vol. 1, p. 416-422; Muslim, 2:66; An-Nasa'i 1:115; Ibn Shayba, *Al-Musannif* 4:140; Ahmad, *Al-Musnad* 6:51; Abu Awana 1:400; Ibn Sa'd in *At-Tabaqat* 2:240; Al-Baghawi 2:415; and Al-Bayhaqi in *As-Sunan al-Kubiya* 4:80.
[2] John 8:32.

Muslim-Christian Dialogue

I ask Allah, Most Glorified, to bless this fine and noble step forward. It encourages me to look sincerely into these topics with you. In our discussions, I will be relying on the Torah, the Bible and the Qur'an.

Moses told us about the coming of the prophets one after another. He said:

> Now this is the blessing with which Moses the man of God blessed the children of Israel before his death. And he said:
> The Lord came from Sinai, and dawned on them from Seir;
> He shone forth from Mount Paran.[1]

Look carefully at the above verses and we find that there were two phases preceding the final message.

He clearly says that "the Lord came from Sinai." Sinai refers to Mount Sinai, where Moses went to talk to his Lord. Seir refers to the land of Palestine where Jesus preached, and Paran refers to Makkah. And I will talk about this in detail later, if Allah wills.

When words like "came", "dawned", and "shone", are used, we know that these are all action verbs. The verb "came" refers to movement during the day or night. Second, the verb "dawned" refers to the action of the light that dispels darkness. As for the "shone", it represents the highest degree of illumination, for there is nothing more than shining.

The Torah, being the first (of the three),[2] which Allah revealed to Moses, peace be upon him, was in a defined form, where there was no room for interpretation. The Ten Commandments came as part of the law revealed to him by Allah. The coming of Jesus is described as "dawned", i.e., the beginning of illumination. So, why did Jesus come? He told the Jews, "Do not think that I came to destroy the Law or the Prophets. I did not come to destroy but to fulfill."[3]

Probing a little further, let us ask what was it that he would fulfill? Jesus says that Moses said, *"You shall not murder*, and whoever murders will be in danger of the judgment. But I say to you that whoever is angry with his brother without a cause shall

---
[1] Deuteronmomy 33:1-2.
[2] i.e., the three messages, Torah, Injil (Gospel) and Qur'an.
[3] Matthew 5:17.

Muslim-Christian Dialogue

be in danger of the judgment."[1] Thus, Jesus came to clarify and explain the Ten Commandments, which Allah had given to Moses.

Interestingly, in the first two testaments (i.e., the Torah and Gospel) we find no mention of a specific identity for religion. Yet, in the Noble Qur'an, we find that Allah says, "This day have I perfected your religion for you, completed My favor upon you, and have chosen for you Islam as your religion."[2]

So Islam is the way of life that Allah chose for humanity. It is the religion of all the previous prophets. It denotes total submission to Allah, Most Glorified, Most Exalted. Undoubtedly, the mission of all the prophets was the same. Jesus Christ says in the Bible that "...the first of all the commandments is: 'Hear, O Israel, the Lord is our God, the Lord is One!'"[3]

Similarly, before him, Moses said it: "Hear, O Israel: the Lord is our God, the Lord is One!"[4]

Moreover, Jesus, before his ascension to the heavens, affirmed this he when said to Mary Magdalene: "...go to My Brethren and say to them, 'I am ascending to My Father and your Father, and to My God and your God.'"[5]

Finally, the Qur'an confirms the call to *tawhid*, as it reiterates, "And your God is one God; there is no god but He, Most Gracious, Most Merciful."[6]

In reality, my dear seekers of truth, do you realize how similar the situation today is to the situation of Jesus during his experience with the Devil when he

> ...took Him up on an exceedingly high mountain, and showed Him all the kingdoms of the world and their glory. And he said to Him, "All these things I will give You if You will fall down and worship me."[7]

But Jesus, who had submitted himself to Allah and who used to turn to Allah to inspire him with the right response,

---

[1] Matthew 5:21-22.
[2] Qur'an 5:4.
[3] Mark 12:29.
[4] Deuteronomy 6:4.
[5] John 20:17.
[6] Qur'an 2:163.
[7] Matthew 4:8-9.

faced the Devil and unequivocally said, "Away with you, Satan! For it is written, *'You shall worship the Lord your God, and Him only you shall serve.'*"[1]

Once Jesus had overcome Satan, he was ready to preach his mission openly. Matthew and Luke narrate this incident in their Gospels, saying that "the devil left Him, and behold, angels came and ministered to Him."[2]

As a direct consequence of this test, Jesus addressed his disciples advising them:

> "For what profit is it to a man if he gains the whole world, and loses his own soul? Or what will a man give in exchange for his soul?"[3]

I welcome your sincere interest in seeking clear answers to your questions. We will try our best to respond to your queries in a scholarly manner. Furthermore, we will ensure absolute integrity, being careful to be honest and sincere in our efforts. Finally, I implore Allah to guide us to the right path.

The topics that I will deal with tonight are related to the following questions:

1. Is Jesus, the son of Mary, a god or a human being?
2. Does he come from the essence of God or from the dust from which Allah created Adam?
3. Is the Holy Spirit a god or one of the angels?
4. Does he come from God's essence or was he created from light?
5. Is the Virgin Mary the mother of God or the mother of a human being, Jesus?
6. Did she come from God's essence or from the dust from which Allah created Adam?
7. How and when did spurious ideas concerning the constituent elements of the Trinity become mixed with original Christian beliefs?
8. Did Jesus prophesize about a prophet succeeding him, and who was that prophet?

---

[1] Matthew 4:11.
[2] Matthew 4:11.
[3] Matthew 16:26.

Seven of the above questions concern Jesus (peace be upon him). The eighth question concerns our noble Prophet Muhammad (may Allah's peace and blessings be upon him). Later, I would like to talk about Prophet Muhammad in the Torah and in the Gospels, and what Moses' prophecy was about Prophet Muhammad (may Allah's peace and blessings be upon him), whom he referred to as being "...from among their brethren",[1] and how the text of Deuteronomy 33:1-2 refers to Prophet Muhammad (may Allah's peace and blessings be upon him), and what the prophecies of Isaiah about the expected prophet were, as narrated in chapters 42 and 60 of Isaiah. Also, what does the verse, "Arise, shine; for your light has come! And the glory of the Lord is risen upon you,"[2] refer to? How do these prophecies relate to the Qur'anic verse: "The religion before Allah is Islam (submission to His Will)"?[3] What did David mean by the sentence: "The stone which the builders rejected has become the chief cornerstone"?[4] And what did Jesus mean when he confirmed this prophecy, saying: "Have you never read in the scriptures: 'The stone which the builders rejected has become the chief cornerstone...'"?[5] What did Daniel mean when he interpreted the dream of Nebuchadnezzar saying, "...inasmuch as you saw that the stone was cut out of the mountain without hands..."?[6]

Perhaps the above is an explanation for the following verses where Allah says, "Verily, this brotherhood of yours is a single brotherhood, and I am your Lord and Cherisher: therefore serve Me (and no other),"[7] and "You are the best of peoples, evolved for mankind, enjoining what is right, forbidding what is wrong."[8]

What were the prophecies of Jesus about the prophet coming after him? And what about the *hadith* of the Prophet: "I have five names..." and its relationship to "Paraclete"? Finally, I will

---

[1] Deuteronomy 18:18.
[2] Isaiah 60:1.
[3] Qur'an 3:19.
[4] Psalms 118:22.
[5] Matthew 21:42.
[6] Daniel 2:45.
[7] Qur'an 21:92.
[8] Qur'an 3:110.

Muslim-Christian Dialogue

talk about the Qur'an and its defense of all prophets, and then conclude with a brief word about the ecumenical councils.

I'd like to begin now by talking about the nature of Jesus. Our reference will be the Bible itself.

The Birth of Jesus

Matthew says, "Now the birth of Jesus Christ was as follows: After His mother Mary was betrothed to Joseph, before they came together, she was found with child of the Holy Spirit."[1]

Relating how the Angel Gabriel came to the Virgin Mary, Luke says, "and having come in, the angel said to her, 'Rejoice, highly favored one, the Lord is with you; blessed are you among women!'"[2]

Then he gives her the good tidings about Jesus. Luke relates that when the Angel Gabriel came to her, "...Mary said to the angel, 'How can this be, since I do not know man?' And the angel answered and said to her, 'The Holy Spirit will come upon you, and the power of the Highest will overshadow you.'"[3]

Now if someone says that Jesus was born by the power of the Holy Spirit, and that this makes him unique in comparison to all other human beings, we say that it is not a distinguishing feature. In fact, one doesn't even have to think—not even for one moment—that Jesus was created from something other than what the rest of mankind was created from. For example, his colleague and relative, John the Baptist, was born by the power of the Holy Spirit. The same angel, Gabriel, talked to his father, Zacharias, when he was in the Temple:

>...the angel said to him, "Do not be afraid, Zacharias, for your prayer is heard; and your wife Elizabeth will bear you a son, and you shall call his name John. And you will have joy and gladness, and many will rejoice at his birth. For he will be great in the sight of the Lord, and shall drink neither wine

---
[1] Matthew 1:18.
[2] Luke 1:28.
[3] Luke 1:34-35.

nor strong drink. He will also be filled with the Holy Spirit, even from his mother's womb."[1]

Later, Luke relates that Zacharias himself was filled with the Holy Spirit:

> Now his father Zacharias was filled with the Holy Spirit, and prophesied, saying: "Blessed is the Lord God of Israel, for He has visited and redeemed His people."[2]

Thus, the Holy Spirit who was with Zacharias and his son John, was the same one with Jesus. Luke says:

> ...in the sixth month the angel Gabriel was sent by God to a city of Galilee named Nazareth, to a virgin betrothed to a man whose name was Joseph, of the house of David. The virgin's name was Mary.[3]

From the preceding verses it is clear that the Holy Spirit was one of the angels of Allah, Most Glorified, Most Exalted. Referring to the angel Gabriel and the Virgin Mary, Luke says:

> ...while they were there, the days were completed for her to be delivered. And she brought forth her first born Son, and wrapped Him in swaddling cloths, and laid Him in a manger, because there was no room for them in the inn.[4]

According to the Law of Moses, the baby that the virgin gave birth to was circumcised, and when his mother was purified she offered a sacrifice to the Lord. Luke relates these events saying:

> ...when eight days were completed for the circumcision of the Child, His name was called Jesus, the name given by the angel before He was conceived in the womb. Now when the days of her purification according to the law of Moses were completed, they brought Him to Jerusalem to present Him to the Lord (as it is written in the law of the Lord, "Every male who opens the womb shall be called holy to the Lord,") and

---

[1] Luke 1:34-35.
[2] Luke 1:67-68.
[3] Luke 1:26-27.
[4] Luke 2:6-7.

to offer a sacrifice according to what is said in the law of the Lord: a pair of turtle-doves or two young pigeons.[1]

It is important to point out that the concept of "holy" in Christianity and Judaism differs from what it is in Islam. The word *quds*—*kadosh* in Hebrew—means "separating or putting aside." In Islam, holiness means de-anthropomorphism[2] and glorification. Consequently, we find in the Old Testament that God said to Moses, "Consecrate to Me all the firstborn, whatever opens the womb among the children of Israel, both of man and beast; it is Mine."[3] "Consecrate" here means separate or put aside the firstborn.

The word "holy" in reference to the Holy Son means consecrated or put aside, or separated as the first-born, the first one to open the mother's womb. Hence it is clear that Jesus was a normal first-born, similar to any other human first-born. Moreover, he and his mother were completely subject to the Law of Moses. We affirm that Jesus came from the same substance as other humans. He was given birth to by the Virgin Mary, who was one of the descendants of Adam. Adam was created from dust. The miracle here was that Allah, Most Glorified, is just as capable of giving a child to a barren woman as He is to a virgin. Allah says, "...the similitude of Jesus before Allah is as that of Adam; He created him from dust, then said to him, 'Be,' And he was."[4]

It was a miracle when Allah, Most Glorified, Most Exalted, created Adam. Similarly, when He created Eve from Adam's body, wasn't that a miracle?

Luke correlates the events as he shows the similarity between Jesus' birth and the birth of John the Baptist. When the Virgin Mary wondered how she could become pregnant and then bear a child when she was not intimate with any man:

> ...Mary said to the angel, "How can this be, since I do not know a man?" And the angel answered and said to her, "The Holy Spirit will come upon you, and the power of the High-

---

[1] Luke 2:21-24.
[2] i.e., elimination of any human element from being associated with Allah in form or attribute.
[3] Exodus 13:2.
[4] Qur'an 3:59.

est will overshadow you; therefore, also, that Holy One Who is to be born will be called the Son of God. Now indeed, Elizabeth your relative has also conceived a son in her old age; and this is now the sixth month for her who was called barren. For with God nothing will be impossible."[1]

The Qur'an declares that

...it is not befitting to (the majesty of) Allah that He should beget a son. Glory be to Him! When He determines a matter, He only says to it, 'Be,' and it is.[2]

The "Son of God"

Let us ask ourselves what the meaning of "son of God" is in the Bible. The Gospel of Matthew says, "Blessed are the pure in heart, for they shall see God. Blessed are the peacemakers, for they shall be called sons of God."[3]

Thus, anyone working for good and for the sake of peace is considered a son of God, according to the language of the Gospel. It is a figurative sonship; it is not a real sonship. For example, some people say that this man is a son of Sudan or a son of Khartoum (i.e., a native of Sudan or Khartoum). These are simply figurative expressions, common in certain languages.

In the Old Testament there is a verse about the creation of man: "So God created man in His own image; in the image of God He created him; male and female He created them."[4] But the Qur'an says, "We have indeed created man in the best of molds."[5] The Qur'anic expression, here, is more accurate and more beautiful than the expression in the Torah. Obviously, Allah has no image, because "there is nothing whatever like unto Him."[6]

Similarly, the Lord said to Moses in the Torah: "Then you shall say to Pharaoh, 'Thus says the Lord: "Israel is My son, My

---

[1] Luke 1:34-37.
[2] Qur'an 19:35.
[3] Matthew 5:8-9.
[4] Genesis 1:27.
[5] Qur'an 95:4.
[6] Qur'an 42:11.

firstborn.""[1] In Hosea God says, "When Israel was a child, I loved him, and out of Egypt I called My son."[2] In I Chronicles we read: "Now He said to me, 'It is your son Solomon who shall build My house and My courts; for I have chosen him to be My son, and I will be his Father.'"[3] No one has ever claimed that Solomon was a god or a son of God.

Furthermore, we have a definition of "son of God" related by the Gospel when it says, "...as many as received Him, to them He gave the right to become children of God, to those who believe in His name."[4]

Later, John, in his first epistle, says, "Behold what manner of love the Father has bestowed on us, that we should be called the sons of God."[5] So, son of God means the servant of the One Who bestows most, or the Most Gracious. Not surprisingly, this is what Allah says in the Qur'an: "And the servants of (Allah) Most Gracious are those who walk on the earth in humility, and when the ignorant address them, they say, 'Peace!'"[6]

Baptism means the human confession of sins and its subsequent purification. It is related that John, the son of Zacharias, went into all the region around the Jordan, preaching "a baptism of repentance for the remission of sins,"[7] such that one could bathe in the Jordan river as a symbol of purification. Now, concerning Jesus' baptism, Matthew says:

> When He had been baptized, Jesus came up immediately from the water; and behold, the heavens were opened to him, and He saw the Spirit of God descending like a dove and alighting upon Him. And suddenly a voice came from heaven, saying, "This is My beloved Son, in whom I am well pleased."[8]

No doubt God is far above committing any sins and is certainly in no need of baptism and purification.

---

[1] Exodus 4:22.
[2] Hosea 11:1.
[3] I Chronicles 28:6.
[4] John 1:12.
[5] John 3:1.
[6] Qur'an 25:63.
[7] Luke 3:3.
[8] Matthew 3:16-17.

Moreover, in the Old Testament we read: "...that the sons of God saw the daughters of men, that they were beautiful; and they took wives for themselves of all whom they chose."[1] Clearly, all sons of Adam are sons of God and it is impossible for the sons of God to be gods. Luke, after mentioning the entire genealogy of Joseph the Carpenter, says at the end that Joseph was "...the son Seth, son of Adam, the son of God."[2] Note that Seth was a real son of Adam and we write 'son' (*ibn*) with an *alif*; and though Adam is a son of God only metaphorically we still write 'son' with an *alif*. Thus, obviously, Adam is not a god.

The Messiah, a Prophet of Allah

Let us go back to see how the Gospels talked about Jesus as a prophet. We find some important passages in the Gospel of Matthew, Mark and Luke. For instance, Matthew relates:

> ...[W]hen He had come to His own country, He taught them in their synagogue, so that they were astonished and said, "Where did this Man get this wisdom and these mighty works? Is this not the carpenter's son? Is not His mother called Mary? And His brothers James, Joses, Simon, and Judas? And His sisters, are they not all with us? Where then did this Man get all these things?" So they were offended at Him. But Jesus said to them, "A Prophet is not without honor except in his own country and in his own house." Now He did not do many mighty works there because of their unbelief.[3]

Mark adds that "...he could do no mighty work there."[4]

Here Jesus was unable to perform miracles. If Jesus was really a god or son of God, he would have been able to perform miracles, regardless of how badly he was received or how he was psychologically affected by the reaction of the people. As a matter of fact, Matthew reports:

---

[1] Genesis 6:2.
[2] Luke 3:38.
[3] Matthew 13:54-58.
[4] Mark 6:5.

> ...when He had come into Jerusalem, all the city was moved, saying, "Who is this?" So the multitude said, "This is Jesus, the prophet from Nazareth of Galilee."[1]

This was the testimony of the witnesses who saw him and witnessed his miracles. Yet none of them claimed that he was a god or son of God. Luke relates another incident where the people acknowledged Jesus as a prophet. Luke says:

> Now what happened, the day after, that He went into a city called Nain: and many of His disciples went with Him, and a large crowd. And when He came near the gate of the city, behold, a dead man was being carried out, the only son of his mother; and she was a widow. And a large crowd from the city was with her. When the Lord saw her, He had compassion on her and said to her, "Do not weep." Then He came and touched the open coffin, and those who carried him stood still. And He said, "Young man, I say to you, arise." So he who was dead sat up and began to speak. And He presented him to his mother. Then fear came upon all, and they glorified God, saying, "A great prophet has risen up among us": and, "God has visited His people."[2]

Bringing the Dead to Life

This wasn't the first the first time that the Jews had seen a prophet give life to a dead body. They had seen Elijah and Elisha give life to the dead before. In fact, even the bones of Elisha in his grave, when touched by a dead man, helped revive the dead man. As a matter of fact, Ezekiel raised an entire dead army, according to the Old Testament. In I Kings we read the following:

> Now it happened after these things that the son of the woman who owned the house became sick. And this sickness was so serious that there was no breath left in him. So she said to Elijah, "What have I to do with you, man of God? Have you come to me to bring my sin to remem-

---
[1] Matthew 21:10-11.
[2] Luke 7:11-16.

brance, and to kill my son?" And he said to her, "Give me your son." So he took him out of her arms and carried him to the upper room where he was staying, and laid him on his own bed. Then He cried out to the Lord and said, "O Lord my God, have You also brought tragedy on the widow with whom I lodge, by killing her son?" And he stretched himself out on the child three times, and cried out to the Lord and said, "O Lord my God, I pray, let this child's soul come back to him." Then the Lord heard the voice of Elijah; and the soul of the child came back to him, and he revived. And Elijah took the child and brought him down from the upper room into the house, and gave him to his mother. And Elijah said, "See, your son lives!" Then the woman said to Elijah, "Now by this I know that you are a man of God, and that the word of the Lord in your mouth is the truth."[1]

Likewise, in II Kings we read the following:

When Elisha came into the house, there was the child, lying dead on his bed. He went in therefore, shut the door behind the two of them, and prayed to the Lord. And he went up and lay on the child, and put his mouth on his mouth, his eyes on his eyes, and his hands on his hands; and he stretched himself out on the child, and the flesh of the child became warm. He returned and walked back and forth in the house, and again went up and stretched himself out on him; then the child sneezed seven times, and the child opened his eyes. And he called Gehazi and said, "Call this Shunammite woman." So he called her. And when she came in to him, he said, "Pick up your son." So she went in, fell at his feet, and bowed to the ground; then she picked up her son and went out.[2]

More amazing than the above was what Elisha's bones did after his death. II Kings narrates:

Then Elisha died, and they buried him. And the raiding bands from Moab invaded the land in the spring of the year. So it was, as they were burying a man, that suddenly they

---

[1] I Kings 17:17-24.
[2] II Kings 4:32-37.

Muslim-Christian Dialogue

spied a band of raiders; and they put the man in the tomb of Elisha; and when the man was let down and touched the bones of Elisha, he revived and stood on his feet.[1]

Also let us mention the miracle of Ezekiel. According to the Book of Ezekiel:

> The hand of the Lord came upon me and brought me out in the Spirit of the Lord, and set me down in the midst of the valley and it was full of bones. Then he caused me to pass by them all around, and behold, there were very many in the open valley; and indeed they were very dry. And He said to me, "Son of man, can these bones live?" So I answered, "O Lord God, You know." Again He said to me, "Prophesy to these bones, and say to them, 'Dry bones, hear the word of the Lord! Thus says the Lord God to these bones: "Surely I will cause breath to enter into you, and you shall live. I will put sinews on you and bring flesh upon you, cover you with skin and put breath in you; and you shall live. Then you shall know that I am the Lord."'"
>
> So I prophesied as I was commanded; and as I prophesied, there was a noise, and suddenly a rattling; and the bones came together, bone to bone. Indeed as I looked, the sinews and the flesh came upon them, and the skin covered them over; but there was no breath in them. Also He said to me, "Prophesy to the breath, prophesy, son of man, and say to the breath, 'Thus says the Lord God: "Come from the four winds, O breath, and breathe on these slain, that they may live."'" So I prophesied as He commanded me, and breath came into them, and they lived, and stood upon their feet, an exceedingly great army.[2]

Finally, we find that Jesus' contemporaries who believed in him believed that he was a prophet and nothing more. Luke says:

> And He said to them, "What things?" So they said to Him, "The things concerning Jesus of Nazareth, who was a

---
[1] II Kings 13:20-21.
[2] Ezekiel 37:1-10.

Prophet mighty in deed and word before God and all the people."[1]

Likewise John says:

> Then those men, when they had seen the sign that Jesus did, said, "This is truly the Prophet who is to come into the world."[2]

The Messiah, a Messenger of Allah

Let us now move on to talk about Jesus as a Messenger of Allah.

John says: "Most assuredly, I say to you, a servant is not greater than his master; nor is he who is sent greater than He Who sent him"[3] On another occasion, John quotes Jesus as saying:

> "I know that you are Abraham's descendants, but you seek to kill Me, because My word has no place in you. ...They answered and said to Him, "Abraham is our father." Jesus said to them, "If you were Abraham's children, you would do the works of Abraham. But now you seek to kill Me, a Man who has told you the truth which I heard from God."[4]

Later, John reports that Jesus accused the Jews of being devilish when he said:

> "You are of *your* father the devil, and the desires of your father you want to do. He was a murderer from the beginning, and does not stand in the truth, because there is no truth in him. When he speaks a lie, he speaks from his own resources, for he is a liar and the father of it."[5]

---

[1] Luke 24:19.
[2] John 6:14.
[3] John 13:16.
[4] 8:37; 39-40.
[5] John 8:44.

Fatherhood and Sonhood in the New Testament

In light of the above, we can understand Jesus' saying to his disciples when he was teaching them what to say in prayer, i.e., "Our Father, Who art in Heaven..." However, when he censured the Jews he referred to their father as the Devil. Although they were physically the descendants of Abraham, in terms of their behavior they were essentially of the Devil. On the other hand, the believers who believed in one God and who believed in Jesus as a prophet, a messenger, and a human being, are referred to by the New Testament as the sons of God. Thus all statements in the Bible about this kind of sonship refer to a figurative sonship. These statements do not convey any meaning of it being an actual, physical sonship.

In the Gospel of John, we find that

> Jesus answered them and said, "My doctrine is not Mine, but His Who sent Me. If anyone wills to do His will, he shall know concerning the doctrine, whether it is from God or *whether* I speak on My own *authority.* He who speaks from himself seeks his own glory; but He who seeks the glory of the One Who sent Him is true, and no unrighteousness is in Him."[1]

On another occasion, John states that "...Jesus cried out and said, 'He who believes in Me, believes not in Me but in Him Who sent Me.'"[2]

Regarding the miracle when Jesus helped give life to the dead, John says:

> Then Jesus, again groaning in Himself, came to the tomb. It was a cave, and a stone lay against it. Jesus said, "Take away the stone." Martha, the sister of him who was dead, said to Him, "Lord, by this time there is a stench, for he has been dead four days." Jesus said to her, "Did I not say to you that if you would believe you would see the glory of God?" Then they took away the stone from the place where the dead man was lying. And Jesus lifted up His eyes and

---

[1] John 7:16-18.
[2] John 12:44.

said, "Father, I thank You that You have heard Me. And I know that You always hear Me, but because of the people who are standing by I said this, that they may believe that You sent Me." Now when He said these things, He cried with a loud voice, "Lazarus, come forth!" And he who had died came out...[1]

Jesus would always pray and ask God before any miracles would take place through his own hands. They used to call him teacher, because a teacher is one who is surrounded by students. When Jesus came, he chose for himself twelve disciples. On one occasion, Matthew narrates about Jesus:

>...when He got into a boat, His disciples followed Him and suddenly a great tempest arose on the sea, so that the boat was covered with the waves. But He was asleep. Then His disciples came to Him and woke Him, saying, "Lord, save us! We are perishing!" But He said to them, "Why are you fearful, you of little faith?" Then He arose and rebuked the winds and the sea, and there was a great calm.[2]

How can a god sleep and neglect the universe? Jesus was a human being. He was subject to everything other humans are subject to, such as sleep, activity, fatigue, rest, fear and peace. In contrast, Allah, Most Glorified, Most Exalted, as the Qur'an states, is One Whom "no slumber can seize Him nor sleep."[3]

Jesus Preached Monotheism

Luke relates: "Now a certain ruler asked Him, saying, 'Good Teacher, what shall I do to inherit eternal life?' So Jesus said to him, 'Why do you call Me good? No one is good but One, that is, God.'"[4] Dr. Muhammad Jamil Ghazi has already elucidated the saying of the Prophet when he said, "Do not exaggerate in praising me as the Christians have exaggerated in praising Jesus the son of Mary." Excessive praise of an individual opens the door to many evils and simply leads one astray. Jesus refused to

---

[1] John 11:35-44.
[2] Matthew 8:23-26.
[3] Qur'an 2:225.
[4] Luke 18:18-19.

acknowledge for himself the trait of goodness; instead, he would always attribute it to Allah alone. After all this, how can anyone say that he was a god or the son of God?

Marks says that once, when

> ...one of the scribes came, and having heard them reasoning together, perceiving that He had answered them well, asked Him, "Which is the first commandment of all?" Jesus answered him, "The first of all the commandments is: 'Hear, O Israel, the Lord is our God, the Lord is one.'"[1]

Clearly, Jesus did not claim that he was a god to be worshipped, but his position towards Allah (swt) was similar to the rest of the Israelites. He called for *tawhid* openly, as stated in the Gospel of John. Therein Jesus says, "And this is eternal life, that they may know You, the only true God, and Jesus Christ whom You have sent."[2]

Also in his conversations with Mary Magdalene, "Jesus said to her, 'Do not cling to Me, for I have not yet ascended to My Father: but go to My brethren and say to them, "I am ascending to My Father and your Father, and to My God and your God."'"[3] The relationship between Jesus and Allah is the same as the relationship between his disciples and Allah: all of them were God's slaves and servants.

When we study the history of the prophets, we find that Moses escaped to the desert after he killed the Egyptian, and stayed there for forty years, tending sheep and contemplating Allah's wonders on earth and in the heavens. Moses lived under the watch of Allah until he was prepared to undertake the mission and bear its pain and hardships.

Likewise, Joseph was exposed to many trials. They began with his brothers conspiring against him, then his being sold to the Pharaoh of Egypt to serve in his house and then being accused of flirting with the King's wife. However, in the end, Allah exonerated him and he became the chief minister to the Pharaoh of Egypt.

---

[1] Mark 12:28-29.
[2] John 17:3.
[3] John 20:17.

Jesus' life was no different. Before he began his mission at the age of thirty, according to Luke, he had gone from his hometown of Nazareth to the countryside. He stayed there for forty days without food. Afterwards, Satan came and tried him with three temptations. Jesus remained steadfast and overcame the Devil, and as such was ready to assume the responsibility of being a prophet of God.

> Then Jesus returned in the power of the Spirit to Galilee, and news of Him went out through all the surrounding regions. And He taught in their synagogues, being glorified by all.[1]

> The Devil left Him, and behold, angels came and ministered to Him.[2]

Jesus was prepared for the mission as all prophets before him were. Here is the testimony of one of the people closest to him, i.e., Peter, the chief of the disciples. He says:

> "Men of Israel, hear these words: Jesus of Nazareth, a Man attested by God to you by miracles, wonders, and signs which God did through Him in your midst, as you yourselves also know..."[3]

Peter never said that Jesus was a god. Instead, he said that he was "...a Man who performed miracles and wonders by the will of God." In fact, Peter elaborates this when he says, "...how God anointed Jesus of Nazareth with the Holy Spirit and with power, who went about doing good and healing all who were oppressed by the devil, for God was with Him."[4] Peter didn't say, "for God was with him as He was with all the other prophets and messengers." All this clearly shows that Jesus was a human being and a messenger of Allah. He was a prophet who came to the Israelites as other prophets had come before him.

---

[1] Luke 4:14-15.
[2] Matthew 4:11.
[3] Acts 2:22.
[4] Acts 10:38.

The Holy Spirit

Now let us talk about the Holy Spirit. The Old Testament says:

> Behold, I send an Angel before you to keep you in the way and to bring you into the place which I have prepared. Beware of Him and obey His voice; do not provoke Him for He will not pardon your transgressions; for My name is in Him.[1]

International convention mandates that an ambassador is a representative of the nation, and of its president in particular. Any ill treatment of the ambassador is considered ill treatment of the president of that nation. The expression, "My name is in Him," means that Jesus is an ambassador between Allah, Most Glorified, Most Exalted, and His creation.

The Old Testament relates (concerning Saul) that

> Samuel took a flask of oil and poured it on his head, and kissed him and said: "Is it not because the Lord has anointed you commander over His inheritance?"...So it was, when he had turned his back to go from Samuel, that God gave him another heart; and all those signs came to pass that day. When they came there to the hill, there was a group of prophets to meet him; then the Spirit of God came upon him, and he prophesied among them.[2]

Later in the same book we find that God was angry at Saul and "...the spirit of the Lord departed from Saul, and an evil Spirit from the Lord troubled him."[3]

In fact, the Holy Spirit would come to a pure and sincere person. However, if a person displeased God, committing sin, then the Holy Spirit would depart from him and an evil spirit would embrace him. Not surprisingly, we see David praying and asking Allah:

> Create in me a clean heart, O God, and renew a steadfast spirit within me. Do not cast me away from Your presence, and do not take Your Holy Spirit from me.[1]

---

[1] Exodus 23:20-21.
[2] I Samuel 10:1, 9-10.
[3] I Samuel 16:14.

Luke adds that,

> When all the people were baptized, it came to pass that Jesus also was baptized; and while He prayed, the heaven was opened. And the Holy Spirit descended in bodily form like a dove upon Him.[2]

The Holy Spirit was active at the time of the other prophets in the Old Testament. Once more, he was with Jesus during his baptism and his trials. Thus, the Holy Spirit is not permanent within a certain human being; instead, he comes to the prophets as circumstances warrant. Finally, one can clearly see that Jesus' being was completely distinct from the being of the Holy Spirit. Mark further clarifies this when he says:

> "Assuredly, I say to you, all sins will be forgiven the sons of Men, and whatever blasphemies they may utter, but he who blasphemes against the Holy Spirit never has forgiveness, but is subject to eternal condemnation."[3]

This is similar to what we have already seen in Exodus, where it was said "...do not provoke...for My Name is in Him."[4] Matthew reiterated the above. He narrated that Jesus said:

> "Therefore I say to you, every sin and blasphemy will be forgiven men, but the blasphemy against the Spirit will not be forgiven men. Anyone who speaks a word against the Son of Man, it will be forgiven him; but whoever speaks against the Holy Spirit, it will not be forgiven him, either in this age or in the age to come."[5]

Needless to say, all the above only confirms that Jesus' being was separate and distinct from the essence or being of the Holy Spirit.

---

[1] Psalms 51:10-11.
[2] Luke 3:21-22.
[3] Mark 3:28-29.
[4] Exodus 23:20-21.
[5] Matthew 12:31-32.

Muslim-Christian Dialogue

The Miracles of Jesus

Let us now discuss Jesus' miracles. He provided for the hungry until they were content, cured lepers and raised the dead—with God's permission. These miracles were not unique to Jesus. They had also taken place at the hands of other prophets before him. For example, at the time of Moses, Allah, Most Glorified, Most Exalted, blessed him by providing manna and quails for the Israelites for forty years.[1] Once, Prophet Elijah visited a poor widow. She told him that she had nothing but some flour and oil and she would cook a cake for her son and then she would die. He told her to make the cake and afterwards she would see that the flour bag and the oil would never run out.[2]

Since this happened at the time of a famine, it was certainly a major miracle of Elijah. Also, in another incident, a woman told Elisha that creditors were demanding payment for some of her debts. Unfortunately, she had nothing except a pot of oil. So Elisha told her to go and gather as many empty vessels as she could and then go home and remain there. At home, she should begin to pour oil into all these vessels. Miraculously, when she began to pour from that little pot of oil, all the vessels were filled. When she told him what had happened, he humbly told her to "...go sell the oil, and pay your debts."[3]

Clearly, this was a miracle at the hands of Prophet Elisha. Among his miracles, Prophet Elisha also cured lepers.[4] As far as raising the dead—by God's will—we have already mentioned how Elijah, Elisha and Ezekiel did it before Jesus. In fact, even Peter also did it,[5] yet no one claimed that Peter was a god. The wisdom behind miracles is that Allah, Most Glorified, through them shows His support for His prophet so that people might believe that he was Allah's messenger, and prophet, and that he was sent by the Most Powerful and the Most Capable. This is what happened with Moses:

---

[1] Exodus 16:4-31.
[2] I Kings 17:8-6.
[3] II Kings 4:1-7.
[4] II Kings 5:8-14.
[5] Acts 9:36-42.

Thus Israel saw the great work which the Lord had done in Egypt; so the people feared the Lord, and believed the Lord and His servant Moses.[1]

Similarly, the same happened with Elijah. Relating this incident, the Bible says:

> Then the woman said to Elijah, "Now by this I know that you are a man of God, and that the word of the Lord in your mouth is the truth."[2]

Finally, this happened with Jesus himself. The Bible states: "Then many of the Jews who had come to Mary, and had seen the things Jesus did, believed in Him."[3]

Jesus Facing the Priests

Having talked about the miracles of Jesus and established that he was human and that he was a prophet and messenger of Allah, let us talk about Jesus' meeting with the priests and influential people of Israel. Regarding Jesus' elucidating understanding of forgiveness, Matthew quotes him as saying

> For if you forgive men their trespasses your heavenly Father will also forgive you. But if you do not forgive men their trespasses, neither will your Father forgive your trespasses.[4]

Clearly, this advice indicates that forgiveness is possible without any need for a crucifixion or the sacrifice of Jesus' blood for the sins of mankind. Had the crucifixion been an absolute necessity such that the forgiveness of sins without it was impossible, then Jesus should have been the first one to draw our attention to this. Instead, he insists on a *quid pro quo*, i.e., if one forgives his brother's sin, then God will forgive his sins. In other words, God's pleasure may be gained by practicing rituals and doing good deeds. In this light, Matthew relates the story of the paralytic:

---

[1]Exodus 14:31.
[2]I Kings 17:24.
[3]John 11-45.
[4]Matthew 6:14-15.

> Then behold, they brought to Him a paralytic lying on a bed. When Jesus saw their faith, He said to the paralytic, "Son, be of good cheer; your sins are forgiven you." And at once some of the scribes said within themselves, "This Man blasphemes!" But Jesus, knowing their thoughts said, "Why do you think evil in your hearts? For which is easier, to say, '*Your* sins are forgiven you,' or to say. 'Arise and walk'? But that you may know that the Son of Man has power on earth to forgive sins"—then He said to the paralytic, "Arise, take up your bed, and go to your house." And he arose and departed to his house.[1]

The result was that "...the multitude saw it, they marveled and glorified God, Who had given such power to men."[2]

Forgiveness of Sins

Jesus explained to us that he had authority to forgive sins, and he could forgive them by merely saying, "Your sins are forgiven."[3] In addition, he taught the people that curing a paralytic is much more difficult than forgiving sins merely with a few words. This clearly shows that the idea of shedding Jesus' blood on the cross as an absolute must for the forgiveness of one's sins is nothing more than a claim which has no truth to it. On another occasion, when Jesus met some leaders of the Israelites, John narrates:

> ...early in the morning He came again into the temple, and all the people came to Him; and He sat down and taught them. Then the scribes and Pharisees brought to Him a woman caught in adultery. And when they had set her in the midst, they said to Him, "Teacher, this woman was caught in adultery, in the very act. Now Moses, in the law, commanded us that such should be stoned. But what do You say?"

---

[1] Matthew 9:2-7.
[2] Matthew 9:8.
[3] Matthew 9:5.

> This they said, testing Him, that they might have something of which to accuse Him. But Jesus stooped down and wrote on the ground with His finger, as though He did not hear. So when they continued asking Him, He raised Himself up and said to them, "He who is without sin among you, let him throw a stone at her first." And again He stooped down and wrote on the ground.
>
> Then those who heard it, being convicted by their conscience, went out one by one, beginning with the oldest even to the last. And Jesus was left alone, and the woman standing in the midst. When Jesus had raised Himself up and saw no one but the woman, He said to her, "Woman, where are those accusers of yours? Has no one condemned you?" She said, "No one, Lord." And Jesus said to her, "Neither do I condemn you; go and sin no more."[1]

From the above, it is clear that Jesus called people to love one another, forgive one another and protect one another. Jesus adhered clearly to the law of God, being careful to observe its details as given in the Old Testament. For example, he adhered to the advice of the Torah when it said:

> Whoever is deserving of death shall be put to death on the testimony of two or three witnesses; he shall not be put to death on the testimony of one witness. The hands of the witness shall be the first against him to put him to death, and afterwards the hands of all the people. So you shall put the evil from among you.[2]

Accordingly, Jesus could not find any positive evidence to execute the law, so he set her free.

The result was that "...as He said these things to them, the scribes and Pharisees began to assail Him vehemently, and to cross-examine him about many things, lying in wait for Him, and seeking to catch Him in something He might say, that they might accuse Him."[3] They were trying to avail any opportunity

---

[1] John 8:1-11.
[2] Deuteronomy 17:6-7.
[3] Luke 11:53-54.

to scrutinize Jesus, as Luke explains. For example, the Bible mentions an incident involving money. Luke says,

> ...they watched Him, and sent spies who pretended to be righteous, that they might seize on His words, in order to deliver Him to the power and the authority of the governor. Then they asked Him, saying, "Teacher, we know that You say and teach rightly, and You do not show personal favoritism, but teach the way of God in truth: Is it lawful for us to pay taxes to Caesar or not?"
>
> But he perceived their craftiness, and said to them, "Why do you test Me? Show Me a denarius; whose image and inscription does it have?" They answered and said, "Caesar's." And He said to them, "Render therefore to Caesar the things that are Caesar's, and to God the things that are God's." But they could not catch Him in His words in the presence of the people. And they marveled at His answer and kept silent."[1]

As a matter of fact, Jesus himself was considered a subject of the Roman empire. Like all other subjects, he also was subject to the taxes to be paid to the Romans. He had to pay taxes for himself and on behalf of his disciples. Matthew relates that,

> [w]hen they had come to Capernaum, those who received the temple tax came to Peter and said, "Does your Teacher not pay the temple tax?" He said, "Yes." And when he had come into the house, Jesus anticipated him, saying, "What do you think, Simon? From whom do the kings of the earth take customs and taxes, from their sons or from the strangers?" Peter said to Him, "From strangers." Jesus said to him, "Then the sons are free. Nevertheless, lest we offend them, go to the sea, cast in a hook, and take the fish that comes up first. And when you have opened its mouth, you will find a piece of money; take that and give it to them for Me and you."[2]

In the Gospel of Luke we find a story about the Sadducees. Among the Jews there were many sects. Two of these sects were known as the Pharisees and the Sadducees. The Pharisees be-

---

[1] Luke 20:20-26.
[2] Matthew 17:24-27.

lieved in resurrection, the Day of Judgment, Paradise and Hell. The Sadducees didn't believe in any of these. Once,

> ...some of the Sadducees, who deny that there is a resurrection, came to Him and asked Him, saying: "Teacher, Moses wrote to us that if a man's brother dies, having a wife, and he dies without children, his brother should take his wife and raise up offspring for his brother. Now there were seven brothers. And the first took a wife, and died without children. And the second took her as wife, and he died childless. Then the third took her, and in like manner the seven also; and they left no children, and died. Last of all the woman died also. Therefore, in the resurrection, whose wife does she become? For all seven had her as wife."
>
> Jesus answered and said to them, "The sons of this age marry and are given in marriage. But those who are counted worthy to attain that age, and the resurrection from the dead, neither marry nor are given in marriage; nor can they die anymore, for they are equal to the angels and are sons of God, being sons of the resurrection. But even Moses showed in the burning bush passage that the dead are raised, when he called the Lord 'the God of Abraham, the God of Isaac, and the God of Jacob'. For He is not the God of the dead but of the living, for all live to Him." Then some of the scribes answered and said, "Teacher, You have spoken well."[1]

Jesus' Attitude towards the Sabbath

Now, let us talk about why the Jews hold Saturday to be a holy day. The Bible tells us that

> ...the heavens and earth, and all the host of them, were finished. And on the seventh day God ended His work which He had done, and He rested on the seventh day from all His work which he had done. Then God blessed the seventh day

---

[1] Luke 20:27-39.

and sanctified it, because in it He rested from all His work which God had created and made.[1]

In contrast, we find that Allah tells us in the Noble Qur'an that "We created the Heavens and the earth and all between them in six days, Nor did any sense of weariness touch us."[2]

In other words, no fatigue whatsoever affects Allah. Naturally, there is no room for talking about rest after the creation of the world in six days. Under the pretext of consecrating Saturday as a holy day, the Jews took issue with Jesus and began censuring him for curing the sick on Saturday. Jesus had taught them that Saturday was created for mankind, and not mankind for Saturday. But their minds were unable to comprehend that. The Gospel of John relates:

> Now as Jesus passed by, He saw a man who was blind from birth. And His disciples asked Him, saying, "Rabbi, who sinned, this man or his parents, that he was born blind?" Jesus answered, "Neither this man nor his parents sinned, but that the works of God should be revealed in him.
>
> "I must work the works of Him Who sent Me while it is day; the night is coming when no one can work. As long as I am in the world, I am the light of the world." When He had said these things, He spat on the ground and made clay with the saliva; and He anointed the eyes of the blind man with the clay. And He said to him, "Go, wash in the pool of Siloam (which is translated Sent)."
>
> So he went and washed, and came back seeing. ...Now it was a Sabbath when Jesus made the clay and opened his eyes... Therefore some of the Pharisees said, "This Man is not from God, because He does not keep the Sabbath." Others said, "How can a man who is a sinner do such signs?" And there was a division among them... So they again called the man who was blind, and said to him, "Give God the glory! We know that this Man is a sinner." He answered and said, "Whether He is a sinner or not I do not know. One thing I know: that though I was blind, now I see."

---

[1] Genesis 2:1-3.
[2] Qur'an 50:38.

> ...Then they reviled him and said, "You are His disciple, but we are Moses' disciples. We know that God spoke to Moses: *as for* this *fellow*, we do not know where He is from." The man answered and said to them, "Why, this is a marvelous thing, that you do not know where He is from; yet He has opened my eyes! Now we know that God does not hear sinners; but if anyone is a worshipper of God and does His will, He hears Him. Since the world began it has been unheard of that anyone opened the eyes of one who was born blind. If this Man were not from God, He could do nothing."[1]

We must note here that in the Bible some attributes of Allah are used for humans, such as Jesus' statement: "As long as I am in the world, I am the light of the world."[2] This does not mean that he is a god or equivalent to God.

At the same time, this is nothing compared to what the Torah mentions about Moses, whom it refers to as a god for both his brother Aaron, and his enemy, Pharaoh. The Old Testament says that the Lord told Moses, about his brother Aaron:

> "...and look, he is also coming out to meet you...Now you shall speak to him and put the words in his mouth. And I will be with your mouth and with his mouth, and I will teach you what you shall do. So he shall be your spokesman to the people. And he himself shall be as a mouth for you, and you be to him as God."[3]

Later, the Bible says that "...the Lord said to Moses: 'See, I have made you as God to Pharaoh, and Aaron your brother shall be your prophet.'"[4]

All these expressions are figurative rather than literal. The entire objective of the story of the blind man who was cured on a Saturday was that Jesus wanted to prove something to the Jews. He wanted to show them that their belief that nothing should be done, not even good, on Saturday, was a fallacious belief. Mark reports that Jesus

---

[1] John 9:1-7,14,16,24-25,28-33.
[2] John 9:5.
[3] Exodus 4:14-16.
[4] Exodus 7:1.

> ...went through the grain fields on the Sabbath; and as they went His disciples began to pluck the heads of grain. And the Pharisees said to Him, "Look! Why do they do what is not lawful on the Sabbath?" But He said to them, "Have you never read what David did when he was in need and hungry, he and those with him: how he went into the house of God *in the days* of Abiathar the high priest, and ate the shewbread, which is not lawful to eat except for the priests, and also gave some to those who were with him?" And He said to them, "The Sabbath was made for man, and not man for the Sabbath. Therefore the Son of Man is also Lord of the Sabbath."[1]

Now, I have to stop here for today. Allah willing, we will resume our discussion of these issues in the next session.

Dr. Muhammad Jamil Ghazi

In the name of Allah, the Compassionate, the Merciful, and may His peace and blessings be upon Muhammad, his family and all of his Companions.

We will ask Allah to grace us all with patience, for the subject is lengthy and there is a lot to talk about. Even a few back-to-back nightly sessions or long discussions are simply not enough. Regardless, we will try to focus on at least some of the crucial areas. Presently, I'd like to talk about the "Christian Law of Faith."[2] We shall see how this law started and how it developed through a number of Church ecumenical councils.

The text of the Law of Faith, which was released by the Council of Nicea in 325 C.E., reads as follows:

> We believe in one God, Father, Controller of everything, Creator of heavens and earth, of what is seen and what is unseen. We believe in one Lord... Jesus the Christ, the only Son of God, begotten by the Father before times, light from light, true God from true God. He was born uncreated. He is

---

[1] Mark 2:23-28.
[2] For further reading in this respect, cf: Abdul-Karim Al-Khatib, *Christ in the Torah, the New Testament and the Qur'an*, published in Arabic.

equivalent to the Father in essence. Because of Him everything was. This is the One Who, for our sake, and for the sake of saving our souls, descended from Heaven. He assumed his physical form by virtue of the Holy Spirit and the Virgin, Mary. Incarnated as the Son of God, He was crucified for us at the time of Pilate, the Nabatean. He suffered, was buried, and rose from the dead on the third day, as reported by the books of the Bible. Then He ascended to the heavens, and sat on the right of His Father. Then He will come in His Glory to judge the living and the dead, He Whose sovereignty is eternal.

Some years after this, an addition was made to this law by the Council of Constantinople in 381 C.E.:

Yes, we believe in the Holy Spirit, the Lord, the One Who grants life, Who came from the Father. We bow down to Him and glorify Him, along with the Father and the Son. He is the One Who talks to the prophets, all of whom come from a line field prophetic church. We acknowledge one Baptism for the forgiveness of all sins. We await the resurrection of the dead and life in the hereafter. Amen!

Then a third addition was made in praise of the Virgin Mary by the Council of Ephesus in 431 C.E. It said:

We appreciate and glorify you, mother of the true light, holy Virgin, for you have delivered to us the Savior of the whole world. He came and saved our souls.

Later a fourth addition was made in praise of Jesus:

Glory be to you, our Master, our King, the Christ, the pride of all Prophets, symbol of martyrdom, cheer and joy of the sincere and truthful, establisher of churches and forgiver of sins.

Finally, one more addition was made concerning the preaching of the holy Trinity. The text was:

We preach and propagate the Holy Trinity as one Godhead. We bow down to it and glorify it. O our Lord, be Merciful to us and, O Lord, Bless us. Amen.

Muslim-Christian Dialogue

These are the Articles of Faith, which we would like to go through and analyze, in order to figure out how they were devised and how their words were collected from the scriptures.

The history of Christianity tells us that in 325 C.E. an ecumenical conference convened in Nicea by order of the emperor, Constantine the Great. At the meeting, the first and the only issue discussed was the nature of Christ. It should be pointed out that this conference was held after the Alexandrian priest, Arius, had declared that Christ was a created being. Ibn Al-Batriq, in his history book, *Nuzum al-Jawhar*, tells of a manuscript by Arius, and how it sparked debate among Christians and caused division among them. He relates what happened to him and the consequences of the letter:

> The Patriarch of Alexandria said to his students: "The Christ has cursed Arius, so be wary of accepting his views. I saw Jesus Christ in my dreams with tattered clothes. I asked him, Master, who has torn your clothes? He said, Arius. So be wary of him and do not let him come with you to the church."

Emperor Constantine summoned the patriarchs and archbishops from all cities. So they assembled in the city of Nicaea after a year and two months. Approximately two thousand forty-eight archbishops attended the conference. They represented many different views and sects. Some of them claimed that Christ and Mary were two gods other than Allah. These were the Maryists. Some said that Christ emanated from the Father much like one flame of fire would give rise to another flame of fire, without the first one taking away anything from the second one. This was the statement of Sibarinon and his followers.

Some said that Mary was not pregnant for nine months; rather, a light passed through her womb, as water passes through a pipe. Similarly, God's word entered her ear and came out from where the baby comes from. This was the belief of Elian and his followers. Others said that Christ was created from the Godhead like us in his essence, but that the beginning of the baby was from Mary. Moreover, he was chosen to be the savior of the human essence, as such divine grace accompanied him with love and a will. That was why he was named the Son of God.

Still others said that God is one essence having three names. Further, they didn't believe in the Word or in the Holy Spirit. This was the statement of Paul of Shamshat, Patriarch of Antioch and his followers. They were known as Paulists. Many said that there are three gods: Good, Bad and Just. This was the statement of Marcion and his followers. Finally, quite a few claimed that God is the Christ. This was the statement of Paul the apostle and three hundred eighteen archbishops.

Later, when Constantine listened to these statements he was amazed. Immediately, he provided them with a place to stay and provisions for their stay. At the same time, he ordered them to debate the subject until they came to a conclusion so that he could follow it. Thereafter, the three hundred eighteen archbishops agreed to have one view of their religion. They debated with the rest of the archbishops and defeated their arguments and insisted on their view.

Perhaps the most important decision made by those three hundred eighteen archbishops was that Jesus was the Son of God and was equal to God in essence. Now we would like to examine the text of the Christian Law of Faith. Where did they collect its text from? Upon close examination, we find that its statements came forth as follows. The origin of each word or phrase is given in the footnotes below.

> We believe in one God,[1] Father,[2] Controller of everything,[3] Creator of the heavens and earth, of what is seen and what is unseen.[4] We believe in one Lord[5]..., Jesus the Christ,[6] the only Son of God,[7] begotten by the Father before all time,[8] light from light,[9] true God from True God.[10] He was born uncreated.[11] He is equivalent to the Father in essence.[1] Be-

---

[1] John 17:3.
[2] I Thessalonians 3:11.
[3] Matthew 1:9-20.
[4] Matthew 11:25, Exodus 20:11.
[5] Hebrews 1:8, Revelation 19:16.
[6] Hebrews 13:18.
[7] John 3:16.
[8] Micah 5:20.
[9] Hebrews 1:3.
[10] John 5:17.
[11] John 17:5.

cause of Him everything was.² This is the One Who, for our sake, and for the sake of saving our souls,³ descended from the heavens. He assumed his physical form⁴ by virtue of the Holy Spirit and the Virgin Mary.⁵ Incarnated as the Son of God,⁶ was crucified for us at the time of Pilate the Nabatean.⁷ He suffered,⁸ was buried,⁹ and rose from the dead on the third day, as reported by the Books of the Bible.¹⁰ Then He ascended to the heavens,¹¹ and sat on the right of his Father¹² Then He will come in His Glory¹³ to judge the living and the dead.¹⁴ He is One Whose sovereignty is eternal.¹⁵

This was the first Christian Law of Faith, before it was developed further. I would like to draw your attention to the fact that the preceding analysis is not ours. Rather, it is according to the conference's decision, which was presented by the attendees with its explanatory note.

If you look beyond this justification and its arbitrariness, you will notice that the concept of Godhead arrived at by their decision is devoid of the third part of the Trinity, namely the Holy Spirit. The faith that this decision preaches is faith in the Father and the Son only. As for the Holy Spirit, it is what entered the body of the Son from the Virgin Mary. This could be the Lord's angel, Gabriel or the Word of God.

We can consider this decision an authenticated historical document proving that the Christian Trinity was unknown be-

---

[1] John 5:26.
[2] John 10:30.
[3] John 1:3.
[4] There is no reference for this in the New Testament; this statement was added by the Ecumenical Council.
[5] John 1:14; Hebrews 10:5.
[6] Luke 1:35.
[7] John 8:42.
[8] John 19:19.
[9] I Peter 1:11.
[10] Isaiah 53:9; Matthew 27:60.
[11] Revelation 14:14; I Cornithians 15:2.
[12] Luke 24:51.
[13] Mark 16:19.
[14] Matthew 25:31.
[15] Matthew 10:30.

fore 325 C.E. Furthermore, the conference held that year did not acknowledge anyone besides the Father and Son. We can also conclude that up to this time Jesus had not been made to be the Son of God associated with His essence as in the Trinitarian concept with the Father and the Holy Spirit. In fact, the most that could be said regarding his sonship was that he was a derivative from the root. Even if Jesus' existence pointed to a God, he himself was not the God.

Thus, in the conference proceedings there is a plain declaration that God the Father is the Creator of the heavens and the earth. The Son had nothing to do with the creation of the heavens and the earth. Yet Christendom afterwards embraced the belief that God the Father did not create anything. Instead it was Christ the Son who created everything. Hence, it was the essence of the Son, as part of the Trinity, that was responsible for creation. This is where the Christian belief ended up in the middle of the fourth century, after several centuries of indecision regarding its central belief, the concept of God. The belief about Jesus was still unsettled, confused and uncertain. After all, was he God or a man? Obviously, this matter needed more discussion for it to be resolved.

Such an issue could not be resolved without another council. Thus, in 381 C.E., that is exactly what happened. Emperor Theodosius the Great called for a holy council in Constantinople to discuss the statements of Macedonius, the Patriarch of Constantinople. Macedonius had been preaching to his church and to his followers that the Holy Spirit was created like the rest of creation. From the above, it is clear that the issue of the Holy Spirit—i.e., as being one of the faces of God or a constituent part of the three-part Godhead equal to the Father and the Son in rank—was still undecided. Eventually, when the council finally convened, one hundred fifty gathered, representing all Christian institutions. Timotheus, the Patriarch of Alexandria, chaired the meeting.

The conference decided to refute the view of Macedonius and any other archbishop who held the same. Instead, it reaffirmed the resolutions of the Council of Nicaea and added the following new text. As before, the origins of the text are provided in the footnotes below.

> Yes, we believe in the Holy Spirit,[1] the Lord,[2] the One Who grants life,[3] Who came from the Father.[4] We bow down to Him and glorify Him, along with the Father and the Son.[5] He is the One Who talks to the prophets,[6] all of whom come forth from a single,[7] unified,[8] prophetic[9] church.[10] We acknowledge one baptism[11] for the forgiveness of all sins.[12] We await the resurrection of the dead[13] and the life in the Hereafter. Amen![14]

This passage from the Christian Law of Faith, like its previous counterpart, was collected from various fabricated tracts from the Gospels and the Epistles. All of its words and phrases are completely out of context. They have been collected here in an extremely incoherent manner. Needless to say, the third of the Trinity manifests itself in this page.

Soon after this addition, Christendom began to look into the idea of a three-part Godhead from theological and philosophical perspectives. In other words, philosophy began to be mixed with theology, and unwarranted imagination began to adulterate reality. Eventually, the Christian mind very skillfully wove a fabulous myth which provided the necessary link between the heavens and the earth and which merged God with man. However, the details of the story still had to be worked out. There were still too many gaping holes which could only be filled at those infamous ecumenical councils by words and phrases taken at

---

[1] John 14:26.
[2] II Corinthians 2:17-18.
[3] Romans 8:11.
[4] John 15:16.
[5] Matthew 18:19-20.
[6] I Peter 1:11, II Peter 1:21.
[7] Romans 13:5.
[8] John 11:52.
[9] Ephesians 3:5.
[10] Ephesians 5:25-26.
[11] Matthew 16:18.
[12] Ephesians 4:5.
[13] Hebrews 8:13, 9:22.
[14] I Corinthians 15:21.

Muslim-Christian Dialogue

random from here and there from the passages of the Gospels or the Epistles.

In 431 C.E., Nestor, the Patriarch of Constantinople, declared that the Virgin Mary did not deliver an incarnate being;[1] rather, she delivered a normal human being. Thereafter, God entered him by His will and not by unity with Him. Thus, God had two natures and two parts. In view of this new declaration, Christians again divided further and took sides. Some sided with Nestor while others opposed him. Many others stood on the sidelines being thoroughly confused. It was because of this chaos that Emperor Theodosius II, called for another holy council. About two hundred archbishops attended the meeting.

After lengthy discussions they concluded that, "...the Word was become flesh;" also, the two natures, the divine and the human, were combined without mixing or blending or transmuting into one another.

What is noticeable in the resolutions of this conference is that they were not like the recommendations of the first two councils. This time it was not in the form of an invitation to accept a new matter in the faith; rather, these more recent resolutions were added as an introduction to the Law of Faith. It was as if the conferees were cognizant of the great danger stemming from the constant changes in the Christian creed and how that could affect the hearts and minds of the people. They were afraid that frequent changes after particular events or manifestations of certain new ideas could cause them to censure the statements presented to them by religious authorities. More importantly, such a state of flux might even cause ordinary Christians to be skeptical in believing that such changes were divinely inspired. After all, they believed that the word of God was immutable.

Thus the conferees comprehended the gravity of the situation and accordingly did not put their resolutions as new additions to the faith. Instead, they used them as a preface to the creed and an introduction to the Faith. This introduction was divided into three parts: the Virgin Mary, Jesus Christ and the

---

[1] i.e., a being incarnated with God.

Trinity. What follows is the text of this introduction, along with a breakdown of its origins:

A. Praise of the Virgin Mary

We appreciate[1] and glorify you,[2] O mother of the true light,[3] holy virgin,[4] for you delivered to us the savior of the whole world.[5] He came and saved our souls.[6]

B. Glorifying Jesus Christ

Glory be to you, our Master,[7] and our King, the Christ,[8] the pride of all Prophets,[9] symbol of martyrdom,[10] the cheer and joy of the sincere and truthful,[11] the establisher of churches[12] and the forgiver of sins.[13]

C. Propagation of The Holy Trinity

We preach and propagate[14] the Holy Trinity[15] as one Godhead.[16] We bow down to it and glorify it.[17] O Lord be merciful to us,[18] O Lord bless us, Amen.[19]

As we have seen, the Law of Faith was developed through the Councils at the same time, it was made up of scattered phrases taken from the scriptures of the Old and New Testa-

---

[1] Luke, 1:48.
[2] Psalms 91:15.
[3] Luke 1:43; John 1:8-10.
[4] Isaiah 7:14; Luke 1:37.
[5] Luke 3:11.
[6] Luke 19-10.
[7] Isaiah 43:8.
[8] Luke 1:33.
[9] Galatians 6:14.
[10] Isaiah 38:5.
[11] John 8:56.
[12] 15:24.
[13] 9:23.
[14] Hebrews 10:43.
[15] Matthew 28:19.
[16] John 5:7.
[17] Matthew 4:10.
[18] Psalms 33:1.
[19] Luke 24:53.

ments. These are simply fabricated passages taken from texts that are inherently contradictory.

Brig. Gen. Ahmad Abdul-Wahhab

I have a simple comment to make. Arius, who said in 313 C.E. that the Messiah is created and is less than God in essence, was not the first one to say that and believe in it. In fact, the belief of the majority of the early Christians was that Jesus was a created human being. Moreover, reference to Jesus as a slave or servant of Allah still exists in the New Testament to this day. Regrettably, the Arabic editions express it in a subtle way, so that the Arabic reader cannot really comprehend it.

Jesus has been described in the Scriptures as a prophet, a messenger, son of man (i.e., Adam's son). This last name was his favorite. Also, he was described in the Scriptures as a slave, but unfortunately, they did not retain this word; instead, they used a synonym to keep the meaning hidden. This is exemplified by a passage from the Gospel of Matthew. This Gospel is famous for quoting the most from the Old Testament (relative to the other gospels). He claimed that they were previous prophecies which were now useful.

But scholars, after exhaustive studies, are convinced that there are many predictions in Matthew's Gospel which have no root or basis in the Old Testament. What concerns us here is how the writer of the Gospel of Matthew took a prophecy from the Old Testament; however, in the process, a noticeable alteration was made which the casual Arab reader would not discern.

So, what does Matthew say? He says:

> ...great multitudes followed Him, and He healed them all. Yet He warned them not to make Him known, that it might be fulfilled which was spoken by Isaiah the prophet, saying: "Behold! My Servant whom I have chosen, My Beloved in whom My soul is well pleased! I will put My Spirit upon Him, and He will declare justice to the Gentiles. He will not quarrel nor cry out, nor will anyone hear His voice in the streets. A bruised reed He will not break, and smoking flax

He will not quench, till He sends forth justice to victory; and in His name Gentiles will trust."[1]

But the prophecy of Isaiah, wherefrom Matthew quoted, says:

Behold! My Servant whom I uphold, My Elect One in whom My soul delights! I have put My Spirit upon Him; He will bring forth justice to the Gentiles. He will not cry out, nor raise His voice, Nor cause His voice to be heard in the street. A bruised reed He will not break, and smoking flax He will not quench; He will bring forth justice for truth. He will not fail nor be discouraged, till He has established justice in the earth; and the coastland shall wait for His law.[2]

But how did those entrusted with the Book of God discharge their trust? The first words of Isaiah, which read "My Servant whom I uphold", were copied in the New Testament as "My Servant whom I have chosen". In the Arabic text the word "servant" is translated as 'slave' in the Old Testament, and as 'boy' in the New Testament. This was done deliberately to keep the Arabic reader far from the idea of Jesus as a slave or servant of Allah. Although the use of the word 'boy', *fata* in Arabic, may give the meaning of slave, as in the Qur'an:

Ladies said in the city: 'The wife of the (great) Aziz is seeking to seduce her slave... '

And Joseph told his servants to put their stock-in-trade into their saddlebags...[3]

it still does not justify the change in words from the Old Testament to the New.

Undoubtedly, we can state that the current Bible acknowledges Jesus as Allah's servant. Jesus' disciples described him likewise. Peter and John would often refer to Jesus as Allah's servant. The Bible states: "The God of Abraham, Isaac and Jacob, the God of our fathers, glorified His Servant Jesus, whom you delivered up and denied in the presence of Pilate, when he

---

[1] Matthew 12:15-21.
[2] Isaiah 42:1-4.
[3] Cf. Qur'an 12:30, 62.

was determined to let Him go."[1] Again, in the Arabic the word "boy" appears instead of "servant."

If it was "glorified His Servant Jesus" it would seek the attention of the Arab reader to the fact that Jesus is Allah's servant. If we review the English translation of the Bible, the pertinent chapters and verses of Isaiah, Matthew and Acts, all concur in using the word "servant". Jesus was mentioned in the scriptures of the New Testament as Allah's servant

On this point, we would like to conclude the fourth session. Allah willing, we will begin the fifth session tomorrow.

---

[1] Acts 3:13.

THE FIFTH SESSION

Dr. Muhammad Jamil Ghazi

In the name of Allah, Most Gracious, Most Merciful. Glory to your Lord, the Lord of Honor and Power. He is free from what they ascribe to Him. And peace be upon the messengers, and praise to Allah, the Lord and Cherisher of the Worlds. May Allah's peace and blessings be upon the final Prophet and upon his family and all of his Companions.

We open the fifth session of this Muslim-Christian discourse by reading a few verses from the Glorious Qur'an. We seek Allah's protection from the accursed Satan. Allah, Most Exalted says:

> One day will Allah gather the Messengers together, and ask: What was the response you received (from men to your teaching)? They will say: "We have no knowledge: it is You Who knows in full all that is hidden."

> Then will Allah say: Jesus, son of Mary! Recount My favor to you and to your mother. Behold! I strengthened you with the holy spirit, so that you did speak to the people in childhood and in maturity. Behold! I taught you the Book and Wisdom, the Law and the Gospel. And behold! You make out of clay, as it were, the figure of a bird, by My leave, and you breathe into it and it becomes a bird by My leave, and you heal those born blind, and the lepers, by My leave. And behold! You bring forth the dead by My leave. And behold! I did restrain the Children of Israel from (violence to) you when you did show them the clear Signs, and the unbelievers among them said: "This is nothing but evident magic."

> And behold! I inspired the disciples to have faith in Me and My Messenger: They said, "We have faith, and do you bear witness that we bow to Allah as Muslims." Behold! The dis-

ciples, said: "Jesus son of Mary! Can your Lord send down to us a table set (with viands) from heaven?" Said Jesus: "Fear Allah, if you have faith." They said: "We only wish to eat thereof and satisfy our hearts, and to know that you have indeed told us the truth; and that we ourselves may be witnesses to the miracle."

Said Jesus the son of Mary: "Allah our Lord! Send us from heaven a table set (with viands), that there may be for us—for the first and the last of us—a solemn festival and a sign from You; and provide for our sustenance, for You are the best Sustainer (of our needs)."

Allah said: I will send it down unto you: But if any of you after that resist faith, I will punish him with a penalty such as I have not inflicted on anyone among all the peoples. And behold! Allah will say: Jesus son of Mary! Did you say unto men, "Worship me and my mother as two gods in derogation of Allah"? He will say: "Glory to You! Never could I say what I had no right (to say). Had I said such a thing, You would indeed have known it. You know what is in my heart, and I know not what is in Yours. For You know in full all that is hidden.

"Never said I to them aught except what You did command me to say, to wit, 'Worship Allah, my Lord and your Lord'; and I was a witness over them while I dwelt among them; when You did take me up You were the Watcher over them, and You are a witness to all things. If You do punish them, they are Your servants: If You do forgive them, You are the Exalted in power, the Wise."

Allah will say: This is a day on which the truthful will profit from their truth: theirs are gardens, with rivers flowing beneath, their eternal Home: Allah well-pleased with them, and they with Allah: That is the great salvation, (the fulfillment of all desires). To Allah belongs the dominion of the heavens and the earth, and all that is therein, and it is He Who has power over all things.[1]

---

[1] Qur'an 5:112-123.

Our topic this evening deals with the prophecies of the coming of the Messenger of Allah [Muhammad] (may Allah's peace and blessings be upon him). We have said it before and we still say again: These Biblical scriptures have been heavily tampered with, for they have been repeatedly changed, altered and edited by man over the years. Nevertheless, there still remains in the Bible some passages which need no special interpretation whatsoever. Certain passages prove absolutely that the person referred to therein is none other than Prophet Muhammad (may Allah's peace and blessings be upon him) who was sent by Allah, Most Glorified, Most Exalted, and who was one of Ishmael's descendants.

Before our esteemed scholar, Ibrahim Khalil Ahmad, speaks, I would like to say that all these prophecies for the believing Muslims represent just one out of thousands of proofs and signs that Prophet Muhammad (may Allah's peace and blessings be upon him) spoke the truth. By far, this is not the only thing we have in our hands to prove his truthfulness. These prophecies are just one of countless signs. As alluded to earlier, these prophecies merely represent a small finger pointing to a great reality; namely, Muhammad, may Allah's peace and blessings be upon him, was the final Prophet and Messenger of Allah.

If we were to embark upon reviewing all proofs and signs concerning the credibility of the Prophet (peace be upon him), then a few nights are simply insufficient for this task. You should know that many voluminous books have been written about the signs of the coming of Prophet Muhammad, may Allah's peace and blessings be upon him. Since our time is too limited to review everything, we will at least refer to some of these prophecies as our scholar Ibrahim Khalil Ahmad sees fit. He will talk to us this evening about these signs and predictions in the holy books of both the Old and the New Testaments.

Mr. Ibrahim Khalil Ahmad

In the name of Allah, Most Gracious, Most Merciful. Praise be to Allah, Lord of the Worlds, and may Allah's peace and blessings be upon Prophet Muhammad, his family and his Companions.

Dear brothers, tonight I'm going to talk to you about the prophecies concerning Prophet Muhammad. Or to put it in another way, I'll talk to you tonight with absolute candor as to why I embraced Islam, how I became a Muslim, and what the reasons were that motivated me to accept Islam.

Frankly speaking, when I came upon the following Qur'anic verse, saying: "Those who follow the Messenger, the unlettered Prophet whom they find mentioned in their own Scriptures, in the Torah and the Injil,"[1] I said to myself: If I look through the Old and the New Testaments and find that Prophet Muhammad is mentioned in them, I will tell people about it and will surely witness that he is most certainly the final Prophet.

Old Testament Predictions of the Final Messenger

My comments to you tonight are those of a person who was able to know Prophet Muhammad from the Old and the New Testaments. From the Torah we see that the Lord talks to Moses about Prophet Muhammad, may Allah's peace and blessings be upon him, when He says:

> I will raise up for them a prophet like you from among their brethren, and will put My words in his mouth, and he shall speak to them all that I command him. And it shall be *that* whoever will not hear My words, which he speaks in My name, I will require *it* of him.[2]

There are a number of points which must be discussed concerning the passage ascribed to Moses. For example, when God says, "I will raise up for them a prophet like you from among *their* brethren," the pronoun "their" carries an important meaning. If God had willed to make the awaited prophet come from the Israelites, He would have said "I will raise up for them a

---
[1] Qur'an 7:157.
[2] Deuteronomy 18:18-19.

prophet like you from among *your* brethren." In other words, the third person pronoun is used instead of the second person pronoun. This indicates that the prophethood this time would go beyond the Israelites, the descendants of Isaac,[1] to some other descendants of Abraham.[2]

Examine the Torah to find out who are the descendants of Abraham. The Torah informs us that Abraham was blessed in the land, said to be the Land of Promise, where initially he was not granted a son, but later he was. Relating this episode, the Bible says, "Abraham said to God, 'Would that Ishmael might live before You!'"[3] In response, Allah says:

> ...as for Ishmael, I have heard you. Behold, I have blessed him, and will make him fruitful, and will multiply him exceedingly. He shall beget twelve princes, and I will make him a great nation.[4]

This was the promise made by Allah to Abraham as mentioned in the Bible. It furnishes proof that the prophet to come would be from Abraham's descendants, and in particular from Ismael's descendants. Moreover, the earlier verses show that the prediction referred to the third person "their", i.e., people other than those addressed by the text. If the future prophet were to come from the Israelites, the text would have clearly been "*your* brethren".

Then we come the phrase "like you". It means that the coming prophet would be like Moses. If we compare the three prophets, Moses, Jesus and Muhammad (may Allah's peace and blessings be upon all of them), Moses and Muhammad are most alike. For example, we find that Moses received a revelation which included the Law. Jesus, on the other hand, did not bring a new Law, as he said, "Do not think that I came to destroy the Law or the prophets. I did not come to destroy but to fulfill."[5] Prophet Muhammad (may Allah's peace and blessings be upon

---

[1] Isaac was the second son of Abraham, along with Ishmael. Thus, Isaac and Ishmael were brothers.
[2] or "brethren" of the Israelites.
[3] Genesis 17-18.
[4] Genesis 17-20.
[5] Matthew 5:17.

him) came with the Glorious Qur'an. This was the final Testament and the Master of all previous revelations. It comprises a complete new code of Law.

Then the text also says, "...and (I) will put My words in His mouth, and He shall speak to them all that I command Him." This is irrefutable proof against the Orientalists, who claim that the Qur'an is Muhammad's word. Yet Allah clearly says, "(I) will put My words in His mouth," because, after all, the Prophet does not "...say (aught) of his own desire."[1] Rather, he would only speak what Allah, Most Glorified, Most Exalted, revealed to him.

But he speaks by revelation from Allah (swt) to him. Furthermore, what is more alarming is when God says, "And it shall be that whoever will not hear My words, which He speaks in My name, I will require it from him."[2]

Woe to the one who disbelieves in Prophet Muhammad, and woe unto any people who oppose the final Prophet!

The Mountains of Paran

Moving on to another text in the Torah, we find that it says:
> Now this is the blessing with which Moses the man of God blessed the children of Israel before his death. And he said: The Lord came from Sinai, and dawned on them from Seir; He shone forth from Mount Paran, and He came with ten thousands of saints: From His right hand came a fiery law for them.[3]

In contemplating the above passage let us take a look at the holy places in this text. Sinai is the first place, Seir is the second and Paran is the third. Sinai was the place of Moses.[4] Seir refers to the Land of Palestine, wherein Esau, the brother of Jacob, i.e., Israel, dwelt.[5] The Law in the Torah mandates that the firstborn should inherit in the name of his father. Esau was the firstborn,

---

[1] Qur'an 53:3.
[2] Deuteronomy 18:19.
[3] Deuteronomy 33:1-2.
[4] Exodus 24:16-18.
[5] Genesis 36:8.

Muslim-Christian Dialogue

while Jacob was the next in line. What is strange is that, because of a trick played by Jacob on his father, Isaac, the birthright was stolen from Esau.[1] Esau, whose story has been concealed, was living in the mountain of Seir.[2] Esau is Edom. Later, the Bible says that "...Jacob sent messengers before him to Esau his brother in the land of Seir, the country of Edom."[3] Thus, Seir is the land of Palestine to which the prophets from Jacob's descendants came. Needless to say, Jesus was one of those descendants.

Now let us come to the Land of Paran. It is so amazing, dear brothers, that Allah, Most Glorified, Most Exalted, had promised to give Abraham the land from the Nile to the Euphrates:

> On the same day the Lord made a covenant with Abram, saying: "To your descendants I have given this land, from the river of Egypt to the great river, the River Euphrates—the Canaanites, the Kenizzites, the Cadmonites, the Hittites, the Perizzites, the Rephaim, the Amorites, the Canaanites, the Girgashites, and the Jebusites."[4]

This was the promise that was given to Abraham though he had no child at that time. Thereafter, Sarai (or Sarah), Abraham's wife, who had not bore him any children, asked him to marry an honorable woman in her house. Her name was Hagar. She had hoped that Hagar would give him a child. He married her and soon after was blessed with Ishmael who was loved by Abraham, Hagar, and Sarai too. The Bible relates the above events:

> Now Sarai, Abram's wife, had borne him no children. And she had an Egyptian maidservant whose name was Hagar. Sarai said to Abram, "See now, the Lord has restrained me from bearing children. Please, go in to my maid; perhaps I shall obtain children by her." And Abram heeded the voice of Sarai.
>
> Then Sarai, Abram's wife, took Hagar her maid, the Egyptian, and gave her to her husband Abram to be his wife, after

---
[1] Genesis 27.
[2] Genesis 36:8.
[3] Genesis 32:2.
[4] Genesis 15:18-20.

Abram had dwelt ten years in the land of Canaan. So he
went in to Hagar, and she conceived.[1]

So, Abram was now blessed with a son, Ishmael, whose descendants would inherit the land from the Nile to the Euphrates. Later, we find that Allah, Most Glorified, Most Exalted, gave Abraham more. He gave him Isaac when Ishmael was fourteen years old. Then, suddenly, as the Bible tells it, jealousy began to take hold of Sarai's heart. She started preferring her own son Isaac over Ishmael. She asked Abraham to drive Hagar and her son out of the house. The Torah says that

> ...Sarah saw the son of Hagar the Egyptian, whom she had borne to Abraham, scoffing. Therefore she said to Abraham, "Cast out this bondwoman and her son; for the son of this bondwoman shall not be heir with my son, *namely* with Isaac." And the matter was very displeasing in Abraham's sight because of his son. But God said to Abraham, "Do not let it be displeasing in your sight because of the lad or because of your bondwoman. Whatever Sarah has said to you, listen to her voice; for in Isaac your seed shall be called. Yet I will also make a nation of the son of the bondwoman, because he is your seed."[2]

Although the words of Sarah concerning Hagar and Ishmael were disturbing and displeasing to Abraham, he had no choice but to listen to her. He had to take his wife Hagar and their son Ishmael to the desert. It is there that Abraham turns to Allah and says, "Our Lord, I have made some of my offspring to dwell in a valley without cultivation, by Your Sacred House."[3]

The Torah says that Ishmael dwelt in the desert of Paran.[4] It relates that

> God heard the voice of the lad. Then the angel of God called to Hagar out of heaven, and said to her, "What ails you, Ha-

---

[1] Genesis 16:14.
[2] Genesis 21:9-13.
[3] Qur'an 14:37.
[4] The name Paran is Hebrew for the Arabic Faran, referring to the valley of Makkah and the surrounding mountains in Saudi Arabia. Makkah was the birthplace of Prophet Muhammad and the seat of the first Qur'anic revelation.

Muslim-Christian Dialogue

gar? Fear not, for God has heard the voice of the lad where he is.

"Arise, lift up the lad and hold him with your hand, for I will make him a great nation." Then God opened her eyes, and she saw a well[1] of water. And she went and filled the skin with water, and gave the lad to drink. So God was with the lad; and he grew and dwelt in the wilderness, and became an archer. He dwelt in the wilderness of Paran: and his mother took a wife for him from the land of Egypt.[2]

Thus, the third part of Moses' statement: "...He shone forth from Mount Paran,"[3] refers to Ishmael and the final Prophet, who will come from Ishmael's offspring. This is exactly what the divine promise was when God said, "Yet I will also make a nation of the son of the bondwoman."[4] "And as for Ishmael, I have heard you. Behold! I have blessed him, and will make him fruitful, and will multiply him exceedingly. He shall beget twelve princes, and I will make him a great nation."[5]

Some of Paul's Alterations

As time passed, Jesus came, born of the Virgin Mary, and carried out his mission. However, in the process some people who had no connection to Jesus, such as Saul, also known as Paul, slipped into his ranks and caused irreparable evil. Saul represented the blind hatred of Christendom towards followers of Muhammad, who were the descendants of Ishmael. Paul said:

> Nevertheless what does the Scripture say? "Cast out the bondwoman and her son, for the son of the bondwoman shall not be heir with the son of the free woman." So then, brethren, we are not children of the bondwoman but of the free.[6]

---

[1] i.e.the well of Zamzam, which still exists in Makkah, supplying water to millions of pilgrims and visitors.
[2] Genesis 21:17-21.
[3] Deuteronomy 33:2.
[4] Genesis 21:13.
[5] Genesis 17:20.
[6] Galatians 4:30, 31.

It is evident that the Crusades between the Christians and the Muslims began with Paul's letters to the Galatians. They believe that they are the offspring of Isaac (may Allah's peace and blessings be upon him), and therefore they are the only ones for whom divine promises will be fulfilled. Moreover, they believe that only they have the right to have the Law and sovereignty over all. Later, we will see when we review other prophecies that their claim is nothing but nonsense.

Habakkuk's Prophecy

After Moses we come to Prophet Habakkuk, who said:

> God came from Teman, the Holy One from Mount Paran. Selah. His glory covered the heavens, and the earth was full of His praise. His brightness was like the light; He had rays *flashing* from His hand, and there His power *was* hidden.[1]

This prophecy of Habakkuk refers to Makkah. His phrase, "God came from Teman," refers to a town southeast of Tabuk, namely Makkah.[2] His phrase, "The Holy One from Mount Paran" is also a reference to Makkah.

What does the statement, "His glory covered the heavens," refer to? Tonight, when we heard the *adhan*[3] for the 'Isha' prayer,[4] we all stopped talking and listened to the caller. It is the call, "God is the Greatest," (*Allahu akbar*) that rings in every corner of the world where Muslims live, whether they are few or many.

---

[1] Habakkuk 3:3-4.
[2] In Hebrew, Teman is Yemen, though it is certainly likely that Habakkuk was referring to the general direction (ed.).
[3] The *adhan* is the Muslim call to prayer, called aloud five times daily. The words are: Allah is the Greatest, Allah is the Greatest, Allah is the Greatest, Allah is the Greatest. I bear witness that there is none deserving of worship but Allah; I bear witness that there is none deserving of worship but Allah. I bear witness that Muhammad is the Messenger of Allah; I bear witness that Muhammad is the Messenger of Allah. Come to prayer, come to prayer. Come to success, come to success. Allah is the Greatest, Allah is the Greatest. There is none deserving of worship but Allah.
[4] *'isha'* is the fifth daily prayer, after the end of twilight.

It is the glory of Allah which covers the heavens and the earth. This verse couldn't possibly be referring to a Jewish synagogue, which uses the trumpet; likewise it couldn't possibly be referring to a Christian church, which uses the bell. Instead, it must be referring to the minaret of a mosque, where the caller stands and witnesses that "There is none worthy of worship but Allah." (*La ilaha illa Allah*) and "Muhammad is His Messenger" (*Muhammadur-rasulu Allah*). He declares to all the people that "God is the greatest" (*Allahu akbar*). Accordingly, when the prayer is called to, Muslims stand, humbly praising, glorifying and then prostrating to Allah with their foreheads touching the ground. Nothing like this happens in a Jewish synagogue or a Christian church; the earth does not become "covered" with those glorifying Allah. Only in the Muslim prayers. As a matter of fact, even outside their prayers, they are always busy praising and glorifying God.

As for the statement, "His brightness was like the light, He had rays flashing from His hand, and there His power was hidden," how great it is for the Qur'an, raised up high, flashing its rays of blessings and guidance, and all that is good! That is what Prophet Habakkuk said.

The Prophecy of David

"The stone which the builders rejected became the chief cornerstone."

Let us now spend a few moments with Prophet David. He said, "The stone which the builders rejected has become the chief cornerstone. This was the Lord's doing; it is marvelous in our eyes."[1]

This means that the many prophets sent to the Israelites represent the many stones used in building the Lord's house. But the cornerstone which will support the whole structure, although it is only one stone, is the most important and crucial one to keep the entire building steady. This refers to the final prophet, Muhammad, without whom all the prophets would not be

---

[1] Psalms 118:22-23.

united. The whole office of prophethood would have no value without him, much like the building would be incomplete without the cornerstone. This was the Lord's doing. Some may say that Jesus is that cornerstone. But Jesus himself talked to the Israelites, censuring them severely.

> Jesus said to them, "Have you never read in the Scriptures: 'The stone which the builders rejected has become the chief cornerstone. This was the Lord's doing; it is marvelous in our eyes'?
>
> "Therefore I say to you, the kingdom of God will be taken from you and given to a nation bearing the fruits of it. And whoever falls on this stone will be broken; but on whomever it falls, it will grind him to powder."[1]

Jesus' statement, "Therefore I say to you, the kingdom of God will be taken from you," means that the final prophet, represented by the cornerstone, will not be from the Israelites; instead, he will come from a pious nation that will enjoin what is right, forbid what is wrong and believe in only one God. This is the Muslim nation.

As for as his statement, "And whoever falls on this stone will be broken; but on whomever it falls, it will grind him to powder," this refers to the sheer power of Islam. Whoever attacks it, Allah will destroy. In fact, this is exactly what history has recorded, whereby a small group of Muslims were able to defeat the two most powerful empires at that time. In other words, they were the two superpowers of that time. The upstart Muslims completely overran the Persian empire, and captured half of the Roman empire, which was rich in land, wealth and human resources. Jesus' prophecy predicting the absolute defeat of the enemies of Islam matches what Moses had said earlier. He warned that God had said, "And it shall be *that* whoever will not hear My words, which He speaks in My name, I will require *it* of him."[2] That is, Allah, Most Glorified, Most Exalted, will punish him.

---

[1] Matthew 21:42-44.
[2] Deuteronomy 18:19.

Prophet Daniel's Explication of Nebuchadnezzar's Dream

What is even more amazing is what happened with Prophet Daniel. Prophet Daniel was a Jew who lived in Babylon at the time of King Nebuchadnezzar. That king had destroyed the Temple and had taken all its property, including the Torah and the golden vessels. Once he saw a dream which no one could interpret, except Daniel. Prophet Daniel, interpreting the king's dream, tells him:

> "You, O king, were watching; and behold, a great image! This great image, whose splendor was excellent, stood before you; and its form was awesome. This image's head was of fine gold, its chest and arms of silver, its belly and thighs of bronze, its legs of iron, its feet partly of iron and partly of clay. You watched while a stone was cut out without hands, which struck the image on its feet of iron and clay, and broke them in pieces. "Then the iron, the clay, the bronze, the silver, and the gold were crushed together, and became like chaff from the summer threshing floors; the wind carried them away so that no trace of them was found. And the stone that struck the image became a great mountain and filled the whole earth. This is the dream. Now we will tell the interpretation of it before the king.
>
> "You, O king, are a king of kings. For the God of heaven has given you a kingdom, power, strength, and glory; and wherever the children of men dwell, or the beasts of the field and the birds of the heaven, He has given them into your hand, and has made you ruler over them all—you *are* this head of gold. But after you shall rise another kingdom inferior to yours; then another, a third kingdom of bronze, which shall rule over all the earth. And the fourth kingdom shall be as strong as iron, inasmuch as iron breaks in pieces and shatters everything; and like iron that crushes, *that kingdom* will break in pieces and crush all the others. Whereas you saw the feet and toes, partly of potter's clay and partly of iron, the kingdom shall be divided; yet the strength of the iron shall be in it, just as you saw the iron mixed with ceramic clay. And as the toes of the feet were partly of iron and

partly of clay, so the kingdom shall be partly strong and partly fragile. As you saw iron mixed with ceramic clay, they will mingle with the seed of men; but they will not adhere to one another, just as iron does not mix with clay.

And in the days of these kings the God of heaven will set up a kingdom which shall never be destroyed; and the kingdom shall not be left to other people; it shall break in pieces and consume all these kingdoms, and it shall stand forever. Inasmuch as you saw that the stone was cut out of the mountain without hands, and that it broke in pieces the iron, the bronze, the clay, the silver, and the gold—the great God has made known to the king what will come to pass after this. The dream is certain, and its interpretation is sure."[1]

In reviewing world history, we find that the oldest kingdom after the Pharaohs was the Babylonian empire, which was symbolized by the golden head. Next was the Persian empire symbolized by silver. Then came the Greek empire symbolized by bronze, after which came the Roman empire symbolized by iron. This last one was divided into two large parts, the eastern and the western. Then it crumbled into many smaller kingdoms. After that came the nation of Islam, which confounded those great kingdoms. It was a nation which emerged from the desert.

It was referred to by the above passage as "the stone (that) ...was cut out of the mountain." This stone defeated all those kingdoms. This stone is Islam, which will last forever. Daniel says: "And in the days of these kings the God of heaven will set up a kingdom which shall never be destroyed; and the kingdom shall not be left to other people; it shall break in pieces and consume all these kingdoms, and it shall stand forever."[2]

Muhammad was born in Makkah, which is surrounded by mountains. Then, Allah, Most Glorified, chose him to be the final Prophet and Messenger. Thus, the promise which was given to Abraham and to Ishmael was now a reality. Daniel's interpretation of the king's dream proved to be true. Barely a few years had passed before Islam became a distinct power in

---

[1] Daniel 2:31-45.
[2] Daniel 2:44.

the world. Its domain did not extend just between the Nile and Euphrates, but it extended from China in the East to the Iberian peninsula in the West.

No matter how hard people with malicious intentions try to eradicate Islam's effect on the world, they will be unable to. I personally tried for fifteen years to work against Islam, but Allah Most Glorified, Most Exalted, subjugated me. So instead of aiding the colonial policy through their missionary movement in this country, I was later prepared by Allah's blessing to embrace Islam, and was prepared by His grace to be an Islamic worker, and to do my best to defend Islam, its lands and its peoples.

The Prophecy of Isaiah

Madinah

Let us now move to the Book of Isaiah. Here we read the following passage:

> Let the wilderness and its cities lift up *their voice.* The villages that Kedar inhabits. Let the inhabitants of Sela sing, let them shout from the top of the mountains. Let them glory to the LORD, and declare His praise in the coastlands. The LORD shall go forth like a mighty man; He shall stir up His zeal like a man of war. He shall cry out, yes, shout aloud; He shall prevail against His enemies.[1]

The above passage is depicting the arrival of the Prophet in Madinah. Sela is one of the mountains close to Mount Uhud in Madinah. The statement "Let the inhabitants of Sela sing" is a prophecy of the reception of the Prophet by the people of Madinah as they sang with joy when he emigrated there. That is exactly what happened. The *Ansar*[2] received him singing: "The full moon has risen upon us."

---

[1] Isaiah 42:11-13.
[2] The group of Muslims from Madinah, called the 'Helpers' because they helped the Prophet (pbuh) and the *Muhajirun*, the 'emigrants' from Makkah.

Makkah

Later we read the following passage in the Book of Isaiah:

> Arise, shine; for your light has come! And the glory of the Lord is risen upon you. For behold, the darkness shall cover the earth, and deep darkness the people; but the Lord will arise over you. And His glory will be seen upon you. The Gentiles shall come to your light, and kings to the brightness of your rising. Lift up your eyes all round, and see: they all gather together, they come to you; your sons shall come from afar, and your daughters shall be nursed at your side.
>
> Then you shall see and become radiant, and your heart shall swell with joy; because the abundance of the sea shall be turned to you, the wealth of the Gentiles shall come to you. The multitude of camels shall cover your land, the dromedaries of Midian and Ephah; all those from Sheba shall come; they shall bring gold and incense, and they shall proclaim the praise of the LORD. All the flocks of Kedar shall be gathered together to you, the rams of Nebaioth shall minister to you; they shall ascend with acceptance on my altar, and I will glorify the house of My glory.[1]

This prophecy is talking about Makkah. The statement "Arise, shine, for your light has come," refers to the beginning of the illumination through the light of Islam, the light of *tawhid*, emanating from Makkah. Second, the sentence, "the darkness shall cover the earth," refers to the presence of polytheism in Arabia at that time, fire worship in Persia, paganism in India, and the heresy and paganism which adulterated Christianity in the Roman empire and its colonies. Indeed, pitch darkness had enveloped all nations. However, in the middle of all that darkness, the light of Islam began to shine from Makkah.

The third statement, "The Gentiles shall come to your light, And kings to the brightness of your rising," means that the whole world will listen to the truth. Even entire nations and kings will come to you. Though Arabia was a desolate desert land without plants and water. Allah, Most Glorified, would

---

[1] Isaiah 60:1-7.

make great wealth pour into it as a response to Abraham's prayer when he said to Allah:

> "O our Lord! I have made some of my offspring to dwell in a valley without cultivation, by Thy Sacred House; in order, O our Lord, that they may establish regular Prayer: So fill the hearts of some among men with love towards them, and feed them with fruits: so that they may give thanks."[1]

Because of this, the wealth of nations came forth and poured into Makkah and into Arabia at large.

Then the next statement, "The multitude of camels shall cover your land," definitely refers to Arabia in general and Makkah as its capital in particular. Makkah was the place where pilgrims would come from everywhere. In the desert Arabian lands, the camel was their only means of transportation; nothing else was as efficient for desert travel. Finally, the passage talks about Nebaioth and Kedar and others. Needless to say, they were children of Ishmael, even by the Bible's admission.[2]

Brig. Gen. Ahmad Abdul-Wahhab

In addition to what Prof. Ibrahim Khalil Ahmad has already said, I would like to suggest that it is quite enough for us to focus on only two scriptural passages. The first is from the Old Testament. i.e., Isaiah, Chapter 42, which Professor Ibrahim has already dealt with. The second passage comes from the New Testament, from the Gospel of John. It is the only Gospel of the four that talks about "the comforter", and the "spirit of truth", which is very different from the "Holy Spirit". John acknowledges and affirms in the Epistles that "the Spirit of Truth" is a "believing human".

In reality, Chapter 42 of the Book of Isaiah is a formidable document which challenges all who refuse to believe in Prophet Muhammad. This is because the description of the Prophet and his people, their characteristics and condition before his coming, and then after his appearance among them, is all clearly spelled

---

[1] Qur'an 14:37.
[2] 25:12-18.

out in that book. Any reader sincere to him-/herself cannot help but admit that these characteristics cannot apply to anyone except Muhammad son of 'Abdullah. So, what does Chapter 42 of the Book of Isaiah say?

Let us divide it into paragraphs. Each one contains some lines or words that go together and that give a complete thought.

1. The first paragraph speaks of a prophet who would become famous as the slave and messenger of Allah. It says "Behold! My Servant whom I uphold, My Elect one in whom My soul delights! I have put My Spirit upon Him; he will bring forth justice to the Gentiles."[1]

2. The second paragraph indicates that the religion will prevail and the Law (*shari'ah*), which he brings will be completed during his lifetime and not afterwards. It is clear—and all Christian scholars know this—that Christianity as we know it today was not completed within the lifetime of Jesus. It is a fact that numerous things were added to the Bible by his disciples, by the Church and by Paul. But the prophet that Isaiah's prophecy talked about, would have the whole law completed during his lifetime. In fact, the whole religion would be complete in his presence so that the coming generations wouldn't be able to add anything to or delete anything from what the Prophet brought. The only responsibility that the Muslims had to shoulder was to practice that religion. The Gospel of Matthew affirms the above, saying, "...He will bring forth justice for truth. He will not fail nor be discouraged, till He has established justice in the earth; and the coastland shall wait for His law."[2]

He states here that the prophet to come will have a law. In contrast, it is well known that Jesus did not bring a new law; rather, he came with a set of morals and ethics, preserving and safeguarding the Law of Moses and motivating people to apply it. As a matter of fact, Jesus' last commandments corroborate what we have said. Matthew relates that

> ...Jesus spoke to the multitudes and to His disciples, saying: "The scribes and the Pharisees sit in Moses' seat. Therefore whatever they tell you to observe, *that* observe and do, but

---
[1] Isaiah 42:1.
[2] Isaiah 42:3-4.

Muslim-Christian Dialogue

do not do according to their works; for they say, and do not do."[1]

3. The third passage indicates that Allah will protect him from the people until he completes his mission. In other words, he will not die or be killed before the completion of the religion. God says, "I, the LORD, have called You in righteousness, and will hold Your hand; I will keep You and give You as a covenant to the people, as a light to the Gentiles."[2]

Clearly, the passage cannot possibly apply to Jesus. According to the Bible, he failed, was defeated and killed a short time after the start of his call. The length of his mission is a controversial issue. Some Christians estimate it to be a year to eighteen months. Some say it could have been as long as three years. Allah's safeguarding of the prophet from the people's violence, as agreed to by Isaiah here, has also been mentioned in the Qur'an:

> O Messenger! Proclaim the (message) which has been sent to you from your Lord. If you did not, you would not have fulfilled and proclaimed His mission. And Allah will defend you from men (who mean mischief).[3]

Thus, Allah, Most Glorified, decreed that His Prophet be protected from the people's mischief. In fact, when this verse was revealed, the Prophet, having bodyguards to defend him from his enemies, let the guards go and said: "Men, you can go, for Allah is guarding us now."

4. The fourth passage informs us that the new prophet will come from the offspring of Ishmael, the son of Abraham. It says: "Let the wilderness and its cities lift up *their voice* the villages that Kedar inhabits. Let the inhabitants of Sela sing, let them shout from the top of the mountains."[4] Kedar was the second son of Ishmael, according to the Bible.[5]

5. There is a glaring difference between the prophecy concerning this new prophet and that of any other prophet like Jesus. The Book of Isaiah clearly shows that his defeated enemies

---

[1] Matthew 23:1-3.
[2] Isaiah 42:6.
[3] Qur'an 5:67.
[4] Isaiah 42:11.
[5] Genesis 25:13.

were idol worshippers. The Jews to whom Jesus came were not idol worshippers. They believed in Allah, the One, the Everliving, Who does not die. The Book of Isaiah reads:

> They shall be turned back, they shall be greatly ashamed, who trust in carved images, who say to the modeled images, "You are our gods."[1]

6. The sixth paragraph shows that this prophet would be a man of war. The Scriptures tell us that man of war is a description that belongs to God. Such a belief is attributed to Moses when he said, "The Lord is a man of war; the Lord is His name."[2]

War is not an easy task. For the soldier it means a lot of physical and mental hardship. Yet this is the real sacrifice, as one Arab poet said, sacrificing oneself is the pinnacle of sacrifice.

After all, the one who is relaxing and reposing in total comfort and then censures those who struggle for the truth, how much is he worth? What positive proof does he have to substantiate that he practices his belief? Moses was a man of war. He prepared his forces to fight and led the Israelites in battles where they achieved victory at times and were defeated at times. This is not a defect at all; it is one of the characteristics of the determined messengers.

Isaiah describes this new prophet as a man of war, daring, courageous and one who defeats his enemies. This passage reads:

> The LORD shall go forth like a mighty man; He shall stir up His zeal like a man of war. He shall cry out, yes, shout aloud; He shall prevail against His enemies.[3]

These were some of the characteristics of Muhammad, the son Abdullah.

7. What about the religion of this prophet?

This paragraph indicates that his religion would be declared loudly from the mountain tops. This would be achieved by prais-

---

[1] Isaiah 42:17.
[2] Exodus 15:3.
[3] Isaiah 42:13.

ing and glorifying the Lord publicly and by convening an annual global conference. It is only in Islam that such an event takes place. All types of pilgrims—leaders and their people from many places and of many ages—assemble annually for the pilgrimage. They do not gather in palaces but on the tops of mountains. The Book of Isaiah says:

> Let them shout from the top of the mountains. Let them Glory to the LORD, and declare His praise in the coastlands.[1]

The pilgrimage is one of the major pillars of Islam.

8. This paragraph indicates that the people which the new prophet would come to would be very weak. They would be easy prey for any outside power. The condition of the Arabs in Arabia before Islam was well known. While its northwestern borders were usurped by the Romans, its northeastern borders were usurped by the Persians. Let us now read the Scripture and see how it describes this community. It says:

> ...this is a people robbed and plundered; all of them are snared in holes, and they are hidden in prison houses; they are for prey, and no one delivers; for plunder, and no one says, "Restore!"[2]

9. However, once this prophet came to them, and the religion spread among them, the blind began to see, the sick became well. Soon thereafter, they spread all over the world, until most of the world came under their sway. This paragraph says that the new prophet was sent

> ...to open blind eyes, to bring out prisoners from prison, those who sit in darkness from the prison house[3]...I will bring the blind by a way they did not know; I will lead them in paths they have not known. I will make darkness light before them, and crooked places straight. These things I will do for them, and not forsake them.[4]

---

[1]Isaiah 42:11-12.
[2]Isaiah 42:22.
[3]Isaiah 42:7.
[4]Isaiah 42:16.

Who would dare say, when looking at a map of the seventh century world, that from this desert, a people would rise and spread all over the world and rule most of it? Anthony Fanting, a former British minister, declared:

> What happened in the history of Islam has no parallel in world history. The average of the area gained daily by Muslims was 250 square kilometers over a period of seventy years. The lightening speed with which Islam spread belittled any previous conquests known to man. Realistically, it even surpasses the achievements of any modern, organized and well-equipped army in the world today.

10. Finally, the Book of Isaiah ends by answering that this prophet would be a prophet of righteousness, who would respect and honor the Law of God. Of course, this is exactly what is known of Prophet Muhammad's compassionate attitude towards all human beings, the needy, women, orphans, children, widows, even animals. He respected human beings no matter who they were.

Let me remind you of a story. Once, when the funeral of a Jew passed by the Prophet, he stood up in respect for the funeral. His companions said, "Messenger of Allah, this is a Jew's funeral." He replied: "Wasn't he a human being?" The Prophet's companions thought it was too much that the Prophet should stand in respect for a dead Jew, due to the torment and intense pain and hardship that the Prophet and his companions had suffered at the hands of Jews. But the Prophet elevated them to a higher set of morals. He once said, "I have been sent to perfect noble manners."

As a Muslim, I believe in Jesus completely, according to the Qur'anic teachings. I believe that he was, according to what the Bible also says, Allah's prophet and messenger, and a pious servant of Allah—and nothing more. But the people who wrote the Gospels incorporated so many errors in them that even Christian scholars themselves dishonor Jesus because of these errors.

Professor Wales of London University says in his book, *The Jesus of the Original Christians*:

> Jesus called for ideal love, saying: Do not resist evil, but whoever slaps you on your right cheek, turn and give him

the other one also. Love your enemies. Bless whoever curses you. Do good to those who detest you. Pray for those who are mean to you and drive you away. Whoever calls his brother a slave deserves a trial of the council. Whoever calls his brother stupid deserves the Hellfire...

But in spite of such teachings, Jesus didn't leave any opportunity to attack his opponents or Jewish enemies, and to heap curses upon them. After all, wasn't he the one who said: "Woe to you, scribes and Pharisees, hypocrites!"[1] "...You serpents, you generation of vipers, how can you escape the damnation of hell!"[2]

But what is known of Prophet Muhammad is that he was a prophet of righteousness and forgiveness, especially when he was capable of revenge. When he entered Makkah triumphantly among ten thousand fighters, the people of Quraysh expected that he would punish and kill them, but he forgave them. He asked them, "What do you think I should do with you?" They answered: "We think you'll do good. You are a noble brother and the son of a noble brother." He said, "Go, you are free."

Let us compare this honorable stand at the time of Prophet Muhammad with what happened at the time of Moses and according to his law, which Jesus upheld. According to the Bible, the Law of Moses mandated the execution of all people defeated in war and the burning of their houses, even if occupied by women and children. Even the animals had to be destroyed. Life was forbidden for all of them (i.e., the people defeated). The Bible says:

> When you go near a city to fight against it, then proclaim an offer of peace to it. And it shall be if they accept your offer of peace, and open to you, then all the people who are found in it shall be placed under tribute to you, and serve you. Now if the city will not make peace with you, but makes war against you, then you shall besiege it. And when the LORD your God delivers it into your hands, you shall strike every male in it with the edge of sword. But the women, the little

---

[1] Matthew 23:14.
[2] Matthew 23:33.

ones, the livestock, and all that is in the city, all its spoils, you shall plunder for yourself; and you shall eat the enemies' plunder which the LORD your God gives you.

Thus you shall do to all the cities which are very far from you, which are not of the cities of these nations. But of the cities of these peoples which the LORD your God gives you as an inheritance, you shall let nothing that breathes remain alive, but you shall utterly destroy them: the Hittite and the Amorite and the Canaanite and the Perizzite and the Hivite and the Jebusite, just as the LORD your God has commanded you.[1]

Now if someone claims that these prophecies were about some other prophet than Muhammad (may Allah's peace and blessings be upon him), why not let the Bible decide this issue? Many prophets came to the Israelites after Isaiah and until the time of Jesus. The Gospel of Matthew tried to apply these prophecies to Jesus, as we saw before (in Chapter 12 of his Gospel).

As Muslims, we respond to such claims as follows: we are ready to submit that this prophecy refers specifically to Jesus on one condition, namely, you must accept the entire prophecy and not small parts of it from here and there. The very first sentence of this prophecy states: "Behold My Servant whom I uphold, My Elect One in whom My soul delights! I have put My Spirit upon Him; He will bring forth justice to the Gentiles."[2]

If you really believe that Jesus is the slave and messenger of Allah and that Allah supported him by the Spirit, we as Muslims agree with you. As such, Muslims and Christians agree that Jesus "was no more than a messenger: many were the messengers that passed before him."[3] Moreover, the fierce debate among Christian sects themselves will come to an end.

Realistically, we must state that the rest of Isaiah's prophecy (in chapter 42) cannot possibly be applied to Jesus. The Jewish people at the time of Jesus were not idol worshippers. Jesus was

---

[1] Deuteronomy 20:10-17.
[2] Isaiah 42:1.
[3] Qur'an 5:75.

Mr. Ibrahim Khalil Ahmad

Jesus' Prophecies

The Helper

What I should really focus on, besides the prophecies of the Old Testament, is what Jesus himself said. For example, he once prayed:

> And I will pray the Father, and He will give you another Helper, that He may abide with you forever—the Spirit of truth, whom the world cannot receive, because it neither sees Him nor Knows Him: but you know Him, for He dwells with you and will be in you.[1]

When we refer to the Old Testament we find that Allah is the God of Abraham, Isaac and Jacob. What is the name of God there? It is Jehovah. They pictured their god as a bloody god who appeared in natural phenomena such as thunderstorms, lightning and fires, a god that fights, destroys, and demolishes by fire. This was God as the Israelites knew Him until Jesus appeared. Jesus wanted to mitigate those attributes which they had assigned to Allah, Most Glorified, Most Exalted. The Jews were more materially oriented. They had not elevated themselves spiritually. Accordingly, Jesus wanted to address the All-Compassionate, All-Merciful Allah, in front of them by saying: "Say, our Father who is in Heaven." He symbolized God as Father, because the father is full of sympathy, pity and care for his dependents. Jesus once advised:

---

[1] John 14:16-17.

"These things I have spoken to you while being present with you. But the Helper, the Holy Spirit, whom the Father will send in My name, He will teach you all things, and bring to your remembrance all things that I said to you.

"But when the Helper comes, whom I shall send to you from the Father, the Spirit of truth who proceeds from the Father, He will testify of Me, and you also will bear witness, because you have been with Me from the beginning."[1]

On another occasion, Jesus said:

"Nevertheless I tell you the truth. It is to your advantage that I go away; for if I do not go away, the Helper will not come to you; but if I depart, I will send Him to you.

"And when He has come, He will convict the world of sin, and of righteousness, and of judgment: of sin, because they do not believe in Me; of righteousness, because I go to My father and you see Me no more; of judgment, because the ruler of this world is judged."[2]

Lastly, Jesus says:

"I still have many things to say to you, but you cannot bear *them* now. However, when He, the Spirit of truth, has come, He will guide you into all truth; for He will not speak on His authority, but whatever He hears He will speak; And He will tell you things to come. He will glorify Me, for He will take of what is Mine and declare *it* to you."[3]

The Spirit of Truth

All the preceding passages came from the Gospel of John. Let us now examine the last text, i.e., John 16:12-14. First, we can see that the disciples were not at the desired level to shoulder the responsibility of the mission. Jesus says, "I still have many things to say to you, but you cannot bear them now." In addition, the disciples would divide and scatter. Jesus says, "In-

---

[1] John 15:25-27.
[2] John 16:7-11.
[3] John 16:12-14.

deed the hour is coming, yes, has now come, that you will be scattered, each to his own, and will leave Me alone."[1]

This passage shows us that the prophet who will come after Jesus is described as the Spirit of Truth. His responsibility is to guide them, the Christians, to the whole Truth.

From the above passage, it appears as if Jesus were pointing the finger at Orientalists, who completely deny the biblical prophecy about Prophet Muhammad. About him, Jesus says that "...He will not speak on His authority, but whatever He hears He will speak; And He will tell you things to come." This is exactly what happened when Prophet Muhammad used to receive the revelation from Allah. It was through the Holy Spirit, the angel Gabriel. Commenting on the Prophet, the Qur'an states: "Nor does he say (aught) of (his own) desire. It is no less than inspiration sent down to him. He was taught by one mighty in power,"[2]—i.e., Gabriel.

As for his words: "and he will tell you things to come", they point to the greatness of Islam and the sublimity of its origin, i.e., Allah. If we were to go through the first two chapters of Genesis, then compare that with what the Qur'an tells us in terms of its wondrous knowledge which couldn't possibly have been known to the Prophet (may Allah's peace and blessings be upon him), being unlettered and living in an unlettered environment of the seventh century, and which even the scholars and wise men of the advanced nations of that time couldn't have possibly known, we can then have at least a little appreciation for how sublime the Qur'an really is. Let us read what the Qur'an says about the creation of the person in his mother's womb and the different stages he passes through. Allah says:

> Man We did create from a quintessence (of clay); then We placed him as (a drop of) sperm in a place of rest, firmly fixed; then We made the sperm into a clot of congealed blood; then of that clot we made a (fetus) lump; then we made out of that lump bones and clothed the bones with

---

[1] John 16:32.
[2] Qur'an 53:3-5.

flesh; then we developed out of it another creature. So blessed be Allah, the best to create![1]

These stages which the human being goes through in his mother's womb have been confirmed by modern science. Surely, this is just another one of the countless signs proving the truthfulness of the Prophet. We find in John's Gospel the following verse in the words of Jesus:

> "...But when the Helper comes, whom I shall send to you from the Father, the Spirit of truth who proceeds from the Father, He will testify to Me, and you also will bear witness, because you have been with Me from the beginning."[2]

By the grace of Allah, I studied Greek so I could learn the truth about the New Testament. Likewise, I studied Hebrew so I could learn more about the Old Testament. In the Greek version of the Bible we find the word "parakletos" (παρακλητος), which was translated as "helper" in some of the English editions of the Bible.[3] The word "parakletos" has four meanings: the Comforter (Mu'azzi), the Praised One (Muhammad), the Praiseworthy One (Mahmud) and the Effacer (Mahi).[4]

Those translators of the Gospels used the word "helper", mistranslating the meaning of "parakletos". Why? They were deliberately being deceitful. "Yet Allah, too, plans, and the best planner is Allah."[5] It actually means 'comforter' or 'consoler'. Accordingly, what Jesus meant was that the one who came after him would be a comforter or consoler to the small group of believers. He would comfort them, affirming the original belief in one God, at a time when this original creed was all but lost to myriad other misguided conceptions of God. Later, when I talk about the councils, we will know exactly how this issue came about.

The "Comforter" who came after Jesus came to comfort the people of *tawhid* who say, "There is none worthy of worship but Allah." One of them was Arius.

---

[1] Qur'an 23:12-14.
[2] John 15:26.
[3] Some English versions use the word "comforter".
[4] These Arabic words are the meanings of parakletos.
[5] Qur'an 8:30.

Muslim-Christian Dialogue

If the writers of the Gospels had used, instead of "helper", the expression "the Praised one" (Muhammad), it would have been irrefutable proof of the prophethood of Muhammad. Even if they had used the word "Effacer" (Al-Mahi), it would be a clear acknowledgment of the prophethood of Muhammad. Why? Because the Prophet said:

> I have five names: I am Muhammad; I am Ahmad; I am Al-Mahi (the effacer), by whom Allah effaces *kufr*; I am Al-Hashir (the gatherer), before whom people are gathered; I am Al-'Aqib (the last).[1]

The Qur'an affirms the above, saying:

> Those who follow the Messenger, the unlettered Prophet, whom they find mentioned in their own (scriptures), in the Law and the Gospel; for he commands them what is just and forbids them what is evil; he allows them as lawful what is good (and pure) and prohibits them from what is bad (and impure).[2]

While conducting missionary work among Muslims, and before being guided by Allah to Islam, I tell you honestly that I was courting and approaching Muslims by saying to them that the Qur'an states that the Christians are people of love, mercy and caring. It says:

> Strongest among men in enmity to the Believers will you find the Jews and Pagans; and nearest among them in love to the Believers will you find those who say, "We are Christians": because among these are men devoted to learning and men who have renounced the world, and they are not arrogant.[3]

Any astute Muslim would automatically say: How can you talk like this and still be a Christian? It seems as if you are playing with words. Do you truly believe in the Qur'an? The Qur'an says, "And nearest among them in love to the Believers will you find those who say, 'We are Christians,'"[4] but it also says,

---

[1] Narrated by Al-Bukhari, *Book of the Virtues and Merits of the Prophet and his Companions.*
[2] Qur'an 7:157.
[3] Qur'an 5:82.
[4] Qur'an 5:82.

"They do blaspheme who say, 'Allah is Christ the son of Mary.'"[1]

Finally, there is something very important in this verse [5:82]. Most Muslims may not pay much attention to it. The Qur'an talks about a relationship of love, not of creed. There is a big difference between the former and the latter.

The Ecumenical Councils

A quick look through the history of Christianity during the first few centuries clearly shows that Christendom was between a rock and a hard place, i.e., between Jewish persecution on the one hand and pagan Roman oppression on the other. In 325 C.E., Constantinople was the capital of the eastern Roman state, where most of Emperor Constantine's citizens were Christians. Most of the pagans of Rome were in the West. In order to strengthen his position, the emperor brought the Christians nearer to himself. But when he saw that the Christians themselves were so divided on the position of Jesus, he invited them to a council to bring these religious differences to an end. This step, he thought, would lend stability to his empire.

For that reason, the Council of Nicaea was convened in 325 C.E. It was attended by 2,048 archbishops who came from every corner of the world for only one reason: to establish who was Jesus.

Heisting, author of *The History of the Church*, says that the participants debated in the meeting. One of them was Arius, a scholar. He said that Jesus was a prophet of Allah and a messenger, a human being and a servant of Allah. Following Arius were 1,731 archbishops. However, Athenasius, a deacon in the church of Alexandria, took advantage of the opportunity to draw closer to the pagan Constantine and quickly declared that Jesus was God in human form. Only 317 of the 2,048 attendees endorsed Athenasius. After reviewing all the opinions, Constantine, still a pagan, ratified Athenasius' view. This endorsement was not

---

[1] Qur'an 5:17, 72.

really surprising, for Athenasius' view accommodated the pagan creeds which promoted belief in humanoid gods and their descending from the heavens. Thus the pagan emperor embraced Athenasius' statement and turned away the rest of the unitarian archbishops along with their leader, Arius. More significantly, he banned the Holy Book and made it illegal for people to circulate it among themselves. Whoever wanted to learn religion would have to learn directly from state-approved priests.

Strangely, this evil heresy continued its sway over Christendom until the year 1516 C.E., when the Holy Bible was finally released by Martin Luther. Such was the Council of Nicaea, whose most critical decision was the deification of Jesus.

Afterword

Dr. Muhammad Jamil Ghazi

I have a few brief comments concerning the prophecies. My comments will be limited to three specific Bible passages. The first passage mentions the angels reciting "Glory to God in the highest, and on earth peace, goodwill toward men!"[1] Second, the Bible says, "And as for Ishmael, I have heard you. Behold! I have blessed him, and will make him fruitful, and will multiply him exceedingly. He shall beget twelve princes, and I will make him a great nation."[2] Finally, in the Gospel of Matthew we read: "For all the prophets and the law prophesied until John. And if you are willing to receive *it*, he is Elijah who is to come."[3]

In reviewing the first passage, let us quote a comment made by 'Abdul-Ahad Dawud, who was formerly the archbishop of Mosul and who later embraced Islam. He presented linguistic research which concluded that the birth of Jesus was really a prophecy—a prophecy of the birth of Muhammad. He proved his contention by using the Gospel of Luke. The Gospel of Luke

---

[1] Luke 2:14.
[2] Genesis 17:20.
[3] Matthew 11:13-14.

narrates that when Jesus was born, Syrian shepherds saw angels coming from the heavens singing, "Glory to God in the highest, and on earth peace, goodwill toward men!"

This is the text present in the currently circulated Arabic version of the Bible; but the text in the edition translated by the Bible Society is: "Praise be to God in the highest, safety be on earth and satisfaction be for people."

Mr. 'Abdul-Ahad says that those angels did not speak Arabic. If they had done so, the Syrians would not have understood. Moreover, they did not speak any language other than their own. Naturally, the shepherds wouldn't be familiar with any other language anyway, due to their lack of knowledge. If the hymn had been in Syriac, the language of the shepherds, then what would have been the original words of that hymn in Syriac? What was the real translation of the words, especially the two words, 'peace' or 'safety', and 'good will' or 'satisfaction'?

Before giving an answer to these questions, Mr. 'Abdul-Ahad assures us that the translations of the two words, peace or safety, and good will or satisfaction, were absolutely wrong.

He asks: What is the meaning of "peace or safety be on earth?" What type of peace has the earth witnessed since its creation? One of Adam's children spoiled it by killing his brother at the dawn of humanity? Thereafter, the descendants of Adam have kept on killing one another without pause till this day. It became normal for mankind to live a life of the almost continuous disasters, disputes and wars which human nature is disposed to.

What was said about this sentence could be repeated for the other one: "Good will be for people, or satisfaction be for people." Where is the good will that people should enjoy compared with the tears, the sweat, the struggle and the pain that mankind suffers? Where is the satisfaction shown by people when greed seems to be unlimited?

What further confirms that this translation is false is that Tolstoy, the famous Russian thinker, summarized the four Gospels into one gospel. He connected the useful verses—as he thought—together. He did not include that verse in his book, saying it was not one of the known, useful verses and was nothing more than nonsense.

After that Mr. Abdul-Ahad analyzed the original two Syriac words. The original words are *irni* and *ayadokya*. He explains in a lengthy linguistic dissertation that *irni* means Islam and *ayadokya* means Ahmad.

Thus, according to him, the general meaning becomes "Praise to God in the highest (heaven), Islam is about to come to earth and will be introduced by Ahmad."

Once more, he reassures us that if the intended meaning of peace was safety or security, the opposite of war, the Syriac word should have been *shaam*, or *shalom* in Hebrew.

Regarding the other two texts, we are going to run a simple calculation related to what is known as the "arithmetic of sentences." This was a type of arithmetic known to the Israelites which they used to interpret their predictions. The following table gives the Arabic letter along with its numeric equivalent.

alif	ba'	jim	dal	ha'	waw	zay	ha'	ta'	ya'
1	2	3	4	5	6	7	8	9	10

kaf	lam	mim	nun	sin	'ayn	fa'	sad	qaf	ra'
20	30	40	50	60	70	80	90	100	200

shin	ta'	tha'	kha'	dhal	dhad	dha'	ghayn
300	400	500	600	700	800	900	1000

Let us now go back to the second passage cited above. It says: "And as for Ishmael, I have heard you. Behold! I have blessed him, and will make him fruitful, and will multiply him exceedingly. He shall beget twelve princes, and I will make him a great nation."[1]

The equivalent for the word "exceedingly" or "very much" in Hebrew is *bim'od m'od*. Also the two words "great nation" give in Hebrew *l'goy gadol*.

---

[1] Genesis 17:20.

Using the arithmetic of sentences method, we can calculate the value of the first two words. The calculations are shown below:

```
B    M    '     D          M    '    D
b'   mim  alif  dal        mim  alif dal
2    40   1     4      +   40   1    4   = 92
```

Similarly, when we calculate the number value of the second Hebrew phrase, *l'goy gadol*, we come to the following result:

```
L    G    W    Y    G    D    W    L
Lam  jim  waw  ya'  jim  dal  waw  lam
30   3    6    10   3    4    6    30  = 92
```

Now, if we calculate the number value of the word "Muhammad" which has in Arabic four letters (m-h-m-d) we come to the same total:

```
M    H   M    D
40   8   40   4   =   92
```

Hence, according to the calculations of the Israelite scholars in examining their prophecies, "the blessing of Ishmael which Allah promised Abraham will come through the presence of Prophet Muhammad (may Allah's peace and blessings be upon him)."

Let us now study the third passage, which was narrated in the Gospel of Matthew: "For all the prophets and the law prophesied until John. And if you are willing to receive *it*, he is Elijah who is to come."[1] When calculating the number value of the word "Elijah", which is in Arabic "Ilya'", and having the following six letters and corresponding numbers, we come to the following total:

---

[1] Matthew 11:13-14.

Alif	ya'	lam	ya'	alif	'[1]	
1	10	30	10	1	1	= 53

Then, when calculating the number value of the name Ahmad, we come to the same result:

Alif	ha'	mim	dal	
1	8	40	4	= 53

Once again, this means that the prophet whom Jesus said would come after him, according to the passage "who is to come,"[2] is Ahmad. And Ahmad is one of the famous names of Prophet Muhammad (may Allah's peace and blessings be upon him).

The Qur'an confirms the above saying:

> And remember, Jesus, the son of Mary, said: "Children of Israel! I am the messenger of Allah (sent) to you, confirming the Law (which came) before me, and giving Glad Tidings of a Messenger to come after me, whose name shall be Ahmad." But when he came to them with Clear Signs, they said, "This is evident sorcery!"

I will conclude here, and leave you with Professor Ibrahim Khalil Ahmad.

Professor Ibrahim Khalil Ahmad

Let us consider the Qur'anic verse where Allah says, "They do blaspheme who say: Allah is one of three in a Trinity: for there is no god except one God."[3]

---

[1] *Hamza* (') is given the same value as *alif*—one. (This is valid, as *hamza* and *alif* are one letter in Hebrew. (ed.)
[2] Matthew 11:14.
[3] Qur'an 5:73.

Muslim-Christian Dialogue

Divisions Within The Church

The Council of Constantinople

Around 381 C.E., Macedonius began to say that the Holy Spirit was not a god but was a messenger of God. This statement was readily accepted by the Christians living in the Roman empire, as they found nothing heretical or distasteful about this. However, some malicious people suggested to the emperor to call another council. As planned, this council was convened in 381 C.E. Only 150 archbishops attended. In comparison with the Council of Nicaea in 325 C.E., when 2,084 archbishops had attended, the number of attendees at the Council of Constantinople was very small. What was decided at the Council was that the Holy Spirit is a god from the same essence of God. The Qur'an warns:

> People of the Book! Commit no excesses in your religion: Nor say of Allah aught but the truth. Christ Jesus the son of Mary was (no more than) a messenger of Allah, and His Word, which He bestowed on Mary, and a Spirit proceeding from Him: so believe in Allah and His Messengers. Say not "Trinity": desist: it will be better for you: for Allah is one God: Glory be to Him: (far exalted is He) above having a son. To Him belong all things in the heavens and on earth. And enough is Allah as a Disposer of affairs.[1]

In reality, the concept of trinity is nothing more than a philosophy that appeared in Alexandria before the coming of Jesus. It was Platonic philosophy which claimed that three powers govern the whole world: the Intellect, the Logos, and the Spirit. Out of this philosophy came the addition in the Gospel of Matthew. He states: "Go therefore and make disciples of all the nations, baptizing them in the name of the Father and of the Son and of the Holy Spirit."[2]

---

[1] Qur'an 4:171.
[2] Matthew 28:19.

In a footnote on the same page we find it saying that this sentence did not exist in the original Greek manuscript. What confirms that the addition was added afterwards is the statement of Jesus to his disciples. The Gospel of Matthew relates:

> These twelve Jesus sent out and commanded them, saying: "Do not go into the way of the Gentiles, and do not enter a city of the Samaritans. But go rather to the lost sheep of the house of Israel, and as you go, preach, saying, 'The kingdom of heaven is at hand.'"[1]

Jesus restricted the mission of his disciples to "the house of Israel", i.e., Israelites. He himself limited his mission to the Israelites, saying, "I was not sent except to the lost sheep of the house of Israel."[2]

If we use our intellect to discuss the problem of the Trinity, we must say that if it is as they claim, that God has three real constituent parts in Himself, then the logical conclusion is that God is a compound entity. Every component needs something other than itself to stay together. That means God is in need, which is, of course, ludicrous. If the connection between God's divine nature and His human nature is real, as they claim, then the essence of the son is limited. And anything which can be increased or decreased is created. And a creation cannot be a god, because Allah is Eternal and not created. The Quran states that Allah's statements are nothing but the truth:

> If there were in the heavens and the earth, other gods besides Allah, there would have been confusion in both! But glory to Allah, The Lord of the Throne: (High is He) above what they attribute to Him![3]

The Deification of Mary

Let us now discuss another problem that has entered into Church thought. The problem concerns the deification of the Virgin Mary. An archbishop known as Nestorius, patriarch of

---

[1]Matthew 10:5-7.
[2]Matthew 15:24.
[3]Qur'an 21:22.

Constantinople, declared that the Virgin Mary was the mother of a human being, Jesus Christ; it was impossible for her to be the mother of God. Christ himself was not a god, but a human being inspired by Allah. This creed prevailed until a council was held in Ephesus. It was attended by two hundred archbishops, who decided that Mary was God's mother.

In this regard the Qur'an says:

> And behold! Allah will say: "Jesus son of Mary! Did you say unto men, 'Worship me and my mother as gods in derogation of Allah'?" He will say: "Glory to You! Never could I say what I had no right (to say). Had I said such a thing, you would indeed have known it. You know what is in my heart, though I know not what is in Yours, for You know in full all that is hidden. Never said I to them aught except what You did command me to say, to wit, 'Worship God, my Lord and your Lord.'"[1]

Will Durant, in his book, *The Story of Civilization*, says:

> When Christianity conquered Rome the ecclesiastical structure of the pagan church, the title and vestments of the *pontifex maximus*, the worship of the Great Mother and a multitude of comforting divinities, the sense of supersensible presence everywhere, the joy or solemnity of old festivals, and the pageantry of immemorial ceremony, passed like maternal blood into the new religion, and captive Rome captured her conqueror. The reins and skills of government were handed down by a dying empire to a virile papacy; the lost power of the broken sword was rewon by the magic of the consoling word; the armies of the state were replaced by the missionaries of the church moving in all directions along the Roman roads; and the revolted provinces, accepting Christianity, again acknowledged the sovereignty of Rome.[2]
>
> Christianity did not destroy paganism, it adopted it. The Greek mind, dying, came to a transmigrated life in the theology and liturgy of the Church; the Greek language, having reigned for centuries over philosophy, became the vehicle of

---

[1] Qur'an 5:116.
[2] The Story of Civilization, "Epilogue," p. 671f.

Christian literature and ritual; the Greek mysteries passed down into the impressive mystery of the Mass. Other pagan cultures contributed to the syncretist result. From Egypt came the ideas of a divine Trinity, the Last Judgment, and a personal immortality of reward and punishment; from Egypt the adoration of the Mother and Child, and the mystic theosophy that made Neoplatonism and Gnosticism, and obscured the Christian creed; there, too, Christian monasticism would find its exemplars and its source. From Phrygia came the worship of the Great Mother; from Syria the resurrection drama of Adonis; from Thrace, perhaps, the cult of Dionysus, the dying and saving god. From Persia came millennarianism, the "ages of the world," the "final conflagration," the dualism of Satan and God, of Darkness and Light; already in the fourth Gospel Christ is the "Light shining in the darkness, and the darkness has never put it out." The Mithraic ritual so closely resembled the eucharistic sacrifice of the Mass that Christian fathers charged the Devil with inventing these similarities to mislead frail minds. Christianity was the last great creation of the ancient pagan world.[1]

The Glorious Qur'an says: "Say: People of the Book! Exceed not in your religion the bounds (of what is proper), trespassing beyond the truth, nor follow the vain desires of people who went wrong in times gone by—who misled many, and strayed (themselves) from the even Way."[2]

The Glorious Qur'an tells us what happened within the Church; i.e., the dissolution of the creed, plurality of gods and the acceptance of pagan beliefs.

Birth of the Egyptian Orthodox Church

Archbishop Dioscorus, the Patriarch of Alexandria, declared that Jesus Christ is of one nature, wherein the divine and the human element combine together. Therefore, he continued, Jesus is from God's essence and he is God incarnated. This creed

---

[1]Op. cit., Chapter 27, p. 595.
[2]Qur'an 5:77.

Muslim-Christian Dialogue

became widespread and eventually led to the Council of Chalcedon in 451 C.E. This Council decided that Christ has a dual nature, where divine and human nature are distinct; however, they are inseparable.

The Council declared Dioscorus a heretic and decided to expel him from Alexandria. But the Egyptians rejected this decision and refused to replace him with anyone else. Soon after, they withdrew from the Church and established the Orthodox Egyptian Church. Admittedly, there may have been other political factors which facilitated this decision. Dioscorus had based his declaration on Paul's statement when he said, "...great is the mystery of Godliness: God was manifest in the flesh."[1]

Paul's letters were sermons that he preached in his own way. His knowledge was very scattered, as he collected the material for these sermons from here and there. In contrast to all this wrangling among the Christians and their unending debate concerning Jesus, the Glorious Qur'an states the truth. It is not biased one way or the other. People are not necessarily pleased with the truth. However, the truth does completely suit their nature and disposition. Allah, Most Exalted, says:

> ...that they rejected Faith; that they uttered against Mary a grave false charge; that they said (in boast), "We killed Christ Jesus the son of Mary, the Messenger of Allah;"—but they killed him not, nor crucified him, but so it was made to appear to them, and those who differ therein are full of doubts, with no (certain) knowledge, but only conjecture to follow, for of a surety they killed him not:—Nay, Allah raised him up unto Himself; and Allah is Exalted in Power, Wise.[2]

Allah Forgives Sins

Brothers and sisters, we have talked much about the Cross. We have also said that according to the Bible, Jesus Christ (may Allah's peace and blessings be upon him) had the authority to

---

[1] I Timothy 3:16.
[2] Qur'an 4:156-158.

forgive. Prophet David (may Allah's peace and blessings be upon him) used to say, whenever he made a mistake, "As You have the forgiveness, so You must be feared." Forgiveness comes from Allah, Most Glorified, Most Exalted. The Qur'an categorically rejects the crucifixion of Jesus Christ. Moreover, the dubious relationship between the Crucifixion and the forgiveness of human sins is no more than superstition and fairy tales. The Qur'an, on the other hand, encourages people to turn to Allah for the remission of sins:

> Say: My servants who have transgressed against their souls! Despair not of the Mercy of Allah: for Allah forgives all sins for He is Oft-forgiving, Most Merciful.[1]

After all, Allah is our Creator. He is our Provider. He is the One Who forgives our sins. Allah, Most Exalted, is very close to all of us. He reminds us that

> When My servants ask you concerning Me, I am indeed close (to them): I listen to the prayer of every supplicant when he calls on Me. Let them also, with a will, listen to My call, and believe in Me, that they may walk in the right way.[2]

Allah addresses all mankind in the Qur'an by saying: "It was We Who created man, and We know what dark suggestions his soul makes to him: for We are nearer to him than (his) jugular vein."[3]

If Allah is closer to a person than he/she is to himself, then why should we have an intermediary between us. Why must we wait for someone other than Allah to forgive our sins?

Birth of the Maronite Church

In 680 C.E., the Council of Constantinople convened in response to what Archbishop John Maron claimed in 667 C.E. He preached a new concept, namely that Jesus Christ has a dual nature, the divine and the human in one person, but he has one will, which is the will of God. Not being very enthusiastic about

---

[1] Qur'an 39:53.
[2] Qur'an 2:186.
[3] Qur'an 50:16.

this view, the patriarchs called the Council of Constantinople in 680 C.E. Two hundred eighty-nine archbishops participated and decided that Jesus Christ has a dual nature and a dual will. The Syrians rejected the resolution of the Council and followed their archbishop. Later, they split off from the Mother Church.

What I want to say is that every new council rejected the decision of the previous council and issued new decisions. Strangely, each council would then claim that its resolutions were inspired by the Holy Spirit!

Sanctification of Images

Let us now move to the Council of Nice, which was held in 787 C.E. Three hundred seventy-seven archbishops attended. They decided to sanctify the images of Jesus Christ, his mother the Virgin Mary, and all other saints. Of course, this decision was in direct conflict with the Law of Moses, which stated as part of the Ten Commandments, that "you shall not make for yourself a graven image, any likeness of anything that is in heaven above, or that is in the earth beneath, or that is in the water under the earth; you shall not bow down to them nor serve them."

Birth of the Roman (Greek) Orthodox Church

Then came the Council of Constantinople of 879 C.E. It decided that the Holy Spirit emanated from God, the Father. Moreover, this Council rejected the decisions taken by the previous Council of Constantinople of 869 C.E., which had stated that the Holy Spirit came from both the Father and the Son. As a result of this new resolution, the Church of Constantinople split from the Mother Church. The Greek Church called itself the Roman Orthodox Church. It doesn't follow the Pope of Rome.

The Pope and the Right of Forgiveness

Thereafter, in a meeting of the council of archbishops, it was decided that the Pope of Rome would be vested with the authority to forgive. Then, as time passed, the Church abused the power to grant forgiveness. They carried it too far, so much so that they established documents called "certificates of forgiveness".[1] The text of these certificates generally stated that "I, by the prophetic authority vested in me, forgive you of all requitals, excessive acts, evil intentions, any sins you committed, no matter how great or severe they were, and all shortcomings and weaknesses. And I return you back to purity and righteousness. Your baptism shall last for many years. If you live many years after that, this blessing will stay with you unchanged till your last hour."

Amazingly, these certificates of forgiveness were bought and sold for a price. This is the way that the Pope and his men exercised their authority to forgive human sins.

Paul and His Bodily Sins

In his Epistle to the Romans, Paul says:

> For we know that the law is spiritual, but I am carnal, sold under sin. For what I am doing, I do not understand. For what I will to do, that I do not practice, but what I hate that I do. If, then, I do what I will not to do, I agree with the law that it is good. But now, it is no longer I who do it, but sin that dwells in me. For I know that in me (that is, in my flesh) nothing good dwells; for to will is present with me, but how to perform what is good I do not find. For the good that I will to do, I do not do; but the evil I will not to do, that I practice. Now if I do what I will not to do, it is no longer I who do it, but sin that dwells in me. I find then a law, that evil is present with me, the one who wills to do good. For I delight in the law of God according to the inward man. But I see another law in my members, warring against the law of

---

[1]These are better known in the West as "indulgences" (ed.).

my mind, and bringing me into captivity to the law of sin which is in my members. O wretched man that I am! Who will deliver me from this body of death? I thank God—through Jesus Christ our Lord! So then, with the mind I myself serve the law of God, but with the flesh the law of sin.[1]

Here Paul admits his human sins and explains how the idea of the Crucifixion did not really fight off the human tendency to commit sins.

The Appearance of Martin Luther

The next major event occurred in 1521 C.E., when Martin Luther appeared. He openly criticized the certificates of forgiveness. He denied the sinlessness of the popes and declared that the Pope's words were not sacrosanct. He exposed the corruption prevailing in the monasteries. Most importantly, he declared that Allah is One, and only One. In response to Luther, the Council of Worms convened in 1521 C.E. The Pope attended the meeting and ordered that Luther be burned at the stake. However, some German youths kidnapped him at the last moment and saved him. Later, they also decided to split from the papal Church and established the Protestant Church. Severe confrontations took place between the Catholic and the Protestant churches. The main thing that saved the Protestants from Catholic oppression was the discovery of America, where the Protestants migrated in huge numbers.

The popes have openly disobeyed Jesus. For example, when he selected his disciples he advised them saying:

> "Provide neither gold, nor silver, nor brass in your purses,
> nor scrip for your journey, neither two coats, neither shoes,
> nor yet staves; for the workman is worthy of his meat."[2]

But the popes have led rich and luxurious lives bedecked with gold and wealth. This lifestyle was certainly not reflective of Jesus' commandments.

---

[1] Romans 7:14-25.
[2] Matthew 10:9-10.

Amid all this confusion and chaos, Islam came to show the truth and to address the People of the Book[1] in a kind and gentle way. Allah says:

> People of the Book! There have come to you Our Messenger, revealing to you much that you used to hide in the Book, and passing over much (that is now unnecessary): There has come to you from Allah a (new) light and a perspicuous Book, wherewith Allah guides all who seek His good pleasure to ways of peace and safety, and leads them out of darkness, by His will, unto the light—guides them to a path that is straight.[2]

Dearly beloved, these were the principal issues which I was able to come to terms with and which led me to embrace Islam. I thank Allah for that. In spite of the hardship that I faced, I did not give up, because I reached a level of certainty by the grace of Allah. On December 25, 1959 C.E., I cabled the American Missionary Office in Egypt telling them that I believed in one God and in His Prophet and Messenger, Muhammad (may Allah's peace and blessings be upon him). As for the issue of the deification of Jesus Christ, the Gospels to this very day confirm that he called people to *tawhid*, i.e., the absolute Oneness of God in His Lordship and Sovereignty, his Names and Attributes, and His worship. The Bible says in Jesus' words, "And this is eternal life, that they may know You, the only true God, and Jesus Christ whom You have sent."[3]

Finally, I pray to Allah:

> Our Lord! Let not our hearts deviate now after You have guided us, but grant us mercy from Your own Presence for you are the Grantor of bounties without measure. Our Lord! You are He that will gather mankind together against a Day about which there is no doubt; for Allah never fails in His promise.[4]

May Allah's peace, mercy and blessing be upon you.

---

[1] Jews and Christians.
[2] Qur'an 5:15-16.
[3] John 17:3.
[4] Qur'an 3:89.

THE SIXTH SESSION

Dr. Muhammad Jamil Ghazi

In the name of Allah, Most Gracious, Most Merciful. Praise be to Allah, Lord of the Worlds. May His peace and blessings be upon His final Prophet and Messenger, his family, and his pious and righteous Companions, and all those who righteously follow in their footsteps till the Day of Judgment. Let me start, my dear brothers and sisters, with the following Qur'anic verses. Our Lord says:

Truly did Allah fulfill the vision for His Messenger: you shall enter the Sacred Mosque, if Allah wills, with minds secure, heads shaved, hair cut short, and without fear. For He knew what you knew not, and He granted, besides this, a speedy victory. It is He Who has sent His Messenger with Guidance and the Religion of Truth, to proclaim it over all religion: and enough is Allah for a Witness. Muhammad is the Messenger of Allah; and those who are with him are strong against Unbelievers, (but) compassionate among each other.

> You will see them bow and prostrate themselves (in prayer), seeking Grace from Allah and (His) Good Pleasure. On their faces are their marks, (being) the traces of their prostration. This is their similitude in the Torah; and their similitude in the Gospel is like a seed which sends forth its blade, then makes it strong; it then becomes thick, and it stands on its own stem, (filling) the sowers with wonder and delight. As a result, it fills the Unbelievers with rage at them. Allah has promised those among them who believe and do righteous deeds forgiveness, and a great Reward.[1]

Tonight, I will respond to your questions concerning Islam. As you can see, there are many questions concerning diverse

---

[1] Qur'an 48:29.

topics; but I will do my best, and within the time limit, to summarize them and give quick responses to them all.

After finishing our discussion on Christian issues, the time has now come to discuss Islamic issues. It seemed the more useful and logical approach to begin with the Christian part so we could have an open and objective scholarly discussion. Once we finished, we thought that we could then address the Islamic part.

Although the questions relating to Christianity were few, we responded with a comprehensive academic study on the subject. As you have seen and heard, we have spent five whole days on these queries. We did that to give the questioners and the entire audience an opportunity to know better about all topics and to discuss and study them in depth.

It was possible from the outset to answer those questions in a different way, i.e., to treat the whole subject briefly and in a short time. But we felt that that was not a useful methodology for a person who wanted to evaluate this issue in a scholarly fashion. More important, we felt that such a methodology would be more useful especially when dealing with serious issues such as the destruction or establishment of a religion. It is not possible to condemn an entire religion in one stroke of the pen. Likewise, it is just as impossible to establish an entire religion with one stroke of the pen.

Religions are not simple or superficial issues. They deal with crucial issues like history, human lives, way of life, the life of this world and the Hereafter. I cannot imagine, along with you, that it is possible for a person to change his whole religion in one sitting or to jump from one religion to another, from his current lifestyle to one that he ought to be embracing.

For this reason we, the participants in this meeting, planned to begin by reviewing some of the commonly accepted Christian beliefs. We know that there are only one or two subjects which make up its foundation; if we discuss those one or two subjects and prove their invalidity, everything else based on them will collapse and disintegrate accordingly.

Christ as a God

The first issue is the claim that Christ is a god. In more precise words, He is one of three constituents which form the one God. This is the belief according to Christian superstition.

We have discussed this subject at length. We have already explained how this idea is merely a pagan concept which came from the annals of ancient paganism which imagined that God may have one son or many children. The ancient pagan ideologies instrumental in devising this great lie—i.e., paganistic polytheism—came from the paganism of the Egyptians, the Greeks, the Romans, the Hindus and the Arabs.

To illustrate with an example of how paganism destroyed the message of Jesus—which many claim was Christianity—let us draw a comparison between Christianity and Mithraism.

Robertson[1] says that Mithraism is a religion of Persian origin. It was the predominant religion in Persia six centuries before Christ. Then it moved to Rome around 70 C.E. and spread in the Roman lands. Thereafter, it moved north till it reached Britain, where some of its monuments were found in the cities of York, Chester, and other British cities. This religion states that:

- Mithra was an intermediary between God and the people.
- Mithra was born in a cave or some secluded spot
- He was born on December 25.
- He had twelve disciples.
- He died to save humans from their sins.
- He was buried, but came back to life, rising from his grave.
- He ascended to the heavens in front of his disciples, who were praying for him and bowing.
- He was called the Redeemer and the Savior.
- He was described as the calm lamb of God.
- Every year a "Lord's Supper" was set up in his memory
- One of his rituals was baptism.
- Sunday was a day of worship and considered a holy day.

---

[1] *Christianity and Paganism*, p. 338.

Robertson says that the religion of Mithra did not disappear from Rome until its basic elements had been incorporated into Christianity, as follows:

Mithraism	Christianity
1. Mithra was an intermediary between God and the people.	Jesus Christ was an intermediary between God and the people: "Nor is there salvation in any other, for there is no other name under heaven given among men by which we must be saved"[1]
2. He was born in a secluded spot.	Jesus was born in a manger: "And she brought forth her firstborn Son, and wrapped Him in swaddling cloths, and laid Him in a manger."[2]
3. He was born on December 25.	The West celebrates Jesus' birthday on December 25.
4. He had twelve disciples.	Jesus had twelve disciples: "And when He had called His twelve disciples to Him, He gave them power over unclean spirits, to cast them out, and heal all kinds of sickness...disease."[3]
5. He died to save humanity from its sins.	Jesus died to save humanity from its sins. Paul says: "...I delivered to you first of all that which I also received: that Christ died for our sins

---

[1] Acts 4:12.
[2] Luke 2:7.
[3] Matthew 10:1.
[4] I Corinthians 15:3.

Muslim-Christian Dialogue

	according to the Scriptures."[4]
6. He was buried but he came back to life from the dead.	Jesus was buried, but rose again on the third day, according to Paul: "and that He was buried, and that He rose again the third day according to the Scriptures."[1]
7. He ascended to the heavens in front of his disciples.	Jesus ascended to the heavens while his disciples watched: "Now when He had spoken these things, while they watched, He was taken up, and a cloud received Him out of their sight."[2]
8. He was called the Redeemer and the Savior.	Paul called him the Redeemer and Savior: "Looking for the blessed hope and glorious appearing of our God and Savior, Jesus Christ."[3]
9. He was described as the lamb of God.	John the Baptist described him as the lamb of God. "The next day John saw Jesus coming toward him, and said, 'Behold! The Lamb of God who takes away the sin of the world!'"[4]
10. He set up the "Lord's Supper".	Paul came up with the "Lord's Supper". He said, "For I received from the Lord that which I also delivered to you: that the Lord Jesus on the same night in which He was betrayed took bread: and when He had given thanks, He broke it and said, 'Take, eat: this is My body which is broken for you: do this in remembrance of Me.'"[5]
11. He set up baptism.	Baptism started in a right way, as

---

[1] I Corinthians 15:4.
[2] Acts 1:3.
[3] I Corinthians 2:13.
[4] John 1:29.
[5] I Corinthians 2:23-24.

	"...[Peter] commanded them to be baptized in the name of Lord."[1] But it ended up with the Trinity: "Go therefore and make disciples of all the nations, baptizing them in the name of the Father and of the Son and of the Holy Spirit."[2]
12. He sanctified Sunday.	Sanctified Sunday: "Now after the Sabbath, as the first day of the week began to dawn."[3] This was despite the fact that the fourth commandment made Saturday the holy day. "Remember the Sabbath, to keep it holy."[4]

The Glorious Qur'an addressed these pagan ideas and discussed them extensively. After all, pagan beliefs and customs are generally similar in form and substance. Accordingly, the Qur'an has branded the Christians with disbelief when they say that Jesus Christ is God, or the Son of God, or a third constituent of the Trinity. Allah, Most Exalted, says:

> In blasphemy indeed are those that say that Allah is Christ, the son of Mary. Say: Who then has the least power against Allah, if His Will were to destroy Christ the son of Mary, his mother, and all—everyone that is on the earth?[5]

> They do blaspheme who say: Allah is Christ the son of Mary. But said Christ: "Children of Israel! Worship Allah, my Lord and your Lord." Whoever joins other gods with Allah Allah will forbid him the Garden, and the Fire will be his abode. There will for the wrongdoers be no one to help. They do blaspheme who say: Allah is one of three in a Trinity: for there is no god except one God. If they desist not

---

[1] Acts 10:48.
[2] Matthew 28:19.
[3] Matthew 28:1.
[4] Exodus 20:8-11.
[5] Qur'an 5:17.

> from their word (of blasphemy), verily a grievous penalty will befall blasphemers among them.
>
> Why turn they not to Allah, and seek his forgiveness? For Allah is Oft-Forgiving, Most Merciful. Christ, the son of Mary was no more than a messenger; many were the messengers that passed away before him. His mother was a woman of truth. They had both to eat their (daily) food. See how Allah does make His signs clear to them, yet see in what ways they are deluded away from the truth.[1]

These verses underscore the following important points:

1. Jesus Christ was no more than a messenger, like many other messengers who came before him. Likewise, Muhammad was a messenger of Allah. Allah says, "Muhammad is no more than a messenger: many were the messengers who passed away before him."[2]

2. His mother was nothing more than a woman of truth. She was not a prophetess. Allah says, "his mother was a woman of truth."[3]

3. Then Allah says that "...they had both to eat their (daily) food." This is one of the clearest human attributes negating divinity, because the eater is in need of food to satisfy his hunger. He is also in need of getting rid of his wastes and relieving himself of harmful materials. Needless to say, these characteristics can never apply to God.

While the Qur'an denies the divinity of Jesus Christ, it affirms that he is a servant of Allah. Allah, Most Exalted says:

> When (Jesus) son of Mary is held up as an example, behold your people raise a clamor thereat (in ridicule) and they say, "Are our gods best, or he?" This they set forth to you, only by way of disputation: yea, they are a contentious people. He was no more than a servant: We granted Our favor to him, and We made him an example to the Children of Israel.[4]

---

[1] Qur'an 5:72-75.
[2] Qur'an 3:114.
[3] Qur'an 5:75.
[4] Qur'an 43:57-59.

As a matter of fact, Allah, Most Glorified, Most Exalted, reminds us that the first words uttered by Jesus while he was in the cradle were his affirmation that he was a servant of Allah. Allah Most Exalted says:

> But she pointed to the babe. They said: "How can we talk to one who is a child in the cradle?" He said: "I am indeed a servant of Allah. He has given me revelation and made me a prophet. And He has made me blessed wheresoever I be, and has enjoined on me prayer and charity as long as I live."[1]

The final Prophet (may Allah's peace and blessings be upon him) said:

> Allah Almighty, Most Exalted, says, "The son of Adam tells a lie against Me, though he has no right to do so. He abuses Me, though he has no right to do so. As for his telling a lie against Me, it is his saying that I will not recreate him as I created him the first time. In fact, the first creation was not any easier for Me than his recreation. As for his abusing Me, it is his saying that Allah has begotten a son, while I am the One, the Self-Sufficient Master, Whom all creatures need. I beget not, nor was I begotten, and there is none like unto Me."[2]

When the Qur'an discusses the Christian Trinity, It discusses the issue of Trinity in its various forms and concepts. Likewise, when the Qur'an discusses the Christian concept of divine sonship, it even discusses the pagan concept of sonship in all its stages and phases of development.

Talking about the Arab pagans and other pagans, the Qur'an says:

> Yet they make the jinn equals with Allah, though Allah did create the jinn; and they falsely, having no knowledge, attribute to him sons and daughters. Praise and glory be to Him! (for He is) above what they attribute to Him![3]

---

[1] Qur'an 19:29-31.
[2] This is an authentic *hadith* of Prophet Muhammad (pbuh), narrated by Abu Hurayrah and collected by Al-Bukhari in *The Book of Tafsir*.
[3] Qur'an 6:100.

Has then your Lord, (O pagans,) preferred for you sons, and taken for Himself daughters among the angels? Truly you utter a most dreadful saying![1]

Now ask them their opinion: Is it that your Lord has (only) daughters, and they have sons? Or that We created the angels female, and they are witnesses (thereto)? Is it not that they say, from their own invention, "Allah has begotten children"? But they are liars! Did He (then) choose daughters rather than sons? What is the matter with you? How judge you? Will you not then receive admonition? Or have you an authority manifest? Then bring your Book (of authority) if you be truthful! And they have invented a blood-relationship between Him and the Jinn: But the Jinn know (quite well) that they have indeed to appear (before His Judgment Seat)! Glory to Allah! (He is free) from the things they ascribe (to Him)![2]

People of the Book! Commit no excesses in your religion: nor say of Allah aught but the truth. Christ Jesus the son of Mary was (no more than) a messenger of Allah, and His Word, which He bestowed on Mary, and a Spirit proceeding from Him: so believe in Allah and His messengers. Say not "Trinity": desist: It will be better for you: For Allah is One God: Glory be to Him: (far Exalted is He) above having a son. To Him belong all things in the heavens and on earth. And enough is Allah as a Disposer of affairs. Christ disdains not to serve and worship Allah, nor do the angels, those nearest (to Allah).[3]

The Jews call Ezra a son of God, and the Christians call Christ the Son of God: that is a saying from their mouths; (in this) they but imitate what the Unbelievers of old used to say. Allah's curse be on them; how they are deluded away from the Truth! They take their priests and their anchorites to be their lords in derogation of Allah and (they take as their Lord) Christ, the son of Mary, yet they were com-

---

[1] Qur'an 17:40.
[2] Qur'an 37:149-159.
[3] Quran 4:171-172.

manded to worship but one God; there is no god but He. Praise and glory to Him: (far is He) from having the partners they associate, (with Him).[1]

The statement: "...they but imitate what the unbelievers of old used to say," is an inimitable and eloquent expression of the trail of ancient paganism which has lived on through the ages. Sadly, it is the same pagan legacy that has led to Zionism and the Universal Crusade.

This is just one of the many amazing facts that the Qur'an enlightens us with. It always puts the whole truth at our disposal in the clearest and most complete fashion, without the least ambiguity or complicated arguments. This is how we find the Glorious Qur'an—inimitable and calm in whatever it says and mandates. It says nothing but what is right. It speaks nothing but the truth.

How often, or how many countless times, have people infringed on the Qur'an and said whatever they wanted, being oblivious to its soothing message, and conjured up perceptions according to their acquired biases, which had nothing to do with its genuine advice. Then the truth became manifest, factually and intellectually, and they realized how presumptuous they had been in their statements and perceptions.

The Qur'anic commandments will always stand strong and firm, and be unshakable and undaunted. People will always return to the Qur'an, whether they accept it or not, to study it, research its truths and contemplate its infinite wisdom! Who would have believed that Christian clerics one day would respond positively to the facts of the Qur'an and study them with full appreciation and admiration! Who would have believed that the medieval vitriol of the clergy would be silenced forever!

The permanent function of that clergy was to attack Islam, and to plot against it at any cost. They would tell lies and weave evil stories about Islam, only to turn people away from it. In fact, once they foolishly uttered that "...the only reason why the Muslims forbid wine and pork is because their Prophet, in his

---

[1] Qur'an 9:30-31.

last days, drank wine until he became drunk. Thereafter, some pigs came and killed him"!

Who would have believed that the old clerical mentality would one day become flexible, and change from one extreme to another?

Today, we find people in Christian European publishing houses, institutes, cultural centers, academies, universities, even some missionaries, studying, admiring and writing on Islam.

Moreover, some great Islamic books were edited and published there, e.g., in Germany and other countries. In fact, one of the most extensive indexes of the Prophetic Traditions was published by the Germans. The first edition of the Qur'an was published there.

Who would have believed that European universities would one day teach courses in Islamic faith and Islamic law, and grant advanced degrees to students studying some of the minutiae of Islamic culture?

The Crucifixion and Vicarious Atonement

For the last five days we have discussed the issues of the Trinity, its three constituents, and the begotten god. We have also discussed the issue of the Crucifixion and the blood-sacrifice. It is really a strange and complicated and yet a critical issue. We don't know why it's so mysterious or what the objective behind it is. All we know is that this issue was founded on superstition and ended up a bigger superstition.

What is the mystery behind this vague story, which started with a conspiracy against Jesus Christ, then his trial, then his crucifixion, then his burial, then his resurrection from the dead? Why all these events? Why did they make him a god, or the son of God? Why did they crucify him?

The Holy Qur'an talks about the story of the Crucifixion and denies it absolutely. It says:

> (They have incurred divine displeasure): In that they broke their covenant; that they rejected the signs of Allah; that they slew the messengers in defiance of right; that they said, "Our hearts are the wrappings (which preserve Allah's

Word; We need no more)." Nay, Allah has set the seal on their hearts for their blasphemy, and little is it they believe: that they rejected Faith; that they uttered against Mary a grave false charge; That they said (in boast), "We killed Christ Jesus the son of Mary, the Messenger of Allah;" but they killed him not, nor crucified him, but so it was made to appear to them, and those who differ therein are full of doubts, with no (certain) knowledge, but only conjecture to follow, for of a surety they killed him not: Nay, Allah raised him up unto Himself; and Allah is Exalted in Power, Wise; And there is none of the People of the Book but must believe in him before his death; and on the Day of Judgment he will be a witness against them.[1]

But why does the Noble Qur'an deny the Crucifixion of Jesus? In other words, is it absolutely unthinkable for Jesus to have been killed or crucified? The answer is no, it is not. After all, the Qur'an speaks of the Final Prophet saying, "Muhammad is no more than a messenger: Many were the messengers that passed away before him. If he died or were slain, will you then turn back on your heels?"[2]

Thus, Muhammad could die or be killed. Likewise, Jesus could die and could be killed, even crucified.

Frankly, the Qur'an categorically denies the incident of the Crucifixion to show the disappointment of the Jews (i.e., in this world and the Hereafter). They will be called to account in the Hereafter as the killers of Jesus Christ, even though they didn't do it. How?

Allah, Most Glorified, Most Exalted, has recorded several points against them. First, they have a previous criminal record in killing former prophets. They are guilty "...of slaying the prophets in defiance of right."[3] Second, they are guilty of premeditation. The Qur'an exposes their plot, saying that what spurred this evil attitude was "...that they rejected faith, that they

---

[1] Qur'an 4:155-159.
[2] Qur'an 3:144.
[3] Qur'an 3:181.

uttered against Mary a grave false charge."[1] Third, they themselves confessed. Of course, this is always the strongest evidence. The Qur'an says, "...that they said (in boast), 'We killed Christ Jesus the son of Mary, the Messenger of Allah.'"[2]

Now if the incident of the Crucifixion is a mere myth, full of contradictions and confusion, then whatever is based upon the Crucifixion is also a myth. In other words, the tale of the Son of God sacrificing himself for the sins of mankind or being the savior of all humanity is only a myth.

These incredible stories simply cannot serve as the basis of human interaction. Such tales completely negate personal responsibility. How can Allah accept for Himself this method of dealing with mankind? Imagine for a moment a person who was caught red-handed killing someone, his hands still bloody; and evidence points to him as the perpetrator; and on top of all this, he confesses to the killing. Does he or his lawyer have any right to defend himself saying, "I am the one who killed him; I am the one who led him to a secluded place and then I murdered him. But there is another person who will absolve me of this responsibility, so please apprehend him and prosecute him instead of me"?

Is this permissible by any human logic or convention? So, if man cannot accept such a travesty of his own legal system—in spite of its countless deficiencies—how can it be permissible before the absolute justice of Allah? How can we refuse favoritism, use of influential friends, discrimination, ethnic superiority in our own ministry of justice and then turn around and expect the justice of Allah, Most Exalted and Most Sublime, to be full of favoritism and discrimination on the basis of race, sex, color or ethnic background? Would you be happy if our Lord, Most Glorified, loved or cared for one group of people while hating and condemning another, for no other reason but race or sex?! Do you want our Lord to be the Lord of the Children of Israel alone, and have him curse the Canaanites and others?!

Permit me to relate a passage from the Gospels in circulation today. The Bible says:

---

[1] Qur'an 4:156.
[2] Qur'an 4:157.

> And behold, a woman of Canaan came from that region and cried out to Him, saying, "Have mercy on me, O Lord, Son of David! My daughter is severely demon-possessed." But He answered her not a word. And His disciples came and urged Him, saying, "Send her away, for she cries out after us." But He answered and said, "I was not sent except to the lost sheep of the house of Israel." Then she came and worshipped Him, saying, "Lord, help me!"
>
> But He answered and said, "It is not good to take the children's bread and throw it to the little dogs." And she said, "Yes, Lord, yet even the little dogs eat the crumbs which fall from their master's table."[1]

This is the image of Jesus Christ portrayed in Christian myth. When a woman asked him to cure her daughter, he said: "It is not good to take the children's bread and throw it to the little dogs"! My goodness! Is this the Jesus whom Christians worship as God? May Allah absolve Jesus, the man, the Prophet, the Messenger, of anything false attributed to him.

Racial Discrimination

It is this type of misunderstanding and this attitude which were the real roots of racial discrimination in Europe and America today. The one who first preached racial discrimination was the Bible itself, not America.

America was not a pioneer in racial discrimination. It only upheld the ideas promoted by the supposed holy passages from the Holy Bible. Isn't it the Bible that curses the entire black race forever because they were the children of Ham?[2] The Old Testament says:

---

[1] Matthew 15:22-27.
[2] In fairness, nowhere in this passage, or in the rest of the Bible, is there mention of Ham or Canaan being black. Such an interpretation was introduced much later, and popularized in the Americas and South Africa, to attempt to provide a religious justification for slavery and apartheid. In fact, a more common story, made up by the same type of religious bigots, was that black skin was the mark of Cain, the slayer of Abel (ed.).

Muslim-Christian Dialogue

> Now the sons of Noah who went out of the ark were Shem, Ham, and Japheth. And Ham was the father of Canaan. These three were the sons of Noah, and from these the whole earth was populated. And Noah began to be a farmer, and he planted a vineyard. Then he drank of the wine and was drunk, and became uncovered in his tent.
>
> And Ham, the father of Canaan, saw the nakedness of his father, and told his two brothers outside. But Shem and Japheth took a garment, laid it on both their shoulders, and went backward and covered the nakedness of their father. Their faces were turned away, and they did not see their father's nakedness.
>
> So Noah awoke from his wine, and knew what his younger son had done to him. The he said: "Cursed be Canaan; a servant of servants he will be to his brethren." And he said: "Blessed be the Lord, The God of Shem, And may Canaan be his servant. May God enlarge Japheth, and may he dwell in the tents of Shem; and may Canaan be his servant."[1]

Later the Old Testament relates that Sarah, Abraham's wife, said to him, "Cast out this bondwoman and her son; for the son of this bondwoman shall not be heir with my son, *namely* with Isaac."[2] However, this "...matter was very displeasing in Abraham's sight because of his son."[3]

Paul quoted this exact text, lighting the fire of racism among people. He said:

> Nevertheless what does the Scripture say? "Cast out the bondwoman and her son, for the son of the bondwoman shall not be heir with the son of the freewoman." So then, brethren, we are not children of the bondwomen but of the free.[4]

The government of South Africa (used to) rely on what was narrated in the Book of Genesis, the description of Canaan, the

---

[1] Genesis 9:18-27.
[2] Genesis 21:10.
[3] Genesis 21:11.
[4] Galatians 4:30-31.

son of Ham, as a slave to others. It uses this to justify its control and suppression of its black citizens.

In contrast, we do not find such racial discrimination in Muslim societies. This is because Islamic law prohibits this evil from appearing or prevailing. Allah, Most Exalted says:

> Mankind! We created you from a single (pair) of a male and female, and made you into nations and tribes, that you may know each other (not that you may despise each other). Verily the most honored of you in the sight of Allah is (he who is) the most righteous of you, and Allah has all knowledge and is well-acquainted (with all things).[1]

In this verse, there is a solemn declaration of a comprehensive equality among nations, peoples and individuals. It is a declaration addressed to all of mankind. Moreover, this verse clarifies that the honor of distinction among human beings is not based on color, sex, or ethnic background; rather it is a function of *taqwa*, a term that is inclusive of piety, righteousness and proper guidance. The Prophet (may Allah's peace and blessings be upon him) says, "All creatures are dependents of Allah. The most beloved to Him is the most beneficial to His dependents."

Accordingly, the Prophet (may Allah's peace and blessings be upon him), by his Lord's command, invited all mankind to his mission—Islam. After all, Allah is "...the Lord and Cherisher of Mankind, the King (or Ruler) of Mankind, the God (or Judge) of Mankind."[2]

He is not the Lord of just one sect or one race or one group of people. Islam razed all barriers among races. The Prophet once spoke about Salman Al-Farsi (may Allah be pleased with him), one of his Companions. Salman was a slave whom the Prophet set free. The Prophet said, "Salman is one of us. He is a member of the family." The Companions of the Prophet (may Allah's peace and blessings be upon him) included Suhayb Ar-Rumi[3] and Bilal Al-Habashi.[4] He considered them among the elite of his Arab Companions.

---

[1] Qur'an 49:13.
[2] Qur'an 114:1-3.
[3] He was from Rome.
[4] He was from Abyssinia (Habash, i.e., Ethiopia).

In fact, the Prophet once appointed a young man of eighteen years as leader of his forces, while a number of the older Companions were under his leadership.

In this way, Islam was responsible for a great miracle in human history. It put everyone on the same footing under the banner of Islam from its outset. The Prophet renewed this commandment and declared it very strictly and frankly in his farewell address. He said, "No Arab is better than a non-Arab, no white is better than a black person, except in terms of God consciousness (*taqwa*)." Then he asked the people who had gathered to listen to his last sermon. He asked, "Did I deliver (the message)?" When the Companions affirmed, he turned to Allah and said, "Allah, be my witness."

The Glorious Qur'an does not mention in any surah or verse the names of any of the Prophet's contemporaries, except for two names, Zayd, his adopted son, and Abu Lahab, his uncle. These were the only two contemporaries of the Prophet mentioned by name in the Qur'an. The Qur'an did not name Abu Bakr, 'Umar, 'Uthman or 'Ali. These were the closest Companions to the Prophet. However, the Qur'an mentions the name of Zayd, his adopted son. It gives him an honorable mention saying:

> Behold, you did say to one who had received the grace of Allah and your favor: "Retain (in wedlock) your wife, and fear Allah." But you did hide in your heart that which Allah was about to make manifest: you feared the people, but it is more fitting that you should fear Allah. Then when Zayd had dissolved (his marriage) with her, with the necessary (formality), We joined her in marriage to you.[1]

In contrast, the Qur'an names Abu Lahab in a defamatory way, cursing him in the following verses. Allah says:

> Perish the hands of Abu Lahab (Father of Flame)! Perish he! No profit to him from all his wealth and all his gains! Burnt soon will he be in a fire of blazing Flame! His wife shall

---

[1] Qur'an 33:37.

carry the (crackling) wood—a fuel, a twisted rope of palm leaf fiber round her neck![1]

Considering blood relationship, Zayd was a stranger to the Prophet (may Allah's peace and blessings be upon him). As for Abu Lahab, he was the Prophet's uncle and a prominent figure in the tribe of Quraysh. In spite of their worldly status, the Qur'an threatens Abu Lahab and his wife with eternal damnation. Thus, the Qur'an decrees a well-known principle, namely, there shall be no preference given to anyone based on their sex, color, race or any other worldly criteria. Distinction and honor can only be achieved through God-consciousness.

The Truth about the Bible and its Authenticity

For the last five days, we have talked about the Holy Book, its Old and New Testaments, and we brought to light the discrepancies and contradictions in that document from beginning to end.

This Book is full of issues that contradict the main objective of sending prophets and revelations, namely, true guidance for mankind. For example, let us take a quick look at the Song of Solomon which is full of rather explicit expressions. It describes the hidden parts of a woman's anatomy. It says:

> By night on my bed I sought the one I love; I sought him, but I did not find him. "I will rise now," I said, "and go about the city; in the streets and in the squares I will seek the one I love." I sought him, but I did not find him. The watchmen who go about the city found me; I said, "Have you seen the one I love?" Scarcely had I passed by them, when I found the one I love. I held him and would not let him go, until I had brought him to the house of my mother, and into the chamber of her who conceived me. I charge you, daughters of Jerusalem, by the gazelles or by the does of the field, do not stir up nor awaken love until it pleases.[2]

---

[1]Qur'an 111:5.
[2]The Song of Solomon (a.k.a. Song of Songs) 3:1-5.

The fourth chapter of the same book says:

Behold, you are fair, my love! Behold, you are fair! You have dove's eyes behind your veil. Your hair is like a flock of goats, going down from Mount Gilead. Your teeth are like a flock of shorn sheep which have come up from the washing, every one of which bears twins, and none is barren among them. Your lips are like a strand of scarlet, and your mouth is lovely. Your temples behind your veil are like a piece of pomegranate. Your neck is like the tower of David, built for an armory, on which hang a thousand bucklers, all shields of mighty men. Your two breasts are like two fawns, twins of a gazelle, which feed among the lilies. until the day breaks and the shadows flee away, I will go away to the mountain of myrrh and to the hill of frankincense. You are all fair, my love, and there is no spot in you.[1]

Later, the same book in another chapter continues:

How beautiful are your feet in sandals, prince's daughter! The curves of your thighs are jewels, the work of the hands of a skillful workman. Your navel is a rounded goblet; it lacks no blended beverage. Your waist is a heap of wheat set about the lilies. Your two breasts are like two fawns, twins of a gazelle. Your neck is like an ivory tower, your eyes like the pools in Heshbon by the gate of Bath Rabbim. Your nose is like the tower of Lebanon which looks toward Damascus. Your head crowns you like Mount Caramel, and the hair of your head is like purple; a king is held captive by your tresses. How fair and how pleasant you are, O love, with your delights! This stature of yours is like a palm tree, and your breasts like its clusters. I said, "I will go up to the palm tree, I will take hold of its branches." Let now your breasts be like clusters of the vine, the fragrance of your breath like apples, and the roof of your mouth like the best wine. The wine goes down for my beloved, moving gently the lips of sleepers. I am my beloved's and his desire is toward me.

---

[1] The Song of Solomon 4:1-7.

Come, my beloved, Let us go forth to the field; let us lodge in the villages.[1]

Can this be a book of guidance? Can it be a revelation from God?! Is this the truth that leads people to the straight path? Even if we were to ignore the immoral sexual overtones and explicit expressions and look elsewhere for discrepancies and contradictions, we would find evidence that one would not believe and are beyond any rationale. These contradictions prove one quite important and significant point.

Allah's Attributes in the Bible

God is subject to sorrow and remorse. The Bible says:

And the Lord was sorry that He had made man on the earth, and He was grieved in His heart. So the Lord said, "I will destroy man whom I have created from the face of earth, both man and beast, creeping thing and birds of the air, for I am sorry that I have made them."[2]

God reconsidered and decided not to destroy humanity again. The Bible says:

And the Lord smelled a soothing aroma. The Lord said in His heart, "I will never again curse the ground for man's sake, although the imagination of man's heart is evil from his youth; nor will I again destroy every living thing as I have done."[3]

The Bible portrays Allah as sorry for creating mankind, so He destroyed it at the time of Noah (may Allah's peace and blessings be upon him). Then He was sorry once more for destroying mankind and vowed not to do it again. This is the way the self-contradictory scriptures talk about God, an indecisive God Who contradicts His own decisions. In short, He is a God who contradicts Himself.

---

[1] The Song of Solomon 7:1-11.
[2] Genesis 6:6-7.
[3] Genesis 8:21.

Allah remembers His covenant with the people by using the rainbow. The Bible says that God said:

> I set My rainbow in the cloud, and it shall be for the sign of the covenant between Me and the earth. It shall be, when I bring a cloud over the earth, that the rainbow shall be seen in the cloud; and I will remember My covenant which is between Me and you and every living creature of all flesh; the waters shall never again become a flood to destroy all flesh. The rainbow shall be in the cloud, and I will look on it to remember the everlasting covenant between God and every living creature of all flesh that is on the earth.[1]

In this way, this passage from Genesis brings to light some new scientific discoveries about the rainbow. Allah has put this rainbow in the sky with its beautiful colors, while it is raining, to remind Him of the covenant with mankind. All this so He won't forget. So the horrific storm comes again. Once again, we seek Allah's forgiveness, and repent to Him and say: "Glory be to You, our Lord; this is a most serious slander...!"

God is jealous of mankind. The Bible relates that

> Now the whole earth had one language and one speech. And it came to pass, as they journeyed from the east, that they found a plain in the land of Shinar, and they dwelt there. Then they said to one another, "Come, let us make bricks and bake them thoroughly." They had brick for stone and they had asphalt for mortar. And they said, "Come, let us build ourselves a city, and a tower whose top is in the heavens; let us make a name for ourselves, lest we be scattered abroad over the face of the whole earth."
>
> But the Lord came down to see the city and the tower which the sons of men had built. And the Lord said, "Indeed the people are one and they have one language, and this is what they begin to do; now nothing that they propose to do will be withheld from them. Come, let Us go down and there confuse their language, that they may not understand one another's speech."

---

[1] Genesis 8:21.

> So the Lord scattered them abroad from there over the whole face of the earth, and they ceased building the city. Therefore its name is called Babel, because there the Lord confused the language of all the earth; and from there the Lord scattered them abroad over the face of all the earth.[1]

Did you hear? Have you read this before?

They say that God was jealous of His creatures when they intended to build the city and the tower. He scattered them and confused their language! I just don't understand! How about the building of huge cities, skyscrapers and tall towers that have been built ever since? Doesn't this type of heavy construction spark a cord of jealousy in the God of the Bible?!

God incited people to steal. The Old Testament says:

> And the Lord said to Moses, "I will bring one more plague on Pharaoh and on Egypt. Afterward he will let you go from here. When he lets you go, he will surely drive you out of here altogether. Speak now in the hearing of the people, and let every man ask from his neighbor and every woman from her neighbor, articles of silver and articles of gold." And the Lord gave the people favor in the sight of the Egyptians.[2]

In another place, the Bible continues, saying:

> Now the children of Israel had done according to the word of Moses, and they had asked from the Egyptians articles of silver, articles of gold, and clothing. And the Lord had given the people favor in the eyes of the Egyptians, so that they granted them what they requested. Then they plundered the Egyptians.[3]

Thus, according to the writers of the Scriptures and the narrators of this news, the Lord was the One Who goaded the Children of Israel to rob the Egyptians. He was the One Who taught them to take their gold, silver and clothing before they left Egypt with Moses!

God wrestles Jacob. Again, the Old Testament testifies that

---

[1] Genesis 11:1-9.
[2] Exodus 11:1-3.
[3] Exodus 12:35-36.

Then Jacob was left alone; and a man wrestled with him until the breaking of day. Now when He saw that He did not prevail against him, He touched the socket of his hip; and the socket of Jacob's hip was out of joint as He wrestled with him. And He said, "Let me go, for the day breaks." But he said, "I will not let You go unless You bless me!"

So He said to him, "What is your name?" He said, "Jacob." And He said, "Your name shall no longer be called Jacob, but Israel; for you have struggled with God and with men, and have prevailed." Then Jacob asked, saying "Tell me Your name, I pray." And He said, "Why is it that you ask about My name?" And He blessed Him there. So Jacob called the name of the place Peniel: "For I have seen God face to face, and my life is preserved."[1]

As the passage confirms, the writers of the Scriptures allege that Jacob had wrestled with God until he defeated him. Then, he did not release Him until he got His blessing! If you think that this image of God conjured up by the imagination of the writers is incredible, then wait till you see what they have to say about the prophets of God. The picture becomes much uglier.

Distorted and Foolish Images of Allah's Prophets and Messengers in the Old Testament

Abraham

Here is what the Old Testament says about Abram:

Now there was a famine in the land, and Abram went down to Egypt to dwell there, for the famine was severe in the land. And it came to pass, when he was close to entering Egypt, that he said to Sarai his wife, "Indeed I know that you are a woman of beautiful countenance. Therefore it will happen, when the Egyptians see you, that they will say,

---

[1]Genesis 32:24-30.

'This is his wife;' and they will kill me, but they will let you live. Please say you *are* my sister, that it may be well with me for your sake, and that I may live because of you."

So it was, when Abram came into Egypt, that the Egyptians saw the woman, that she was very beautiful. The princes of Pharaoh also saw her and commended her to Pharaoh. And the woman was taken to Pharaoh's house. He treated Abram well for her sake. He had sheep, oxen, male donkeys, male and female servants, female donkeys and camels. But the Lord plagued Pharaoh and his house with great plagues because of Sarai, Abraham's wife.

And Pharaoh called Abram and said, "What is this you have done to me? Why did you not tell me that she was your wife? Why did you say, 'She is my sister'? I might have taken her as my wife. Now therefore, here is your wife; take her and go your way." So Pharaoh commanded his men concerning him; and they sent him away, with his wife and all that he had.[1]

Would anyone who has the least sense of honor or morality use the beauty of his wife to be successful in business? Is it fair, or is it acceptable for anyone who has morals and a sense of honor, to use his wife in such a way? How about Allah's prophet and messenger, Abraham!

Lot

The Old Testament claims that

...Lot went up out of Zoar and dwelt in the mountains, and his two daughters were with him; for he was afraid to dwell in Zoar. And he and his two daughters dwelt in a cave. Now the firstborn said to the younger, "Our father is old, and there is no man on the earth to come in to us as is the custom for all the earth. Come, let us make our father drink wine, and we will lie with him, that we may preserve the lineage of our father."

---

[1] Genesis 12:10-20.

So they made their father drink wine that night. And the firstborn went in and lay with her father, and he did not know when she lay down or when she arose. It happened on the next day that the firstborn said to the younger, "Indeed I lay with my father last night; let us make him drink wine tonight also, and you go in and lie with him, that we may preserve the lineage of our father."

Then they made their father drink wine that night also. And the younger arose and lay with him, and he did not know when she lay down or when she arose. Thus both the daughters of Lot were with child by their father.[1]

In spite of the fact that this tale is full of lies, our question is, what is the wisdom or the lesson which the readers of the Bible could benefit from by relating such an immoral tale? If this is the level of the prophets, who are carriers of Allah's word and guidance, then what stone have they left unturned for the transgressors and the fools?

How They Address Allah

If we were to acquaint ourselves with the proper etiquette of supplicating to and imploring Allah, we would be shocked. This way of talking to Allah takes the form of daring and accusation. For example, let us take the following text. The Bible says, "Then he cried out to the LORD and said, 'O LORD my God, have You also brought tragedy on the widow with whom I lodge, by killing her son?'"[2]

ISLAM

Now, having talked about Christianity clearly, let us talk about Islam.

First of all, I already know that one lecture, or even a number of lectures, about Islam cannot possibly cover this topic. Is-

---

[1] Genesis 19:30-36.
[2] I Kings 17:20.

lam is much greater than anyone can imagine. Islam is a tremendous cultural entity. It is an unparalleled school of knowledge and sciences. It is well established that, historically and civilizationally, no other topic has solicited the amount of voluminous studies and extensive research that the Qur'an, the Book of Allah, has. It is out of the Glorious Qur'an that much knowledge has come. Allah, Most Exalted, says:

> Those who reject (Truth), among the People of the Book and among the polytheists, were not going to depart (from their ways) until there should come to them Clear Evidence, a Messenger from Allah, rehearsing scriptures kept pure and holy: wherein are laws (or decrees) right and straight.[1]

If we were to note that normally every book has many pages, we would note that each page of the Qur'an speaks volumes. In truth, a single page of the Glorious Qur'an can furnish us with knowledge that would produce valuable books. This is what we have seen and witnessed. This is what the historians of civilization have witnessed as well.

Many branches of knowledge evolved to serve this Glorious Book. These disciplines include the sciences of the Qur'an, of exegesis of the Qur'an, sciences of the Arabic language, sciences of the traditions of Prophet Muhammad (may Allah's peace and blessings be upon him), Islamic law, history, etc. Many books have been written in various branches of knowledge and culture, aiming to expound upon the guidance of the Holy Qur'an. The Arabs were not the only people who carried out this praiseworthy task, but many others participated also. They were scholars and masters of Islamic jurisprudence from among the non-Arabs.

We all know about Abu Hanifah, Al-Bukhari and At-Tabari. Then there was Sibawayh, Zamakhshari and Al-Jirjani. All of this points to the fact that the spread of Islam was not only religious; it also affected the language, progress, culture and civilization of the peoples who welcomed it.

---

[1] Qur'an 98:1-3.

The Holy Qur'an is not just a book of creed and sermons. It is also a book of science, culture, legislation, politics and morals.

Islamic culture conquered other cultures very quickly. It had numerous successive triumphs and spread rapidly. So fast was its expansion that historians to this day are unable to explain such an amazing phenomenon. They are still unable to find an answer to the question: how could Muhammad within eight years open and conquer one million square kilometers? How did it happen, at a time when transportation was limited and the roads were not passable? How did it happen with the least amount of human casualties. The number of Muslim martyrs and non-Muslims being killed was not more then a total of 1,002, as recorded. Answers to such questions are impossible if we use human criteria. However, if we take into consideration Allah's laws and the working of such laws in societies and nations, then the answer will be easily available.

Islam Was the Religion of All the Prophets

Islam is the religion of Allah. There is no other true religion. Allah, Most Glorified, Most Exalted, has promised to make it victorious, powerful, and to master all other religions.

But what is this religion of Islam? Are there any other religions competing with it in their relationship with Allah? Truly, Allah, Most Glorified, Most Exalted, did not send different religions to people. He sent only one single religion, through His prophets—Islam. Allah, Most Exalted, says, "The religion before Allah is Islam (submission to His Will)."[1] It is this one religion that all the messengers and prophets of Allah brought.

Noah Brought the Message of Islam

Allah, Most Exalted, says:

Relate to them the story of Noah. Behold! He said to his people: "My people, if it be hard on your (mind) that I

---

[1] Qur'an 3:19.

should stay (with you) and commemorate the Signs of Allah, yet I put my trust in Allah. Get you then an agreement about your plan and among your partners, so your plan be not to you dark and dubious. Then, pass your sentence on me, and give no respite. But if you turn back, (consider): No reward have I asked of you: my reward is only due from Allah, and I have been commanded to be of those who submit to Allah's Will (in Islam)."[1]

Abraham Brought the Message of Islam

Allah, Most Exalted, says:

And remember Abraham and Ishmael raised the foundations of the House (with this prayer): "Our Lord! Accept (this service) from us: For You are the All-Hearing, the All-knowing. Our Lord! make of us Muslims, bowing to Your (Will), and of our progeny a people Muslim, bowing to Your (Will); and show us our place for the celebration of (due) rites; and turn unto us (in Mercy); for You are the Oft-Returning, Most Merciful.

"Our Lord! Send among them a messenger of their own, who shall rehearse Your Signs to them and instruct them in scripture and wisdom, and sanctify them: For You are the Exalted in Might, the Wise."

And who turns away from the religion of Abraham but such as debase their souls with folly? Him We chose and rendered pure in this world: And he will be in the Hereafter in the ranks of the Righteous. Behold! his Lord said to him: "Bow (your will to Me):" He said: "I bow (my will) to the Lord and Cherisher of the Universe."

And this was the legacy that Abraham left to his sons, and so did Jacob; "My sons! God has chosen the Faith for you; then die not except in the state of (submission to Allah)."[2]

---

[1] Qur'an 10:71-72.
[2] Qur'an 2:127-132.

Jacob Brought the Message of Islam

Allah, Most Exalted, says:
Were you witnesses when Death appeared before Jacob? Behold, he said to his sons: "What will you worship after me?" They said: "We shall worship your God and the God of your fathers, of Abraham, Ishmael and Isaac, the one (True) God: To Him we bow (in Islam.)"[1]

Lot Brought the Message of Islam

Allah, Most Exalted, says:
(Abraham) said: "And what, O Messengers, is your errand (now)?" They said, "We have been sent to a people (deep) in sin to bring on them, (a shower of) stones of clay (brimstone), marked as from your Lord for those who trespass beyond bounds. Then We evacuated those of the Believers who were there, but We found not there any just (Muslim) persons except in one house."[2]

Joseph Brought the Message of Islam

Allah, Most Exalted, says:
"My Lord! You have indeed bestowed on me some power, and taught me something of the interpretation of dreams and events. Creator of the heavens and the earth! You are my Protector in this world and in the Hereafter. Take my soul (at death) as one submitting to Your will (as a Muslim), and unite me with the righteous."[3]

Moses Brought the Message of Islam

Allah, Most Exalted, says:

---

[1] Qur'an 2:133.
[2] Qur'an 51:31-36.
[3] Qur'an 12:101.

Moses said: "My people! If you do (really) believe in Allah, then in Him put your trust if you submit (your will to His)."[1]

Islam Was the Religion of the People of Moses (i.e., the Children of Israel)

Allah, Most Exalted, says:

We took the Children of Israel across the sea: Pharaoh and his hosts followed them in insolence and spite. At length, when overwhelmed with the flood, he said: "I believe that there is no god except Him Whom the Children of Israel believe in: I am of those who submit (to Allah in Islam)."[2]

Islam Was the Religion of the Sorcerers who [Repented and then] Believed in Moses:

Allah, Most Exalted, says:

But the sorcerers fell down prostrate in adoration, saying: "We believe in the Lord of the Worlds, the Lord of Moses and Aaron." Said Pharaoh: "Believe you in Him before I give you permission? Surely this is a trick which you have planned in the city to drive out its people: but soon shall you know (the consequences). Be sure I will cut off your hands and your feet on opposite sides, and I will cause you all to die on the cross."

They said: "For us, we are but sent back unto our Lord: but you wreak your vengeance on us simply because we believed in the Signs of our Lord when they reached us! Our Lord! Pour out on us patience and constancy, and take our souls unto You as Muslims (who bow to Your Will)!"[3]

---

[1] Qur'an 10:84.
[2] Qur'an 10:90.
[3] Qur'an 7:120-126.

Islam Is the Religion of the Prophets of the Children of Israel

Allah, Most Exalted, says:

> It was We Who revealed the Law (to Moses): therein was guidance and light. By its standard have been judged the Jews, by the prophets who bowed (as in Islam) to Allah's will, by the rabbis."[1]

Solomon Brought the Message of Islam

Allah, Most Exalted, says

> It is from Solomon, and is (as follows): "In the name of Allah, Most Gracious, Most Merciful: Be not arrogant against me, but come to me in submission (to the true Religion)."[2]

Then Allah, Most Exalted, says (about the Queen of Sheba):

> He said (to his own men): "Chiefs! Which of you can bring me her throne before they come to me in submission?"[3]

In another place, Allah, Most Exalted, says:

> So when she arrived, she was asked, "Is this your throne?" She said, "It was just like this; and knowledge was bestowed on us in advance of this, and we have submitted to Allah (in Islam)."[4]

Finally, Allah, Most Exalted, says:

> She said: "My Lord! I have indeed wronged my soul: I do (now) submit (in Islam), with Solomon, to the Lord of the Worlds."[5]

Islam Was the Religion of Jesus and His Disciples

Allah, Most Exalted, says:

---

[1] Qur'an 5:44.
[2] Qur'an 27:30-31.
[3] Qur'an 27:38.
[4] Qur'an 27:42.
[5] Qur'an 27:44.

When Jesus found unbelief on their part he said, "Who will be my helpers in (the work of) Allah?" Said the disciples, "We are Allah's helpers: We believe in Allah, and do you bear witness that we are Muslims."[1]

Also, Allah, Most Exalted, says:

And behold! I inspired the disciples to have faith in Me and My messengers: They said, "We have faith, and do you bear witness that we bow to Allah as Muslims."

Islam Is the Religion of the Rightly-Guided Jinns

Allah, Most Exalted says:

Among us are some that submit their wills (to Allah), and some that swerve from justice. Now those who submit their wills—they have sought out (the path) of right conduct. But those who swerve, they are (but) fuel for Hellfire...[2]

Islam Is the Religion of the People of the Book

That is, those who were dedicated to the truth before Muhammad (may Allah's peace and blessings be upon him):

Allah, Most Exalted, says:

Those to whom We sent the Book before this, they do believe in this (revelation): And when it is recited to them, they say: "We believe therein, for it is the Truth from our Lord: indeed we have been Muslims (bowing to Allah's Will) from before this."[3]

Islam Is the Religion of Muhammad, the Final Prophet (may Allah's peace and blessings be upon him):

Allah, Most Exalted, says:

---

[1] Qur'an 3:52.
[2] Qur'an 72:14-15.
[3] Qur'an 28:52-53.

> The Religion before Allah is Islam (submission to His Will): Nor did the People of the Book dissent therefrom except through envy of each other, after knowledge had come to them. But if any deny the Signs of Allah, Allah is swift in calling to account. So if they dispute with you, say: "I have submitted my whole self to Allah and so have those who follow me."
>
> And say to the People of the Book and to those who are unlearned: "Do you (also) submit yourselves?" If they do, they are in right guidance, but if they turn back, your duty is to convey the Message; and in Allah's sight are (all) His servants.[1]

Also, Allah, Most Exalted, says:

> Say: I have been forbidden to invoke those whom you invoke besides Allah, seeing that the Clear Signs have come to me from my Lord; and I have been commanded to bow (in Islam) to the Lord of the Worlds.[2]

In another place, Allah, Most Exalted, says:

> This day have I perfected your religion for you, completed My favor upon you, and have chosen for you Islam as your religion.[3]

In fact, the Glorious Qur'an states clearly that Islam is the religion of everyone in the heavens and on earth. Allah, Most Exalted, says:

> Do they seek for other than the Religion of Allah, while all creatures in the heavens and on earth have, willing or unwilling, bowed to His Will (accepted Islam), and to Him shall they all be brought back?[4]

It is for this religion, Islam, that the Prophet sent his representatives and letters to all the kings and religious leaders around him at that time. He requested them to witness that he and his companions were following Islam. Allah, Most Exalted, says:

---

[1] Qur'an 3:19-20.
[2] Qur'an 40:66.
[3] Qur'an 5:3.
[4] Qur'an 3:83.

Say: People of the Book! Come to common terms as between us and you: that we worship none but Allah; that we associate no partners with him; that we erect not, from among ourselves, lords and patrons other than Allah. If then they turn back, say: Bear witness that we (at least) are Muslims (bowing to Allah's Will).[1]

The Final Prophet

Allah, Most Glorified, Most Exalted, wanted His religion to be perfect, and His blessings to be complete, so He sent Prophet Muhammad as the final prophet. Moreover, He made the Law brought by the Prophet general and universal in time and place.

Allah, Most Glorified, Most Exalted, wanted the mission of Prophet Muhammad (may Allah's peace and blessings be upon him) to be global, perfect and final. He supported Islam for it to spread and to be eternal. In the history of the final message of Islam, there are some points which all students and researchers should take note of.

One of these points is the accuracy in recording the Prophet's biography and teachings. The extreme care taken to record accurately every detail regarding what the Prophet said and did has no parallel in the history of mankind. Never, for any other prophet or even any other personality up to this day, has as much literature been available. Those who claim to follow Moses and Jesus have very little authentic information concerning the details of their lives or the revelations they brought. To this day, not a single complete authentic document exists telling us clearly about Jesus' life, even though he was the final prophet from the Israelites.

What we have in hand today is something that gives us mere glimpses of only the last fifty days in Jesus' life. A priest, Dr. Charles Anderson Scott, says in his article in the *Encyclopedia Britannica*:

---

[1] Qur'an 3:64.

> Frankly, one should forgo any attempts to write a book on the biography of Jesus. In reality, no real material or information exists that could help us to accomplish this task. The number of days for which some information exists does not exceed fifty.[1]

What the priest has stated, and the Encyclopedia Britannica has published, conflicts with popular understanding in the Christian world until very recently.

The general notion in the Christian world used to be that the books of the New Testament contained information about the last three years of Jesus' life. That is what Christian scholars agree upon even today. Yet this completely contrasts with what narrators tell us about the life of Prophet Muhammad. They have furnished us with a comprehensive and reliable record about all facts and details of his life.

His companions recorded his life from the beginning to the end. They documented everything with the utmost care and precision in the books of the Sunnah,[2] the *maghazi*,[3] and the *siyar*.[4]

There are many books which narrate the life of Prophet Muhammad. Some of these books concentrate on his biography in detail; others provide details of his missions to invite other leaders to faith, his scouting missions, the etiquette that he practiced during his battles, and how he dealt with those hostile to his mission once he conquered them. Another category of books are known as the Books of Guidance, such as *Provisions for the Journey to the Hereafter form the Guidance of the Best of Mankind*. Such books shed light on the lifestyle and guidance of the Prophet, in his worship, his rituals, his marriages, his treatment of relatives and his behavior with people in general.

Books known as *shama'il* focus specifically on his moral and physical character, i.e., his mental, spiritual and physical attributes. Still other books, known as books of *khasa'is*, deal with the unique qualities of Prophet Muhammad, in other words,

---

[1] *Encyclopedia Britannica*, 14th ed. vol. 13, p. 171.
[2] i.e., books documenting the Prophet's sayings, actions, tacit approvals, and his physical appearance and character.
[3] i.e., books documenting information concerning the battles the Prophet participated in.
[4] i.e., books documenting the Prophet's biography (*sirah*).

particulars that nobody else shares with him. Then, there are the books of *adhkar* and *Works of the Day and Night*. These books show us how the Prophet would remember his Lord, glorify Him, and pray to Him under all conditions and concerning even the most trivial things. Finally, there are the major works of Hadith known as *Sihah*, *Sunan* and *Masanid*.[1]

I daresay that the most authenticated Christian books do not reach even the fourth or perhaps the third level of authenticity.[2] All this information about the Prophet documented in various ways is in addition to what the Qur'an narrates about the Prophet's life, behavior and morals.

'A'isha[3] (may Allah be pleased with her) was once asked about the conduct of the Prophet. She responded with her famous words, "His conduct was the Qur'an."

In conclusion, the Prophet's life, and the extraordinary care taken to preserve a record of all his statements, actions and affirmations, are undeniable indications he indeed was the Final Prophet and Messenger of Allah.

The Mission of Christ, A Specific Mission

The mission of Christ was specifically to the Children of Israel. He explicitly stated that he was sent solely to look after the lost sheep of Israel: "I am not sent but unto the lost sheep of the House of Israel."[4]

For that reason his message was limited to their villages and lands and those affiliated with them. When a Canaanite woman came to him, appealing to him to pray for her sick daughter, he

---

[1] i.e., documentary records of the Prophet's sayings, actions, tacit approvals, and a description of his physical and moral attributes.
[2] Muslim scholars apply the science of authenticating narrations by evaluating narrations, especially those related by the Prophet, according to a list of rigorous criteria that scrutinized the credibility of the text of the narration as well as the narrator(s). Accordingly, they apply different degrees of authenticity. Needless to say, no Christian document, particularly the Bible, received such intense scrutiny.
[3] The favorite wife of the Prophet.
[4] Matthew 15:24.

Muslim-Christian Dialogue

told her what we previously quoted, namely, "It is not fair to take children's bread and throw it to the dogs."[1]

There are also verses in the Noble Qur'an which indicate that Jesus was a messenger to the Children of Israel, among them the statement of Allah, the Most Exalted:

> (And remember) when the angels said: Mary! Lo! Allah gives you glad tidings of a word from Him, whose name is the Messiah, Jesus, son of Mary, illustrious in the world and the Hereafter, and one of those brought near (unto Allah). He will speak unto mankind in his cradle and in his manhood, and he is of the righteous. She said: My Lord! How can I have a child when no mortal has touched me? He said: So (it will be). Allah creates what He will. If He decrees a thing, He says unto it only: "Be," and it is. And He will teach him the Scripture and wisdom, and the Torah and the Gospel; and will make him a messenger unto the Children of Israel, (saying):
>
> "Lo! I come unto you with a sign from your Lord. Lo! I fashion for you out of clay the likeness of a bird, and I breathe into it and it is a bird, by Allah's leave. I heal him who was born blind, and the leper, and I raise the dead, by Allah's leave. And I announce unto you what you eat and what you store up in your houses. Lo! There is a sign in that for you, if you are believers. And (I come) confirming that which was before me of the Torah, and to make lawful some of that which was forbidden unto you. I have come to you with a clear proof from your Lord, so keep your duty to Allah and obey me. Lo! Allah is my Lord and your Lord, so worship Him. That is a straight path."[2]

Also the statement of the Most Exalted:

> And when Jesus son of Mary, said: "Children of Israel! I am the Messenger of Allah (sent) to you, confirming that which was revealed before me in the Torah, and bringing good tid-

---

[1] Matthew 15:26.
[2] Qur'an 3:45-51.

ings of a messenger coming after me, whose name shall be Ahmad.[1]"[2]

And Allah said:

You who believe! Be Allah's helpers; as Jesus son of Mary said to the disciples, "Who are my helpers for Allah?" They said, "We are the helpers of Allah." So a party of the Children of Israel believed, while a party disbelieved. Then We strengthened those who believed against their enemy, and they became uppermost.[3]

One aspect of Muhammad's prophethood, being the Seal of Prophethood, is that Allah protected the Noble Qur'an from all changes, alterations and distortions. By this unique distinction, the Qur'an differs from all other revealed scriptures.

The French Orientalist, Ettienne Denée, hit the nail on the head when describing the Gospels known as the New Testament and assessing their scholastic and historical value:

Surely God revealed the Gospel to Jesus in His own language, the language of his people. There is no doubt that this Gospel has been lost and vanished without leaving a trace, or it was obliterated.[4]

People, permit me to say something to you quite frankly: it would be easy for anyone who wanted to go to a publisher with an altered copy of the Gospel, get it printed, then distribute it in the market. No one would get upset by this action. In fact, Christian circles would greet it with acceptance. After a while it would become a reference and a source for Christian doctrine.

This statement of mine is not a flight of fancy. It really happened. Listen to this story:

In 1970, the Jewish Publishing House in Jerusalem issued an altered edition of the New Testament; it then translated it into various world languages, including an English version, which was distributed by the Reed Agency in London. In the introduc-

---

[1] "Most praised,". a variant form of the name Muhammad.
[2] Qur'an 61:6.
[3] Qur'an 61:14.
[4] Quoted in *Rays of Light on Christianity*, Mutawalli Yusuf Shalabi, p. 52f.

tion to this altered edition of the New Testament was the following:

> This authoritative Jewish translation of the New Testament may be described as the New Testament devoid of anti-Semitism.
>
> The modifications introduced into the 1611 translation (the standard English edition until now) can be proved by reference to the earliest sources, which were chosen with one aim: to get rid of—as much as reality permits—the bigotry of that translation which aimed at sowing enmity between Christians and Jews.
>
> The true translation of the New Testament consists of love instead of that murderous antipathy. Based on that, we can rightfully say that this Jewish translation is the true Christian translation. Aside from those changes, the text of this translation remains as they were in the translation of 1611.
>
> This translation represents a long overdue proclamation of reconciliation between Christianity and Judaism.

Allah is certainly free from all imperfections.

The Jews set out to alter the New Testament, the text of Christianity, to sift out all that which offended them so that love would prevail between them and the Christians.

And what was the reaction of the Christians to this momentous action? Not a thing! The Christians remained completely silent, as if the issue didn't concern them in the slightest! None of them made the slightest movement; no clerics nor any writer or thinker.

In fact, the only ones who called attention to the Jewish horseplay with the texts of Christianity were Muslim authors. They raised the issue of the alteration to the Gospel and the rest of the texts of the New Testament at Muslim-Christian conferences held in Cordova, Tripoli, and Cairo. The position of the Christian religious figures was total silence, merely staring at the faces of the Muslim scholars holding the distorted copy in their hands!

And what a difference between the silence of the Christians with regard to their Holy Book and the stance of Muslims with

Muslim-Christian Dialogue

regard to the Noble Qur'an. As for the Qur'an, its status differs completely from that of all other divinely revealed scriptures. Allah has taken responsibility for protecting and preserving it from every alteration and change, whether by deletion or addition. Allah, the Exalted, said:

> Lo! We, even We, revealed the Reminder, and lo! We verily are its Guardian."[1]

> It is an unassailable Scripture. Falsehood cannot come at it from before it or behind it: It is sent down by One Full of Wisdom, Worthy of all Praise. (It is) a revelation from the Wise, the Owner of Praise."[2]

> Do not move your tongue with it to hasten it. Lo! upon Us (rests) its compilation and its recitation. So when We recite it, follow its recitation; then lo! upon Us (rests) its explanation.[3]

The Orientalists and meritorious researchers of the West agree that the Noble Qur'an is unchanged, guarded on paper and in the hearts. Not a word of it has been deleted, nor has any word been added. Among them is Sir William Muir, who said in his book *The Life of Muhammad* — and he is well-known for his prejudice against Islam and Prophet Muhammad (may Allah's peace and blessings be upon him):

> A quarter century had not passed after the death of Muhammad before violent disputes developed and factions arose, and 'Uthman fell a victim to this turmoil, and the differences still remain. However, the Qur'an remained the only scripture of these factions. The reliance of all these factions upon the Qur'an for recitation is a manifest proof that the book in our hands today is the same text which the ill-treated Caliph 'Uthman ordered to be collected and written. It is, perhaps, the only Book in the world whose text has remained free of alteration throughout one thousand two hundred years.

Another Orientalist, Waheiry, in his *Commentary on the Qur'an*, said:

---

[1] Qur'an (15: 9).
[2] Qur'an (41: 41-42).
[3] Qur'an 75:16-19.

The Qur'an is absolutely the furthest removed of all ancient texts from commingling and insertion and is the purest and most authentic of them.

Another of them, Yammer, the noted translator of the Qur'an into English, mentions in his book: "The text of the Qur'an which 'Uthman arranged as one book remains accepted and approved by Muslims."

Finally, Ben Bole says:

The greatest distinction of the Qur'an is that there is no doubt about its authenticity. We can be sure every sentence we read today has undergone no alteration for thirteen centuries.

The life of the Prophet, recorded with great integrity and meticulousness, and the Noble Qur'an, preserved and transmitted by countless human hearts and on paper, all that may be counted as a true sign that Muhammad's (may Allah's peace and blessings be upon him) prophethood was the Seal of Prophethood. The time and the place and all the conditions and circumstances were ready to receive the culmination of prophethood. It was a prophethood which inaugurated the age of knowledge and reason and the human aspirations to explore the universe and fathom its mysteries. It was a prophethood which gave impetus, not impediment. It is a message which opens the field for reason to reach its utmost, and praises the human being to the higher levels of righteous behavior, guidance, and a sense of duty to one's creator.

The Qur'an makes it clear with the plainest evidence that Muhammad is the Seal of Prophethood. Allah, the Exalted, said, "Muhammad is not the father of any man among you, but he is the Messenger of Allah, and the Seal of the prophets."[1]

Likewise, authentic *hadiths* of the Prophet (may Allah's peace and blessings be upon him) have been reported which corroborate this. He said (may Allah's peace and blessings be upon him):

---

[1] Qur'an (33-40).

The Children of Israel were led by the prophets; whenever a prophet died, a prophet succeeded (him). Lo! There will be no prophet after me, and there will be *khalifas*.[1]

And he said:

> My example and the example of the prophets before me is like that of a man who built a house, doing a fine job, making it lovely, except for the space of one brick from one corner. People began to circle around it, marveling at it and they said, "If only you had placed a brick there." I am that brick, and I am the Seal of the Prophets.[2]

And he said:

> I was favored over the (other) prophets with six (things): I was granted concise, comprehensive speech; I was granted victory due to fear (of me placed in the hearts of my enemies); spoils of war were made lawful for me; the whole earth was made a place of prayer as well as a means of purification for me; I was sent to the whole of creation, and the (line of) prophets was sealed with me.[3]

On another occasion, he said: "Lo! The sending of messengers and prophets has come to an end, there will be no messenger or prophet after me."[4] Once, he said:

> I am Muhammad, and I am Ahmad, and I am Al-Mahi, by whom Allah extinguishes the rejection of faith, and I am Al-Hashir, at whose feet the people will be resurrected, and I am Al-'Aqib, after whom there will be no prophet.[5]

The Qur'an has explicitly stated that this religion has reached its final stage of perfection and capacity for fulfilling the needs of humanity and fitness for permanence. The Most Exalted said:

---

[1] Reported by Al-Bukhari and Muslim.
[2] Reported by Al-Bukhari and Muslim.
[3] Reported by Muslim, At-Tirmidhi and Ibn Majah
[4] Reported by Ahmad and At-Tirmidhi
[5] Reported by Al-Bukhari and Muslim

> This day I have perfected your religion for you, and completed my favor upon you, and have chosen for you Islam as a religion.[1]

The verse was revealed at 'Arafah during the Farewell Pilgrimage, in the tenth year after the Hijrah.[2] No legislative verses were revealed after it, according to the majority of reports, and the Messenger of Allah did not live more than eighty-one nights after that day.

The Prophet said in his sermon on that day, with more than one hundred thousand people listening and memorizing:

> People! There will be no prophet after me, nor an *Ummah*[3] after you. Listen well! (If you) worship your Lord and pray your (daily prayers) and fast your month (Ramadan) and pay the *zakah* on your wealth willingly and cheerfully, and obey those in charge of your affairs, you will enter the Paradise of your Lord.[4]

The Universality of the Message of Muhammad

Muslim reported on the authority of Abu Hurayrah that the Messenger (peace be upon him) said:

> I was favored over the (other) prophets with six (things): I was granted concise comprehensive speech; I was granted victory due to fear (of me placed in the hearts of my enemies); spoils of war were made lawful for me; the whole earth was made a place of prayer as well as a means of purification for me; I was sent to the whole of creation; and the (line of) prophets was sealed with me.[5]

On another occasion he said:

---

[1] Qur'an 5: 3.
[2] The emigration from Makkah to Madinah, which marks the start of the Muslim calendar.
[3] An *Ummah* is the group of people to whom a prophet is sent.
[4] Reported by Ibn Jarir in *Tahdib al-Athar* and by Ibn Asakir. See *Kanz al-'Ummal* [5:295], printed in Aleppo.
[5] *Sahih Muslim*.

> Each prophet used to be sent to his people in particular, while I was sent to all mankind, and Allah, glory to Him, the Exalted said in the Noble Qur'an: "Say: Mankind! Lo! I am the Messenger of Allah to you all, (the Messenger) of Him to Whom belongs the dominion of the Heavens and the earth."[1]

And the Mighty and Glorious said:

> We have not sent you (Muhammad), save as a bringer of good tidings and a warner to all mankind.[2]

One strange and amazing opinion is the view of some Christians that Muhammad was a prophet for the Arabs in particular. They say this, then repeat it and vaunt it, while numerous texts of the Qur'an and Sunnah emphasize the comprehensiveness of his message to the whole of the creation.

In fact, numerous texts of the Qur'an and Sunnah contain the invitation directed to the People of the Book, Jews and Christians, as well as members of other religions and sects of every locality and region. The mission of the Messenger and his couriers and his jihad directed towards the Jews, Christians, Magians and pagans among the Arabs and others, is a true witness to what we say.

In countless places the Noble Qur'an discusses and criticizes the disbelief of the rejecters of faith among the Jews and Christians. It orders fighting against the oppressors and tyrants among them, and inviting them to embrace Islam, the true religion of God.

The Exalted says:

> Say: People of the Book! Come to an agreement between us and you: that we shall worship none but Allah, and that we shall ascribe no partner unto Him, and that none of us shall take others as lords beside Allah. And if they turn away, then say: Bear witness that we are they who have surrendered (unto Him). People of the Book! Why will you argue about Abraham, when neither the Torah nor the Gospel were revealed until after him? Have you no sense? Lo! You are

---

[1] Qur'an 7:158.
[2] Qur'an 34:28.

those who argue about that of which you have some knowledge. Why then do you argue about that of which you have no knowledge?

Allah knows; you know not. Abraham was not a Jew, nor a Christian; but he was an upright man who had surrendered (to Allah), and he was not of the idolaters. Lo! Those of mankind who have the best claim to Abraham are those who followed him, and this Prophet and those who believe (with him); and Allah is the Protecting Friend of the Believers. A party of the People of the Book long to make you go astray; and they make none to go astray except themselves, but they perceive not.

People of the Book! Why do you disbelieve in the revelations of Allah, when you (yourselves) bear witness (to their truth)? People of the Book! Why do you confound truth with falsehood and knowingly conceal the truth? And a party of the People of the Book say: "Believe in that which has been revealed unto those who believe at the beginning of the day, and disbelieve at the end of it, in order that they may return."[1]

In another place Allah says:

Say: People of the Book! Why do you disbelieve in the revelations of Allah, when Allah (Himself) is Witness of what you do? Say: People of the Book! Why do you drive back believers from the way of Allah, seeking to make it crooked, when you are witnesses? Allah is not unaware of what you do. You who believe! If you obey a party of those who have received the Scripture they will make you disbelieve after your belief.[2]

Allah also says:

You unto whom the Scripture has been given! Believe in what We have revealed confirming that which you possess, before We obliterate faces so as to confound them, or curse

---

[1] Quran 3:64-72.
[2] Qur'an 3:98-100.

them as We cursed the Sabbath-breakers (of old). The commandment of Allah is always executed.[1]

Later, in the same *surah* (chapter), Allah says:

People of the Book! Do not exaggerate in your religion or say anything concerning Allah except the truth. The Messiah, Jesus son of Mary, was only a messenger of Allah, and His word which He conveyed to Mary, and a spirit from Him. So believe in Allah and His messengers, and do not say "Three"—Stop! (It is) better for you!—Allah is only one God. Far is it removed from His Transcendent Majesty that He should have a son. All that is in the heavens and earth belongs to Him. And Allah is Sufficient an Advocate. The Messiah will never scorn to be a slave of Allah, nor will the favored angels. Whosoever scorns His service and is proud, all such will He assemble unto Him.[2]

Again, Allah advises the People of the Book, saying:

People of the Book! Now has Our messenger come to you, expounding unto you much of what you used to hide in the Scripture, and forgiving much. Now has a light from Allah come unto you and a clarifying Scripture, whereby Allah guides him who seeks His pleasure to the paths of peace. He brings them out of darkness into the light by His decree, and guides them unto a straight path.

They indeed have disbelieved who say: Lo! Allah is the Messiah, son of Mary. Say: Who then could do anything against Allah, if He had willed to destroy the Messiah, son of Mary, and his mother and everyone on earth? Allah's is the Sovereignty of the heavens and the earth and all that is between them. He creates what He will. And Allah is Able to do all things.

The Jews and the Christians say: "We are sons of Allah and His loved ones." Say: Why then does He punish you for your sins? Nay, you are only mortals of His creating. He forgives whom He will, and punishes whom He will. Allah's

---

[1] Qur'an 4:47.
[2] Qur'an 4: 171-172.

Muslim-Christian Dialogue

is the Sovereignty of the heavens and the earth and all that is between them, and unto Him is the journeying.

People of the Book! Now has Our messenger come to you to make things plain after an interval (of cessation) of the messengers, lest you should say: No messenger of glad tidings or warnings came to us. Now a messenger of glad tidings and warnings has come to you. Allah is Able to do all things.[1]

Further on, Allah, the Exalted, says:

Say: People of the Book! Do you blame us for anything else than that we believe in Allah and that which is revealed unto us and that which was revealed before, and because most of you are rebellious?[2]

A few verses later, Allah says:

Say: People of the Scripture! You are not on anything (of guidance) until you observe the Torah and the Gospel and that which was revealed to you from your Lord. That which is revealed unto you (Muhammad) from your Lord is certain to increase the contumacy and disbelief of many of them. But grieve not for the disbelieving folk.[3]

Later, Allah, the Exalted, says:

Say: People of the Scripture! Do not stress in your religion other than the truth, and do not follow the vain desires of a people who erred in the past and led many astray, and strayed from the straight path.[4]

Some may ask: Isn't there a contradiction between these verses and other verses which say:

Allah verily has shown grace to the believers by sending to them a messenger of their own who recites to them His revelations, and causes them to grow, and teaches them the Scripture and wisdom; although before (he came to them) they were in flagrant error.[5]

---
[1] Qur'an 5:15-19.
[2] Qur'an 5:59.
[3] Qur'an 5:68.
[4] Qur'an 5:77.
[5] Qur'an 3:164.

> Lo! We have revealed it, a recitation in Arabic, that you may understand.[1]
>
> And lo! it is a revelation from the Lord of the Worlds, which the True Spirit has brought down upon your heart, that you may be (one) of the warners, in plain Arabic speech.[2]
>
> And you were not beside the mountain when We called; but (the knowledge of it is) a mercy from your Lord that you may warn a people unto whom no warner came before you, that they might take heed.[3]?

We say in response:

There is not a single verse in the Noble Qur'an which indicates or hints that Muhammad's mission was solely to the Arabs. These verses merely confirm that he was sent to the Quraysh. Moreover, there is no contradiction when the Noble Qur'an directs certain verses at the People of the Book (as previously cited) and other verses at the Children of Israel and still others at the Children of Adam, as in the following statements of the Exalted:

> Children of Israel! Remember My favor with which I favored you, and fulfill your (part of the) covenant, I will fulfill My (part of the) covenant, and fear me.[4]
>
> Children of Israel! Remember My favor which I favored you and how I preferred you to (all) creatures.[5]
>
> Children of Adam! We have revealed unto you clothing to conceal your shame, and ornaments, but the clothing of restraint from evil, that is best. This is of the signs of Allah, that they may remember.[6]
>
> Children of Adam! Do not let Satan seduce you as he caused your (first) parents to go forth from the Garden.[7]

---

[1] Qur'an 127:12:2.
[2] Qur'an 26:192-95.
[3] Qur'an 28:46.
[4] Qur'an 2:40.
[5] Qur'an 2:47.
[6] Qur'an 7:26.
[7] Qur'an 7:27.

> Children of Adam! Don your adornment at every place of worship, and eat and drink, but do not be extravagant.[1]
>
> Children of Adam! If messengers from among yourselves come to you who narrate unto you My revelations, then whosoever refrains from evil and amends, there will be no fear on them neither will they grieve. But they who deny Our revelations and scorn them, such are denizens of the Fire, they will abide therein.[2]

Addressing a particular people in certain statements of the Islamic Call in no way negates the universality of the message to all humanity and all jinns.[3]

Because of this, all of humanity, and not only humanity but the jinns as well, are addressed by the message of Muhammad (may Allah's peace and blessings be upon him), and they will be held responsible for the extent to which they respond to and follow it.

It is stated in an authentic *hadith* of the Prophet: "Lo! Allah looked upon the inhabitants of the earth and despised them, the Arabs and non-Arabs among them, except for a few remnants of the People of the Book." The remnants whom the Messenger (may Allah's peace and blessings be upon him) meant in this *hadith* were holding fast to the true religion of Christ before the commissioning of Muhammad as a prophet. However, since Muhammad was commissioned, whoever has not believed in him is a rejecter of faith, a dweller in Hellfire. As he said, "By the One in Whose hand is my soul, whoever hears about me from the *Ummah*, whether a Jew or a Christian, then dies without believing in me, he will be a dweller in Hellfire."[4]

It is well known that the Children of Israel were the *Ummah* to whom most prophets were sent. Moses was sent to them, and many prophets after him. Some people even say their number

---

[1] Qur'an 7:31.
[2] Qur'an 7:35-36.
[3] Jinns are beings invisible to us but present in the world. Created from fire, they also have limited free choice like human beings and are thus responsible for their actions and will be judged accordingly on the Day of Resurrection.
[4] Reported by Muslim.

reached a thousand prophets, all of them observing the legal code of the Torah.

Then Christ came to them with a different code; he changed some of the legal code of the Torah by the decree of Allah. So if the sending of Moses and the prophets after him did not prevent the sending of Christ to the Children of Israel, why do they reject Muhammad being a messenger to the Jews and Christians (People of the Book) when no prophet had come to them since Christ? As the Most Exalted Allah says:

> People of the Scripture! Now has Our messenger come to you to make things plain after an interval (of cessation) of the messengers, lest you say: "No messenger of glad tidings or warnings came to us." Now a messenger of glad tidings and warnings has come to you. Allah is Able to do all things.[1]

The Truthful, The Trustworthy

If someone says, I am assailed by doubts regarding Muhammad's truthfulness in claiming prophethood, we say to him:

A. Those who reject Muhammad as objectionable should know that their rejection of him is a rejection of other prophets besides him, and doubt about him means doubt about other prophets besides him. Conversely, exonerating prophets besides him is all the more reason to exonerate him. The life of Prophet Muhammad was more momentous than those of the other prophets, as is his legal code, his *Ummah*, the Scripture revealed to him by the Lord, his miracles, and his guidance. So anyone who denies him or doubts him has all the more reason to doubt the other prophets. And whoever believes in the prophets besides him and calls for them to be followed, for him to believe in Muhammad is more fitting and more correct.

B. Muhammad proclaimed the religion of the prophets before him, attested to their truthfulness, and praised them. We would even be justified in saying that many of those who believe in prophets like Moses and Jesus (peace be upon them) and

---

[1] Qur'an 5:19.

others besides them believe in them only by way of him. And we would be justified in saying that, had it not been for Muhammad and what he narrated to them, many nations would not have believed in them! "If the Noble Qur'an had not mentioned what it did about the birth of Christ and the signs of Allah in him and his mother, people would have considered this subject ancient legend." This statement was made by a Christian author!

C. Many verses of the Noble Qur'an establish the testimony of the People of the Book on his behalf, and the belief of many of them in him. Allah, the Exalted says:

> Lo! Those who have received the Scripture know that (this revelation) is the truth from their Lord. And Allah is not unaware of what they do.[1]

> Those whom we gave the Scripture recognize him as they recognize their sons. But Lo! A party of them knowingly conceal the truth.[2]

> Say (Muhammad): What thing is of most weight in testimony? Say: Allah is Witness between me and you. And this Qur'an has been inspired in me, that I warn you by it and whomsoever it may reach. Do you really bear witness that there are gods beside Allah? Say: I bear no such witness. Say: He is only one God. Lo! I am innocent of that which you associate (with Him). Those unto whom We gave the Scripture recognize (this revelation) as they recognize their sons. Those who ruin their own souls will not believe.[3]

> And lo! Of the People of the Scripture there are some who believe in Allah and that which is revealed to you and that which was revealed to them, humbling themselves before Allah. They do not purchase a measly gain at the price of the revelations of Allah. Verily their reward is with their Lord. Lo! Allah is swift to take account.[4]

> Say: I am no new thing among the messengers (of Allah), nor do I know what will be done with me or with you. I do

---

[1] Qur'an 2:144.
[2] Qur'an 2:146.
[3] Qur'an 6:19-20.
[4] Qur'an 3:199.

but follow that which is inspired in me, and I am but a plain warner. Say: Will you not consider: If it is from Allah and you disbelieve in it, while a witness of the Children of Israel has already testified to the like of it and has believed, and you are too proud (what will happen to you)? Lo! Allah does not guide wrongdoers.[1]

Those who disbelieve say: "You are not sent by Allah." Say: Allah, and whosoever has true knowledge of the Scripture, is sufficient witness between me and you.[2]

Muhammad is the Messenger of Allah. And those with him are hard against the disbelievers and merciful among themselves. You (Muhammad) see them bowing and falling prostrate (in worship), seeking bounty from Allah and (His) acceptance. Their marks are on their faces from the traces of prostration. That is their likeness in the Torah, and their likeness in the Gospel—like a seed that sends forth its shoot, then strengthens it, then rises firm on its stalk, delighting the sowers, that He may enrage the disbelievers with (the sight of) them. Allah has promised, unto such of them as believe and do good deeds, forgiveness and immense reward.[3]

These Qur'anic verses allude to considerable evidence present in the Scriptures of the Jews and Christians, of which we have previously quoted examples. If someone were to say he doesn't concede or acknowledge that the Holy Scriptures of the Old and New Testament contain any allusion or prophecies about Muhammad, we would say to him that two points result as a consequence of his position.

The first point is that no Jewish or Christian book believes in Muhammad (may Allah's peace and blessings be upon him), on the pretext that the Qur'an says he was "described in the Torah and the Gospels (which) are with them,"[4] and he is not described in the Torah and Gospels (which are) with them.

However, the contrary is established historical fact. Surely, those who believed in Muhammad and followed him from

---

[1] Qur'an 46:9-10.
[2] Qur'an 13:43.
[3] Qur'an 48:29.
[4] Qur'an 7:51.

among the Jews and Christians, long ago and in this time—a vast number who can scarcely be counted—did not believe in him until they had read these verses and found these prophecies in their Scriptures.

The second point is that Muhammad appeared and subdued the Jews and Christians, the People of the Book, taking some of them captive in war, killing some of their men, and driving the disbelievers among them from their homes to the first exile. There has to have been some mention of him and the momentous events that would happen to them in his era. And if he were a liar or impostor—God forbid—there would have to be a warning in their books about his followers.

It is known that the People of the Book take two points of view (on this). The first point of view is that he is not present in their books. The second point of view is that he is present and is mentioned with praise and acclaim.

There is no third point of view; no proponent claims he is mentioned with condemnation and warning. If he had been present in their books with condemnation and warning, that would have been the most prominent evidence used in arguments against him in his lifetime, or against his followers after his death. Those who didn't accept Islam would have argued on that basis against those who had.

It is well known that many People of the Book used to—and still do—hate him (may Allah's peace and blessings be upon him), concealing and manifesting considerable enmity and denial of him. In fact, this has spurred them to invent empty and imaginary things and attribute them to him. Some of them went so far as to interpret the Muslim slogan *Allahu akbar*—'God is Great'—that Akbar is the name of an idol, and that the Prophet ordered them to exalt and worship him! Surely, a people who would go to such lengths of fabrication and lying would be capable of bringing to light anything in their books to discredit him and warn against him; however, they did not do so, because their Scriptures are devoid of such claims!

D. Whoever claimed to be a prophet and told the truth would be one of the best of Allah's creation and among the most complete in knowledge and religion. There is no doubt that the messengers of Allah and His prophets were the best of humanity, the most just, the most pious, the most rightly guided of mankind, even though some of them were more excellent than others. Allah says about the messengers: "Those are the messengers, some of whom We have caused to excel others, some of them Allah spoke to, and He raised some of them in degree,"[1] And as Allah, Who is free from imperfections, said about the prophets, "And we preferred some of the prophets above others and we gave David the Psalms."[2]

As for one who claims prophethood and is lying, he is one of the greatest disbelievers from among Allah's creation, the most corrupt and evil of them. As Allah, the Exalted, says, "Who is guilty of more wrong than one who invents a lie against Allah, or says 'I am inspired,' when he is not inspired at all; and who says, 'I will reveal the like of what Allah revealed.'"[3]

Also, the Exalted says:

> And who does greater wrong than one who tells a lie against Allah and denies the truth when it comes to him. Is there not an abode in Hell for the disbelievers? And whoever brings the truth and believes in it—those are the dutiful. They will have whatever they want from their Lord. That is the reward of the good.[4]

Later, Allah described the end of such people:

> And on the Day of Resurrection you (Muhammad) shall see those who lied about Allah with their faces blackened. Is there not in Hell any abode for the arrogant?[5]

Lying is the basis of evil, and the most outrageous lie is the one told about Allah, the Mighty and Glorious. And truthfulness is the basis of good, and the greatest truth is conveying the message of Allah, the blessed and Exalted. The Prophet said:

> Stick to truthfulness, for truthfulness leads to piety and piety leads to Paradise. A man will continue to strive for truthfulness until he dies and is recorded in Allah's sight as emi-

---

[1] Qur'an 2:253.
[2] Qur'an 17:55.
[3] Qur'an 6:93.
[4] Qur'an 39:32-34.
[5] Qur'an 39:60.

nently truthful. And watch out for lying, for lying leads to depravity, and depravity leads to Hellfire. A man will continue to tell us lies until he is recorded in Allah's sight as an inveterate liar.[1]

This is a reality known to all sensible human beings. Therefore it is appropriate for us to quote the following perceptive and precise discussion which took place between Heraclius and Abu Sufyan. It is an exchange which reveals understanding, knowledge, and intelligence on Heraclius' part.

Heraclius was a king of the Christians in the era of the Prophet. When the Prophet (may Allah's peace and blessings be upon him) sent him a letter inviting him to Islam, he asked about ten matters.

Ibn 'Abbas (may Allah be pleased with him and his father) said: "Abu Sufyan Ibn Harb told me, from his mouth to mine:[2]

"'I set out during the period of truce between me and the Messenger of Allah. While I was in Palestine, a letter was brought from the Messenger of Allah to Heraclius. Al-Kalbi had brought it and presented it to the Governor of Basra, who sent it on to Heraclius.

"Heraclius asked, 'Is there anyone here from the people of this man who claims he is a prophet?'

"They said, 'Yes.'

"Abu Sufyan continued: 'I was summoned along with a group of Qurayshis. We entered upon Heraclius, who had us seated before him.

"'He said: "Which of you is most closely related to this man who calls himself a prophet?"

"'I (Abu Sufyan) said, "I am." They sat me in front of him and seated my companions behind me. He called his interpreter and said to him, "Tell them I will ask about this man who claims he is a prophet. If he tells a lie inform me." I

---

[1] Narrated by 'Abdullah Ibn Mas'ud and collected by Al-Bukhari and Muslim.
[2] i.e., I heard it from him and I am now relating it.

said, "By Allah, if not for fear of being caught in a lie, I would have lied about him." Then he told his interpreter to ask me how his lineage was among us.

"'I said, "He is from a good family among us."

"'He said, "Did he have any kings among his ancestors?"

"'I said, "No."

"'He said, "Did you ever curse him before he said what he said?"

"'I said, "No."

"'He said, "And who follows him, the nobles of the community or the weak?"

"'I said, "The weak among them."

"'He said, "Are they increasing or decreasing?"

"'I said, "They are increasing."

"'He said, "Does anyone apostatize from his religion after entering it out of discontent with it?"

"'I said, "No."

"'He said, "Have you fought with him?"

"'I said, "Yes."

"'He said, "How did your fighting with him go?"

"'I said, "The war between us and him goes back and forth. He causes us losses and we cause him losses."

"'He asked, "Does he act treacherously?"

"'I said, "No, but we are currently in a truce with him. We don't know what he will do during it." By Allah, he didn't give me a chance to put in a word against him other than this.

"'He asked, "Has anyone made a claim like this before him?"

"'I said, "No."

"'He asked, "What does he order you (to do)?"

"'I said, "He says, 'Worship Allah Alone and do not worship anything along with Him, and leave what your forefathers [used to] say,' and he commands prayer, truthfulness, chastity, and maintaining good ties with our relatives."

"'He told his interpreter, "Tell him I asked you about his lineage, and you said he is from a respected family among you. Just so, the messengers are commissioned from among the respected families of their peoples.

""'And I asked you if there was a king among his forefathers, and you claimed there wasn't. If there had been a king among his ancestors, I would have said he is a man seeking the kingdom of his ancestors.

""'And I asked you about his followers, if they are from the weaker classes or the nobility. You said from the weak. Those are (always) the followers of the messengers.

""'I asked you if you had accused him of a lie before he said what he said. You claimed not, so I know he would not forgo lying against people, then lie against Allah. And I asked you if anyone apostatizes from his religion after entering into it out of discontent with it; you claimed not. That is the way of true faith when its delight penetrates and permeates the hearts.

""'And I asked you if they are increasing or decreasing, and you claimed they are increasing. That is the way of true faith until it reaches completion. And I asked you if you had fought with him. You claimed you have fought with him and that the war goes back and forth between you; he inflicts a defeat on you and you inflict one on him. Likewise the prophets do not act treacherously.

""'And I asked you if anyone before him had made a claim like this. You claimed no. If one before him had made such a claim, I would have said he is a man imitating something said before him.

""'Then I asked what he commands you. You said he commands you with prayer, (paying) the poor-due, maintaining good relations with relatives, and chastity. If what you say

Muslim-Christian Dialogue

about him is true, he is a prophet. I was expecting his emergence, but I didn't think he would be from among you. If I knew I could definitely meet him I would love to do so, and if I were in his presence I would wash his feet, and surely his kingdom will reach (this land) beneath my feet."

"'Then he called for the letter of the Messenger of Allah (may Allah's peace and blessings be upon him). In it was the following: "In the name of Allah, the Merciful, the Compassionate. From Muhammad, the Messenger of Allah, to Heraclius, ruler of the Byzantines. Peace be on him who follows the guidance. To proceed:

""'I invite you to Islam. If you become a Muslim you will be safe, and Allah will double your reward. If you turn away, the sins of your peasants and the masses will be on you. 'Say: People of the Book! Come to an agreement between us and you: that we will worship none but Allah, and that we will ascribe no partner unto Him, and that none of us will take others as lords beside Allah. And if they turn away, then say: Bear witness that we have surrendered (unto Him).'[1]""

In another version, Heraclius asked: "What does he command you?"

He said, "He commands us to worship Allah and not worship anything along with Him, and he forbids us that which our forefathers used to worship. and he commands of us prayer, truthfulness and chastity, fulfilling covenants and discharging trust."[2]

He said, "That is the description of a prophet."

E. The revelation of the Qur'an was revealed to him, even though he was illiterate. He never went to school or sat with a teacher, nor did he travel in search of knowledge.

Allah says:

> You (Muhammad) did not use to read any Scripture before it, nor did you write it with your right hand, for then the fol-

---

[1] Qur'an 3:64.
[2] Reported by Al-Bukhari and Muslim.

314

lowers of falsehood would have (had cause) to be suspicious.[1]

And the Exalted says:

> And when our clear revelations are recited to them, those who do not look forward to meeting us say: Bring a recitation other than this, or change it. Say (Muhammad): it is not for me to change it of my own accord; I only follow that which is revealed to me. Lo! If I disobey my Lord I fear the retribution of an awful Day. Say: If Allah had so willed, I would not have recited it to you, nor would He have made it known to you. I dwelt among you a lifetime before it. Have you then no sense?[2]

And contemplate, if you will, the statement of Allah, the Exalted: "I dwelt among you for a lifetime before it." During this lifetime, in which he dwelt among them for up to forty years, he was not known for any knowledge, poetry or eloquence. When he reached forty, he began to preach. In fact, he spoke extensively, with beneficial knowledge, sound guidance, and comprehensive good. The illiterate became a teacher, not the teacher of a school or a locality, a city, tribe or nation, nor the teacher for just one era or single generation; rather, he became the teacher of the whole world, with all its colors and nationalities, and a teacher for all eras and times.

Allah the Exalted, says:

> Allah recited the Scripture and wisdom unto you and taught you that which you did not know. The grace of Allah upon you has been infinite.[3]

He did not speak from his own self, or articulate by the power of his own soul, or by the charm of his eloquence, or the fluency of his tongue. Rather, Allah, the Glorious and Exalted, was the One Who taught him wisdom and incisive speech.

Allah had taught him to say in his supplication: "My Lord, increase me in knowledge."[4]

---

[1] Qur'an 29:48.
[2] Qur'an 10:15-16.
[3] Qur'an 4:113.
[4] Qur'an 20:114.

And Allah the Exalted made clear the tremendous transformation in the life of the Messenger and how it was He alone, Glory to Him, Who taught him, trained him, and made him grow. He said:

> And it was not [granted] to any mortal that Allah should speak to him except by revelation or behind a veil, or (that) he sends a messenger who reveals what He will by His leave. Lo! He is Exalted, wise. And thus have We inspired in you (Muhammad) a spirit of Our command. You did not know what the Scripture was nor the faith. But We have made it a light whereby We guide whom We will of Our slaves. And lo! You verily lead to a straight path, the path of Allah to Whom belongs whatsoever is in the heavens and whatsoever is in the earth. Listen! The end of all affairs is to Allah.[1]

On another occasion, Allah, said about him and to him:

In the name of Allah, the Merciful, the Compassionate.

> By the morning hours, and by the night when it is still, your Lord has not forsaken you nor does He hate you, and verily the latter portion will be better for you than the former, and verily your Lord will give unto you so that you will be content. Did He not find you an orphan and give you shelter? Did He not find you wandering and direct (you)? Did He not find you destitute and enrich (you)? Wherefore do not oppress the orphan; wherefore do not repel the beggar; wherefore of the bounty of your Lord speak.[2]

The Noble Qur'an is the major miracle of the Prophet (may Allah's peace and blessings be upon him). It is the only remaining text of the religion of Allah and His guidance, showing what He wants from the worshippers. It is recited as an act of devotion, and its shortest *surah* represents a challenge (to bring the like thereof). This is the secret of the spread of Muhammad's message (may Allah's peace and blessings be upon him) in both East and West, despite the meager effort expended in its propa-

---

[1] Qur'an 42:51-53.
[2] Qur'an 93:1-11.

gation—especially in this era—when measured against all the impediments set in its path by its enemies.

Truly Islam, the Qur'an, and the Shari'ah[1] of Muhammad (may Allah's peace and blessings be upon him) is spreading, and the pace of its spread is increasing, even in those countries they call the New World, the lands of enlightenment, freedom and human rights!

The famous English writer, George Bernard Shaw, wrote:

> If there is any effect in the predictions of prominent people, I predict that the religion of Muhammad, which is beginning to find acceptance in Europe today, will be more acceptable to it tomorrow, and will be the religion of all mankind before the final sound (of the Trumpet).[2]

In an authentic *hadith*, the Messenger of Allah (may Allah's peace and blessings be upon him) said:

> There was no prophet who was not given some signs by the like of which people came to believe in him. The special thing Allah gave me was a revelation revealed to me, and I hope I will have the most followers among them on the day of resurrection...

F. The evidence and proofs which testify to Muhammad's (may Allah's peace and blessings be upon him) truthfulness and the authenticity of his prophethood are more than can be counted or exhaustively listed, for his Companions (may Allah be pleased with them) are signs of his truthfulness. Anyone who studies their lives before Islam and after it, whether individuals or groups, will find marvels.

They were a nation given to insulting each other and disputing among themselves. Between them were enmity and feuds handed down from generation to generation. Wars would get going among them; no sooner had one ended than another would be started. These perpetual wars were ignited by the most trivial causes and could not be extinguished by countless people's striving and efforts.

---

[1] The divinely revealed legal code of Islam, contained in the Qur'an, the Prophet's explanation of it, and his sayings and actions.
[2] i.e., the final moment before the end of this world.

This *Ummah* changed—with the help of Allah—to an *Ummah* mutually allied, harmonious, bonded by mutual solidarity, and one that was powerful. The Messenger said about them, " Muslims' blood is all on a par. The least of them may extend protection (to one who must be observed by all of them), and they are one hand against those not of them."

Allah, Who is free from all imperfections, said about them:

> You who believe! Observe your duty to Allah with right observance, and do not die except as those who have surrendered (unto Him). And hold fast, all of you together, to the rope of Allah, and do not split up. And remember Allah's favor to you: how you were enemies and He made friendship between your hearts so that you became brothers by His grace; and you were upon the brink of an abyss of fire, and He saved you from it. Thus does Allah make clear His signs to you, that you may perhaps be guided.[1]

And the Exalted says:

> And if they would deceive you, then lo, Allah is sufficient for you. He is the One Who supported you with His help and with the believers, and has attuned their hearts. If you had spent all that is in the earth you could not have attuned their hearts, but Allah has attuned them. Lo! He is Mighty, Wise.[2]

In short, the life of the Messenger is among his signs, and his character, his statements, his actions, his legal code are from among his signs. His *Ummah* is among his signs, his expeditions are among his signs. The knowledge and religious practice of his *Ummah* are among his signs, the miracles performed by pious members of his *Ummah* are among his signs. They are all signs of his credibility.

Physical Miracles

If someone were to ask, "Where are Muhammad's physical miracles?" we would respond that it would require pages and pages, in fact, books and volumes. However, we will make do

---

[1] Qur'an 3:102-103.
[2] Qur'an 8:62-63.

Muslim-Christian Dialogue

with a few indications and allusions. Whoever wants more details can look for them in books of Hadith and biographies of the Prophet, and histories. They are full of what will quench thirst and fill the bill.[1]

Among his many miracles are the following;

1. His informing his Companions about (Islam's) conquest of Makkah, Jerusalem, Yemen, Greater Syria, and Iraq.

2. That Khaybar would be conquered at the hands of 'Ali (may Allah be pleased with him) the following day.

3. That they would divide the treasures of the Persian and Roman emperors.

4. That the Persian empire, after a blow or two, would come to a complete end forever. However, the Romans (Byzantium, the West, Christian civilization) would resist for centuries, each passing generation being replaced by another, a power on land and sea, but to the end of time? No way!

5. That Allah contracted the earth before him, so he could see its eastern and western regions, and that the dominion of his *Ummah* would extend to what he saw contracted for him.

6. That there will always continue to be a portion of his *Ummah* manifestly on the truth. No one who differs from and opposes them will harm them until the order of Allah comes (for removing the last Muslim as precursor to the Day of Judgment).

7. That turmoil and dissension would not appear as long as 'Umar remained alive.

8. That 'Uthman would be killed while reading the Qur'an.

9. That the most wretched besides 'Uthman's killers would be one who dyed 'Ali's beard with the blood of his head.

10. That 'Ammar would be killed by a rebellious faction.

11. That the caliphate would remain after him thirty years and then it would be replaced by a kingdom grasping for power and clinging to it tenaciously.

---

[1] Ibn Taymiyyah says of the physical miracles of the Messenger (pbuh), "I have compiled about one thousand miracles." in *The Criterion Between the Allies of the Allies of the Most Merciful and the Allies of Satan*, p. 25.

12. That the Banu Thaqif would produce a great liar and a great murderer. They consider Mukhtar to be that liar and Hajjaj to be that murderer.

13 That his *Ummah* would take to the sea for jihad, looking like kings on thrones. Al-Bukhari and Muslim reported:

> The Messenger of Allah used to visit Umm Haram bint Milhan, an aunt of the Prophet by fostering. She was married to 'Ubadah Ibn As-Samit. He visited her one day and she served him food, and then she sat and picked lice from his hair. Later, he went to sleep, then woke up smiling. She inquired, "What makes you smile?" He said, "People from my *Ummah* were shown to me on a military expedition in the path of Allah, riding over the waves of the sea, kings upon thrones (or he said "like kings upon thrones")."
>
> She said, "Ask Allah to make me one of them." He said, "You will be one of the first." She did embark on a naval expedition during Mu'awiyah's reign. Afterwards, she was thrown from her mount and died.[1]

14. That Fatimah (may Allah be pleased with her) would be the first of his family to follow him; and she did die six months after his death (peace be upon him)

15. He said about Al-Hassan Ibn 'Ali (May Allah be pleased with them), "My (grand)son here is a leader. Allah will use him to bring about reconciliation between two major parties." It happened as he reported. Allah used him to reconcile his followers and the people of Syria.

16. That Abu Dharr would live alone and die alone.

17. That the first of his wives to follow him would be the one who was most generous. The first of his wives to follow him was Zaynab bint Jahsh known for her generous spending in charity.

18. That Suraqah Ibn Ja'sham would wear the bracelets of Chosroe (the emperor of Persia).

---

[1] Reported by Muslim in the *Book of Government* (*Imarah*): the chapter on the excellence of naval expeditions, 3:1518 (#1912).

19. And he told Khalid (Ibn Al-Walid, may Allah be pleased with him) when he sent him to Ukaydar: "You will find him hunting cattle."

20. Al-Baydawi and others reported:

> When the Quraysh appeared from Al-Uqunqul, the Prophet said, "This is Quraysh coming with its arrogance and pride, denying your Messenger. O Allah: I ask You what You promised me." Then Jibril came and told him to take a fistful of dust and throw it at them. When the two armies met, he took a handful of dust and threw it in their faces, and said, "May their faces be distorted." Not one idolater was left who was not preoccupied with his eyes, whereupon they were defeated. The Muslims pursued them, killing them and taking them captive. When they had finished they started boasting to one another. A man would say, "I killed and I captured." *It was about this that Allah said, "And you (Muhammad) did not throw when you threw, but Allah threw."*[1]

21. Water gushed from between his fingers on numerous occasions. This miracle is greater than water gushing from a rock, as happened for Moses, since that happens regularly and often with rocks. But this never happened from fingers composed of flesh and blood, other than his fingers.

Anas Ibn Malik (may Allah be pleased with him) said:

> I saw the Messenger of Allah when the time came for the mid-afternoon (*'Asr*) prayer. The people were looking for water for ablution but couldn't find any. Water was brought to the Messenger of Allah. The Messenger of Allah placed his hands in the container and ordered the people to perform ablution from it. I saw water gushing from between his fingers, and the people performed ablution from it until the last one of them (had done so). This miracle occurred at Az-Zawra at the market place of Al-Madinah.

And Jabir (may Allah be pleased with him) reported:

> The people grew thirsty on the day of Al-Hudaybiyyah. The Messenger of Allah had a small pot in front of him. He performed ablution and people gathered in his vicinity. They

---

[1] Qur'an 8:17.

said, "We have no water except what is in your pot." The Prophet (peace be upon him) placed his hands in the pot. Water began to gush between his fingers like springs, and the number of people present was one thousand four hundred.

22. Jabir (may Allah be pleased with him) reported that a man came to the Prophet (may Allah's peace and blessings be upon him) asking for food. He gave him a lot of barley. He continued to eat from it, along with his wife and guests. Then, (one day), he measured it. Then he came to the Prophet (may Allah's peace and blessings be upon him) and informed him (that it was used up). He said, "If you had not measured it, you would have eaten from it, and it would have remained with you."[1]

The miracles of a dramatic increase in food have been narrated by approximately fifteen Companions, a huge number of *Tabi'un*,[2] and by countless numbers after them. Similar incidents occur in narrations concerning previous prophets, for instance, the miracle of Elijah (may Allah's peace and blessings be upon him) increasing bread and oil in the house of a widow.[3] Likewise, there was the miracle of Elisha, when he increased twenty loaves of barley bread and fresh ears of grain in a sack until one hundred men ate from it and had some left.[4] Also, there was the miracle of Jesus in increasing five loaves and two fish.[5]

23. Jabir reports that the roof of the mosque was supported by date palm trunks. When the Prophet delivered a sermon, he would stand beside one of these trunks. When a *minbar*[6] was built for him we heard a sound from that trunk like a pregnant animal. In a version reported by Anas, (the trunk sounded) until the mosque shook from its lowing; and in a version reported by Sahl many people began to weep at what they saw of (its anguish); and in a version reported by Al-Muttalib, it got to the

---

[1] Reported by Ahmad in the *Musnad* [3:337], and Ibn Majah in his *Sunan, The Book of the Merits of the Messenger*, 2:642.
[2] The Successors, the generation which followed the Companions of the Prophet (pbuh).
[3] I Kings, Chapter 17.
[4] II Kings 5:42.
[5] Matthew, Chapter 14.
[6] A three-step platform, from which the Friday sermon is delivered.

Muslim-Christian Dialogue

point of cracking and splitting, until the Prophet came and laid his hand upon it and it fell silent.

24. Ibn 'Abbas (may Allah be pleased with him) reports:

> There were three hundred sixty idols around the Ka'bah, their legs anchored with lead to the stones. When the Messenger of Allah entered the mosque in the Year of Victory (of Makkah) he began pointing a staff in his hand at them without touching them. Whenever he pointed at the face of an idol it would fall over on its back, and whenever he pointed at the back of one's head it would fall on its face. He did this until no idol was left.

25. Sa'd Ibn Abi Waqqas (may Allah be pleased with him) reported:

> The eye of Qatadah Ibn Nu'man was hit so that it popped out and lay on his cheek. The Messenger of Allah put it back in place and it became the better of his two eyes.

26. Anas Ibn Malik (may Allah be pleased with him) narrated:

> My mother said, "Messenger of Allah, Anas has served you. Please pray to Allah on his behalf." He said, "O Allah, increase his wealth and children, and bless him in what you gave him." I said, "By Allah, my wealth is great and my children and grandchildren today number about a hundred."

27. His Night Journey to Jerusalem in a single night and his ascent from there to Heaven [was another miracle]. The Exalted said:

> Free from all imperfection is He Who carried His slave by night from the Inviolable Place of Worship[1] to the Far Distant Place of Worship,[2] whose vicinity We have blessed, that We might show him of Our signs. Lo! Only He is All-hearing, All-seeing.[3]

No Christian is entitled to deny the Night Journey and ascension of the Prophet, because the like of it is established about Elijah in the Old Testament:

---

[1] The *Masjid al-Haram*, in Makkah.
[2] The *Masjid al-Aqsa*, in Jerusalem.
[3] Qur'an 17:1.

Now when the Lord was about to take Elijah up to the heaven by a whirlwind, Elijah and Elisha were on their way from Gilgal.[1] ...and as they still went on and talked, behold, a chariot of fire and horses of fire separated the two of them. And Elijah went up by a whirlwind into heaven.[2]

28. The splitting of the moon, based on the statement of the Exalted: "The hour drew near and the moon was split. And if they behold a sign they turn away and say: prolonged illusion."[3] It is reported that Hudhayfah Ibn Al-Yaman delivered a sermon in Mada'in, in which he said, "Listen! The hour has drawn near, and verily the moon did split during the lifetime of your Prophet."

29. The Prophet prayed against the Persian emperor when he tore up his letter, asking Allah to tear up his empire. Of course, nothing remained of it.

30. There were rocks that would greet him with salaams and stones would hymn Allah's Glory in his hands.

Space does not permit us to keep going, so we will make do with what we have mentioned. Anyone wanting greater detail should refer to two books:

1. *Al-Jawab as-Sahih liman Baddala Din al-Masih*, by Shaykh al-Islam Ibn Taymiyyah (*The Complete Response to Those Who Changed Christ's Religion*).

2. *Izhar al-Haqq*, by Shaykh Rahmatullah Al-Hindi (*Bringing Out the Truth*).[4]

If someone were to say: "We haven't seen, witnessed, or experienced any of what you have mentioned of these physical miracles, so they aren't proof for us," we would say to him, "Likewise we never saw, witnessed or experienced any of the miracles of Christ and the other prophets."

If someone were to say, "But we have so many reliable reports about them from different sources," we would say to him, "The Islamic narrations are absolutely the most precisely documented of any historical reporting. As for the Christian narra-

---

[1] II Kings 2:1.
[2] II Kings 2:11.
[3] Qur'an 56:1-2.
[4] This has been published and is available at Islamic bookstores.

tions, they are assailed by doubt from every quarter." Moreover, the physical miracle is everything with respect to these other religions. If they are verified, these religions are authentic and if they are disqualified or doubt is raised about them, these religions become untenable. As for Islam, the final religion, the one brought by the Final Prophet, Muhammad, it wasn't established on the basis of physical miracles only; it was established on abstract miracles, the pinnacle of which is the Noble Qur'an.

The Noble Qur'an is an intellectual, lasting miracle, undiminished by the passage of time. In fact, the passage of time has only strengthened and reemphasized its miraculous nature, for time is a component of the miracle of the Qur'an.

Islam is a miraculous religion by every facet of meaning in the word "miraculous."

It is miraculous in its legislation.
It is miraculous in its history.
It is miraculous in the extent of its knowledge.
It is miraculous in its victories and conquests.

If someone were to say that the Qur'an denies physical miracles at the hands of the Prophet (may Allah's peace and blessings be upon him), as can be found in Surat Al-An'am:

> And they swear a solemn oath by Allah that if a sign came to them they would surely believe in it. Say: Signs are only with Allah and (so) is that which informs you that if they did come to them they would not believe.[1]

Further, it is mentioned in Surat Al-Isra':

> And they say, "We will never believe in you until you cause a spring to gush from the earth for us; or you have a garden of date-palms and grapes, and cause rivers to gush forth therein abundantly; or you cause the heavens to fall upon us piecemeal, as you claimed; you bring Allah and the angels before us, or you have a house of gold; or you ascend up into the heaven; and even then we will not believe in your ascent until you bring down for us a book that we can read."

---

[1] Qur'an 6:109.

Muslim-Christian Dialogue

> Say (Muhammad): "My Lord be Glorified. Am I anything but a mortal messenger?"[1]

We would say in response to him: What may be understood from these and similar verses is the negation of miracles on demand. It doesn't follow that all miracles are denied, as it is not the duty of prophets to produce a miracle every time their deniers demand one. On the contrary, they do not produce a miracle when the request for them is based on obstinacy, testing, and mockery.

There are examples of this in their own scriptures. I do not know why they overlook them. The New Testament says:

> The Pharisees came and began to argue with him. And he sighed deeply in his spirit, '"Why does this generation seek a sign? Truly I say to you, no sign shall be given to this generation."[2]

The meaning of this passage is that the Pharisees demanded a miracle from Jesus as a test. However, he did not perform a miracle, nor did he try to perform a miracle at that time or promise to perform a miracle later. Rather, he said that that generation would not be given a sign. This would indicate that no miracle would issue from him at all, since the word "generation" covers all those living at his time.

This is not the only passage on the issue conveyed to us by the New Testament. There are other such passages. For instance, the Gospel of Luke relates that when Herod saw Jesus, he was very glad, for he had long desired to meet him, because he had heard about him, and he was hoping to see some sign by him. So he questioned him at some length; but he made no answer. The chief priests and the scribes stood by, vehemently accusing him. And Herod with his soldiers threatened him with contempt and mocked him; then, arraying him in gorgeous apparel, he sent him back to Pilate.

Also, the Gospel of Luke in another passage relates:

> Now the men who were holding Jesus mocked him and beat him; they also blindfolded him and asked him, "Prophesy!

---
[1] Qur'an 17:90-93.
[2] Mark 8:11-12.

Muslim-Christian Dialogue

who is it that struck you?" And they spoke many other words against him, reviling him.[1]

And the Gospel of Matthew says:

> And those who passed by derided him, wagging their heads and saying, "You who would destroy the temple and rebuild in three days, save yourself! If you are the son of God, come down from the cross." So also the chief priests, with the scribes and elders, mocked him, saying, "He saved others; he cannot save himself. He is the King of Israel; let him come down from the cross and we will believe in him. He trusts in God; let God deliver him now, if He desires him; for he said, 'I am the Son of God.'" And the robbers who were crucified with him also reviled him in the same way.[2]

In another place, Matthew relates:

> Then some of the scribes and Pharisees said to him, "Teacher, we wish to see a sign from you." But he answered them, "An evil and adulterous generation seeks for a sign; but no sign shall be given to it except the sign of the prophet Jonah. For as Jonah was three nights and three days in the belly of the whale, so will the Son of Man be three days and three nights in the heart of the earth."[3]

We have some comments on this passage.

The first observation: Christ promised a miracle which didn't issue from him, since Christ was crucified around noon, Friday, as is known from chapter 19 of the Gospel of John, and he died in the ninth hour, and Joseph (of Arimathea) asked Pilate for his body that evening, then shrouded and buried him, as is clear from the Gospel of Mark. So his burial must have been Friday night. And his body was missing from the grave before sunrise on Sunday, as is clear from the Gospel of John, so he didn't remain in the earth three days and three nights, as he said; he only remained one day and two nights!

The second observation: The scribes and Pharisees didn't see his preservation with their own eyes, because they were the

---

[1] Luke 22:63-65.
[2] Matthew 27:39-44.
[3] 12:38-40.

ones who demanded the sign, and because they were the ones threatened by it!

Also in the Gospel of Matthew:

> And the Tempter came to him and said to him, "If you are the Son of God, command these stones to become loaves of bread," but he answered, "It is written, 'Man shall not live by bread alone, but by every word that proceeds from the mouth of God.'" Then the Devil took him to the holy city and set him on the pinnacle of the temple, and said to him, "If you are the Son of God, throw yourself down, for it is written, 'He will give His angels charge of you,' and 'On their hands they will bear you up, lest you strike your foot against a stone.'" Jesus said to him, "Again it is written, 'You shall not tempt the Lord your God.'"[1]

We see in this passage that the Devil demanded from Jesus (may Allah's peace and blessings be upon him), by way of a test, two miracles, and he didn't respond to either of them.

Jihad in Islam

I have before me a question about the sword and the spread of Islam by the sword. That is a constantly recurring question. Obviously, this is not the first time it has been raised, and it won't be the last. Just as this is not the first time it was answered, nor will it be the last. We must understand that the prop of the false sects is a memorized prop, tossed up without understanding or insight.

It is as if Allah, Most Exalted, Most Glorified, intended for the clergy to maintain the prop of these accusations and spread them among their followers and those they wish to entangle in their nets and snares, intending it as a deterrent from the path of Allah and a means of diverting people from the religion of guidance and truth. But it turns into a token of guidance, a sign of innocence, and a glad tidings of truth—as Allah intended it to

---

[1] Matthew 4:3-7.

Muslim-Christian Dialogue

be. Needless to say, there is a huge difference between what Allah wants and what the oppressors want.

Indeed, Allah has commanded the Muslims to debate all people in the best way, whether they are the People of the Book or not. Allah, Most Exalted says:

> Do not argue with the People of the Book unless it is the better way, except for those who do injustice among them; and say: We believe in that which has been revealed to us and revealed to you; our God and your God is one and unto Him we surrender.[1]

If they are from any other group, then Allah, the Exalted, says:

> Call unto the way of your Lord with wisdom and fair exhortation, and reason with them in the better way, Lo! Your Lord knows best who strays from His path and He knows best who is guided. And if you punish, then punish with the like of that with which you were afflicted; but if you endure patiently (Muhammad,) your endurance is only by (the help of Allah). Do not grieve for them, and do not be in distress because of what they plot. Lo! Allah is with those who keep their duty to Him and those who are doers of good.[2]

These verses and those similar to them do not contradict Allah's statement:

> Will you not consider those unto whom it was said: Withhold your hands, establish prayer and pay *zakat*, but when fighting was prescribed for them, behold! a party of them fear mankind as much as the fear of Allah or with greater fear, and say, "Our Lord! Why have you ordained fighting for us? If only you would grant us a delay a little longer." Say (to them, Muhammad): The comfort of this world is measly; the Hereafter will be better for whoever is careful of his duty (to Allah); and you will not be wronged (by so much as) the down on a date-stone.[3]

The combination of debate and jihad is the procedure of Islam and its methodology. Each approach has its place, as each is

---
[1] Qur'an 29:46.
[2] Qur'an 16:125-128.
[3] Qur'an 4:77.

beneficial where the other is not. Employing both of them is more effective in manifesting guidance and the religion of truth.

Whoever is a non-Muslim living under Muslim political authority,[1] or is visiting Muslim lands with their permission, or is a citizen of a nation with whom the Muslims have a treaty, may not be striven against militarily. They are included in Allah's command to invite and debate them in the best way. They are not included with those whom Allah has commanded to be fought against.

In *Sahih al-Bukhari* it states that, at the time of his death, 'Umar Ibn Al-Khattab delivered a sermon in which he said:

> I advise the *khalifah*[2] after me regarding the covenant of protection by Allah and the covenant of protection by His Messenger, to fulfill their covenant, and fight those outside the borders (to protect them), and not to burden them with more than they are capable of.

This is in accord with the statement of the Prophet:

> Listen! Whoever oppresses a non-Muslim living under Muslim authority by a covenant, or deprives him of any of his rights, or burdens him beyond his capabilities, or takes something from him against his will, I will be his disputant on the Day of Resurrection.[3]

Abu 'Ubayd said in *The Book of Wealth*, on the authority of Abu Az-Zubayr, that the Prophet

> ...wrote to the people of Yemen that whoever accepts Islam among the Jews or Christians would be one of the Believers, having the same rights and responsibilities as the rest of them. And whoever wished to remain a Jew or a Christian should not be coerced to leave his religion, and is required to pay the *jizyah*.[4]

As for those who do wrong and are unjust, Allah advises us, "Do not argue against the People of the Book unless it is in the

---

[1] Called *ahl adh-dhimmah*, or *dhimmi*, in Arabic.
[2] i.e., caliph.
[3] Reported by Abu Dawud.
[4] *jizyah*— a tax on non-Muslims in the Muslim state, paid in lieu of military service; they, on the other hand, are not required to pay *zakah*.

better way, except for those who do injustice among them."[1] We have not been commanded to debate them in the best way. Naturally, someone perpetrating injustice is not interested in knowledge, religion, or truth, and therefore deserves to be fought against.

As for a person seeking safe passage through Muslim lands who is of a people at war with the Muslims, Allah has ordered that he be extended protection until evidence of the truth has been presented to him, then safe passage to a place he feels secure. Allah, the Exalted says:

> If one of the polytheists seeks your protection (Muhammad), then protect him so that he may hear the word of Allah, and afterwards convey him to his place of safety. That is because they are a people who do not know.[2]

The impetus for an Islamic declaration of war is mercy, for it is conducted with mercy and concluded with mercy. If it is an act of mercy to a human body to cut some diseased portion from it to prevent the spread of disease or gangrene, then it is an act of mercy to humanity collectively to amputate elements of corruption such as tyrants, oppressors and dictators. Only in this way can the rest of mankind live in security and peace, with their lives unthreatened by fear, injustice or oppression.

The motivating factor for an Islamic war, as mentioned in the Noble Qur'an, is to repel aggression and oppose tyranny. Allah, Most Exalted, says:

> Sanction is given to those who fight because they have been wronged; and Allah is indeed Able to give them victory.[3]

And Allah, Most Exalted, says:

> Fight in the way of Allah against those who fight against you, but do not act brutally.[4] Lo! Allah has no love for aggressors.[5]

In another place, Allah says:

---

[1] Qur'an 29:46.
[2] Qur'an 9: 6.
[3] Qur'an 22:39.
[4] An alternative translation: "but do not begin hostilities."
[5] Qur'an 2:190.

And fight them until persecution is no more, and religion is for Allah. But if they desist, then let there be no hostility except against the unjust.[1]

And Allah, the Absolutely Perfect, made it clear that treatment of aggressors should only be according to the extent of their aggression. The Exalted says:

The forbidden month for the forbidden month, and forbidden things in retaliation. And one who attacks you, attack him in like manner as he attacked you. Observe your duty to Allah, and know that Allah is with those who ward off (evil).[2]

From these and other passages—and there are a lot of them—we see that the beginning of hostilities was on the part of the idolaters. It was an attack on religious freedom. Repeated attempts were made by a variety of methods to persecute the Believers for their beliefs, drive them from their religion, and deter them from the path of their Lord.

Likewise, it became clear from these passages and many others that when the Muslims were called upon to repel aggression, they were also called upon to observe two important rules:

1. To avoid aggression: "And do not begin hostilities. Lo! Allah has no love for aggressors."[3] Aggression here is to fight against someone who does not initiate fighting against them and does not lay down obstacles and impediments in the path of the Islamic preachings and guidance.

2. And *taqwa*: "And keep your duty to Allah, and know that Allah is with those who ward off evil."[4] *Taqwa* here is adherence to moral excellence, lest the current of the enemy sweep them into copying their enemies' actions in their assault on people's honor, mutilating the dead, and all the other ignorant, terrorist, despicable methods of the polytheists.

Moreover, whoever reviews the life of the Prophet and what the Muslims went through in terms of oppression and torture, persecution and expulsion, knows that the motivation for Islamic

---

[1] Qur'an 2:193.
[2] Qur'an 2:194.
[3] Qur'an 2:190.
[4] Qur'an 2:194.

Muslim-Christian Dialogue

warfare was to repel aggression and stop the savage and terrorist spread of injustice and oppression, "until persecution is no more and religion is for Allah."[1]

Here is a summary discussion about warfare in the Arabian peninsula, and a condensed explanation of its causes and motives.

Polytheism gathered all its power and armies and brought forth its last ounce of strength to strike Islam in its stronghold in the midst of its supporters in Madinah.

Then Allah's command was revealed:

> And wage war on all the polytheists as they are waging war on all of you, and know that Allah is with those who keep their duty (to Him).[2]

These were the circumstances of Islamic warfare in the Arabian Peninsula. As for the circumstances of those wars outside the peninsula, the Messenger directed his letters and couriers to the kings and leaders, to Heraclius, to Maqauqus,[3] to Chosroes,[4] even to some of the leaders of distant Arab lands.

The response of most of them was insulting, whether in words or deeds. Whoever traces the historical events will see that the motive for Islamic war was to ward off injury and make the invitation (to Islam) possible, to oppose evil and combat tyranny. It was never to force religious conversion or coerce anyone to believe. Allah, the Exalted says:

> There is no compulsion in religion. The right direction has been made distinct from errors. So whoever rejects false deities and believes in Allah has grasped the firm handhold which will never come apart. And Allah is All-Hearing, All-Knowing.[5]

In addition, the Most Exalted says:

---

[1] Qur'an 2:193.
[2] Qur'an 9:36.
[3] Ruler of Egypt.
[4] Emperor of Persia.
[5] Qur'an 2:257.

Muslim-Christian Dialogue

> And if your Lord had so willed, everyone on earth would have believed together. Would you (Muhammad,) compel humanity until they are believers?[1]

There is no evidence that Muhammad forced anyone to convert. On the contrary, there is evidence of just the opposite. Some of the *Ansar* wanted to force their children to accept Islam, and the Prophet forbade them. Allah says:

> And if one of the polytheists seeks your protection (Muhammad), then protect him so that he may hear the word of Allah, and afterwards convey him to his place of safety.[2]

Let us now pause to examine some of the texts which cast light on the manner of the Prophet and his instructions about war, during its preparation, its engagement and in its aftermath.

1. The Prophet used to call on the Believers not to wish for encountering the enemy, for he used to say: "Do not wish for encountering the enemy, but when you meet them be steadfast."[3]

2. He was very enthusiastic in forbidding fighting until all alternatives had been exhausted. He said to Mu'adh Ibn Jabal (may Allah be pleased with him), when sending him to Yemen as a commander:

> Do not fight them until you invite them (to Islam). If they refuse, do not fight them unless they start it against you. If they start it, do not fight them unless they kill someone among you. Then show them that and say to them, "Isn't there a better way than this?" For if Allah were to guide at your hands one man, it would be better than everything on which the sun rises and sets.

3. The Prophet said in describing himself, "I am the prophet of mercy, and I am the prophet of battle."

Mercy and battle are inseparable in the wars of the Prophet, for true mercy lies in excising the sources of corruption and halting the spread of crime and evil.

---

[1] Qur'an 10:99.
[2] Qur'an 9:6.
[3] Reported by Al-Bukhari in his *Book of Jihad*, chs. 32, 112 & 156, and by Muslim in his *Book of Jihad*, chs. 29, 20, and by Abu Dawud's *Book of Jihad*, Ch. 89.

4. And the Prophet (may Allah's peace and blessings be upon him) used to instruct his soldiers to try to reconcile hearts and not to destroy lives:

> Try to reconcile people and give them time, and do not attack them until you have invited them. Your bringing all the tent-dwellers and city-dwellers of the earth to me as Muslims is more beloved to me than your bringing their women and children to me (as slaves) and killing their men.

5. The Prophet used to advise his army not to lay waste to crops or cut down trees or kill the weak, whether women or children or men who had neither a decision-making or advisory role in the fighting nor direct or indirect participation in it. For instance he said:

> Proceed with the name of Allah. Do not exceed the proper bounds; do not act treacherously; do not mutilate; do not kill children.

And he said to Khalid Ibn Al-Walid (may Allah be pleased with him): "Do not kill any child or any worker."[1]

6. The Prophet used to emphasize the prohibition against killing children, women, and the elderly who do not fight or advise those conducting the fighting. Once, he was passing by the corpses after a battle and he happened to see a woman who had been killed. He said, "This one should not have been killed." And he said:

> What is the matter with people who get carried away with killing until they kill children? Listen! Do not kill children! Listen! Do not kill children!

7. The Prophet used to prohibit mutilation of the dead, even if the idolaters did it to the Muslims. He said, "Don't you dare mutilate the dead."

8. The Prophet used to order those killed among the idolaters to be buried. He did not allow their corpses to be left for wild animals to despoil. For example, he ordered the corpses of the slain Quraysh (at the battle of Badr) to be placed in Qulayb, a dry well. Likewise, he used to forbid finishing off wounded men.

---

[1] i.e., non-combatant.

9. The Prophet's battles used to end in one of three outcomes:

First: a mutual cessation of hostilities. Allah says:

> And if they incline toward peace, you also incline to it. And trust in Allah. Lo! He is All-Hearing, All-Knowing.[1]

And Allah says:

> You who believe! Enter, all of you, into peace; and do not follow the footsteps of Satan. Lo! he is an open enemy to you.[2]

Second: a peace treaty and an end to the war. This peace treaty was on the basis of justice and fulfillment of the agreed-upon conditions. Therefore, it had necessarily to be linked to the open propagation of Islam in the lands where victory went to the believers.

Third: outright victory, which was achieved when the word of Allah was made uppermost. As Allah, the Exalted, said:

> ...those who, if We give them power in the land, establish worship *(salah)* and pay the poor-due *(zakah)* and enjoin what is right and forbid what is wrong. And to Allah belongs the outcome of all affairs.[3]

10. The Prophet's attitude toward his defeated enemies was one of extreme generosity. We will give one example of his noble humanitarianism.

The Prophet's last war with the Quraysh ended with the conquest of Makkah by Islam and the Muslims. Then what? Then the Prophet met those people who had caused him immense suffering, had been his untiring enemies, and had persecuted his Companions and tortured them severely, until some of them had even died under torture.

What did the Prophet say to them? And what did they say to him? He said to them: "What do you think I'm going to do with you?" They said, "(You will do) good. You are a noble brother and son of a noble brother."

---

[1] Qur'an 8:61.
[2] Qur'an 2:208.
[3] Qur'an 22: 41.

He said, "I will not say anything to you except what my brother Joseph said: 'There will be no censure upon you today. May Allah forgive you, and He is the Most Merciful of all who show mercy.'[1] Go, for you are released."[2]

11. His attitude toward prisoners was so generous and well-known that it needs no mention. He said, "Treat the prisoner well." His Companions complied with his orders so well that Allah praised them with his statement: "And they provide food to the needy, the orphan, and the prisoner, out of love for Him."[3]

War in the Holy Scriptures

After this brief but faithful presentation of the methods of Islamic war as discussed in the Noble Qur'an and the pure Sunnah, we present a comparative picture of religious war as spoken about in the Holy Books of the Jews and the Christians. Things are distinguished by comparison with their opposites, as our early scholars used to say. We will see how loathsome and repulsive this other picture is. We want to minimize our comments, because we want the texts to speak for themselves and tell everything.

In Chapter 20 of Deuteronomy, starting from verse 10, the Old Testament says:

> When you draw near to a city to fight against it, offer terms of peace to it. And if its answer to you is peace and it opens to you, then all the people who are found in it shall do forced labor for you and shall serve you. But if it makes no peace with you, but makes war against you, then you shall besiege it; and when the Lord your God gives it into your hand you shall put all its males to the sword, but the women and the little ones, the cattle, and everything else in the city, all its spoil, you shall take as booty for yourselves; and you shall enjoy the spoil of your enemies, which the Lord your

---

[1] Qur'an 12:92.
[2] Reported by Al-Bukhari in the *Book of Military Expeditions*, and Ahmad in the *Musnad* (3:190, 286).
[3] Qur'an 76:8.

God has given you. Thus you shall do to all the cities which are very far from you, which are not the cities of the nations here.

But in the cities of these peoples that the Lord your God gives you in inheritance, you shall save alive nothing that breathes, but you shall utterly destroy them, the Hittites and the Amorites, the Cannanites and the Perizzites, the Hivites and the Jebusites, as the Lord your God has commanded; lest they teach you to do according to all their abominable practices which they have done in the service of their gods, and so to sin against the Lord, your God.[1]

It appears from this passage (which is supposedly sacred) that God ordered every living man, woman, and child to be put to the sword from among the following people:

1. the Hittites
2. the Amorites
3. the Canaanites
4. the Perizzites
5. the Hivites
6. the Jebusites

And He ordered that all those besides them be called upon to enter a treaty. If they agreed and accepted obedience, submission, and payment of tribute, then so be it. Second, if they didn't agree, they would be fought against. Last, if victory was completed over them, every male would be put to the sword; their women and children would be enslaved, and their animals and wealth seized and distributed among the warriors. That was what was to be done to every nation other than the six nations.

The Bible also says:

When my angel goes before you, and brings you in to the Amorites, and the Hittites, and the Perizzites, and the Canaanites, the Hivites, and the Jebusites, and I blot them out, you shall not bow down to their gods, nor serve them, nor do according to their works, but you shall utterly overthrow them and break their pillars in pieces.[2]

Regarding the treatment of these six nations the Torah spells out some more details. It says:

---

[1] Deuteronomy 20:10-18.
[2] Exodus 23:23-24.

Observe what I command you this day. Behold, I will drive out before you the Amorites, the Canaanites, the Hittites, the Perizzites, the Hivites, and the Jebusites. Take heed to yourself, lest you make a covenant with the inhabitants of the land whither you go, lest it become a snare in the midst of you. You shall tear down their altars, and break their pillars, and cut down their Asherim.[1]

Then it continues:

And the Lord said to Moses in the plains of Moab by the Jordan at Jericho, "Say to the people of Israel, when you pass over the Jordan into the land of Canaan, then you shall drive out all the inhabitants of the land from before you, and destroy all their figured stones, and destroy all their molten images, and demolish all their high places; and you shall take possession of the land and settle in it, for I have given the land to you to possess it. You shall inherit the land by lot according to your families; to a large tribe you shall give a large inheritance; wherever the lot falls to any man, that shall be his; according to the tribes of your fathers you shall inherit. But if you do not drive out the inhabitants of the land from before you, then those of you whom you let remain shall be as pricks in your eyes and thorns in your sides, and they shall trouble you in the land where you dwell. And I will do to you as I thought to do to them."[2]

In another place the Bible says:

When the Lord your God brings you into the land which you are entering to take possession of it, and clears away many nations before you, the Hittites, the Girgashites, the Amorites, the Canaanites, the Perizzites, the Hivites, and the Jebusites, seven nations greater and mightier than yourselves, and when the Lord your God gives them over to you, and you defeat them; then you must utterly destroy them, and show no mercy to them. You shall not make marriages with them, giving your daughters to their sons or taking their daughters for your sons. For they would turn away your sons

---

[1]Exodus 34:11-13.
[2]Numbers 33:50-56.

from following me, to serve other gods; then the anger of the Lord would be kindled against you, and he would destroy you quickly. But thus shall you deal with them: you shall break down their altars, and dash in pieces their pillars, and hew down their Asherim, and burn their graven images with fire. For you are a people holy to the Lord your God.[1]

We learn from these passages (which are holy, of course) that God ordered the extermination of every living member of the seven nations, without mercy toward them, without making any covenant with them. Moreover, He ordered the destruction of their sacrificial sites, the breaking of their idols, the burning of their craven images, and the shattering of their pillars. He demanded their annihilation with phenomenal vehemence, to the extent that He said if they didn't carry it out: "I will do to you as I thought to do to them."

Moreover, there are observations—which are not trivial—connected to the numbers of those nations and peoples. The text says they are "greater and mightier than yourselves." In order to arrive at a rough estimate of these peoples we say: It is established in the first chapter of the Book of Numbers that the number of the Children of Israel fit for fighting i.e., twenty years of age or older, were 603,550 men. The Levites and those younger than twenty years old were excluded from this number. If we take all those numbered (as fighters) from the Children of Israel and add to them all male and female non-combatants, their numbers would reach at the very least a million and a half. Let us quote the relevant text in its entirety to determine for ourselves these numbers. The Bible says:

> The people of Reuben, Israel's first-born, their generations, by their families, by their fathers' houses, according to the number of names, head by head, every male from twenty years old and upward, all who were able to go forth to war: the number of the tribe of Reuben was **forty-six thousand five hundred**.
>
> Of the people of Simeon, their generations, by their families, by their fathers' houses, those of them that were numbered,

---

[1]Deuteronomy 7:1-6.

according to the number of names, head by head, every male from twenty years old and upward, all who were able to go forth to war: the number of the tribe of Simeon was **fifty-nine thousand three hundred**.

Of the people of Gad, their generations, by their families, by their fathers' houses, according to the number of the names, from twenty years old and upward, all who were able to go forth to war: the number of the tribe of Gad was **forty-five thousand six hundred and fifty**.

Of the people of Judah, their generations, by their families, by their fathers' houses, according to the number of names, from twenty years old and upward, every man able to go forth to war: the number of the tribe of Judah was **seventy-four thousand six hundred**.

Of the people of Issachar, their generations, by their families, by their fathers' houses, according to the number of names, from twenty years old and upward, every man able to go forth to war: the number of the tribe of Issachar was **fifty-four thousand four hundred**.

Of the people of Zebulun, their generations, by their families, by their fathers' houses, according to the number of names, from twenty years old and upward, every man able to go forth to war: the number of the tribe of Zebulun was **fifty-seven thousand four hundred**.

Of the people of Joseph, namely, of the people of Ephraim, their generations, by their families, by their fathers' houses, according to the number of names, from twenty years old and upward, every man able to go forth to war: the number of the tribe of Ephraim was **forty thousand four hundred**.

Of the people of Manasseh, their generations, by their families, by their fathers' houses, according to the number of names, from twenty years old and upward, every man able to go forth to war: the number of the tribe of Manasseh was **thirty-two thousand and two hundred**.

Of the people of Benjamin, their generations, by their families, by their fathers' houses, according to the number of names, from twenty years old and upward, every man able to go forth to war: the number of the tribe of Benjamin was **thirty-five thousand and four hundred.**

Of the people of Dan, their generations, by their families, by their fathers' houses, according to the number of names, from twenty years old and upward, every man able to go forth to war: the number of the tribe of Dan was **sixty-two thousand seven hundred.**

Of the people of Asher, their generations, by their families, by their fathers' houses, according to the number of names, from twenty years old and upward, every man able to go forth to war: the number of the tribe of Asher was **forty-one thousand five hundred.**

Of the people of Naphtali, their generations, by their families, by their fathers' houses, according to the number of names, from twenty years old and upward, every man able to go forth to war: the number of the tribe of Naphtali was **fifty-three thousand four hundred.**

These are those who were numbered, whom Moses and Aaron numbered with the help of the leaders of Israel, twelve men, each representing his father's house. So the whole number of the people of Israel, by their fathers' houses, from twenty years old and upward, every man able to go forth to war in Israel—their whole number was **six hundred and three thousand five hundred and fifty.**

But the Levites were not numbered by their ancestral tribe along with them.[1]

From all of this it becomes clear that these seven nations which were more numerous than the Israelites—their population must have been many millions.

A priest, Doctor Keith, wrote a book called *Archaeology in the Stories of the Israelite Prophets*, in which he says that it is known from ancient writings that the number of people in the Jewish lands 550 years before the Exodus was eighty million.

---

[1]Numbers 1:30-47.

This, then, is the number which the "Sacred Scripture" ordered to be killed and exterminated—eighty million!

As we continue to sift through the "Sacred Scriptures" which contain vehement commands for murder and extermination we find plenty to alarm one and turn one's hair white. For instance, the Bible says that "Whoever sacrifices to any god, save to the Lord only, shall be utterly destroyed."[1]

Later, talking about the calf-worshippers, the Old Testament relates:

> And when Moses saw that people had broken loose (for Aaron had let them break loose, to their shame among their enemies), then Moses stood in the gate of the camp, and said, "Who is on the Lord's side? Come to me." And all the sons of Levi gathered themselves together to him. And he said to them, "Thus says the Lord God of Israel, 'Put every man his sword on his side, and go to and fro from gate to gate throughout the camp, and slay every man his brother, and every man his companion, and every man his neighbor.'" And the sons of Levi did according to the word of Moses; and there fell of the people that day about three thousand men.[2]

Also, the Bible says:

> While Israel dwelt in Shittim the people began to play the harlot with the daughters of Moab. These invited the people to the sacrifices of their gods, and the people ate, and bowed down to their gods. So Israel yoked himself to Ba'al of Pe'or. And the anger of the Lord was kindled against the Children of Israel; and the Lord said to Moses, "Take all the chiefs of the people, and hang them in the sun before the Lord, that the fierce anger of the Lord may turn away from Israel." And Moses said to the judges of Israel, "Every one of you slay his men who have yoked themselves to the Ba'al of Pe'or."
>
> And behold, one of the people of Israel came and brought a Midianite woman to his family, in the sight of Moses and in

---

[1] Exodus 22:20.
[2] Exodus 32:25-28.

the sight of the whole congregation of the people of Israel, while they were at the door of the tent of meeting. When Phinehas the son of Eleazar, son of Aaron the Priest, saw it, he rose and left the congregation, and took a spear in his hand and went after the man of Israel into the inner room, and pierced both of them, the man of Israel and the woman, through her body. Thus the plague was stayed from the people of Israel. Nevertheless those that died by the plague were twenty-four thousand.[1]

Later, in the same book, the Bible says:

And Moses sent them to the war, a thousand from each tribe, together with Phinehas the son of Eleazar the priest, with the vessels of the sanctuary and the trumpets of the alarm in his hand. They warred against Midian with the rest of their slain, Evi, Rekem, Zur, Hur, and Reba, the five kings of Midian; and they also slew Balaam the son of Be'or with the sword. And the people of Israel took captive the women of Midian and their little ones; and they took as booty all their cattle, their flocks, and all their goods. All their cities in the places where they dwelt, and all their encampments, they burned with fire, and took all the spoil and all the booty, both of man and of beast. Then they brought the captives and the booty and the spoil to Moses, and to Eleazar the Priest, and to the congregation of the people of Israel, at the camp on the plains of Moab by the Jordan at Jericho.

Moses, and Eleazar the Priest, and all the leaders of the congregation, went forth to meet them outside the camp. And Moses was angry with the officers of the army, the commanders of thousands and the commanders of hundreds, who had come from service in the war. Moses said to them, "Have you let all the women live?"[2] He then ordered, "Kill every male among the little ones, and kill every woman who has known man by lying with him. But all the young girls

---

[1] Numbers 25:1-9.
[2] 31:6-15.

who have not known man by lying with him, keep alive for yourselves."[1]

And they did as he ordered. The booty included 675,000 sheep, 72,000 cattle, 61,000 donkeys, and 32,000 women and young girls. Here we must ask: If the number of women and young girls was thirty-two thousand, what was the total number of males killed, i.e., adult men, youth and children? And how many women were killed who had "known men by lying with them?"

If we turn to Joshua, we find that he set about killing millions after the death of Moses. This is according to the Book of Joshua.

Elsewhere, we find that Samson killed a thousand men with the jawbone of an ass. The Bible says:

> And he found a fresh jawbone of an ass, and put out his hand and seized it, and with it he slew a thousand men. And Samson said, "With the jawbones of an ass, heaps upon heaps, with the jawbone of an ass have I slain a thousand men."[2]

Also it says:

> Now David and his men went up, and made raids upon the Geshurites, the Gerizites, and the Amalekites; for these were the inhabitants of the land from of old as far as Ashur, to the land of Egypt. And David smote the land, and let neither man nor woman alive, but took away the sheep, the oxen, the asses, the camels, and the garments, and came back to Lachish.[3]

This is the David as presented to us by "the Sacred Text". It presents him as a man who assaults a country, ruins the houses, and then leaves no man or woman alive, and leaves no cattle or property unplundered.

Then, David also defeated Hadadezer the son of Rehab, king of Zobah, as he went to restore his power at the river Euphrates. And David took from him a thousand and seven

---

[1] Numbers 31:17-18.
[2] Judges 15:15-16.
[3] I Samuel 27:8-9.

hundred horsemen, and twenty thousand foot soldiers; and David hamstrung all the chariot horses, but left enough for a hundred chariots. And when the Syrians of Damascus came to help Hadadezer king of Zobah, David slew twenty-two thousand men of the Syrians. Then David put garrisons in Aram of Damascus; and the Syrians became servants to David and brought tribute. And the Lord gave victory to David wherever he went.[1]

In another narration, the Bible says:

> So David gathered all the people together and went to Rabbah, and fought against it and took it. And he took the crown of their king from his head; the weight of it was a talent of gold, and in it was a precious stone; and it was placed on David's head. And he brought forth the spoil of the city, a very great amount. And he brought forth the people who were in it, and set them to labor with saws and iron picks and iron axes, and made them toil at the brick-kilns; and thus he did to all the cities of the Ammonites.[2]

That is how the books of the Old Testament spoke. And that is how the priests of the Old Testament believed. So what do the books of the New Testament say? And what do the priests of the New Testament believe?

Paul comments on all this and other similar texts from the Old Testament—and they are very many—in his letter to the Hebrews. He says:

> And what more shall I say! For time would fail me to tell of Gideon, Barak, Samson, Jephthah, of David and Samuel and the prophets—who through faith conquered kingdoms, enforced justice, received promises, stopped the mouths of lions, quenched raging fire, escaped the edge of the sword, won strength out of weakness, became mighty in war, put foreign armies to flight.[3]

---

[1] II Samuel 8:3-6.
[2] II Samuel 12:29-31.
[3] Hebrews 11:32-34.

So Paul, the most prominent church leader of the New Testament, saw that what those whom he named did was nothing other than piety, faith, fear of God, improvement, and good!

Like him, the clergy of the past and present pass on these reports of demolition, destruction, murder, and expulsion with delight and praise, as a veritable hatchery of miracles and signs, And as the poignant hymns play in the background, they repeat Christ's words: "Do not think that I have come to bring peace on earth; I have not come to bring peace, but a sword."[1]

The Documents Speak Out

Now I will quote some passages from *The History of Christian Persecution*, and I would like to divide this persecution into two types: the first type is when the Christians were themselves the victims of persecution; the second type is when they became the persecutors.

We are obliged to take a critical look to get acquainted with the traits of these people in both circumstances. We have to know what their enemies put them through at the dawn of Christian history, then, what the Christians did to their enemies and those who disagreed with them after they gained strength, became established and began to rule.

At the beginning of their era, the Christians were weak; they were subjected to a variety of tortures, injustices, humiliation and barbarism. Then their turn came as power fell into their hands, and they subjected their enemies and opponents to a variety of murders, massacres, and expulsions. They even initiated a ministry for savage torture, which they named "The Holy Office," and courts, which they named "The Courts of Inquisition."

As for the teachings of mercy and forgiveness, and as for the proclamations of Christ which they proudly quote:

> "You have heard that it was said, 'an eye for an eye and a tooth for a tooth.' But I say to you, Do not resist one who is evil. But if anyone strikes you on the right cheek, turn to him the other also; and if anyone would sue you and take

---

[1]Matthew 10-34.

your coat, let him have your cloak as well; and if anyone forces you to go one mile, go with him two miles. Give to him who begs from you, and do not refuse him who would borrow from you. You shall have heard that it was said, 'You shall love your neighbor and hate your enemy.' But I say to you, love your enemies and pray for those who persecute you."[1]

These teachings and advice were taken away by the wind.

Christians Under Fire of Persecution

Persecution of Christians began early, and Christ himself, according to their legends, fell victim to this persecution. Also his followers after him were subjected to great oppression and injustice. The Jews were the source of this cruelty.

However, Christianity began to spread despite the Jews and got the upper hand on them. At that point in time the Romans stepped in to perform their famous role of persecuting Christians. That was because the Romans didn't recognize the new religion as anything more than an extension of Judaism, and Judaism was an object of Roman disdain and revulsion. This was a departure from the usual policy of the Roman empire of granting its subjects religious freedom. That was because Judaism, with its zealotry and exclusivism, inspired hatred and rancor in the hearts of outsiders. Moreover, the Romans, before Christ, had their hands full trying to put down the stormy movement of Jewish zealotry for national liberation. That was from one angle.

From another angle, what stirred Roman rancor specifically at Christians was that they had taken the spirit of zealotry from Judaism. They had proclaimed, even in the time of their weakness, their hostility towards other religions. Moreover, they openly declared that they would work to dismantle Roman civilization whenever the opportunity presented itself.

This transformation which Christianity proclaimed, from forbearance, tolerance, and mercy to rancor and vengeance, exemplifies the transformation of Christianity from the teachings

---

[1] Matthew 5:38-44.

of Jesus to the ideas of Paul, a fact that is confirmed by numerous historians and researchers.

Perhaps the most gruesome policy of persecution suffered by the Christians in that first century was that inflicted on them by the tyrant, Nero, starting in the year 68 C.E. Some of them were fed to ravenous beasts who tore them to pieces; others were coated with tar on his orders and then set on fire to provide lighting for the parties Nero held in the gardens of his palace.

In the second century, the Christians were considered unclean and were not permitted in the public baths and other public places. Nero's policy of throwing them to wild beasts continued. This went on in coliseums where their opponents gathered to witness the spectacles as a form of amusement.

The third century recorded other scenes of the most hideous forms of torture and persecution of the Christians. That was in the era of the emperor Gladionus. He ordered the demolition of Christian churches, the destruction of their sacred Scriptures and the relics of the "Fathers" of the church. He declared them to be sinners, abolished their civil rights, and ordered the arrest and torture of priests and other religious leaders.

These orders were carried out in every province. The prisons became filled with Christians. Many of them died after being lacerated with whips, torn with iron hooks, set on fire, separated limb from limb, thrown to wild beasts, and other forms of torture. The Christians called the period from 281 to 305 C.E. the "Era of Martyrs".

Near the beginning of the fourth century, conditions changed when the emperor Constantine issued the edicts of toleration in 311 and 313 C.E., then accepted Christianity some ten years later. Christianity rapidly gathered strength until it had the upper hand, then proceeded to take the offensive against its enemies, killing, torturing, and attacking. It organized revolutionary orders in the name of religion. The most famous being the order of the Holy Cross in Turin, which took up the burden of uprooting the lingering remnants of Roman paganism.

The Balance of Power Shifts

Speak after that if you wish about the blood spilled and the souls snuffed out of their bodies. This is what led Harthman to describe "The Christian Vengeance" as the most heinous massacre of humanity in recorded history.

Christian persecution didn't stop with the pagans; rather it carried over to Christian targets as well. That was because the Christianity which triumphed and gained political mastery was not the religion of Jesus; rather, it was the Christianity of Paul, the Christianity of Greek philosophy. But it still bore—and continues to bear—the name of Christianity. This Christianity innovated things which true Christians find unacceptable, such as the divinity of Christ, the Trinity, the Crucifixion and vicarious atonement, and other things. A new struggle began in which the true Christians were considered heretics. Greek (or Pauline) Christianity unleashed a campaign of harassment and persecution against them, and the Church continued on its hatchery of innovations, circulating fantasies like the Lord's Supper and certificates of forgiveness.

The Church encountered Christians who opposed these fairy tales. Such people were then subjected to such unparalleled cruelty and savagery that it makes one's skin crawl. Do you want some examples of the coercion and persecution inflicted by Christians upon their Christian brethren?

In the fourth century, Arius opposed the doctrine of Christ's divinity, which led to the convening of the Council of Nicaea in 325 C.E. This Council resolved to condemn Arius, to burn his writings and forbid anyone to possess them, to strip his supporters of all positions in the Church and excommunicate them, and to impose the death penalty on anyone caught secretly possessing any of Arius' or his supporters' writings.

In Theodosius' reign the first Court of Inquisition appeared. Its organization was eventually completed in the twelfth century. Its members were monks whose job was uncovering those whose beliefs differed from Church doctrine. They had great authority and couldn't be questioned about what they did.

The history of the Inquisition is the history of religious persecution in its extreme form, the killing of freedom of thought by the most disgusting methods.

One of their most perverted procedures was their announcement that every person must report without delay or collusion any information about heretics, and it threatened anyone who delayed doing so with severe punishment in this world and in the Hereafter. As a result of this decree of terror a whole system of spies spread, even among members of the same family. In the following centuries the victims of this system proliferated. Large groups underwent hanging and other forms of execution because, in the view of the Church and its monks, they were heretics.

The Church frequently resorted to slow executions to accentuate the torture. They would press candles against the body of the victim and pull his teeth out, as they did to Benjamin, Bishop of Egypt, because he refused to submit to the Decree of Chalcedonia, which stated that Jesus had two natures, divine and human.

Executions would be preceded by agonizing tortures such as branding with fire and excruciating beatings, so that the victims would confess. If they didn't confess, they would be tortured to death. The axiom of these courts was that the accused was guilty until proven innocent; not that the accused was innocent until proven guilty. When the accused confessed, his torture continued prior to actually finishing him off, in order to make him reveal the names of his helpers and cohorts. The laws dictated that the sons and grandsons bore responsibility for crimes of which the father was accused.

The Language of Documents and Numbers

The Roman Catholic Church frequently employed persecution and expulsion against the Protestants in the Kingdoms of Europe. The number of those branded came close to 230,000 of those who believed in Jesus but not the Pope. In France, thirty thousand people were killed in one day. In the city of Toulouse 10,000 were killed. In Calabria, Italy, in the year 1560 C.E., thousands and thousands of Protestants were killed. One Catholic writer said:

> I tremble whenever I remember that executioner, the bloody dagger between his teeth, the handkerchief dripping blood in his hand, his arms smeared with blood to the tops of his elbows, dragging one prisoner after another as a butcher does to sheep.

Charles V issued an edict in 1521 for the expulsion of Protestants from Holland, on the advice of the Pope. This caused the killing of 500,000. After Charles, his son, Philip II, came to power. When he went to Spain, he left the Duke of Alva in charge of the suppression and expulsion of the Protestants. Historians say that within a few months he had killed 18,000 people. After that he used to boast that he had killed, in all parts of the kingdom, 30,000 people.

That is what the Catholics did to the Protestants. What, then, did the Protestants do to the Catholics once they were able to? The Protestants issued the following laws:

1. A Catholic might not inherit from his own parents.

2. None of them might purchase land after passing the age of eighteen unless he converted to Protestantism.

3. None of them might work as a teacher. Anyone caught defying this law would be jailed for life.

4. Catholics would pay twice the normal tax.

5. If one of them sent his son outside England for education, he and his son would be killed and all his wealth and livestock would be surrendered.

6. They would not be given any position in the state.

7. Whoever among them did not attend Sunday and holiday services in the Protestant church would be fined a large monthly fine and would be considered to be outside the community.

8. Any legal cases they brought as plaintiffs would not be heard by the court.

9. Their marriages would not be legally recognized, their dead would not be prepared or buried, and their children would not be baptized, unless it were done according to the rites of the Church of England.

10. No priest would be present at their executions nor when their bodies were prepared or buried.

11. None of them would be permitted to own a weapon.

12. If one of their priests performed any service associated with his office, he would be imprisoned for life.

Many of their monks and scholars were transported on ships, by the order of Queen Elizabeth, then thrown into the sea and drowned. Her soldiers came to Ireland to forcibly convert the Catholics to Protestantism. They burned Catholics, killed their scholars, and hunted them as one would hunt wild animals. They would grant no one safety, and if they should happen to do so, they would kill him even after extending a promise of clemency.

In Spain alone the Courts of Inquisition burned 31,000 souls at the stake and sentenced 290,000 to punishments short of execution.

In 1568 C.E., the Holy Office issued its order condemning all the inhabitants of the low countries and ordering their execution, with the exception of a handful of individuals whose names were stipulated in the decree. Within ten days of the issuance of that decree, millions of men, women and children were beheaded.

One of the biggest massacres organized by Catholics against Protestants was the massacre of Paris on August 24, 1572 C.E. There, Catholics pounced on their guests, Protestants who had been invited to Paris to work out an agreement bridging their differences of opinion, killing them treacherously while they were sleeping. When Paris awoke the next morning the streets were flowing with the blood of the victims. Congratulations were showered on Charles IX by the Pope, Catholic kings and their clergy for this heroic and noble deed.

We have already mentioned that when the Protestants gained power, they played the same role, i.e., the role of cruelty towards and religious persecution of the Catholics. They were no less savage in their treatment of their old enemies.

And so on, and so on. The history of Christianity has documented stories of oceans of blood, piles of the corpses of human victims converted to burnt ashes, and moans, tears and sobs, savagery and barbarism, and cries for help.

Christian Persecution of the Jews

Ibn Al-Batriq says:

The King ordered that no Jew could live in Jerusalem or pass by it, and whoever didn't accept Christianity should be killed. So many Jews accepted Christianity, and Christianity prevailed. It was then said to Emperor Constantine:

"The Jews are accepting Christianity out of fear of death, but they are actually still following their own religion."

The King said, "How can we know that about them?"

The Patriarch Paul said, "Swine is prohibited in the Torah and the Jews don't eat its meat. So order swine to be slaughtered and the meat to be cooked, then feed them from it. Whoever doesn't eat it we will know is still practicing Judaism."

The Emperor said, "If swine is prohibited in the Torah, how is it permissible for us to eat pork and feed it to people?"

The Patriarch Paul said: "Our Master, Christ, has nullified all that is in the Torah and has come with another revelation, a new Torah, which is the Gospel. In the Holy Gospel, it says that whatever goes into the stomach is neither forbidden nor unclean, and the only thing which can make a person unclean is what comes out of his stomach."

The King ordered swine to be slaughtered, the meat to be cooked, then cut into fine pieces, and the test was conducted on Sunday at the door of every church in the Kingdom. Whoever came out of the church was to swallow a piece of pork. Whoever didn't was killed, and thus a large number of people were killed.

This was not an isolated incident. Throughout the years and ages there has been incident after incident of Christians persecuting Jews. We will summarize from them a few of them:

Muslim-Christian Dialogue

The Catholics believed the Jews were non-believers, wherefore they imposed a number of laws on them:

1. Whoever protected a Jew from a Christian had excommunicated himself.
2. No Jew might be given a position in any Catholic state.
3. If any Christian were enslaved to a Jew, then he was free.
4. No one might eat with a Jew or do business with him.
5. Their children should be taken away from them and taught the Christian doctrine.

The Jews were expelled from France seven times.

The number of Jews expelled from Austria alone was 11,000 families. In Austria, also, many of them were killed and their property was plundered. Only a few escaped—by becoming Christians. In Austria, many of them died after being locked into their own houses, then destroyed by burning or drowning.

In England the Jews tasted an assortment of humiliating conditions and expulsions. Edward I, upon assuming power, issued his order for all their properties to be seized, then he had them expelled from his kingdom. More than fifteen thousand were expelled in the most extreme condition of poverty and need.

A traveler in Portugal named Soutie reported:

> The condition of the Portuguese is that they take a Jew and burn him with fire. Their men and women gather on his burning like a gathering for a holiday celebration, and then make merry with the utmost merriment. The women shout at the time of the burning happily and joyfully.

If we add to these edicts and numbers what the Christians did to the Muslims in the Crusades and in Spain after the fall of Granada,[1] then what Crusader imperialism, past and present, has done in Muslim lands, it will become clear that Christianity, whose adherents insist is "the religion of mercy and tolerance," was nothing more than a door among the many doors of torture and mistreatment, an unbearable hell of murder, hatred and rancor. It is a wound which won't heal in the heart of humanity, and its soul overflows with blood and pus.

---

[1] We have presented in our book, *Ancient Tears*, a sampling of what the Inquisition did to the Muslims after the fall of Granada.

In summary, Christianity throughout its history, with its numbers and documents and realities must be regarded as a source of worry, suffering and evil for mankind and for the history of mankind wherever it took up residence on Allah's earth.

That is the Christianity of the Crusaders, whose clergy are determined to scatter ashes in people's eyes. We see them daily spreading among the people support for the false religion which they invented to deter people from the religion of Allah and from His guidance!

True, they said Islam was spread by the sword. But it has become manifest in what has just passed that this claim of theirs is pure forgery and invention. We have already told them in previous discussions that Christianity was spread on an ocean of blood, and its cross was erected on a pyramid of the corpses of the murdered and tattered remains of victims.

And we say to them: If you live in a glass house, don't throw stones!

Polygamy and its Wisdom

Among the questions put to me is one sitting before me, a two-part question on polygamy. The questions read as follows: Muslims can marry more than one wife. Is there a verse of the Qur'an which clarifies that? Second, for what reason did the Prophet marry more than four wives?

As for marrying more than one wife, there is no doubt that the Qur'an establishes its lawfulness, for Allah the Exalted says:

> And if you fear that you will not deal fairly with the orphans marry of the women what seems good to you, (some of you) two, (some of you) three, (some of you) four. And if you fear that you cannot do justice (to so many) then one (only) or (the captives) that your right hands possess. Thus it is more likely that you will not do injustice.[1]

In connection with this topic, in the same *surah*, the following is stated:

---

[1] Qur'an 4:3.

> You will not be able to deal perfectly equally between your wives, however much you wish (to do so). But do not turn away completely (from one), leaving her as in suspense. If you do good and keep away from evil, lo! Allah is ever Forgiving, Merciful.[1]

The interpretation of the two verses depends on their contexts and the circumstances which led to their revelation. The latter verse was directly related to the former in terms of its context. When it was stated in the first verse, "And if you fear that you cannot do justice (to so many) then one (only)," it was understood that justice between the wives was obligatory. Moreover, their immediate impression was that absolute justice—including even the inclination of one's heart—was the intention of the verse. This troubled the Believers, and they had a right to be troubled, since justice according to this definition is impossible. Then the second verse came to clarify what type of justice was required by the first verse, and to dispel the difficulty they had imagined. Accordingly, the statement of Allah, the Exalted, was revealed: "You will not be able to deal (perfectly) equally between your wives, however much you wish (to do so). But do not turn away completely (from one), leaving her as in suspense."[2]

From this it becomes clear that polygamy is permissible, as long as the Believer does not fear injustice in dividing his time and maintenance between the wives and if he fears that it is obligatory for him to save himself from sin by not limiting himself to one wife. Furthermore, it is clear from the two verses that the permissibility of polygamy is not conditional on anything besides justice and an absence of the fear of injustice. For example, it is also permissible in the case of sterility (of the first wife), or of her being ill in a way which precludes the husband from satisfying his sexual urges with her, or of an excessive number of females such that it is feared that they will not be able to find monogamous marriages and will be driven, as a result, to fornication, as during wars and other circumstances.

---

[1] Qur'an 4:129.
[2] Qur'an 4:129.

Besides that, the noble verse establishes polygamy as the primary solution to the problem of injustice towards orphans. Then the verse mentions limiting oneself to a single wife in case one fears a lack of justice between wives. If a Believer is just between girl orphans, then he will also be just between his wives.

The Wisdom of Polygamy

Polygamy is a result of natural differences in male and female sexuality. The male's sex drive remains constant and his readiness for sex is extended. At the same time female sexuality results in periods of time when she is unable or less able to accommodate him, as during her menstrual periods, pregnancy, childbirth and the post-partum bleeding which follows it. Likewise, a woman's period of sexual readiness ends with menopause, which is usually complete by the age of sixty. Therefore, a man's sexual drive remains a threat to his health or disposition, or both.

Some scholars are of the opinion that polygamy is a result of a divine natural law which has determined that the number of women always exceeds the number of men, and at the same time has determined that male mortality is higher than female mortality.

If there were no other natural factors besides the on-going wars in every corner of the world, they alone would be sufficient evidence for this view. So what if we add to the phenomenon of wars—which kill men and leave predominant populations of women and children—the fact that men are exposed to many grueling hardships in life. This is especially true among the working classes, where men engage in jobs working with steel and fire, and in the depths of oceans and in other dangerous situations where death is always a possibility. All of this only supports the above view on the viability of polygamy.

Europe and Polygamy

The scholars of Europe have known and acknowledged the law of polygamy and its merits. We will mention some proof of that. This is not to increase our own certainty and belief, for we believe in the Word of our Lord and the Sunnah of our Prophet. We mention it only for the benefit of those who are amused when they hear that these words and thoughts are also admitted by the West.

Western thinkers have discovered a correlation between the prohibition of polygamy and a rise in the rate of abandoned and murdered newborns. In a conference convened by the French government in 1901 C.E. to investigate the best methods for fighting prostitution, the following statement was made:

> The number of abandoned children gathered in the orphanages of the Seine County[1] alone, whose upbringing is ongoing at the expense of the province, has reached 50,000 foundlings. Some of those in charge of these orphanages are committing indecencies with the girls in their charge. The foundlings themselves are sexually active among themselves and no impediments serve to restrain them.

In this vein an English author wrote that

> ...the number of runaways among our young girls has increased and become a problem for the whole society. Very few researchers have studied the causes for this. I, as a woman, look at these girls and my heart breaks for them. But what good is my sorrow and anxiety and pain to them, even if everyone joins me?

This is the sickness. The French brought it up and the English woman discussed it. So where is the cure?

An English author says:

> May God bless the incisive scholar, Thomas, for he saw the sickness and prescribed the cure. The solution is to allow a

---

[1] The administrative unit which includes Paris.

man to marry more than one wife. With this solution the affliction will come to an end. Our daughters will become housewives. The calamity of calamities has been to force the European man to make do with one wife. This limitation is what has turned our girls into tramps and driven them to look for men's jobs. There is no escaping the alarming increase of evil if men are not permitted to marry more than one wife. If polygamy had been permitted this calamity would not have afflicted us.

Before the French conference or the English author mentioned it, the Noble Qur'an had already dealt with it when it legislated polygamy and allowed latitude in it.

Moreover, it demands that men get married to prevent deviation and dissolution. The Exalted says:

> All beyond those mentioned (as incestuous) are lawful to you, as long as you seal them with your wealth in honest wedlock, not fornication.[1]

And the Exalted said:

> So wed them by permission of their folk, and give them their due presents according to what is customary, in honest wedlock, not fornicating or taking lovers.[2]

Fornication and the taking of intimate companions before marriage are at the head of the plague and calamities afflicting the Western nations. They found no remedy for them in their religion and law and went looking for the remedy in our religion and law!

In the Muslim East

We have explained the condition of the West. As for the East, this is what has happened to one country, Turkey. Turkey abandoned Islam in an unbecoming fashion and turned its face to Europe, looking to it for legislation and hoping to acquire advancement and civilization from it. It adopted a civil code for itself which forbids polygamy.

---

[1] Qur'an 4:24.
[2] Qur'an 4:25.

That was in 1926. Eight years passed, and the number of illegitimate births, common-law wives, and murdered infants increased. Refer to what appeared in the Egyptian magazine *Last Hour*, No. 556, dated June 3, 1945. An article by the well-known Egyptian writer, Muhammad At-Tabi'i, who was then living in Turkey:

> We are in need of polygamy. We do not need to forbid it or attack it. The Qur'an has treated the issue of polygamy logically, humanely, clearly and in a straight-forward manner. It is a treatment which improves and promotes well-being.

How did the Church deal with the same issue? Polygamy was permissible in Christian Europe until the reign of Charlemagne, who was married to more than one woman. Then the priests ordered those married to more than one wife to choose one of them and call her wife, and call the others "consorts". That is how the church spoke according to its way!

The Messenger's Many Wives

Some non-Muslim writers and speakers accuse Muhammad of being a man of lust, because he married around thirteen women, of whom he was still married to nine at the time of his death.

In so doing they have exceeded the limits and perpetrated an offense—deliberately and with malicious intent—against truth, reality and fair-minded scholarship. They claim that the Prophet was lying in claiming to be a prophet because he married a number of wives.

As for us, we stress that one of the signs of his truthfulness and evidence of his prophethood was his marrying a number of wives. That is because those ladies (may Allah be pleased with them) reported on his domestic life and his conduct at home and among his family. And lo and behold, it is a report on the most pious conduct and purest soul.

These "co-wives"—if the term is valid—laid open for us his private life with all transparency. We have never found any blemish or fault therein. Thus, his family life was consistent with his honesty, trustworthiness, mercy, piety, and virtue.

Muslim-Christian Dialogue

Many people, except those whom our Lord has favored with His mercy, have hypocritical dispositions. They make a show of honesty, a concern for improving the world, and integrity, while in reality they are liars, corrupt, and foolish. Unfortunately, they don't realize or know this. These hypocrites and show-offs who hide behind masks cannot maintain this phony manner for long. Their salient qualities must show through, especially in their homes and among their wives and children.

If such a person had even one wife in his home, not more, she might eventually reveal information about him and his secrets and spread them among the people. The Messenger didn't have just one wife in his home; he had many wives. If he had been lying, God forbid, the first sign of his lying would have appeared among these wives, and any one of them could have begun to spread that among her neighbors and relatives.

As a matter of fact, we have before us something that confirms the above. In an incident related by the Noble Qur'an. Allah, the Exalted, says:

> When the Prophet confided a fact to one of his wives and when she afterwards divulged it, and Allah informed him of that, he made known (to her) part of that and passed over part. And when he told it to her she said: "Who informed you of this?" He said, "The All-Knowing, the Aware, has informed me."[1]

It was a trivial secret which the Prophet (may Allah's peace and blessings be upon him) disclosed to two of the best of his wives ('A'ishah and Hafsah, may Allah be pleased with them both). He told them to keep it private. However, it so happened that the secret got out and spread from tongues to ears until in later eras the books of Qur'anic commentary where filled with it. Which leads us to affirm that the Messenger's life and psyche were pure, whether in his house or outside it.

Moreover, we say to these writers and religious speakers among the non-Muslims, the multiple marriages of the Prophet was not lascivious conduct, as you conceive it and present it.

---

[1] Qur'an 66:3.

Muslim-Christian Dialogue

It suffices that you know that the Prophet married the first of his wives, the Mother of the Believers, Khadijah (may Allah be pleased with her) when he was a mature young man of twenty-five, while she was forty years old. He lived with her twenty-six years. In other words, she remained with him until she had reached sixty-six. He took no other wife while she was alive. He remained devoted to her after her death, to the point that 'A'ishah (may Allah be pleased with her) used to feel jealous of her, even though her married life had not overlapped with hers, nor had she even seen her.

Once, when he mentioned her, she ventured to say to him, "Wasn't she just an old woman, whom Allah has replaced for you with someone better (i.e., herself)?" He got angry at her and told her:

> No! By Allah. Allah didn't replace her with someone better. She believed in me when all the people disbelieved, and testified to my truthfulness when the people were calling me a liar. And Allah bestowed children on me from her instead of from other women.

She said, "I never spoke badly of her after that."

Al-Bukhari and Muslim reported that 'A'ishah (may Allah be pleased with her) said:

> I wasn't jealous of any woman the way I was of Khadijah, and I never did see her, but the Prophet used to talk about her frequently. Sometimes he might slaughter a sheep and send it to some of Khadijah's friends. And I might have said to him, "It's as if there was never a woman in the world except Khadijah." He said, "She was (this)," and "She was (that)," and "I had children by her."

After Khadijah (may Allah be pleased with her) died, the Prophet remarried and began to have more than one wife. We should ask at what stage of his life his polygamous marriages were. It was by acknowledgment of both friend and foe, the busiest period of his life, full of sacrifice, jihad, teaching and other responsibilities.

Moreover, what kind of lust is there in a man so far from the world and its glitter. Allah wanted his wives also to be far from the world and its glitter, for Allah tells him:

> O Prophet! Say to your wives: if you desire the world and its adornment, come! I will content you and release you with a fair release. But if you desire Allah and his Messenger and the abode of the Hereafter, then lo, Allah has prepared for the good among you an immense reward.[1]

A sensual man would want his wife or wives to adorn themselves with the most dazzling jewelry and the most charming dresses.

Likewise, a fair-minded researcher into the causes of his multiple marriages would find that they had weighty and noble purposes and goals. For instance, the wives of some of his Companions who strove and fought with him and died after emigrating from their homes had no family in Madinah. Their families were still idol worshippers. The alternatives facing them were to return to their families and undergo punishment or psychological pressure to leave Islam, or they would be left without a husband to protect them and stand beside them to face the vicissitudes of life. Also, they weren't much sought after due to age or lack of beauty.

Another purpose was to strengthen and cement relations with those who helped him convey the message. In this way, he would emphasize the connection of mutual belief with connection through marriage. Nor was the Prophet always the one to receive in this situation. He married the daughters of Abu Bakr and 'Umar, and he married his two daughters Ruqayyah and Umm Kulthum to 'Uthman, the latter after the death of the former. When the second died he said, "If we had a third available we would have married her to you."

Another motive was to free a woman or her people from bondage.

Another goal was to clarify a rule of the Shari'ah and apply it practically, so as to provide a model for people to emulate and combat deeply rooted ignorance and its customs.

Also, he married to have women who could learn from him and then convey his words and deeds to others, especially to the women. He wanted his wives to convey to Muslim women in-

---

[1] Qur'an 33:28-29.

formation he would feel shy about teaching them himself. There were other goals beside these.

This is a summary, which requires more details. We will present more details when discussing the Prophet's marriage to each of his wives.

The Mothers of the Believers

1. Khadijah bint Khuwaylid
— His first wife.
— He stayed married to her for about twenty-six years, as previously mentioned.
— She bore him six children: Al-Qasim and At-Tayyib, who both died before he was commissioned as a prophet, and Ruqayyah, Umm Kulthum, Zaynab, and Fatimah. They all died before him, except Fatimah, who died six months after him.
-He did not marry another woman during her lifetime, as we mentioned.

2. Sawdah bint Zam'an
— The Prophet married her after Khadijah died and before the Hijrah.
— She was about Khadijah's age, i.e., about sixty, but she didn't have Khadijah's beauty.
— She had accepted Islam along with her husband, and had emigrated with him to Abyssinia, fleeing the injuries inflicted by the ignorant among the Quraysh. Her husband had died after their return.
— Her family remained idol worshippers. If she had returned to them they would have pressured her and enticed her away from her religion. So the Prophet married her to protect her from that trial.

3. 'A'ishah bint Abi Bakr As-Siddiq
— She was about nine years old at the time of marriage. She hadn't yet attained puberty, being somewhat thin, and the marriage wasn't consummated until after the Hijrah. Thus his marriage to her wasn't motivated by lust; it was only to strengthen

his companionship with her father, Abu Bakr as-Siddiq (may Allah be pleased with him).

— All his pure wives were previously married (widows), except for 'A'ishah (may Allah be pleased with her) who was the only virgin.

— Although most of his wives had been previously married, he encouraged others to marry virgins. He was the one who said to Jabir Ibn 'Abdullah, when he came to him with signs of perfume and happiness on his face, "Did you get married?" He said, "Yes." He said, "A virgin or a previously married woman?" He said, "A previously married woman." He said. "Why not a virgin? You could play with her and she with you; you could banter with her and she with you."

4. Hafsah bint 'Umar Ibn Al-Faruq

— The Prophet married her after the Hijrah. Her husband had been Khunays Ibn Hadaqah, who had died as a Believer.

— His marriage to her was to cement friendship with her father (may Allah be pleased with him) who was his second minister, so to speak.

The events leading to his marrying her indicate that his love for his Companions was the impetus for this marriage. When 'Uthman's wife Ruqayyah died—as the battle of Badr was being fought—'Umar was interested in marrying Hafsah to 'Uthman. But when he suggested it to him, 'Uthman remained silent. 'Umar complained about that to the Prophet who said, "Someone will soon marry her who is better than 'Uthman, and 'Uthman will soon marry someone better than Hafsah." The Prophet then married Hafsah, and married his daughter, Umm Kulthum, to 'Uthman. We can see from this that his marriage to her was to foster affection and content the hearts.

5. Umm Habibah (Ramlah) bint Abi Sufyan:

— The Prophet married her during a state of war with the *mushrikun*[1] who were under the leadership of her father, Abu Sufyan.

---

[1] i.e.Polytheists, or pagans.

Muslim-Christian Dialogue

She had traveled with her husband, 'Abdullah Ibn Jaysh, to Abyssinia, but he became a Christian and left Islam. She had two choices, either to return to her father, who was then the leader of the *mushrikun* and be pressured to abandon her religion, or to proceed to Madinah with no one to shelter her. The Prophet sheltered her by marrying her.

— The Prophet sent 'Amar Ibn Umayyah Ad-Damari to Abyssinia to convey his proposal to her. An-Najashi, the king of Abyssinia, gave her a wedding present of four hundred dinars and arranged her journey to the Prophet.

— By this marriage the Prophet achieved two goals: first, he protected her from idolatry and religious persecution; second, he established a link by marriage to Abu Sufyan, who was pleased by that. He said, "What a fine, virile man; may his nose not be cut off," referring to Muhammad.

6. Zaynab bint Khuzaymah:

— She was sixty when the Prophet married her, and she only lived with him two years.

— She was nicknamed "Mother of the Poor."

— Her husband had been killed at the battle of Uhud. Marriage to her was a way of providing her shelter and security and a way of encouraging her to help the poor.

7. Zaynab bint Jahsh

— She had been the wife of Zayd Ibn Harith.

— She had married him when he was called the son of Muhammad, because the Prophet had adopted him and given him that name.

— When Allah's statement was revealed:

Nor has He made those whom you claim (to be your sons) your sons. This is but a saying of your mouths. But Allah says the truth and he shows the way: proclaim their real parentage; that is more just in the sight of Allah. And if you do not know their fathers, then (they are) your brothers in the faith, and your *mawlas*."[1],[2]

Zaynab became restless about remaining with Zayd, and he became disgruntled with her pride. He asked the Prophet for permission to divorce her, but he told him, "Fear Allah and hold on to your wife." Allah had ordered his Prophet to marry her after Zayd divorced her, but he concealed that, fearing that people would say, "Muhammad has married his son's wife!" Then Allah, the Exalted, said:

> It is not (permitted) for a believing man or a believing woman, when Allah and His Messenger have decided an affair (for them), that they should (after that) have a choice in their affair. And whoever disobeys Allah and His Messenger have surely gone astray in manifest error. And when you said to him on whom Allah has bestowed favor: "Hold on to your wife and fear Allah," and you concealed in your mind that which Allah was to reveal, and you feared the people, whereas Allah has a better right that you fear Him.
>
> So when Zayd had no further interest in her, we gave her to you in marriage, so that (from now on) there will be no difficulty for the Believers in (marrying) the wives of their adopted sons when they have no further interest in them. The commandment of Allah must be fulfilled. There is no reproach for the Prophet in that which Allah has made his due. That was Allah's way for those who passed away previously—and the command of Allah is certain destiny—who delivered the messages of Allah and feared Him and feared no one except Allah. And Allah is sufficient as a Reckoner. Muhammad is not the father of any of you men, but He is the Messenger of Allah and Seal of the Prophets; and Allah has the knowledge of all things.[3]

---

[1] *Mawla* is translated as 'client', but there is no real equivalent. It is a relationship of mutual rights and responsibilities between people not related by blood.
[2] Qur'an 33:4-5.
[3] Qur'an 33:36-40.

These verses present the matter of the Prophet's marriage with Zaynab after Zayd had divorced her. There are some important points to be made here.

a. The custom of the Days of Ignorance was to consider an adopted son exactly like a natural son in every respect. Allah abolished that by saying, "[P]roclaim their real parentage."

b. Likewise, the wisdom of Allah dictated the nullification of the ignorant custom of including in a family whoever is not of it, which depreciates authentic family ties. And He used the Prophet's action as emphasis for this nullification, as he married the wife of his adopted son after Zayd divorced her. As the Exalted said: "So that there will be no difficulty for the Believers in (marrying) the wives of their adopted sons when they have no further interest in them."

c. The verse indicates that Muhammad wasn't the father of any Arab man.

d. The marriage to Zaynab was by the command of Allah, the Perfect, without defect, the Exalted, and it was not because of the wish of the Prophet. Allah the Exalted said, "When Zayd had no further interest in her We gave her to you in marriage." For that reason it is reported that Zaynab used to say, "Your fathers got you married, while my Lord got me married."

8. Umm Salamah, Hind bint Abi Umayyah

— She was from the Banu Makhzum clan of the Quraysh. Her husband, Abu Salamah had died, leaving her a widow. His name was 'Abdullah Ibn 'Abdul-Asad.

— When her husband was dying, he asked her to remarry, as she was still fairly young, and he prayed sincerely for her to remarry someone better than him.

— The Prophet saw that she had dependent children and needed someone to help look after them,

— Both she and her husband were *Muhajirun*. She had no relatives in Madinah.

9. Juwayriyyah bint Al-Harith

Ibn Hisham says about her marriage:

When the Messenger of Allah was returning from the expedition against Banu Al-Mustaliq, he had with him Juwayriyyah bint Al-Harith.[1] He ordered Juwayriyyah over to a man of the *Ansar* to look after and guard her on his behalf. When the Prophet got back to Madinah, her father, Al-Harith Ibn Abi Dirar came with a ransom for his daughter. When he reached the wadi of Aqiq, he looked at the camels that he had brought for ransom. Two of the camels appealed to him, so he hid them in the Aqiq valley. Thereafter, he came to the Prophet, and said, "Muhammad, you took my daughter and this is her ransom." The Messenger of Allah said, "Where are the two camels you hid in Aqiq in such and such a valley?" He said, "I bear witness that nothing is worthy of worship except Allah, and that you are the Messenger of Allah, for by Allah, no one saw that beside me." Harith and two of his sons who were with him accepted Islam.

About one hundred of her people were prisoners of war. When the Prophet married her, after agreement from her father, she had accepted Islam. Immediately, everyone holding one of her people captive freed them. They said, "How can we hold captive the in-laws of the Messenger of Allah!" Thus the guardians of a hundred households of the Banu Al-Mustaliq were released as a result of his marriage to her. Commenting on this, Mother of the Believers, 'A'ishah said: "No woman was more blessed for her people than Juwayriyyah. Because of her a hundred houses of her people were freed."

So this marriage was not due to lust; it was to secure freedom and release people from captivity.

10. **Safiyyah bint Huyay Ibn Akhtab**

She was taken captive at the battle of Khaybar, along with her sister. Bilal took them past their people, the Jews of Khaybar. The Prophet reproached Bilal, saying, "Is there no mercy in your heart? How could you take two girls past the slain members of their people?"

---

[1] She had been captured in the battle.

He presented the two girls to some of his Companions so that someone would marry them. Her sister was married but she remained. So the Prophet married her as an act of charity, benevolence and mercy.

11. **Maymunah bint Al-Harith**

— Al-'Abbas Ibn Muttalib chose her as a wife for the Prophet as a means of strengthening the ties between him and some of the Arab tribes. Al-'Abbas gave her a present of 400 dirhams.

— It is reported that she was one of those who offered herself to the Prophet. That is because when she found that the Prophet had proposed to her, she said, "The camel and what is on it are for Allah and His Messenger." Then Allah revealed:

> ...And a believing woman, if she gives herself to the Prophet and the Prophet desires to marry her—a privilege for you only, not for the rest of the believers—We are of what We have imposed on them concerning their wives and those whom their right hands possess, so that there should be no constriction upon you, and Allah is Forgiver, Merciful.[1]

These are the wives with whom he consummated the marriages. They are the ones who are called "Mothers of the Believers", since Allah said, "And his wives are (as) their mothers."[2] Also, in forbidding their marriage after him, Allah says: "And it is not for you to cause annoyance to the Messenger of Allah, nor that you ever marry his wives after him."[3]

Narrators tell us that:

— The number of the Prophet's wives was thirteen.

— He consummated the marriage of eleven of them. Accordingly, they are known as "Mothers of the Believers."

— He was married to nine when he died; Khadijah and Zaynab, Mother of the Poor, died during his lifetime.

— He married two with whom he didn't consummate the marriage: Asma' bint An-Nu'man Al-Kindiyyah, and Umaymah bint An-Nu'man Ibn Sharahabil.

---

[1] Qur'an 33:50.
[2] Qur'an 33:6.
[3] Qur'an 33:53.

This is the number that Allah made lawful for the Prophet and by which all the societal, educational, and legislative goals associated with the mission were realized. Regarding this, Allah, the Exalted says:

> You can defer whom you will of them and receive whom you will, and whomsoever you desire of those whom you have set aside (temporarily) it is no sin for you (to receive her again); that is better; that they may be comforted and not grieve, and may all be pleased with what you give them. Allah knows what is in your hearts (O men) and Allah is Forgiving, Clement. It is not allowed for you to take (other) women after this, nor that you should change them for other wives, even though their beauty pleases you, except those whom your right hand possesses. And Allah is Watcher over all things.[1]

This passage indicates that

— the prophet was prohibited from taking more wives than the number he already had.

— the Prophet used to defer the turn of some among them and receive to himself whom he willed. Also, the Noble Qur'an indicates that this number was especially for him. The Exalted says that this was "...a privilege for you only, not for the rest of the believers."[2]

Truly, the wives of the Prophet were the Mothers of the Believers. They were schools for the teaching of knowledge and disseminating good.

As for their engagement in teaching knowledge, many women used to feel bashful to ask the Prophet about certain matters of Islamic law, especially those related to them, such as rules about menstruation, post-partum bleeding, (purification after) intercourse, marital issues, and other rules. Sometimes a woman would be overcome by shyness when she wanted to ask the Prophet about some of these issues. Likewise, modesty was a part of the Prophet's character. He was described in the recorded collections of the Sunnah as "shier than a virgin in her private quarters".

---

[1] Qur'an 33:51-52.
[2] Qur'an 33:50.

Muslim-Christian Dialogue

Naturally, he was not always able to answer with complete frankness and plainness each question put to him by women, but sometimes he would employ euphemistic allusions. And sometimes the woman questioner would not understand what he meant by his euphemism.

Mother of the Believers 'A'ishah reports that a woman from the *Ansar* asked the Prophet how to bathe after completing her menstrual period. The Prophet instructed her how to bathe. Then he said, "Take an absorbent disk, that is, a piece of cotton with a trace of perfume on it, and clean yourself with it." She said, "How should I clean myself with it?' He said, "Clean yourself with it." She said, "How, Messenger of Allah, should I clean myself with it?" 'A'ishah said, "I pulled her by the hand and said, 'Place it in such-and-such a place and use it to check for any trace of blood.'"

It is almost too well known to require saying that many of the rules which especially concern women were reported by Mother of the Believers, 'A'ishah.

It is reported that Abu Musa Al-Ash'ari said:

> Whenever any *hadith* confused us, the Companions of the Messenger of Allah, we would then ask 'A'ishah about it and we found her to have knowledge about it.

Masruq said, "I saw the majority of the learned elders among the Companions of the Messenger of Allah asking her about inheritance."

'Urwah Ibn Zubayr said, "I never saw a woman more learned in medicine, jurisprudence, or poetry than 'A'ishah."

This is not surprising, for the books of Hadith testify to her copious knowledge and her formidable intellect. No man has reported more authentic *hadiths* than she did except Abu Hurayrah and 'Abdullah Ibn 'Umar.

Perhaps one of the reasons for the divine order that they should not remarry after him, i.e., "It is not for you to cause annoyance to the Messenger of Allah, nor that you ever marry his wives after him,"[1] was so that they could devote themselves exclusively to teaching the women the rules of the religion and its

---

[1] Qur'an 33:56.

excellent qualities and its etiquette, and to convey the reports about the Prophet at home and within his family.

Their Responsibility for Disseminating Good

They were examples for all women in their chastity, purity, obedience, and fine character. And Allah, the Perfect without defect, the Exalted, attended to the instruction and refinement of the wives of the Prophet because they were models and examples. The Exalted said:

> O Prophet! Say to your wives: If you desire this world's life and its adornments, come, I will content you and will release you with a fair release. But if you desire Allah and His Messenger and the abode of the Hereafter, then lo, Allah has prepared for the good among you an immense reward.
>
> Wives of the Prophet! Whosoever of you commits manifest lewdness, the punishment for her will be doubled, and that is easy for Allah. And whosoever of you is submissive to Allah and His Messenger and does right, We shall give her reward twice over, and We have prepared for her a rich provision.
>
> Wives of the Prophet! You are not like any other women. If you keep your duty (to Allah), then do not be soft of speech, lest he in whose heart is disease aspire (to you), but utter customary speech. And stay in your homes, do not bedizen yourselves with the bedizenment of the Time of Ignorance. Be regular in prayer, and pay the poor-due, and obey Allah and His Messenger. Allah's wish is but to remove uncleanness far from you, folk of the household, and cleanse you with a thorough cleansing. And bear in mind that which is recited in your houses of the revelations of Allah and wisdom. Lo! Allah is Subtle, Aware.[1]

---

[1] Qur'an 33:28-34.

A Look at the Holy Book[1]

After this detailed, careful examination of the life of the Messenger and his conduct, and how and why he undertook his multiple marriages, let us return and leaf through the pages of the Holy Bible to see what it says about the prophets and their wives. We will make do with examining three prophets, Gideon, David and Solomon.

Gideon

Gideon the son of Joash the Abiezrite was one of the prophets of the Old Testament. The Bible says:

> When the people of Israel cried to the Lord on account of the Midianites, the Lord sent a prophet to the people of Israel; and he said to them, "Thus says the Lord, the God of Israel: I led you up from Egypt, and brought you out of the house of bondage; And I delivered you from the hand of the Egyptians, and from the hand of all who oppress you, and drove them out before you, and gave you their land; and I said to you, 'I am the Lord your God; you shall not pay reverence to the gods of the Amorites, in whose land you dwell.' But you have not given heed to my voice."
>
> Now the angel of the Lord came and sat under the oak at Ofrah, which belonged to Joash the Abiezrite, as his son Gideon was beating out wheat in the wine press, to hide from the Midianites. And the angel of the Lord appeared to him and said to him, "The Lord is with you, you mighty man of valor." And Gideon said to him, "Pray, sir, if the Lord is with us, why then has all this befallen us? And where are all his wonderful deeds which our fathers recounted to us, saying, 'Did not the Lord bring us up from Egypt?' But now the Lord has cast us off, and given us into the hand of Midian." And the Lord turned to him and said, "Go in this might of

---

[1] i.e., the Bible.

yours and deliver Israel from the hand of Midian; do not I send you?"[1]

Likewise his prophethood is discussed in the Letter to the Hebrews. The Bible says:

> ...and what more shall I say? For time would fail me to tell of Gideon, Barak, Samson, Jephthah, of David and Samuel and the prophets—who through faith conquered kingdoms, enforced justice, revived promises, stopped the mouths of lions.[2]

The question is: How many wives did Gideon marry? The answer as given by the Old Testament that

> ...Gideon had seventy sons, his own offspring, for he had many wives. And his concubine who was in Shechem also bore him a son, and he called his name Abimelech.[3]

David

Allah has proclaimed his innocence of what they falsely accuse him of. The Scriptures say he married many wives.

He first married Michal, the daughter of Saul, in exchange for a brideprice of which the world had never heard the like before. That was a hundred foreskins of the Philistines. I don't know what Saul wanted with those foreskins, or what he wanted to do with them, or what he might do with them for his daughter! Anyway, according to the Bible, David was more generous than Saul, for he presented a dower of two hundred foreskins, not just one hundred. The Bible narrates that

> ...the days were not expired wherefore David arose and went, he and his men, and slew of the Philistines two hundred men; and David brought their foreskins, and they gave them in full tale to the king, that he might be the king's son-in-law. And Saul gave him Michal his daughter to wife.[4]

---

[1] Judges 6:7-14.
[2] Hebrews 11:32-33.
[3] Judges 8:30-31.
[4] I Samuel 18:26-27.

David married six other women: Ahino'am the Jezreelitess, Abigail, Maacah the daughter of Talmai, king of Geshur, Haggith, Abital, and Eglah.

In another passage the Bible adds that

> ...sons were born to David at Hebron: his first-born was Amnon, of Ahino'am of Jezreel; and his second, Chil'ab, of Abigail, the widow of Nabal of Carmel; and the third, Absalom the son of Maacah, the daughter of Talmai, king of Geshur; and the fourth, Adonijah the son of Haggith; and the fifth, Shephatiah the son of Abital; and the sixth, Ithre'am of Eglah, David's wife. These were born to David in Hebron.[1]

After that David married other women and took concubines whose number the "Holy Bible" doesn't explicitly state. It merely says that "...David took more concubines and wives from Jerusalem, after he came from Hebron; and more sons and daughters were born to David."[2]

In fact, the "Holy Bible" speaks about a blanket permission to David to marry whom he would, whenever he would, and however he would.

> Thus says the Lord, the God of Israel, "I anointed you king over Israel, and I delivered you out of the hand of Saul; and I gave you your master's house, and your master's wives into your bosom, and gave you the house of Israel and of Judah; and if this were too little, I would add to you as much more."[3]

The marriage of David to the wife of Uriah the Hittite is one of those cases surrounded by question marks in every way. We will quote it in its entirety and lay it before the minds of the Christians and Jews and place a question with it, one brief question: how does this compare with Muhammad?

The story as related by the Holy Bible is as follows:

> In the spring of the year, the time when kings go forth to battle, David sent Joab, and his servants with him, and all Israel; and they ravaged the Ammonites, and besieged Rab-

---

[1] II Samuel 3:2-5.
[2] II Samuel 5:13.
[3] II Samuel 12:7-8.

bah. But David remained at Jerusalem. It happened late one afternoon, when David arose from his couch and was walking upon the roof of the king's house, that he saw from the roof a woman bathing; and the woman was very beautiful. And David sent and inquired about the woman. And one said, "Is not this Bathsheba, the daughter of Eliam, the wife of Uriah the Hittite?"

So David sent messengers and took her; and she came to him, and he lay with her. (Now she was purifying herself from uncleanness.) Then she turned to her house and told David, "I am with child." David sent word to Joab, "Send me Uriah the Hittite." And Joab sent Uriah to David. When Uriah came to him, David asked how Joab was doing, and how the people fared, and how the war prospered. Then David said to Uriah, "Go down to your house and wash your feet."

And Uriah went out of the king's house, and there followed him a person from the king. But Uriah slept at the door of the king's house with all the servants of his lord, and did not go down to his house. When they told David, "Uriah did not go down to his house," David said to Uriah, "Have you not come from a journey? Why did you not go down to your house?" Uriah said to David, "The ark and Israel and Judah dwell in booths; and my lord Joab and the servants of my lord are camping in the open field; shall I then go to my house, to eat and to drink, and to lie with my wife? As you live, and as your soul lives, I will not do this thing."

Then David said to Uriah, "Remain here today also, and tomorrow I will let you depart." So Uriah remained in Jerusalem that day, and the next. And David invited him, and he ate in his presence and drank, so that he made him drunk; and in the evening he went out to lie on his couch with the servants of his lord, but he did not go down to his house.

In the morning David wrote a letter to Joab, and sent it by the hand of Uriah. In the letter he wrote, "Set Uriah in the forefront of the hardest fighting, and then draw back from him, that he may be struck down, and die." And as Joab was

Muslim-Christian Dialogue

besieging the city, he assigned Uriah to the place where he knew there were valiant men. And the men of the city came out and fought with Joab; and some of the servants of David among the people fell. Uriah the Hittite was slain also.

Then Joab sent and told David all the news about the fighting; and he instructed the messenger, "When you have finished telling all the news about the killing to the king, then, if he says to you, 'Why did you go so near the city to fight? Did you not know that they would shoot from the wall? Who killed Abimelech the son of Jerubbesheth? Did not a woman cast an upper millstone upon him from the wall, so that he died at Thebez? Why did you go so near the wall?' Then you shall say, 'Your servant Uriah the Hittite is dead also.'"

So the messenger went, and came and told David all that Joab had sent him to tell. The messenger said to David, "The men gained an advantage over us, and came out against us in the field; but we drove them back to the entrance of the gate. Then the archers shot at your servants from the wall; some of the king's servants are dead; and your servant Uriah is dead also." David said to the messenger, "Thus shall you say to Joab, 'Do not let this matter trouble you, for the sword devours now one and now another; strengthen your attack upon the city, and overthrow it.' And encourage him."

When the wife of Uriah heard that Uriah her husband was dead, she made lamentation for her husband. And when the mourning was over, David sent and brought her to the house, and she became his wife, and bore him a son. But the thing that David had done displeased the Lord.

This long and dubious story claims that David saw the wife of Uriah, one of his warriors, bathing naked on her roof, and that she pleased him. So he "took her" and committed adultery with her. Soon after, she conceived an illegitimate child by him. Wanting to avoid any embarrassment, he sent for her husband, summoning him for the war and thus for him to spend the night with his wife so that the pregnancy could conceivably be attributed to him. But that valiant soldier refused to sleep with his wife while his companions in the army were fighting in the desert. So what did David do but write a letter to the commander of the army and send it with poor Uriah, commanding the general to set Uriah in the forefront of the hardest fighting with the enemy so that he would be killed. That is exactly what happened, and Uriah was killed according to the plot devised by David. After Uriah's death, David sent for Uriah's wife and added her to his wives. Did you follow along? Do you see?

This is the way the books of the Old Testament talk about Allah's prophets and messengers. May Allah exonerate them from what the transgressing slanderers say about them!

I neglected to mention the rest of this biblical legend. This legend has it that this Bathsheba became the mother of Solomon the Wise.[1]

Furthermore, David married near the end of his life a virgin named Abishag the Shunammite. The Bible reports that

> ...King David was old and advanced in years; and although they covered him with clothes, he could not get warm. Therefore his servants said to him, "Let a young maiden be sought for my lord the king, and let her wait upon the king, and be his nurse; let her lie in your bosom, that my lord the king may be warm." So they sought for a beautiful maiden throughout all the territory of Israel, and found Abishag the Shunammite, and brought her to the king. The maiden was very beautiful; and she became the king's nurse and ministered to him; but the king knew her not.[2]

Solomon

It will suffice for us to mention concerning exactly what is in the Holy Bible. The Holy Bible explains that

> ...King Solomon loved many foreign women: the daughter of Pharaoh, and Moabite, Ammonite, Edomite, Sidonian, and Hittite women, from the nations concerning which the Lord had said to the people of Israel, "You shall not enter

---

[1] II Samuel 12:24.
[2] I Kings 1:1-4.

into marriage with them, neither shall they with you, for surely they will turn away your heart after their gods"; Solomon clung to these in love. He had seven hundred wives, princesses, and three hundred concubines; and his wives turned away his heart. For when Solomon was old his wives turned away his heart after other gods; and his heart was not wholly true to the Lord his God, as was the heart of David his father.[1]

This is how they talk about Solomon, namely, that he was so extravagant in marrying idolatrous women, that he married a thousand women, strayed at the end of his life and disbelieved and took other gods through the enticement of those beautiful idolatresses. That is how the books of these people speak about Solomon!

As for the Noble Qur'an, it says that

> ...they (the Jews) follow that which the devils falsely related against the kingdom of Solomon. Solomon did not disbelieve, but the devils disbelieved...[2]

The devils were those who perverted the language of the Scriptures, and those like them who insulted the messengers of Allah and killed the prophets unjustly.

In conclusion, there is not a single passage in the books of the Old Testament that prohibit the marrying of more than one wife. If marrying more than one wife was prohibited or blameworthy, Moses would have called attention to that.

On the contrary, there are passages which affirm its permissibility. I will suffice with this passage:

> When you go forth to war against your enemies, and the Lord your God gives them into your hands, and you take them captive, and see among the captives a beautiful woman, and you have desire for her and would take her for yourself as a wife, then you shall bring her home to your house, and she shall shave her head and pare her nails. And she shall put off her captive's garb, and shall remain in your house and bewail her father and mother a full month; after

---

[1] I Kings 11:1-4.
[2] Qur'an 2:102.

that you may go in to her, and be her husband, and she shall be your wife.

Then, if you have no delight in her, you shall let her go where she will; but you shall not sell her for money, you shall not treat her as a slave, since you have humiliated her.

If a man have two wives, the one loved and the other disliked, and they have borne him children, both the loved and the disliked, then on the day when he assigns his possessions as an inheritance to his sons, he may not treat the son of the loved as the first-born in precedence to the son of the disliked, who is the first-born, but he shall acknowledge the first-born, the son of the disliked, by giving him a double portion of all that he has, for he is the first issue of his strength; the right of the first-born is his.[1]

After this presentation I have nothing more to say except to quote the poet who said:
>   If the virtues by which I'm recognized
>   Are my faults, then tell me, how do I apologize?

Abrogation

People ask us, concerning the Qur'an, how it could abrogate the books that came before it.

And why didn't the Muslims take the same position the Christians took toward the books of the Old Testament; they acknowledged and affirmed them. Not only that, they printed them along with their Gospels in one book, and they called it the Holy Bible.

In response to these questions, we would like to say that what you are claiming is a matter of superficial appearances, which are contradicted by the actual situation and the reality of the matter. Even when you print the two Testaments together, you do not accept what is in the two Testaments together.

For example, let us examine the laws of divorce.

---
[1] Deuteronomy 21:10-17.

A. Divorce

In the Old Testament, a man is permitted to divorce his wife for any reason, and another man may marry the divorcée after she leaves the house of the first man.

> When a man takes a wife and marries her, if then she finds no favor in his eyes because he had found some indecency[1] in her, and he writes her a bill of divorce and puts it in her hand and sends her out of his house, and if she departs out of his house and if she goes and becomes another man's wife...[2]

Instead, in the New Testament, it is not permitted to divorce except for reason of adultery, nor is it permitted to marry a divorcée. That is condemned as adultery.

The Bible says:

> It was also said, "Whoever divorces his wife, let him give her a certificate of divorce." But I say to you that everyone who divorces his wife, except on the grounds of unchastity, makes her an adulteress; and whoever marries a divorced woman commits adultery."[3]

> On another occasion, the Pharisees came up to Jesus and tested him by asking, "Is it lawful to divorce one's wife for any cause?" He answered, "Have you not read that He Who made them from the beginning made them male and female, and said, 'For this reason a man shall leave his father and mother and be joined to his wife, and the two shall become one flesh? What, therefore, God has joined together, let no man put asunder.'" They said to him, "Why then did Moses command one to give a certificate of divorce, and to put her away?" He said to them, "For your hardness of heart Moses

---

[1] An alternative translation is "some unnecessary thing." "The school of Shammai translated those words by 'a thing of indecency' and maintained that divorce could only be allowed if the wife was guilty of unchastity; whereas the school of Hillel rendered it as 'indecency in anything,' implying that a wife may be divorced for reasons other than unchastity." J.H. Hertz, *The Pentateuch and the Haftorahs, Deuteronomy*, Oxford U. Press, London, Humphrey Oxford, 11936, p. 291.
[2] Deuteronomy 24:1-2.
[3] Matthew 5:31-32.

Muslim-Christian Dialogue

allowed you to divorce your wives, but from the beginning it was not so. And I say to you: whoever divorces his wife except for unchastity, and marries another commits adultery."[1]

It is thus known from Jesus' answer to the Pharisees that this law was abrogated twice, once in the Old Testament and once in the New Testament.

B. Prohibitions

Many animals were prohibited in the Law of the Old Testament. Subsequently, their prohibition was abrogated in the law of the New Testament. Their permissibility was affirmed in the legal opinions of Paul. We can observe this when reading the following two passages:

> I know and am persuaded in the Lord Jesus that nothing is unclean in itself; but it is unclean for anyone who thinks it is unclean.[2]

> To the pure all things are pure, but to the corrupt and unbelieving nothing is pure; their very minds and consciences are corrupted.[3]

C. The Sabbath

The rule of the Sabbath was an eternal rule in the legal code of the Old Testament. No one was allowed to do the smallest act of labor on that day. Whoever performed an act of labor and did not preserve the sanctity of the day was killed. The importance of this law is repeatedly explained in the books of the Old Testament:

> Remember the Sabbath day to keep it holy. Six days you shall labor, and do all your work; but the seventh day is a Sabbath to the Lord your God; in it you shall not do any work, you, or your son, or your daughter, your manservant,

---

[1] Matthew 19:3-9.
[2] Romans 14:14.
[3] Titus 1:15.

or your maidservant, or your cattle, or the sojourner who is within your gates; for in six days the Lord made heaven and earth, the sea, and all that is in them, and rested the seventh day; therefore the Lord blessed the Sabbath day and hallowed it.[1]

...the Lord said to Moses, "Say to the people of Israel. 'You shall keep my Sabbath, for this is a sign between me and you throughout generations, that you may know that I, the Lord, sanctify you. You shall keep the Sabbath, because it is holy for you; everyone who profanes it shall be put to death; whoever does any work on it, that soul shall be cut off from among his people. Six days shall work be done, but the seventh day is a Sabbath of solemn rest, holy to the Lord; whoever does any work on the Sabbath day shall be put to death. Therefore the people of Israel shall keep the Sabbath, observing the Sabbath throughout generations, as a perpetual covenant. It is a sign forever between me and the people of Israel that in six days the Lord made heaven and earth, and on the seventh day he rested, and was refreshed.'"[2]

Jews who were contemporaries of Jesus used to harm him. They maneuvered to kill him, and hoped for his destruction on the basis that he was not giving the Sabbath its proper respect: And this was why the Jews persecuted Jesus, because he did this on the Sabbath. But Jesus answered them, "My Father is working still, and I am working." This was why the Jews sought all the more to kill him, because he not only broke the Sabbath but also called God his own Father, making himself equal with God."[3] As a matter of fact, "...some of the Pharisees said, 'This man is not from God, for he does not keep the Sabbath.'"[4]

D. Circumcision

Circumcision was an eternal provision in the legal code of Abraham. The Old Testament says:

---

[1] Exodus 20:8-11.
[2] Exodus 31:12-17.
[3] John 5:61-18.
[4] John 9:16.

> God said to Abraham, "As for you, you shall keep My covenant, you and your descendants after you throughout their generations. This is My covenant which you shall keep, between Me and you and your descendants after you; every male child among you shall be circumcised; and you shall be circumcised in the flesh of your foreskin, and it shall be a sign of the covenant between Me and you.
>
> He who is eight days old among you shall be circumcised, every male child in your generation, he who is born in your house or bought with money from any foreigner who is not your descendant. He who is born in your house and he who is bought with your money must be circumcised, and My covenant shall be in your flesh for an everlasting covenant. And the uncircumcised male child who is not circumcised in the flesh of his foreskin, that person shall be cut off from his people; he has broken my covenant.[1]

This law has remained in practice among the children of Ishmael and the children of Isaac (peace be upon them). And Jesus was himself circumcised, as is found in the New Testament:

> And at the end of eight days, when he was circumcised, he was called Jesus, the name given by the angel before he was conceived in the womb...[2]

This law remained operative until Paul came along and abolished it:

> Now I, Paul, say to you that if you receive circumcision, Christ will be of no advantage to you. I testify again to every man who receives circumcision that he is bound to keep the whole law. You are severed from Christ, you who would be justified by the law; you have fallen away from grace. For through the Spirit, by faith, we wait for the hope of righteousness. For in Christ Jesus neither circumcision nor uncircumcision is of any avail, but faith working through love.[3]

---

[1] Genesis 17:9-14.
[2] Luke 2:21.
[3] Galatians 5:26.

Abrogation of the Laws of the Old Testament

Afterwards, the disciples embarked upon the abrogation of all the laws governing actions in the Old Testament, leaving only four laws operative: These laws dealt with sacrifice to an idol, blood, a strangled animal, and adultery.

They maintained the prohibition against these four things and sent a letter instructing all the churches to observe them. What follows is the text of the letter:

> Then it seemed good to the apostles and the elders, with the whole church, to choose men from among them and send them to Antioch with Paul and Barnabas. They sent Judas, called Baesabbas, and Silas, leading men among the brethren, with the following letter:
>
> "The brethren, both the apostles and the elders, to the brethren who are of the Gentiles in Antioch and Syria and Cilicia, greeting. Since we have heard that some persons from us have troubled you with words, unsettling your minds, although we gave them no instruction, it has seemed good to us, having come to one accord, to choose men and send them to you with our beloved Barnabas and Paul, men who have risked their lives for the sake of our Lord Jesus Christ. We have therefore sent Judas and Silas, who themselves will tell you the same things by word of mouth. For it has seemed good to the Holy Spirit and to us to lay upon you no greater burden than these necessary things: that you abstain from what has been sacrificed to idols, and from blood, and from what is strangled, and from unchastity. If you keep yourselves from these, you will do well. Farewell."[1]

What next? Then Paul proceeded to the second step. He abrogated the prohibitions of the first three laws until none of the laws of the Old Testament governing actions remained except the prohibition against adultery. Even adultery can be considered abrogated since there is no prescribed penalty for it.

Thus all the laws of the Old Testament have been abrogated. Paul says:

---

[1] Acts 15:22-29.

I have been crucified with Christ; it is no longer I who live, but Christ who lives in me; and the life I now live in the flesh I live by faith in the Son of God, who loved me and gave himself for me. I do not nullify the grace of God; for if justification were through the law, then Christ died to no purpose.[1]

Commenting on the verse, Dr. Hammond says:

...He (Paul) says one cannot rely for salvation on observance of the law, nor should it be understood that the laws of Moses are necessary, because the Gospel of Jesus would, in that case be superfluous.

Moreover, Paul also says:

...all who rely on works for the law are under a curse; for it is written, "Cursed be everyone who does not abide by all things written in the books of the law, and do them." Now it is evident that no man is justified before God by the law; for "He who through faith is righteous will live," but the law does not rest on faith, for "He who does them shall live by them." Christ redeemed us from the law, it having become a curse for us.[2]

In his commentary on this passage, Lard says that what the Apostle means here is that the law was nullified, or rendered useless, by the death of Christ and his Crucifixion. Then he continues, saying that the Apostle makes it very clear that the formal laws of the (Pentateuch) legal code were abolished as a result of Jesus' death.[3]

Thus the New Testament nullified the laws of the Old Testament, even if the preservation of its form and appearance creates the opposite impression. Nevertheless, Christians persist in arranging their sacred books immediately after the sacred books of the Jews.

As for the Noble Qur'an, it is the guardian of all the Scriptures. What it says is true without doubt. What it negates is false without doubt. What it remains silent about[4] is knowledge with-

---

[1] Galatians 2:20-21.
[2] Galatians 3:10-13.
[3] Lard, *Exegesis of the Bible*, vol. 9, p. 487.
[4] i.e., in matters related to belief.

out benefit, and ignorance of it is harmless. Surely, the Noble Qur'an is the brilliant, radiant morning which came and extinguished all candles and all lights.

The Qur'an and the Scriptures of the Past

The issue of abrogation gives rise to another question, namely, what is the Qur'anic position on the divinely revealed scriptures of the past, such as the books of the Old Testament, and the books of the New Testament? We will first respond with a brief answer and then explain it in detail.

Briefly, any narrations or passages in these older books, if corroborated by the Noble Qur'an, are fully acceptable. Conversely, if any passages are declared false by the Noble Qur'an, they are rejected outright. If the Noble Qur'an remains silent on a certain issue, i.e., not declaring as to the truth or falsehood of a certain passage or text, then we also remain silent. We neither believe it nor reject it.

Now the details.

The Qur'an Attests To The Truth

Allah, Most Exalted, declares: "We sent the Scriptures to you in truth confirming the Scriptures that came before it and guarding it in safety."[1] Moreover, Allah adds:

> ...Allah! There is no god but He, the Living, the Self-Subsisting, the Supporter of all. It is He Who sent down to you (step by step) in truth the Book, confirming what came before it, and He sent down the Torah (of Moses) and the Gospel (of Jesus) before this as a guide to mankind. And He sent down the Criterion (of judgment between right and wrong).[2]

Perhaps some may understand the Qur'an's "confirming the Scriptures that came before it" as if the Qur'an absolves the previous Scriptures of any charges against them and affirms every-

---
[1] Qur'an 5:48.
[2] Qur'an 3:2-4.

thing in them despite the fact that they were edited, altered and distorted. Obviously this is a gross misunderstanding and far from truth.

The Qur'an Preserves the Truth of Previous Scriptures

While calling the Qur'an, an attestation to the truth, i.e., *musaddiq*, Allah simultaneously calls the Qur'an *muhaymin*. Allah says, "We sent the Scripture to you in truth confirming what came before it and guarding it in safety."[1] The word *muhaymin* means more than "guarding"; it also means that which "safeguards, watches over, stands witness, preserves and upholds." Thus the Qur'an bears witness to any truths found in the previous Scriptures. Second, it clearly points out the numerous distortions found therein. Then it upholds and issues its rulings based on what Allah has ordained and commanded us to do. Moreover, it nullifies what Allah has nullified in the previous Scriptures. In short, the Qur'an has been entrusted to preserve and uphold all of the above.

"The Qur'an," Ibn Jurayj once said, "is the master of all previous Scriptures. So if you find that whatever the People of the Book tell you about their books is in the Qur'an, believe it. Otherwise, deny it."

Bukhari, may Allah be merciful to him, narrates on the authority of the Ibn 'Abbas (may Allah be pleased with him) in the *Book of Witnesses* and others, that he (Ibn 'Abbas) said,

> Muslims, how can you turn to the People of the Book (i.e., for answers to your questions) when your Book, revealed to the Prophet of Allah (i.e., Muhammad), is the most recent news from Allah? You can read it unadulterated and pure, whereas, Allah has already told you that the People of the Book altered what Allah revealed and distorted their books with their own hands and then claimed that "...this is from Allah, to traffic with it for a paltry price!"[2]

---

[1] Qur'an 5:48.
[2] Qur'an 2:79.

Shouldn't the knowledge given to you prevent you from asking them? I swear by Allah that we have never seen one of them asking you about the revelation brought to you.

Ahmad narrates on the authority of Jabir, who attributes the Prophet as saying:

Don't inquire of anything (i.e., pertaining to religion) from the People of the Book. They've already gone astray and they will never guide you aright.

Previous Scriptures Support The Qur'an

Allah, Most Exalted, says:

If you are in doubt as to what We have revealed unto you, then ask those who have been reading the Book before you. The truth has indeed come to you from your Lord so do not be like those in doubt.[1]

This eminent verse does not indicate doubt on the part of the Prophet (may Allah's peace and blessings be upon him) or that he was inclined to asking (the People of the book). Assuredly, the Prophet (may Allah's peace and blessings be upon him) never doubted nor did he ever ask any of them. Rather, he is reported to have said on this subject: "I swear by Allah that I have no doubts nor do I ask (i.e., the Christians and Jews)." The real objective of this verse is to announce that the People of the Book have much proof and evidence which supports Prophet Muhammad and corroborates the truth which he brought and which the disbelievers reject outright.

In other distinguished verses, Allah, Most Exalted, says:

The disbelievers say: "You are no messenger." Say: Enough for a witness between me and you is Allah and such as have knowledge of the Book.[2]

Say: See? If (this teaching) be from Allah, and you reject it, and a witness from among the Children of Israel testifies to its similarity (with earlier scripture), and has believed while

---

[1] Qur'an 10:94.
[2] Qur'an 13-43.

you are arrogant, (how unjust you are)! Truly, Allah guides not a people unjust.[1]

Is it not a sign to them that the learned of the Children of Israel knew it (as true)?[2]

Now have We caused the Word to reach them themselves, in order that they may receive admonition. Those to whom We sent the Book before this—they do believe in this (Revelation); and when it is recited to them, they say: "We believe therein, for it is the truth from our Lord; indeed we have been Muslims (bowing to Allah's Will) from before this."[3]

...it is true that those who were given knowledge beforehand, when it is recited to them, fall down on their faces in humble prostration and they say: "Glory to our Lord! Truly has the promise of our Lord been fulfilled!" They fall down on their faces in tears and it increases their (earnest) humility.[4]

Strong among men in enmity to the Believers will you find the Jews and Pagans; and nearest among them in love to the Believers will you find those who say, "We are Christians": Because among these are men devoted to learning and men who have renounced the world, and they are not arrogant. And when they listen to the revelation received by the Messenger, you will see their eyes overflowing with tears, for they recognize the truth: They pray: "Our Lord! We believe; record us among the witnesses."[5]

But those among them who are well grounded in knowledge, and the believers, believe in what has been revealed to you and what was revealed before you: and (especially) those who establish regular prayer and practice regular charity and believe in Allah and in the Last Day: to them shall We soon give a great reward.[6]

---

[1] Qur'an 46:10.
[2] Qur'an 26:197.
[3] Qur'an 28:51-53.
[4] Qur'an 17:107-109.
[5] Qur'an 5:82-83.
[6] Qur'an 4:162.

> Before you, also, the messengers We sent were but men to whom We granted inspiration: If you realize this not, ask of those who possess the Message.[1]

> The People of the Book know this as they know their own sons; but some of them conceal the truth which they themselves know.[2]

The above verses clearly assure us that the previous Scriptures were full of signs and prophecies of the coming of Muhammad (may the peace and blessings of Allah be upon him), his religion and his people. One may ask if these verses don't imply that the Scriptures of the People of the Book were authentic and never distorted. In response, we say that these verses do not address the subject of distortion. That is another topic addressed elsewhere in the Noble Qur'an. We shall certainly deal with it in our discussion later, if Allah wills.

Nevertheless, these verses bring out a number of facts which the disbelievers disavow, yet they are known to the People of the Book and recorded in their Scriptures. These facts are discussed below.

A. Former scriptures confirm that Moses and other prophets (may Allah's peace and blessings be upon them) invited people to worship Allah alone and forbade *shirk*.[3] This was ample proof against those who thought that *shirk* was an accepted way of life. Allah, Most Exalted, says:

> And do you question our messengers whom We sent before you; did We appoint any deities other than (God) Most Gracious, to be worshipped?[4]

> Not a messenger did We send before you without this inspiration sent by Us to him: that there is no god but I; therefore worship and serve Me.[5]

---

[1] Qur'an 21:7.
[2] Qur'an 2:146.
[3] *Shirk*— associating or considering as equal or better beings or other things with Allah in His lordship, names and attributes, or worship.
[4] Qur'an 43:45.
[5] Qur'an 21:25.

> For We assuredly sent among every people a messenger (with the command), "Serve Allah, and eschew evil." Of the people were some whom Allah guided, and some on whom error became inevitably (established). So travel through the earth, and see what was the end of those who denied (the Truth).[1]

B. The People of the Book know that Allah sent men like themselves as prophets. He did not send angels to them. It is only pagans who would maintain that Allah would not send a prophet unless he were an angel or he were a man sent along with an angel. Instead they would be amazed to see a human prophet without any apparent angel accompanying him. Allah, Most Exalted, relates:

> What kept men back from belief when guidance came to them was nothing but this: they said, "Has Allah sent a man (like us) to be (His) messenger?" Say: If there were settled on earth angels walking about in peace and quiet, We should certainly have sent them down from the heavens an angel for a messenger.[2]

> Before you, also, the messengers We sent were but men, to whom We granted inspiration: If you realize this not, ask of those who possess the Message.[3]

C. The People of the Book should be asked—no doubt, they must have some knowledge of it—about what transpired between the prophets and their peoples. What happened to the believers and what became of those who disbelieved?

D. The People of the Book should be questioned about the basic fundamentals of the message which Allah sent via the prophets and which He revealed in the Scriptures; namely, the message was Islam. They must be asked about His commandments and prohibitions, commandments such as maintaining the oneness of

---

[1] Qur'an 16:36.
[2] Qur'an 17:94-95.
[3] Qur'an 21:7.

Muslim-Christian Dialogue

God, or upholding the truth, justice, righteousness, fulfilling one's promise, maintaining strong family ties, and prohibitions such as the outlawing of *shirk,* tyranny, and evil deeds, privately and publicly.

E. They must be asked about how former prophets described their Lord. Do these descriptions agree or disagree with how Prophet Muhammad (may Allah's peace and mercy be upon him) spoke about Him?

F. The Jews and Christians must be asked about the evidence and prophecy of the prophethood of Muhammad (may Allah's peace and mercy be upon him) mentioned by the Noble Qur'an. For example, Allah, Most Exalted, says:

> And ordain for us that which is good in this life and in the Hereafter: For we have turned to You.
>
> He said: "With My punishment I visit whom I will; But My mercy extends to all things. That (mercy) I shall ordain for those who do right, and practice regular charity, and those who believe in Our signs. Those who follow the Messenger, the unlettered Prophet, whom they find mentioned in their own (Scriptures), in the law and the Gospel, for he commands them what is just and forbids them what is evil; he allows them as lawful what is good (and pure) and prohibits them from what is bad (and impure); he releases them from their heavy burdens and from the yokes that are upon them. So it is those who believe in him honor him, help him, and follow the light which is sent down with him: it is they who will prosper.[1]
>
> And remember, Jesus, the son of Mary, said: "I am a messenger of Allah (sent) to you, confirming the Law (which came) before me, and giving Glad Tidings of a messenger to come after me, whose name shall be Ahmad." But when he came to them with Clear Signs, they said, "This is evident sorcery!"[2]

---

[1] Qur'an 7:156-157.
[2] Qur'an 61:6.

If anyone says the Jews and the Christians do not believe these prophecies, nor do they speak of them, then we respond by saying that is impossible. It doesn't make sense. It must be remembered that multitudes of Jews and Christians, scholars and others, have embraced Islam and have become great Muslims. They surely wouldn't have blindly embraced a faith which refutes clearly what was believed to be basic truths.

If someone were to say, "Since you (Muslims) are citing our Scriptures to confirm the prophethood of Muhammad (may Allah's peace and mercy be upon him) and its prophecy of it, then based on this, our books must be correct and free from any alterations or distortions, as you have described," then, in response, we would say that the Torah (i.e., Old Testament) and the Injil, or Gospel (New Testament) contain truth and falsehood mixed up with each other. Prophet Muhammad (may Allah's peace and mercy be upon him) once said, "Don't believe everything the People of the Book (have in their scriptures), or deny (everything) they (have)."

> But say, "We believe in the revelation which has come down to us and in that which came down to you; our God and your God is one; and it is to Him we bow (in Islam)."[1]

Ibn Hajr, a great scholar of Hadith, relates the following statement of Ash-Shafi'i in his explanation of the above *hadith*:

> Concerning information related to you by them (i.e., Jews and Christians) which could be true or false, do not deny it summarily, for it could contain some truth. Similarly, do not believe it absolutely, for it could contain something false; otherwise you will find yourself in an embarrassing position. No revealed text prohibits us from disbelieving in what contradicts our Islamic law nor believing in what agrees with our Islam.

Without a doubt, the prophecies concerning the Final Prophet (may Allah's peace and mercy be upon him) agree in content with what was revealed in the Noble Qur'an and what their Scriptures endorse. We have already discussed some of these details in Shaykh Ibrahim Khalil Ahmad's discourse.

---

[1] Qur'an 29:46.

Muslim-Christian Dialogue

There is much more for whoever wants to follow up and research more.

One may say that he finds many verses in the Noble Qur'an which testify to the authenticity of the Torah—as it is today—and to the authenticity of the Gospel—as it is today—and confirm that the two Testaments do not suffer from distortion or forgery. For example, the Qur'an says:

> But why do they come to you for decision, when they have (their own) Law before them?—therein is the (plain) command of Allah; yet even after that, they would turn away, for they are not (really) people of faith.[1]

And in another place, it says:

> Let the people of the Gospel judge by what Allah has revealed therein. If any do fail to judge by (the light of) what Allah has revealed, they are (no better than) those who rebel.[2]

Our response is as follows. First, let us respond by using the verses of the Noble Qur'an which confirm that mischievous forces tampered with these books. For instance, Allah, Most Exalted, says:

> Can you (men of faith) entertain the hope that they will believe in you?—seeing that a party of them heard the Word of Allah, and perverted it knowingly after they understood it. Behold! when they meet the men of faith, they say: "We believe": But when they meet each other in private, they say: "Shall you tell them what Allah has revealed to you, that they may engage you in argument about it before your Lord?"—Do you not understand (their aim)? Know they not that Allah knows what they conceal and what they reveal? And there are among them illiterates, who know not the Book, but (see therein their own) desires, and they do nothing but conjecture. Then woe to those who write the Book with their own hands, and then say: "This is from Allah," to

---
[1] Qur'an 5:43.
[2] Qur'an 5:47.

traffic with it for a miserable price! Woe to them for what their hands do write, and for the gain they make thereby.[1]

But because of their breach of their covenant, We cursed them and made their hearts grow hard; they change the words from their (right) places and forget a good part of the message that was sent them, nor will you cease to find them—barring a few—ever bent on (new) deceits: But forgive them, and overlook (their misdeeds): for Allah loves those who are kind. From those, too, who call themselves Christians, We did take a covenant, but they forgot a good part of the message that was sent them: so we estranged them, with enmity and hatred between the one and the other, to the Day of Judgment. And soon will Allah show them what it is they have done.

People of the Book! There has come to you Our Messenger, revealing to you much that you used to hide in the Book, and passing over much (that is now unnecessary): There has come to you from Allah a (new) light and a perspicuous Book.[2]

O Messenger! Let not those grieve you who race each other into unbelief: (whether it be) among those who say "We believe" with their lips but whose hearts have no faith; or it be among the Jews—men who will listen to any lie—who will listen even to others who have never so much as come to you. They change the words from their (right) times and places: they say, "If you are given this, take it, but if not, beware!" If any one's trial is intended by Allah, you have no authority in the least for him against Allah. For such it is not Allah's will to purify their hearts. For them there is disgrace in this world, and in the Hereafter a heavy punishment.[3]

---

[1] Qur'an 2:75-79.
[2] Qur'an 5:13-15.
[3] Qur'an 5:41.

Muslim-Christian Dialogue

Imam Ahmad,[1] on the authority of Jabir, narrates a *hadith* attributed to the Prophet (may Allah's peace and blessings be upon him):

> Don't ask the People of the Book about anything (pertaining to Islam). They will not guide you right for they have gone astray.

All in all, the evidence given here from Qur'an and Hadith proves that they have distorted their books and have thus been oblivious to genuine revelation and divine guidance. These Scriptures, after what happened, were totally unable to provide humanity with a proper sense of conduct, guidance and a mature sense of righteousness.

We have already presented our detailed findings by Brigadier General Ahmad 'Abdul-Wahhab concerning the validity of the Gospels. I proved therein that, according to the writings of Christian writers and others, in these Scriptures there are hundreds of issues which defy reason, revelation and science.

Second, it is true that their (i.e., Christians and Jews) Scriptures do contain some truth, despite their being altered and their words changed due to translation or due to personal motives.

When we read verses 43 and 47 from Surat Al-Ma'idah (i.e., Chapter 5 of the Qur'an) in their proper context, any ambiguity is removed immediately and the facts become crystal clear.

Allah, Most Exalted—and how perfect He is!—says:

> O Messenger! let not those grieve you, who race each other into unbelief: (whether it be) among those who say, "We believe," with their lips but whose hearts have no faith; or it be among the Jews—men who will listen to any lie—will listen even to others who have never so much as come to you. They change the words from their (right) times and places: they say, "If you are given this, take it, but if not, beware!" If anyone's trial is intended by Allah, you have no authority in the least for him against Allah. For such—it is not Allah's will to purify their hearts.

---

[1] Imam Ahmad, one of the four major scholars whose opinions are still widely followed by many Muslims. He was also a major compiler of Hadith.

For them there is disgrace in this world, and in the Hereafter a heavy punishment. (They are fond of) listening to falsehood, of devouring anything forbidden. If they do come to you, either judge between them, or decline to interfere. If you decline, they cannot hurt you in the least. If you judge, judge in equity between them, for Allah loves those who judge in equity. But why do they come to you for decision, when they have (their own) law before them? Therein is the (plain) command of Allah; yet even after that, they would turn away, for they are not (really) people of faith.

It was We Who revealed the Law (to Moses): therein was guidance and light. By its standard have been judged the Jews, by the prophets who bowed (as in Islam) to Allah's will, by the rabbis and the doctors of law: For to them was entrusted the protection of Allah's Book, and they were witnesses thereto: Therefore fear not men, but fear Me, and sell not My Signs for a miserable price. If any do fail to judge by (the light of) what Allah has revealed, they are (no better than) Unbelievers.

We ordained therein for them: "Life for life, eye for eye, nose for nose, ear for ear, tooth for tooth, and wounds equal for equal." But if anyone remits the retaliation by way of charity, it is an act of atonement for himself. And if any fail to judge by (the light of) what Allah has revealed, they are (no better than) wrongdoers.

And in their footsteps we sent Jesus the son of Mary, confirming the Law that had come before him: We sent him the Gospel: therein was guidance and light, and confirmation of the Law that had come before him: a guidance and an admonition to those who fear Allah. Let the people of the Gospel judge by what Allah has revealed therein. If any do fail to judge by (the light of) what Allah has revealed, they are (no better than) those who rebel.

To you We sent the Scripture in truth, confirming the Scripture that came before it, and guarding it in safety: so judge between them by what Allah has revealed, and follow not their vain desires, diverging from the Truth that has come to you. To each among you have We prescribed a law and an open way. If Allah had so willed, He would have made you a single people, but (His Plan is) to test you in what He has given you: so strive as in a race in all virtues. The goal of you all is to Allah; it is He That will show you the truth of the matters in which you dispute; And this (He commands): judge between them by what Allah has revealed, and follow not their vain desires, but beware of them lest they beguile you from any of that (teaching) which Allah has sent down to you.

And if they turn away, be assured that for some of their crime it is Allah's purpose to punish them. And truly most men are rebellious. Do they then seek after a judgment of (the days of) ignorance? But who, for a people whose faith is assured, can give better judgment than Allah?[1]

From the above verses, one can see that Allah has commanded the People of the Torah (the Jews) to make legal decisions on what Allah revealed in their book. Similarly, He ordered the People of the Injil (the Christians) to make their decisions based on what Allah had revealed in their book. Moreover, Allah had ordered the Torah (the Old Testament) as well as in the Injil (the Gospel, or the New Testament) to obey and follow Muhammad (may Allah's peace and blessings be upon him). Consequently, if they refused to judge according to the injunctions of Prophet Muhammad (may Allah's peace and blessings be upon him), then it is as if they have refused to judge according to the Torah and the Gospel. Furthermore, if they fail to believe in him, it is as if they have failed to believe in the Torah and the Gospel!

Disavowal of what was revealed to them in their books has been documented in the collections of Hadith.

In a narration in *Sahih Al-Bukhari* and *Sahih Muslim*,[2] on the authority of 'Abdullah Ibn 'Umar (may Allah be pleased with them), he said:

---

[1] Qur'an 5:41-50.
[2] Two of the most authentic collections of Hadith.

Muslim-Christian Dialogue

> Some Jews came to Allah's Prophet (may Allah's peace and blessings be upon him) and informed him of a man and a woman from among them who had committed adultery. The Prophet (may Allah's peace and blessings be upon him) asked them, "What can you find in the Torah concerning stoning?" They answered, "We only expose them and then they are flogged." At this 'Abdullah Ibn Salam[1] interjected, "You are lying! It mentions stoning. Bring the Torah!" When they brought the Torah, they spread it out and found the verse. However, one of the Jews placed his hand over the verse regarding stoning. Then he proceeded to read what was before it and what came after the verse. So 'Abdullah told him, "Lift your hand!" When he removed his hand, there was the verse of "stoning". The Jews then said. "He was right, Muhammad!" So the Prophet (may Allah's peace and blessings be upon him) ordered that both of them be stoned.[2]

In a variant *hadith* on the authority of 'Abdullah Ibn 'Umar, Al-Bukhari narrates that 'Abdullah Ibn 'Umar said:

> A Jewish man and a Jewish woman were brought to Allah's Prophet (may Allah's peace and blessings be upon him). They had committed adultery. The Prophet (may Allah's peace and blessings be upon him) left and visited them in their Jewish school. There he inquired, "What do you have in the Torah concerning adultery?" They responded, "...we blacken their faces and then they are paraded all over town." He said, "Then bring forth the Torah, and read it for me if what you are saying is true."[3]
>
> So they brought it forth and read from it. When they reached the verse of stoning, the young man reading the text put his hand on the verse of stoning and read what was before it and what came after it. So 'Abdullah Ibn Salam, who was with the Prophet (may Allah's peace and blessings be upon him) said to him, "Ask him to move his hand." When he moved

---

[1] A Companion of the Prophet who had been a Jew but embraced Islam.
[2] Reported authentically by Al-Bukhari and Muslim.
[3] Qur'an 3: 93.

his hand, there appeared the verse of stoning. They (the Jews) immediately concurred saying, "He's right, it (the Torah) does carry the verse of stoning. However, we keep this to ourselves. Our rabbis came up with the idea of tying the adulterer and adulteress, with their faces blackened, back-to-back on a donkey and parading them all over town."

So Allah's Prophet (may Allah's peace and blessings be upon him) ordered both of them to be stoned.[1]

In a (similar) narration by Muslim, Al-Barra' Ibn Azib (may Allah be pleased with him) says:

A Jew who was whipped and his face blackened passed by the Prophet (may Allah's peace and blessings be upon him). So he asked them about it. He said, "Is this the punishment for adultery you find in your book?" They said yes. He then called upon one of their scholars and asked him, "I ask you in the name of Allah Who revealed the Torah to Moses: is this the way you find the punishment for adultery in your book?"

He said, "No, and had you not asked me in the name of Allah, I wouldn't have told you about the punishment by stoning. This crime was on the rise among our nobles, so if we caught one of our nobles we would let him go. However, if we caught one of the lower class people doing it we would punish him (i.e., by stoning). So we said to each other: 'Come, let us come together on something which we can implement for the upper class as well as the lower class.' Accordingly, we replaced stoning with blackening the faces (of the adulterer and the adulteress) and whipping them publicly."

(Hearing this) the Prophet (may Allah's peace and blessings be upon him) said, "O Allah! I am the first one to revive Your injunction which they had stifled." Then he ordered him to be stoned, and so he was. Therefore, Allah, Most Exalted, revealed the following verses:

---

[1] Reported by Al-Bukhari.

"O Messenger! let not those aggrieve you, who race each other into unbelief: (whether it be) among those who say, 'We believe' with their lips but whose hearts have no faith; or it be among the Jews—men who will listen to any lie— who will listen even to others who have never so much as come to you. They change the words from their (right) times and places: they say, 'If you are given this, take it, but if not, beware!' If anyone's trial is intended by Allah, you have no authority in the least for him against Allah. For such it is not Allah's will to purify their hearts. For them there is disgrace in this world, and in the Hereafter a heavy punishment. (They are fond of) listening to falsehood, of devouring anything forbidden. If they do come to you, either judge between them or decline to interfere. If you decline, they cannot hurt you in the least. If you judge, judge in equity between them. For Allah loves those who judge in equity. But why do they come to you for decision, when they have (their own) Law before them? Therein is the (plain) command of Allah; yet even after that, they would turn away. For they are not (really) people of faith. It was We Who revealed the Law (to Moses): therein was guidance and light. By its standard have been judged the Jews, by the prophets who bowed (as in Islam) to Allah's will, by the rabbis and the doctors of law: For to them was entrusted the protection of Allah's Book, and they were witnesses thereto. Therefore fear not men, but fear Me, and sell not My Signs for a miserable price. If any do fail to judge by (the light of) what Allah has revealed, they are unbelievers. We ordained therein for them: 'Life for life, eye for eye, nose for nose, ear for ear, tooth for tooth, and wounds equal for equal.' But if anyone remits the retaliation by way of charity, it is an act of atonement for himself. And if any fail to judge by (the light of) what Allah has revealed, they are wrongdoers. And in their footsteps we sent Jesus the son of Mary, confirming the Law that had come before him: We sent him the Gospel: therein was guidance and light, and confirmation of the Law that had come before him: A guidance and an admonition to those who fear Allah. Let the people of the Gospel judge by what Allah has revealed therein. If any do fail to judge by (the light of) what Allah has revealed, they are among those who rebel."[1]

Then he (may Allah's peace and blessings be upon him) said, "...this applies to all disbelievers."

In a narration related in *Sahih Muslim*, Jabir Ibn 'Abdullah (may Allah be pleased with them) says that the Prophet (may Allah's peace and blessings be upon him) had a Muslim and a Jew stoned.

Ibn 'Umar said that a group of Jews came and called the Messenger of Allah to Quff. So he visited them in their school. They said, "Abu'l-Qasim, a man among us has committed fornication with a woman; so pronounce judgment upon them."

They placed a cushion for the Messenger of Allah, who sat on it and said, "Bring the Torah." It was brought. He then withdrew the cushion from beneath him and placed the Torah on it, saying: "I believe in you and in Him Who revealed you." He then said, "Bring me one who is learned among you," and a young man was brought.[2] The transmitter then cited the rest of the *hadith* by Malik from Nafi':

> Abu Hurayrah said (this is Ma'mar's version, which is more perfect): A man and a woman of the Jews committed fornication. Some of them said to others: "Let us go to this Prophet, for he has been sent with an easy law. If he gives a judgment lighter than stoning, we shall accept it, and argue from it with Allah, saying, 'a judgment of a prophet from Your prophets.'"
>
> So they came to the Prophet, who was sitting in the mosque among his Companions, and they said, "Abu'l-Qasim, what do you say about a man and a woman who committed fornication?" He did not speak to them a word till he went to their school. He stood at the gate and said, "I adjure you by Allah, Who revealed the Torah to Moses, what (punishment) do you find in the Torah for a person who commits fornication if he is married?" They said, "He shall be blackened

---
[1] Qur'an 5:41-47.
[2] *Sahih Muslim*, Hadith no. 4434.

with charcoal, taken round among the people on a donkey, and flogged." A young man among them kept silence. When the Prophet emphatically adjured him, he said, "By Allah, since you have adjured us, (we inform you that) we find stoning in the Torah (as punishment for fornication)." The Prophet said, "So when did you take Allah's command easy?"

He said, "A relative of a certain king of ours had committed fornication, but he suspended stoning for him. Then a man of a family of commoners committed fornication, and he intended to have him stoned, but his people intervened and said, 'Our man shall not be stoned until you bring your man and stone him.' So they made a compromise on this punishment between them." The Prophet said, "Therefore, I decide in accordance with what the Torah says." He then ruled regarding them and they were stoned to death.[1]

According to what we have related above, we can easily see that the objective was to use the former books for legal judgments as long as they conformed to the Qur'an and did not contradict or conflict with it.

Now, a Christian may say that the Noble Qur'an praises them and considers them the nearest to the Believers in love. After all, Allah, Most Exalted, says:

> Strong among men in enmity to the Believers will you find the Jews and Pagans; and nearest among them in love to the Believers will you find those who say, "We are Christians": because among these are men devoted to learning and men who have renounced the world, and they are not arrogant.[2]

This appreciation refers only to those among them (the Christians) who believed in Muhammad (may Allah's peace and blessings be upon him). Undoubtedly, there were many more Christians than Jews who became Muslims. The proof of this comes from the three verses [5:83-85], following verse 5:82, cited by our friend:

---

[1] *Sahih Muslim*, Hadith no. 4435.
[2] Qur'an 5: 82.

And when they listen to the revelation received by the Messenger, you will see their eyes overflowing with tears, for they recognize the truth: They pray: "Our Lord! We believe; record us among the witnesses."

What cause can we have not to believe in Allah and the truth which has come to us, seeing that we long for our Lord to admit us to the company of the righteous? And for this their prayer has Allah rewarded them with gardens, with rivers flowing underneath—their eternal home. Such is the recompense of those who do good.

As seen above, the Most Exalted, Allah, does not promise any reward in the Hereafter except to those who believe in Muhammad (may Allah's peace and blessings be upon him). They are those who "...when they listen to the revelation received by the Messenger, you will see their eyes overflowing with tears, for they recognize the truth. They pray, 'Our Lord! We believe; record us among the witnesses.'"

These "witnesses" refers to people who bear witness to the message brought by the Prophet (may Allah's peace and blessings be upon him). Accordingly, they testify that there is none to be worshipped but Allah and that Muhammad is the Messenger of Allah. For this reason, we find that Ibn 'Abbas[1] and others explain the passage, "...and record us among the witnesses" as "record us along with Muhammad and his people as witnesses to the truth.' Obviously, anyone who believes in Muhammad (may Allah's peace and blessings be upon him) is a "witness". As a matter of fact, the disciples of Jesus reiterated this when they declared, "Our Lord! We believe in what you have revealed, and we follow the Messenger; then write us down among those who bear witness."[2]

It is true that the Noble Qur'an does praise priests and monks who sincerely studied the truth, testified to it and then followed it. On the other hand, it reproaches others who treated their religion as a business to make profit, who hoarded gold and silver, and who appointed themselves as pseudo-gods legalizing

---

[1] A famous Companion of the Prophet (peace be upon him).
[2] Qur'an 3:53.

what they sought and making unlawful what they wished, and declaring those whom they liked as people who would enter Paradise, and prohibiting it to those whom they disliked. Allah, Most Exalted, says:

> The Jews call Ezra the son of God, and the Christians call Christ the son of God. That is a saying from their mouth; (in this) they but imitate what the Unbelievers of old used to say. Allah's curse be on them: how they are deluded away from the Truth!
>
> They take their priests and their anchorites to be their lords in derogation of Allah, and (they take as their Lord) Christ the son of Mary; yet they were commanded to worship but one God: there is no god but He. Praise and glory to Him: (Far is He) from having the partners they associate (with Him).
>
> Fain would they extinguish Allah's light with their mouths, but Allah will not allow but that His light should be perfected, even though the Unbelievers may detest (it). It is He Who has sent His Messenger with Guidance and the Religion of Truth, to proclaim it over all religion, even though the Pagans may detest (it).
>
> You who believe! There are indeed many among the priests and anchorites who in falsehood devour the substance of men and hinder (them) from the way of God. And there are those who bury gold and silver and spend it not in the way of God: announce unto them a most grievous penalty: on the Day when heat will be produced out of that (wealth) in the fire of Hell, and with it will be branded their foreheads, their flanks, and their backs, "This is the (treasure) which you buried for yourselves: taste, then, the (treasures) you buried!"[1]

---

[1] Qur'an 9:30-35.

The Disciples

A question often raised is concerning how the Muslims believe in Jesus' disciples as being chosen by him and whom he entrusted, as mentioned in the New Testament, with the responsibility of spreading the Gospel to all peoples.

Christians claim that these disciples were messengers commissioned by Allah and that they brought the Torah (i.e., the Old Testament) and the Injil (i.e., the New Testament) and that they performed miracles. Their contention that they are God's messengers can only be based on the claim that Jesus is God; hence, these disciples are God's messengers.

The great Islamic scholar, Ibn Taymiyyah, writes in his well-documented book, *The Sound Rebuttal of Those Who Altered the Religion of Jesus*:

> Their premise is baseless. However, in view of discussing these issues in the best and most gracious way, we politely refuse to believe their above contention. Moreover, we demand proof that they are messengers of God. Frankly, they have no evidence in this regard. If there is no proof that Jesus is God, then it cannot be proven that they (i.e., the disciples) are messengers of God. To prove their contention that Jesus is God, one must use either reason or revelation. Surely reason cannot attest to this; on the contrary, it views it as inconceivable. Accordingly, they (i.e., the Christians) do not claim to establish this based on reason and logic. What they want is only to prove its possibility by way of reason and not necessarily its actual existence. Of course, this view is also groundless.
>
> Instead, they claim to prove this by way of revelation. However, they must be told at this juncture that you cannot prove that Jesus is God without citing these Scriptures (i.e., the Old and New Testaments). Likewise, you cannot authenticate the Scriptures without establishing that the disciples were infallible messengers of God. Finally, you cannot prove that they were actual prophets of God unless you establish that Jesus is God. All of the above becomes a vicious circle leading to no end.

In other words, Jesus' divinity cannot be established unless the authenticity of the Scriptures is ascertained. Likewise, the Scriptures cannot be validated unless the disciples are acknowledged as God's messengers. Obviously, this cannot be accepted unless Jesus is accepted as God. Thus, proving Jesus' divinity hinges on establishing his divinity. Similarly, acceptance of the disciples as God's messengers is contingent upon accepting them as God's messengers. Needless to say, the above is a vicious circle which proves nothing.

Later, he further refutes their claims. For instance, in response to their claim that these disciples performed miracles and are thus considered prophets, he says:

> ...they may allege that the disciples, along with church officials after them, were infallible. They claim that the disciples and these church dignitaries were responsible for many extraordinary miracles. For example, they may mention that some of them gave life to the dead. This, if it were true—even though the one who performed the miracles never claimed to be a prophet or messenger—still does not prove his infallibility.
>
> It is true that many extraordinary events—recounting of which would prolong our discussion—did occur in the personal lives of saints from among the Companions and the succeeding pious generations and all other Muslim and non-Muslim saints. However, not one of them was infallible such that everything he/she said must be accepted. On the contrary, each one of them could have erred. Needless to say, with the exception of the prophets—may Allah's peace be upon them all—the statements of every other human are subject to acceptance or rejection. For this reason, Allah has obliged us to believe in everything given to the prophets and not everything every saint says.[1]

Allah, Most Exalted, says:

> Say: We believe in Allah, and the revelation given to us, and to Abraham, Ishmael, Isaac, Jacob, and the Tribes,

---

[1] Ibn Taymiyyah, op. cit.

and that given to Moses and Jesus, and that given to (all) prophets from their Lord. We make no difference between one and another of them: And we bow to Allah (in Islam).[1]

So when the Muslims declare that disciples of Jesus were not infallible, they maintain the same position for their own saints whom they view as much better, such as Abu Bakr and 'Umar. Thus, if they say that Jesus was created a servant of Allah and that he was not God, they have already acknowledged this in those—such as Muhammad and Abraham, may Allah's peace and blessings be upon them both— who they believe as being better than Jesus.[2]

We believe that the disciples were Jesus' companions and his ambassadors. They were like the ambassadors of Moses, the ambassadors of Abraham and the ambassadors of Muhammad (may Allah's peace and blessings be upon all of them) in that they were commissioned by their prophets to carry their message to the people far and wide. They were summoned to do this to teach and propagate the religion.

The Christians, however, feel that these disciples were prophets of God, i.e., Jesus! Jesus' disciples are mentioned in three places in the Noble Qur'an. First, Allah, Most Exalted, says:

When Jesus found unbelief on their part he said: "Who will be my helpers to (the work of) Allah?" Said the disciples: "We are Allah's helpers: We believe in Allah, and do you bear witness that we are Muslims."[3]

Then Allah, Most Exalted, says:

And behold! I inspired the disciples to have faith in Me and My Messenger: They said, "We have faith, and do you bear witness that we bow to Allah as Muslims." Behold, the disciples said: "Jesus son of Mary! Can your Lord send down to us a table set (with viands) from heaven?" Said Jesus: "Fear Allah, if you have faith." They said: "We only wish to

---

[1] Qur'an 2:136.
[2] Ibn Taymiyyah, op. cit.
[3] Qur'an 3:52.

eat thereof and satisfy our hearts, and to know that you have indeed told us the truth; and that we ourselves may be witnesses to the miracle."

Said Jesus the son of Mary: "O Allah, our Lord! Send us from heaven a table set (with viands), that there may be for us—for the first and the last of us—a solemn festival and a Sign from You; and provide for our sustenance, for You are the best Sustainer (of our needs)." Allah said: I will send it down unto you: But if any of you after that resists faith, I will punish him with a penalty such as I have not inflicted on anyone among all the peoples.[1]

Finally, Allah, Most Exalted, says:

You who believe! Be helpers of Allah: As Jesus the son of Mary said to the disciples, "Who will be my helpers to (the work of) Allah?" Said the disciples, "We are Allah's helpers!" Then a portion of the Children of Israel believed, and a portion disbelieved: But We supported those who believed against their enemies, and they became the ones who prevailed.[2]

Now, someone may ask whether the verses of *Surat Ya Sin*[3] relating the story of Jesus' messengers to Antioch prove that they (i.e., the disciples) were God's messengers? To begin with, the verses cited above are as follows:

Set forth to them, by way of a parable, the (story of) the Companions of the City. Behold! There came messengers to it. When We (first) sent to them two messengers, they rejected them: But We strengthened them with a third: they said, "Truly, we have been sent on a mission to you." The (people) said: "You are only men like ourselves; and (Allah) Most Gracious sends no sort of revelation: You do nothing but lie." They said: "Our Lord knows that we have been sent on a mission to you: And our duty is only to proclaim the clear Message."

---

[1] Qur'an 5:111-115.
[2] Qur'an 61:14.
[3] The 36th *surah* (chapter) of the Qur'an.

Muslim-Christian Dialogue

The (people) said: "For us, we augur an evil omen from you: if you desist not, we will certainly stone you, and a grievous punishment indeed will be inflicted on you by us." They said: "Your evil omens are with yourselves: (Deem you this an evil omen) if you are admonished? Nay, but you are a people transgressing all bounds!"

Then there came running, from the farthest part of the City, a man, saying, "My people! Obey the messengers: Obey those who ask no reward of you (for themselves), and who have themselves received Guidance. It would not be reasonable of me if I did not serve Him Who created me, and to Whom you shall (all) be brought back. Shall I take (other) gods besides Him? If (Allah) Most Gracious should intend some adversity for me, of no use whatever will be their intercession for me, nor can they deliver me. I would indeed, if I were to do so, be in manifest error. For me, I have faith in the Lord of you (all): listen, then, to me!"

It was said: Enter the Garden. He said: "Ah me! Would that my people knew (what I know)! For that my Lord Has granted me forgiveness and has enrolled me among those held in honor!"

And We sent not down against his people, after him, any hosts from heaven, nor was it needful for Us so to do. It was no more than a single mighty blast, and behold, they were (like ashes) quenched and silent. Ah! Alas for (My) servants! There comes not a messenger to them but they mock him! See they not how many generations before them We destroyed? Not to them will they return: But each one of them—all—will be brought before Us (for judgment).[1]

Ibn Taymiyyah—may Allah shower him with mercy—says:

...the messengers mentioned in Surat Ya Sin are not the same disciples (i.e., of Jesus), nor were they Jesus' messengers. In fact this delegation was sent before Jesus. When the people of the town refused to believe these messengers, Allah destroyed them. Accordingly, Allah, Most Exalted, says,

---

[1] Qur'an 36:13-32.

"And We sent not down against his people, after him, any hosts from heaven, nor was it needful for Us so to do. It was no more than a single mighty blast, and behold, they were (like ashes) quenched and silent."[1]

There were three messengers mentioned in the *surah*. There was only one man in the town who believed them. This delegation to this town, even if it was Antioch, was before Jesus. Also, only two of Jesus' companions went to Antioch *after* his ascension to the heavens. Moreover, these two were not "strengthened...with the third",[2] nor was the beloved carpenter present at that time. Finally, the people of Antioch *believed* in Jesus, may Allah's peace be upon him. In actuality, it was the first town that believed in him.[3]

Before concluding this session of the debate, I would like to examine some more pages of the books of the New Testament. More importantly, I would like to pull out some excerpts concerning these disciples, who are thought to be infallible prophets.

> Now the names of the twelve apostles are these: first, Simon, who is called Peter, and Andrew his brother; James the son of Zebedee, and John his brother; Philip and Bartholomew; Thomas, and Matthew the tax collector; James the son of Alphaeus, and Lebbaeus, whose surname was Thaddaeus; Simon the Canaanite, and Judas Iscariot, who also betrayed Him.[4]

> But He turned and said to Peter, "Get behind Me, Satan! You are an offense to Me, for you are not mindful of the things of God, but the things of men."[5]

> And when they had come to the multitude, a man came to Him, kneeling down to Him and saying, "Lord, have mercy on my son, for he is an epileptic and suffers severely; for he often falls into the fire and often into the water. So I brought

---

[1] Qur'an 36: 28-29.
[2] Qur'an 36: 14.
[3] Ibn Taymiyyah, op. cit.
[4] Matthew 10: 2-4.
[5] Matthew 16: 23.

him to your disciples, but they could not cure him." Then Jesus answered and said, "Faithless and perverse generation, how long shall I be with you? How long shall I bear with you? Bring him here to Me." And Jesus rebuked the demon, and it came out of him; and the child was cured from that very hour. Then the disciples came to Jesus privately and said, "Why could we not cast it out?" So Jesus said to them, "Because of your unbelief."[1]

Peter answered and said to Him, "Even if all are made to stumble because of You, I will never be made to stumble." Jesus said to him, "Assuredly, I say to you that this night, before the rooster crows, you will deny Me three times."[2]

The Gospel confirms, as we mentioned earlier, that Judas Iscariot was one of the twelve disciples. In fact, he was one of the major disciples, for he was the treasurer. Yet he was the one who plotted against Jesus along with Jewish elders for a paltry price of thirty silver pieces.

Here, a question comes up. Did Judas know or believe that Jesus, whom he sold out to for thirty silver pieces, was the son of God, as they (i.e., Christians) claim? Did Peter, the chief disciple who, according to the narrations of the Gospel, denied Jesus three times then declared himself free of him, actually believe that he was the son of God, as they claim? If both of them knew or believed this, how could the former (Judas) betray him and the latter (Peter) deny him? On the other hand, if they did not know this, despite Peter being the head disciple, then how did they deify him afterwards and declare that Jesus is the son of God?

The Gospels insist that Judas was a traitor:

Then one of the twelve, called Judas Iscariot, went to the chief priests and said, "What are you willing to give me if I deliver Him to you." And they counted out to him thirty pieces of silver. So from that time he sought opportunity to betray him.[3]

---

[1] Matthew 17: 14-20.
[2] Matthew 26: 33-34.
[3] Matthew 26: 14-16.

The Gospels also provide a sketch of the two sons of Zebedee. They (i.e., the two sons) brought their mother to Jesus so she could ask him to let one of them be on his right and the other on his left in the Kingdom of God:

> Then the mother of Zebedee's sons came to Him with her sons, kneeling down and asking something from Him. And He said to her, "What do you wish?" She said to Him, "Grant that these two sons of mine may sit, one on Your right hand and the other on the left, in Your Kingdom."
>
> But Jesus answered and said, "You do not know what you ask. Are you able to drink the cup that I am about to drink, and be baptized with the baptism that I am baptized with?" They said to Him, "We are able."
>
> So He said to them, "You will indeed drink My cup, and be baptized with the baptism that I am baptized with; but to sit on My right hand and on My left is not Mine to give, but *it is for those* for whom it is prepared by My Father." And when the ten heard *it*, they were greatly displeased with the two brothers.[1]

As a matter of fact, all the disciples were looking for personal gain. For example, Peter, their leader, speaks on their behalf to Jesus. The Gospels relate:

> Then Peter answered and said to Him, "See, we have left all and followed You. Therefore what shall we have?" So Jesus said to them, "Assuredly I say to you, that in the regeneration, when the Son of Man sits on the throne of His glory, you who have followed Me will also sit on twelve thrones, judging the twelve tribes of Israel. And everyone who has left houses or brothers or sisters or father or mother or wife or children or lands, for My name's sake, shall receive a hundredfold, and inherit eternal life."[2]

Twelve thrones, matching the number of disciples as twelve! Did the authors of the Gospels forget to leave out Judas the betrayer from this episode of the thrones? Apparently, Judas Iscariot still holds his throne, in spite of everything that happened!

---

[1] Matthew 20: 20-24.
[2] Matthew 19: 27-29.

Alcohol[1]

A question was presented to me about wine, saying: Wine is forbidden in the Noble Qur'an; however, it isn't prohibited in the New Testament. How do you explain that? Is there a verse in the Qur'an forbidding intoxicants? We have related the question exactly as it reads, though its beginning contradicts its ending. Our response:

Allah, Most Perfect, Most Exalted, prohibits wine and other intoxicants in the Noble Qur'an. He revealed several verses regarding this topic. Allah, Most Exalted, says:

> They ask you concerning wine and gambling. Say: In them is great sin, and some profit, for men; but the sin is greater than the profit. They ask you how much they are to spend; Say: What is beyond your needs. Thus does Allah make clear to you His Signs: in order that you may consider.[2]

> You who believe! Approach not prayers with a mind befogged, until you can understand all that you say, nor in a state of ceremonial impurity (except when traveling on the road), until after washing your whole body. If you are ill, or on a journey, or one of you comes from answering the call of nature, or you have been in contact with women, and you find no water, then take for yourselves clean sand or earth, and rub therewith your faces and hands.

> For Allah does blot out sins and forgives again and again.[3]

> You who believe! Intoxicants and gambling, (dedication of) stones, and (divination by) arrows, are an abomination—of Satan's handwork: Eschew such (abomination), that you may prosper. Satan's plan is (but) to excite enmity and hatred between you, with intoxicants and gambling, and hinder you from the remembrance of Allah, and from prayer: Will you not then abstain?[4]

---

[1] *Khamr* is an Arabic term for grape wine and any other intoxicant.
[2] Qur'an 2: 219.
[3] Qur'an 4:43.
[4] Qur'an 5:90-91.

Muslim-Christian Dialogue

'Umar Ibn Al-Khattab said, "O Allah, tell us about wine in clear terms, for it destroys wealth and the mind." Thereafter this verse was revealed, i.e., "They ask you about wine and gambling...," and 'Umar was called and this verse was recited to him. When he repeated, "O Allah, tell us about wine in clear terms," soon after, the verse of *Surat An-Nisa'* was revealed, i.e., "You who believe! Approach not prayers with a befogged mind."

After this, the Prophet's caller to prayer, when he would call out for prayer would say, "Let no drunkard approach the prayer." As before, 'Umar was called and the verse was recited to him. Once more, 'Umar said, "O Allah, tell us about wine in clear terms!" Finally, the verse in *Surat Al-Ma'idah* came down. 'Umar was summoned as before and the verse was read to him. When the reciter reached the end, saying, "...will you not then abstain?" 'Umar repeated, "We are finished (with it)! We are finished!"[1]

'Uthman, may Allah be pleased with him, once said:

Avoid wine, for it is the root of all evils. Long ago, there lived a very pious man. It so happened that a very flirtatious woman fell in love with him. She sent her maid to him, inviting him to her, saying, "We would like to invite you to seek some advice."

Promptly, the man left and went with the maid to the woman's home. Every door he would enter, the maid would lock it behind him, until he ended up in a room where he found a beautiful woman. Beside her was a young man and a jug of wine, and the woman said, "I swear by Allah I didn't invite you here to seek your advice; rather, I called you here to either make love to me, drink a cup of this wine or kill this young man."

So the man said, "Give me a cup of this wine." She gave him the cup to drink. Then he said, "Give me more." They gave him more. Soon after he started drinking more and more, he made love to her. Then he also killed the young man. So stay away from wine, for I swear by Allah that

---
[1] Narrated by Imam Ahmad, Abu Dawud and al-Tirmidhi.

strong faith and drunkenness cannot coexist. One will throw out the other.[1]

Wine is called *khamr* because "it beclouds or obscures the mind."[2] Ibn Al-Anbari[3] said it was called *khamr* because it mixes up the mind or disorients it and takes over the mind. It is often said that a disease has overwhelmed him, i.e., it has overcome him and made him disordered.

Undoubtedly, the mind is the most precious and most valuable thing in a human being. Thus if one loses his/her mind what else is left for him/her?

An alcoholic poet once said that drunkenness cannot be produced until the drunkard eats his shoes and thinks a cat is an elephant and an elephant an ant.

Al-Qurtubi said:

> One who drinks wine becomes the laughingstock of sensible people, for he may play with his own urine and excrement. He may even touch his face with hands soiled by human waste. In fact, some of them have been observed to wipe their faces with urine. Then they have been heard saying, "O Allah, make me join the ranks of the repentant and the pure." Some of them have been seen with a dog licking his face, saying, "May Allah honor you as you have honored me."[4]

This is a quick and brief survey of evidence from the Noble Qur'an and the pure and unadulterated Sunnah concerning the prohibition of intoxicants. What remains now is to take a look at biblical texts and what they contain about wine and its prohibition.

> Wine is a mocker,
> Strong drink is a brawler,
> And whoever is led astray by it is not wise.[5]

---

[1] Narrated by An-Nasa'i.
[2] Az-Zajjaj— a famous scholar of Arabic.
[3] Ibn Al-Anbari— a famous scholar of Arabic.
[4] Al-Qurtubi— a famous Muslim scholar.
[5] Proverbs 20:1.

> Who hath woe? Who hath sorrow? Who hath contentions? Who hath babbling? Who hath wounds without cause? Who hath redness of eyes?
>
> They that tarry long at the wine; they that go to seek mixed wine. Look not thou upon the wine when it is red, when it giveth his color in the cup, when it moveth itself aright. At the last it biteth like a serpent, and stingeth like an adder.
>
> Thine eyes shall behold strange women, and thine heart shall utter perverse things.
>
> Yea, thou shall be as he that lieth in the midst of the sea, or as he that lieth upon the top of a mast.
>
> They have stricken me, shalt thou say, and I was not sick; they have beaten me, and I felt it not; When shall I awake? I will seek it yet again.[1]
>
> Woe to men mighty at drinking wine,
> Woe to men valiant for mixing intoxicating drink.[2]
>
> But they also have erred through wine,
> And through intoxicating drink are out of the way;
> Priest and prophet have erred through intoxicating drink,
> They are swallowed up by wine,
> They are out of the way through intoxicating drink;
> They err in vision, they stumble in judgment.
> For all tables are full of vomit and filth;
> no place is clean. [3]
>
> Harlotry, wine, and new wine enslave the heart.[4]

The Bible did not permit anyone consecrating an offering to drink during the designated period:

> Then the LORD spoke to Moses, saying, "Speak to the children of Israel, and say to them: 'When either a man or woman consecrates an offering to take the vow of a Nazirite, to separate himself to the LORD, he shall separate himself from wine and *similar* drink; he shall drink neither vinegar

---
[1] Proverbs 23:29-35.
[2] Isaiah 5:22.
[3] Isaiah 28:7-8.
[4] Hosea 4:11.

Muslim-Christian Dialogue

made from wine nor vinegar made from *similar* drink; neither shall he drink any grape juice, nor eat fresh grapes or raisins. All the days of his separation he shall eat nothing that is produced by the grapevine, from seed to skin.'"[1]

Likewise, it did not permit the priest to drink when entering to work in the tabernacle:

> Then the LORD spoke to Aaron, saying: "Do not drink wine or intoxicating drink, you, nor your sons with you, when you go into the tabernacle of meeting, lest you die. It *shall be* a statute forever throughout your generations, that you may distinguish between holy and unholy, and between unclean and clean..."[2]

As a matter of fact, the Bible declares that poverty is linked to drinking wine:

> He who loves pleasure *will be* a poor man: He who loves wine and oil will not be rich.[3]

Furthermore, it prohibits even sitting together with those who drink wine:

> Do not mix with winebibbers, or with gluttonous eaters of meat. For the drunkard and the glutton will come to poverty, and drowsiness will clothe *a man* with rags.[4]

Also, the Bible forbids one to be drunk on wine, and explains how drunkenness is wrong:

> Now Hannah spoke in her heart; only her lips moved, but her voice was not heard. Therefore Eli thought she was drunk. So Eli said to her, "How long will you be drunk? Put your wine away from you!" But Hannah answered and said, "No, my lord, I am a woman of sorrowful spirit. I have drunk neither wine nor intoxicating drink, but have poured out my soul before the LORD. Do not consider your maidservant a wicked woman, for out of abundance of my complaint and grief I have spoken until now."[5]

---

[1] Numbers 6:1-4.
[2] Leviticus 10.
[3] Proverbs 21.
[4] Proverbs 2.
[5] Samuel 1.

Muslim-Christian Dialogue

The Bible threatens and reviles the wine drinker, saying:

> Woe to those who rise early in the morning, that they may follow intoxicating drink; who continue until night, till wine inflames them! The harp and the strings, the tambourine and flute, and wine are in their feasts; but they do not regard the work of the LORD, nor consider the operation of His hands.
>
> Therefore my people have gone into captivity, because they have no knowledge; their honorable men are famished, and their multitude dried up with thirst.
>
> Therefore Sheol has enlarged itself and opened its mouth beyond measure; their glory and their multitude and their pomp, and he who is jubilant, shall descend into it. People shall be brought down, each man shall be humbled, and the eyes of the lofty shall be humbled.[1]

Let us now leave the above evidence of the Old Testament and turn our attention to evidence from the New Testament. We find that both Testaments are in agreement in prohibiting wine and censuring it. In the first Epistle of Paul to the Corinthians:

> But now I have written unto you not to keep company, if any man that is called a brother be a fornicator, or covetous, or an idolator, or a reveler or a drunkard, or an extortioner; with such a one one is not to eat.[2]

Also in the same Epistle it says:

> Know you not that the unrighteous shall not inherit the Kingdom of God? Be not deceived: neither fornicators, nor idolaters, nor adulterers, nor abusers of themselves with mankind, nor thieves, nor covetous, nor drunkards, nor revelers, nor extortioners, shall inherit the Kingdom of God.[3]

In his Epistle to the Galatians, Paul says:

> Now the works of the flesh are evident, which are: adultery, fornication, uncleanness, lewdness, idolatry, sorcery, hatred, contentions, jealousies, outbursts of wrath, selfish ambitions, dissections, heresies, envy, murders, drunkenness, revelries,

---

[1] Isaiah 5:11-15.
[2] I Corinthians 5:11.
[3] I Corinthians 6:9-10.

and the like; of which I tell you beforehand, just as I also told *you* in time past, that those who practice such things will not inherit the Kingdom of God.[1]

Then in Paul's letter to the Ephesians, he says:

And do not be drunk with wine, in which is dissipation; but be filled with the Spirit.[2]

In the first Epistle of Peter, it says:

For we *have spent* enough of our past lifetime in doing the will of the Gentiles—when we walked in lewdness, lusts, drunkenness, revelries, drinking parties, and abominable idolatries.[3]

This is what the Old and New Testaments say about wine. Yet what absolutely shocks us is when we read the second chapter of the Gospel of John. This Gospel narrates the initial miracles of Jesus. Interestingly, one of them is to turn water into wine! The Gospel says:

And the third day there was a marriage in Cana of Galilee; and the mother of Jesus was there: And both Jesus was called, and his disciples, to the marriage. And when they wanted wine, the mother of Jesus said unto him, "They have no wine." Jesus said unto her, "Woman, what have I to do with you? My hour is not yet come." His mother said unto the servants, "Whatsoever he says unto you, do it."

And there were set there six waterpots of stone, after the manner of the purifying of Jews, containing two or three firkins apiece. Jesus said unto them, "Draw out water," and they filled them up to the brim. And he said unto them, "Draw out now, and bear unto the governor of the feast." And they bore it.

When the ruler of the feast had tasted the water that was made wine and knew not whence it was: (but the servants which drew the water knew;) the governor of the feast called the bridegroom and said unto him, "Every man at the beginning does set forth good wine; and when men have well

---

[1] Galatians 5: 19-21.
[2] Ephesians 5:18.
[3] I Peter 4:3.

> drunk, then that which is worse: but you have kept the good wine until now."
>
> This beginning of miracles did Jesus in Cana of Galilee and manifested for his glory; and his disciples believed on him.[1]

But the New Testament takes us by no little surprise. Indeed, it alarms us when it narrates that Jesus himself was found extremely drunk once, so much so that he took off his clothes. Let us leave it to the Gospel to tell us what happened.

> He rose from supper and laid aside His garments, took a towel and girdled Himself. After that, He poured water into a basin and began to wash the disciples' feet, and to wipe *them* with the towel with which He was girdled.[2]

The passage leaves one full of unanswered questions and astonished. Regardless, we won't discuss this passage here. We'll only relate it without any commentary from us. Instead, we will leave it to one of the Christian commentators, namely, Fender, in his book *The Balance of Truth*. He says:

> ...this (i.e., passage) implies that Jesus' body had wine in it such that he did not know what he was doing. Washing people's feet does not require disrobing completely.

As for me, I say this is like a suspect saying: "Take me, I am guilty."

I will conclude this discourse on wine with two excerpts from the New Testament, though there are many more. The first passage reads:

> "For John the Baptist came neither eating bread nor drinking wine, and you say, 'He has a demon.' The Son of Man has come eating and drinking, and you say, 'Look, a glutton and a winebibber, a friend of tax collectors and sinners!'"[3]

The second passage complements and completes what the first passage mentions:

> Then one of the Pharisees asked Him to eat with him. And he went to the Pharisee's house and sat down to eat. And behold, a woman in the city who was a sinner, when she

---
[1] John 2: 1-11.
[2] John 13: 4-5.
[3] Luke 7:33-34.

knew that Jesus sat at the table in the Pharisee's house, brought an alabaster flask of fragrant oil, and stood at His feet behind Him weeping; and she began to wash His feet with her tears, and wiped them with the hair of her head; and she kissed His feet and anointed them with the fragrant oil.

Now when the Pharisee who had invited Him saw this, he spoke to himself, saying, "This man, if He were a prophet, would know who and what manner of woman this is who is touching Him, for she is a sinner."[1]

The above passage continues:

Then He turned to the woman and said to Simon, "Do you see this woman? I entered your house; you gave Me no water for My feet, but she has washed My feet with her tears and wiped them with the hair of her head. You gave Me no kiss, but this woman has not ceased to kiss My feet since the time I came in. You did not anoint My head with oil, but this woman has anointed My feet with fragrant oil. Therefore I say to you, her sins, *which are* many, are forgiven, for she loved much. But to whom little is forgiven, *the same* loves little."[2]

In this manner, the New Testament continues to relate its "sacred" passages. Let us now stop and move on to another topic.

Swine

There is a question about the pig. Why does the Qur'an prohibit pork? Is there a verse which forbids it?

There are several verses in the Noble Qur'an which absolutely prohibit swine. Allah, Most Exalted, says:

You who believe! Eat of the good things that We have provided for you, and be grateful to Allah, if it is Him you worship. He has only forbidden you dead meat, and blood, and

---

[1] Luke 7:36-39.
[2] Luke 7:44-47.

the flesh of swine, and that on which any other name has been invoked besides that of Allah.[1]

Forbidden to you (for food) are: dead meat, blood, the flesh of swine, and that on which has been invoked the name of other than Allah; that which has been killed by strangling, or by a violent blow, or by a headlong fall, or by being gored to death; that which has been (partly) eaten by a wild animal; unless you are able to slaughter it (in due form); that which is sacrificed on stone (altars); (forbidden) also is the division (of meat) by raffling with arrows: that is impiety.

This day have those who reject faith given up all hope of your religion: Yet fear them not but fear Me. This day have I perfected your religion for you, completed my favor upon you, and have chosen for you Islam as your religion. But if any is forced by hunger, with no inclination to transgression, Allah is indeed Oft-forgiving, Most Merciful.[2]

Say: I find not in the message received by me by inspiration any (meat) forbidden to be eaten by one who wishes to eat it, unless it be dead meat, or blood poured forth, or the flesh of swine—for it is an abomination—or, what is impious, (meat) on which a name has been invoked other than Allah's. But (even so), if a person is forced by necessity, without willful disobedience, nor transgressing due limits, Your Lord is Oft-Forgiving, Most Merciful.[3]

So eat of the sustenance which Allah has provided for you, lawful and good; and be grateful for the favors of Allah, if it is He Whom you serve. He has only forbidden you dead meat, and blood, and the flesh of swine, and any (food) over which the name of other than Allah has been invoked. But if one is forced by necessity, without willful disobedience, nor transgressing due limits, then Allah is Oft-Forgiving, Most Merciful.[4]

---

[1] Qur'an 2:172-173.
[2] Qur'an 5:3.
[3] Qur'an 6:145.
[4] Qur'an 16:114-115.

A question frequently asked is what is the real reason for the prohibition of swine. We are thankful to several people who have put together interesting studies and written valuable articles concerning the reasons for its prohibition from a health and medical perspective. They assure us that the flesh of swine is a breeding ground for microbes and lethal germs as well as tapeworms and its eggs lodged in well-protected sacs.

Others argue that it is possible to kill this worm by cooking its meat at a high temperature. In response to this the first group of researchers observe that it took us a long time after Allah's prohibition of swine to discover these worms. Who can tell what we'll find in the future?

Surely Allah, Whose Will and Wisdom are indomitable, has endowed man with the ability to make great efforts. Concurrently, He has also directed him to what will benefit him in his religion and his worldly life. Similarly, He has warned him about what can harm his religious life and his worldly life. Accordingly, we should not let our research into the reasons for the prohibition of swine lead us to neglect one very important truth, namely, what is permissible (*halal*) is because Allah permitted it; conversely, what is prohibited (*haram*) is because Allah prohibited it. Authentic divine revelation has a certain respectful precedence over any human judgment, research or justification.

Adam's first mistake was that he ate from the forbidden tree. Later he repented dearly. He did not know the reason for its prohibition. He did not stop, though he was forbidden and warned not to go near that tree.

We must keep in mind what happened to Adam when we discuss issues of *halal* and *haram*—the permissibility and prohibition of things. We must do this so we don't lose our way to the truth or inadvertently slip into error.

The Noble Qur'an is not the only book which mandates the prohibition of the flesh of swine. In fact, passages from the New and Old Testaments confirm this and requite it likewise.

A. The pig is forbidden because it doesn't chew its cud:
> Now the Lord spoke to Moses and Aaron, saying to them, "Speak to the children of Israel, saying, 'These *are* the ani-

Muslim-Christian Dialogue

mals which you may eat among all the animals that *are* on the earth: Among the animals, whatever divides the hoof, having cloven hooves *and* chewing the cud—that you may eat.

Nevertheless these you shall not eat among those that chew the cud or those that have cloven hooves: the camel, because it chews the cud but does not have cloven hooves, is unclean to you; the rock hyrax, because it chews the cud but does not have cloven hooves, *is* unclean to you; the hare, because it chews the cud but does not have cloven hooves, *is* unclean to you; and the swine, though it divides the hoof, having cloven hooves, yet does not chew the cud, *is* unclean to you. Their flesh you shall not eat, and their carcasses you shall not touch. They *are* unclean to you.'"[1]

You shall not eat any detestable thing. These *are* the animals which you may eat: the ox, the sheep, the goat, the deer, the gazelle, the roe deer, the wild goat, the mountain goat, the antelope, and the mountain sheep. And you may eat every animal with cloven hooves, having the hoof split into two parts, and that chew the cud, among the animals.

Nevertheless, of those that chew the cud or have cloven hooves, you shall not eat, *such as* these: the camel, the hare, and the rock hyrax; for they chew the cud but do not have cloven hooves; they *are* unclean for you. Also the swine *is* unclean for you, because it has cloven hooves, yet *does* not *chew* the cud; you shall not eat their flesh or touch their dead carcasses.[2]

The Dictionary of the Bible[3] comments on this passage, saying:

> ...this is because it is a filthy animal. It does not chew its cud. Moreover, its flesh causes diseases if it is not cooked well done. The Arabs were forbidden to breed them. The Qur'an, like the Torah, has categorically prohibited eating it.

---

[1] Leviticus 11:1-8.
[2] Deuteronomy 14:3-8.
[3] *The Dictionary of the Bible*, p. 305.

The Phoenicians, Ethiopians, and Egyptians looked at the pig as unclean. However, in Egypt, at the annual feast, they used to offer a pig as sacrifice to the moon god. Despite this it was mandatory for whoever even touched a pig inadvertently to take a complete bath. Once more, a pig farmer was not allowed to enter the temple. In fact, he could only marry the daughters of other pig breeders like himself. After all, no one wanted to marry his daughter to a pig farmer.[1]

B. Pigs are unclean:

> As a ring of gold in a swine's snout,
> so is a lovely woman who lacks discretion.[2]

Let us now leave the Old Testament and move on to the New Testament. We find that it says:

> Do not give what is holy to the dogs; nor cast your pearls before swine, lest they trample them under their feet, and turn and tear you in pieces.[3]

But it has happened to them according to the true Proverbs:

> A dog returns to his own vomit, and, a sow, having washed, to her wallowing in the mire.[4]

The books of the New Testament mandate that pig breeding is the lowest and most ignoble profession. Only the absolutely destitute turn to it:

> Then He said: "A certain man had two sons, and the younger of them said to his father, 'Father, give me the portion of goods that falls to me.' So he divided to them his livelihood. And not many days after, the younger son gathered all together, journeyed to a far country, and there wasted his possessions with prodigal living. But when he had spent all, there rose a severe famine in that land, and he began to be in want. Then he went and joined himself in his fields to feed swine."[5]

---

[1] Heroditz, vol. II, p. 47.
[2] Proverbs 11:22.
[3] Matthew 7:6.
[4] II Peter 2:22.
[5] Luke 15:11-15.

Now a large herd of swine was feeding there near the mountains. So all the demons begged Him, saying, "Send us to the swine, that we may enter them." And at once Jesus gave them permission. Then the unclean spirits went out and entered the swine (there were about two thousand); and the herd ran violently down the steep place into the sea, and drowned in the sea.[1]

Having cited all this, we must keep one very important fact in mind, namely, Jesus came to confirm and uphold what was in the Torah:

"Do not think that I came to destroy the Law or the prophets. I did not come to destroy but to fulfill. For assuredly, I say to you, till heaven and earth pass away, one jot or one tittle will by no means pass away from the Law till all is fulfilled."

This is what Jesus said. But what did Peter say? Peter opened the doors wide. He permitted what had been prohibited. He annulled the Law of the prophets—especially the Law of Moses. We have already presented the Christian view on prohibitions when we discussed abrogation. Here we'll add the story of the great sheet of Peter:

The next day, as they went on their journey and drew near the city, Peter went up on the housetop to pray, about the sixth hour. Then he became very hungry and wanted to eat; but while they made ready he fell into a trance and saw heaven opened and an object like a great sheet bound at the four corners, descending to him and let down to the earth. In it were all kinds of four-footed animals of the earth, wild beasts, creeping things, and birds of the air.

And a voice came to him, "Rise, Peter; kill and eat." But Peter said, "Not so, Lord! For I have never eaten anything common or unclean." And a voice *spoke* to him again the second time, "What God has cleansed you must not call common." This was done three times, and the object was taken up into heaven again.[2]

---

[1] Mark 5:11-13.
[2] Acts 10: 9-16.

What a shock! Everything permitted? All the animals of earth? Even the wild animals, reptiles and pigs—nothing was left to be prohibited!

But this was Peter! Peter had the right to make permissible what he wanted and prohibit what he wanted! The will of God was subservient to the will of Peter! After all, hadn't God already told him:

> "And I say also unto you, that you are Peter, and upon this rock I build my church; and the gates of hell shall not prevail against it. And I will give unto you the keys of the Kingdom of heaven: and whatsoever you shall bind on earth shall be bound in heaven; and whatsoever you shall loose on earth shall be loosed in heaven."[1]

The Holy Spirit in the Qur'an and the Bible

Among the questions forwarded to us is a question about the Holy Spirit and what the Noble Qur'an says about it. The Qur'an uses the term *ruh* to refer to the angel Jibril.[2]

We begin by first talking about what is attributed to Allah or added on to the name "Allah" in the Qur'an. There are two ways something is attributed to Allah. This can either be some descriptive noun, which cannot exist by itself and is attributed to Allah, such as knowledge, ability, speech, or life, or something which exists by itself.

The first case refers to something descriptive attributed to Allah. For example:

> Allah! There is no god but He—the Living, the Self-Subsisting, Eternal. No slumber can seize Him nor sleep. His are all things in the heavens and on earth. Who is there can intercede in His presence except as He permit? He knows what (appears to His creatures as) before or after or behind them. Nor shall they compass aught of His knowledge except as He will. His Throne extends over the heavens and

---

[1] Matthew 18:19.
[2] i.e., Gabriel, the angel of Revelation.

the earth, and He feels no fatigue in guarding and preserving them for He is the Most High, the Supreme (in glory).[1]

For Allah is He Who gives (all) sustenance—Lord of Power—Steadfast (forever).[2]

Now the 'Ad behaved arrogantly through the land, against (all) truth and reason, and said: "Who is superior to us in strength?" What! Did they not see that Allah, Who created them, was superior to them in strength? But they continued to reject Our Signs![3]

Or the authentic *hadith* of the Prophet (may Allah's peace and blessings be upon him) known as the *istikhara hadith*:

If any of you decides to do anything, he should offer two units of prayer other than the compulsory ones and say (after the prayer): O Allah, I seek guidance from Your knowledge, and power from Your might and I ask for Your great blessings...[4]

The second type of thing attributed to Allah is something that actually exists. For example, He says:

Behold! We gave to Abraham the site of the (Sacred) House, (saying): Associate not anything (in worship) with Me; and sanctify My House for those who compass it round, or stand up, or bow, or prostrate themselves (therein in prayer).[5]

But the Messenger of Allah said to them: "It is a she-camel of Allah! And (bar her not from) having her drink!"[6]

A Fountain where the devotees of Allah do drink, making it flow in unstinted abundance.[7]

Thus what was attributed to Allah in the first case is an uncreated attribute of Allah associated with Allah. In the second case, what is attributed to Allah is what belongs to Allah. It has been created and is separate from him; however, it is attributed

---

[1] Qur'an 2:255.
[2] Qur'an 51:58.
[3] Qur'an 41:15.
[4] *Hadith Al-Bukhari*, Chapter "Tahajjud" 25.
[5] Qur'an 2:26.
[6] Qur'an 91:13.
[7] Qur'an 76:6.

to Him, since it is something held in great honor and respect because of certain special characteristics bestowed upon it by Allah.

Accordingly, Allah adds Prophet Salih's camel to Himself. Likewise, He chose His House as one of the houses of Makkah. Also, He rewards His pious servants from among all His servants. It is the second type which is mentioned in the verse:

> She placed a screen (to screen herself) from them; then We sent her Our angel, and he appeared before her as a man in all respects.[1]

This *ruh* angel is described by Allah as "a man in all respects." Moreover, Mary sought Allah's protection and warned "...(come not near) if you fear Allah."[2] In response he said, "Nay, I'm only a messenger from your Lord."[3] All of the above proves that this *ruh*, or angel, was an individual by itself, separate from Allah.

Later, Allah, Most Exalted, mentions in His Noble Book that He breathed into Mary from His Spirit (i.e., His *ruh*). He says:

> And (remember) her who guarded her chastity: We breathed into her of Our spirit, and We made her and her son a sign for all peoples.[4]

> And Mary the daughter of 'Imran, who guarded her chastity; and We breathed into (her body) of Our spirit; and she testified to the truth of the words of her Lord and of His Revelations, and was one of the devout (servants).[5]

Elsewhere, Allah, Most Exalted, mentions His supporting Jesus (may Allah's peace be upon him) with the Holy Spirit. He says:

> We gave Moses the Book and followed him up with a succession of messengers; We gave Jesus the son of Mary clear (signs) and strengthened him with the Holy Spirit. Is it that whenever there comes to you a messenger with what you

---

[1] Qur'an 19:17.
[2] Qur'an 19:18.
[3] Qur'an 19:19.
[4] Qur'an 21:91.
[5] Qur'an 66:12.

yourselves desire not, you are puffed up with pride? Some you called impostors, and others you slay![1]

Those messengers we endowed with gifts, Some above others: to one of them Allah spoke; others He raised to degrees (of honor); to Jesus the son of Mary we gave clear (signs), and strengthened him with the Holy Spirit. If Allah had so willed, succeeding generations would not have fought among each other, after clear (signs) had come to them, but they (chose) to wrangle, some believing and others rejecting. If Allah had so willed, they would not have fought each other; but Allah fulfills His plan.[2]

Then will God say:

Jesus son of Mary! Recount My favor to you and to your mother. Behold! I strengthened you with the Holy Spirit, so that you did speak to the people in childhood and in maturity. Behold! I taught you the Book and Wisdom, the Law and the Gospel and behold! You make out of clay, as it were, the figure of a bird, by My leave, and you breathe into it and it becomes a bird by My leave, and you heal those born blind, and the lepers, by My leave. And behold! you bring forth the dead by My leave. And behold! I did restrain the Children of Israel from (violence to) you when you did show them the Clear Signs, and the unbelievers among them said: "This is nothing but evident magic."[3]

Not surprisingly, if Allah, Most Perfect and Exalted, said this of Jesus (may Allah's peace be upon Him) then He had already said this about our Prophet Muhammad (may Allah's peace and blessings be upon him) and about the Qur'an He revealed. He, Most Exalted, says:

When We substitute one revelation for another—and Allah knows best what He reveals (in stages)—they say, "You are but a forger": But most of them understand not. Say: The Holy Spirit has brought the revelation from your Lord in

---

[1] Qur'an 2:87.
[2] Qur'an 2:53.
[3] Qur'an 5:110.

Truth, in order to strengthen those who believe, and as a Guide and Glad Tidings to Muslims.[1]

Or:

Verily this is a Revelation from the Lord of the Worlds: With it came down the spirit of Faith and Truth—to your heart and mind, that you may admonish.[2]

Or:

Say: Whoever is an enemy to Gabriel—for he brings down the (revelation) to your heart by Allah's will—a confirmation of what went before. And guidance and glad tidings for those who believe.[3]

Thus the Holy Spirit, who brought the Qur'an from Allah is "the Spirit of Faith and Truth" or in other words he is Jibril, may Allah's peace be upon him.

We should add here that the verse of the Most Exalted, "...We breathed into her of Our Spirit,"[4] is similar to the verse about Adam (may Allah's peace be upon him) when He says: "When I have fashioned him (in due proportion) and breathed into him of My spirit, fall down in obeisance unto him."[5]

In fact, Allah says that Jesus is similar to Adam, when He, Most Exalted, says:

The similitude of Jesus before Allah is as that of Adam; He created him from dust, then said to him: "Be!" And he was.[6]

Confused Dreams

We have surveyed the Noble Qur'an for what it says about the "Holy Spirit". Let us turn to what the Bible says about this term.

It was Paul who determined how the Torah and the Injil, i.e., the Old and New Testaments, should be accepted. He says:

---

[1] Qur'an 16:101-102.
[2] Qur'an 26:192-194.
[3] Qur'an 2:97.
[4] Qur'an 21:91.
[5] Qur'an 15:29.
[6] Qur'an 3:59.

"...all Scripture is given by inspiration of God."[1] When we trace how this inspiration takes place, we find that, according to him, it involves a person falling into a trance. Luke, in the Book of Acts, describes how Paul fell into a trance and then said:

> "Now it happened, when I returned to Jerusalem and was praying in the temple, that I was in a trance and saw Him saying to me, 'Make haste and get out of Jerusalem quickly, for they will not receive Your testimony concerning Me.' So I said, 'Lord, they know that in every synagogue I imprisoned and beat those who believe in You. And when the blood of Your martyr Stephen was shed, I also was standing by, consenting to his death and guarding the clothes of those who were killing him.' Then He said to me, 'Depart, for I will send you far from here to the Gentiles.'"[2]

Paul propagated a Gospel different from the Gospel of Jesus. He says:

> And I went up by revelation, and communicated to them that gospel which I preach to the Gentiles, but privately to those who were of reputation, lest by any means I might run, or had run, in vain.[3]

Holding the disciples of Jesus in disdain, he says:

> But of these who seemed to be somewhat, (whatsoever they were, it makes no matter to me: God accepts no man's person): for they who seemed to be somewhat in conference, added nothing to me: But contrariwise, when they saw that the gospel of the uncircumcised was committed unto me, as the gospel of the circumcised was unto Peter; (for he that wrought effectuality in Peter to the apostleship of the circumcision, the same was mighty in me toward the Gentiles).
>
> And when James, Cephas, and John, who seemed to be pillars, perceived the grace that was given unto me, they gave to me and Barnabas the right hands of fellowship; that we should go unto the heathen, and they unto the circumcised.

---

[1] II Timothy.
[2] Acts 22:17-21.
[3] Galatians 2:2.

Only they would that we should remember the poor; the same which I also was forward to do.[1]

In this way, Paul uprooted the message of Jesus from its roots, which were based on the Torah and were a completion of the Torah. Jesus used to say, "Do not think that I came to destroy the Law or the prophets. I did not come to destroy but to fulfill."[2] Instead, he changed it to a Christianity which derived its fundamental principles from Greek philosophy.

What is more amazing than this is when Peter states how the sacred scriptures were really compiled. He says, "for prophecy never came to the will of man, but holy men of God spoke as they were moved by the Holy Spirit."[3]

To determine how Peter received the revelation, Luke tells us about Peter, saying:

> The next day, as they went on their journey and drew near the city, Peter went up on the housetop to pray, about the sixth hour. Then he became very hungry and wanted to eat; but while they made ready, he fell into a trance.[4]

What happened as a result of this trance? Luke informs us:

> Then he said to them: "You know how unlawful it is for a Jew to keep company with or go to one of another nation. But God has shown me that I should not call any man common or unclean."[5]

Interestingly, when Peter saw the faith of the people in Jesus as a prophet and after they had received the Holy Spirit as part of them, he said, "And he commanded them to be baptized in the name of the Lord. Then they asked him to stay a few days."[6]

Then there was Philip, one of the disciples who insisted on using the name of the Lord. The Bible says:

---

[1] Galatians 2:6-10.
[2] Matthew 5:17.
[3] Peter 1: 21.
[4] Acts 10:9-10.
[5] Acts 10:28.
[6] Acts 10:48.

But when they believed Philip as he preached the things concerning the Kingdom of God and the name of Jesus Christ, both men and women were baptized.[1]

The real message was to convey "...the things concerning the Kingdom of God", which in reality is telling the people to submit to the message of God (i.e., Islam) which He ordained for all of humanity.

Henceforth, we will see clear contradictions in Paul's perspective. He says, "But we preach Christ crucified, to the Jews a stumbling block and to the Greeks foolishness."[2]

So, when exactly was Jesus crucified? Of course, we will now disprove this with irrefutable proof.

Let us leave Paul and Peter and their contradictions. Instead, let us ask, what is the status of the Gospels? Is it revelation from Allah, or is it something that the disciples of Jesus composed? Luke answers this question when he says:

> Inasmuch as many have taken in hand to set in order a narrative of those things which have been fulfilled among us, just as those who from the beginning were eyewitnesses and ministers of the word delivered them to us, it seemed good to me also, having had perfect understanding of all things from the very first, to write to you an orderly account, most excellent Theophilus, that you may know the certainty of those things in which you were instructed.[3]

Once more, John reaffirms this when he says:

> And truly Jesus did many other signs in the presence of His disciples, which are not written in this book.[4]

As a matter of fact, the Gospels confirm that Jesus escaped crucifixion and then died. Here let us pause for a moment and ask: isn't it possible to consider Paul's contention, "...we preach Christ crucified", as the product of one of his trances?

John, in his Gospel, states:

---

[1] Acts 8:11.
[2] I Corinthians 1:23.
[3] Luke 1:1-4.
[4] John 18:4-6.

Muslim-Christian Dialogue

> Jesus, therefore, knowing all things that would come upon Him, went forward and said to them, "Whom are you seeking?" They answered Him, "Jesus of Nazareth." Jesus said to them, "I am he." And Judas, who betrayed Him, also stood with them. Now when He said to them, "I am He," they drew back and fell to the ground.[1]

Here let us think and reflect and ask, what startled them that they moved back and fell on the ground despite being armed against an unarmed individual? There must have been something that put fear in their hearts. What if we add to the previous passage a portion of the following text, narrated in the Gospel of Luke, concerning the birth of Jesus. It reads:

> And there were in the same country shepherds abiding in the field, keeping watch over their flock by night. And lo, the angel of the Lord came upon them, and the glory of the Lord shone round about them: and they were sore afraid. And the angel said unto them, "Fear not: for behold, I bring you good tidings of great joy, which shall be to all people. For unto you is born this day in the city of David a Savior, which is Christ the Lord."[2]

The point to be added comes from the ninth verse of the second chapter of the Gospel of Luke. Let us take the pertinent portion mentioned in Luke 2:9, i.e., "...the angel of the Lord came upon them, and the glory of the Lord shown round about them, and they were sore afraid..." and place it after Jesus' statement "I am He", related in John 18:6. Once we insert the deleted portion, the text reads:

> Jesus therefore, knowing all things that would come upon Him, went forward and said to them, "Whom are you seeking?" They answered Him, "Jesus of Nazareth." Jesus said to them, "I am He." and Judas, who betrayed Him, also stood with them. Now when He said to them, "I am He," the angel of the Lord came upon them, and the glory of the Lord

---

[1] John 18: 4-6.
[2] Luke 2:8-11.

shone round them, and they were sore afraid, they drew back and fell to the ground.[1]

Thereafter, the Holy Spirit led him to a safe and secure place as he had done in the past. Once before he had led Jesus to the wilderness, as narrated by Luke in the following passage:

> Then Jesus, being filled with the Holy Spirit, returned from the Jordan and was led by the Spirit into the wilderness.[2]

Arguments Supporting how Jesus was Saved (and not Crucified)

A. Luke relates how the statements of the prisoner (i.e., Jesus) were given no credence. He says:

> As soon as it was day, the elders of the people, both chief priests and scribes, came together and led Him into their council, saying, "If You are the Christ, tell us." But He said to them, "If I tell you, you will by no means believe. And if I also ask *you*, you will by no means answer Me or let Me go. Hereafter the Son of Man will sit on the right hand of the power of God."[3]

B. Another proof is the screams of the one crucified. According to Matthew:

> And about the ninth hour Jesus cried out with a loud voice, saying, "Eli, Eli, lama sabachthani?" that is, "My God, My God, why have You forsaken Me?"[4]

In contrast, Jesus was quite confident in Allah's help, for he says:

> "And He Who sent Me is with Me. The Father has not left Me alone, for I always do those things that please Him."[5]

---

[1] Luke 2:9.
[2] Luke 4:1.
[3] Luke 22:66-69.
[4] Matthew 27:46.
[5] John 8:29.

Muslim-Christian Dialogue

C. Another strong piece of evidence is when Jesus foretells his disciples' abandoning him and fleeing during hard times:

"Indeed the hour is coming, yes, has now come, that you will be scattered, each to his own, and will leave Me alone, because the Father is with Me."[1]

Matthew relates the feeling of the disciples, saying:

But all this was done, that the Scriptures of the Prophets might be fulfilled. Then all the disciples forsook him, and fled.[2]

Now, notice what John related in his narration. He said:

Jesus therefore, knowing all things that would come upon Him, went forward and said to them, "Whom are you seeking?"[3]

1. Allah had already informed Jesus of the intentions of the betrayer, for Jesus said:

"The Son of Man indeed goes just as it is written of Him, but woe to that man by whom the Son of Man is betrayed! It would have been good for that man if he had not been born." Then Judas, who was betraying Him, answered and said, "Rabbi, is it I?" He said to him, "You have said it."[4]

2. The threat of the Jews who had plotted to kill him:

The Pharisees heard the crowd murmuring these things concerning Him, and the Pharisees and the chief priests sent officers to take Him. Then Jesus said to him, "I shall be with you a little while longer, and *then* I go to Him Who sent Me. You will seek Me and not find *Me*, and where I am you cannot come."[5]

Moreover, Jesus himself confirmed this. John relates:

Then Jesus said to them again, "I am going away, and you will seek Me, and will die in your sin. Where I go you can-

---

[1] John 16:32.
[2] Matthew 26:56.
[3] John 18:4.
[4] Matthew 26:24-25.
[5] John 7:32-34.

not come." So the Jews said, "Will He kill Himself, because He says, 'Where I go you cannot come'?"[1]

This is further confirmed by his statement to his disciples:

"Little children, I shall be with you a little while longer. You will seek Me; and as I said to the Jews, 'Where I am going, you cannot come,' so now I say to you."[2]

This is the Jesus whom Allah raised to Himself. We thank Allah that He, Most Exalted, conclusively stated in His Noble Qur'an:

...that they said (in boast), "We killed Christ Jesus the son of Mary, the Messenger of Allah," but they killed him not, nor crucified him, but so it was made to appear to them, and those who differ therein are full of doubts, with no (certain) knowledge, but only conjecture to follow, for of a surety they killed him not. Nay, Allah raised him up unto Himself; and Allah is Exalted in Power, Wise.[3]

Undoubtedly, the story of the crucifixion is baseless and absolutely untrue. Needless to say, anything based on falsehood can only be false and invalid. Then how could Paul say, "...but we preach Christ crucified."[4]

So true is what Tolstoy said. He denied the divinity of Prophet Jesus. He asserted that Paul misunderstood the teachings of Prophet Jesus; rather he destroyed them and went astray. At one time it was an extension of God's Law as Allah revealed to His servant and messenger, Moses. Then it became Hellenic teachings deeply rooted in Greek philosophy. He also declared that all statements related in the New Testament about Prophet Jesus do not really prove that he is God or the Son of God. Additionally, he boldly states that the New Testament was definitely corrupted, changed and altered.

One last question remains: who is the Holy Spirit? Let us answer this by using biblical texts.

Luke in his Gospel talks about the Virgin Mary:

---

[1] John 8:21-22.
[2] John 13:33.
[3] Qur'an 4:147-158.
[4] I Corinthians 1:23.

Muslim-Christian Dialogue

> And in the sixth month the angel Gabriel was sent from God unto a city of Galilee, named Nazareth, to a Virgin espoused to a man whose name was Joseph, of the House of David; and the Virgin's name was Mary. And the angel came in unto her, and said, "Hail, you that are highly favored, the Lord is with you: blessed are you among women."[1]

In his Gospel Luke talks about John, the son of Zacharias:

> But the angel said unto him, "Fear not, Zacharias: for your prayer is heard; and your wife Elizabeth shall bear you a son, and you shall call his name John; and you shall have joy and gladness; and many shall rejoice at his birth. For he shall be great in the sight of the Lord, and shall drink neither wine nor strong drink; and he shall be filled with the Holy Spirit, even from his mother's womb."[2]

Then he mentions the pregnancy of the Virgin Mary:

> Then Mary said to the angel, "How can this be, since I do not know a man?" And the angel answered and said to her, "The Holy Spirit will come upon you, and the power of the Highest will overshadow you; therefore, also, that Holy One Who is to be born will be called the Son of God."[3]

Moreover, Luke states in his Gospel that pregnancy and any miraculous birth is by Allah's Will (i.e., divine decree) for nothing is impossible to Allah. He states:

> "Now indeed, Elizabeth your relative has also conceived a son in her old age; and this is now the sixth month for her who was called barren. For with God nothing will be impossible."[4]

In the Old Testament, Jeremiah is filled with the Holy Spirit in the womb of his mother:

> Then the word of the LORD came to me, saying: "Before I formed you in the womb I knew you; Before you were born I sanctified you; I ordained you a prophet to the nations."[5]

---

[1] Luke 1:26-28.
[2] Luke 1:13-15.
[3] Luke 1:34-35.
[4] Luke 1:36-37.
[5] Jeremiah 1:4-5.

"[S]anctified you" means filled with the Holy Spirit. The Holy Spirit is reputed to have helped the Children of Israel to the land of Canaan:

> Behold, I send an angel before you to keep you in the way and to bring you into the place which I have prepared. Beware of Him and obey His voice; do not provoke Him; For He will not pardon your transgressions; for My name is in Him.[1]

Regarding the meaning of "...and do not provoke Him, for He will not pardon your transgression, for my name is in Him," Prophet Jesus states:

> "Therefore I say to you, every sin and blasphemy will be forgiven men, but the blasphemy against the Spirit will not be forgiven men. Anyone who speaks a word against the Son of Man, it will be forgiven him; but whoever speaks against the Holy Spirit, it will not be forgiven him, either in this age or in the age to come."[2]

Later Luke relates Prophet Jesus as saying:

> "And anyone who speaks a word against the Son of Man, it will be forgiven him; but to him who blasphemes against the Holy Spirit, it will not be forgiven. Now when they bring you to the synagogues and magistrates and authorities, do not worry about how or what you should answer, or what you should say. For the Holy Spirit will teach you in that very hour what you ought to say."[3]

Matthew in his Gospel relates what Jesus says about the Holy Spirit as being a Spirit coming from Allah:

> "But when they deliver you up, do not worry about how or what you should speak. For it will be given to you in that hour what you should speak; for it is not you who speak, but the Spirit of your Father who speaks in you."[4]

---

[1] Exodus 23:20-21.
[2] Matthew 12:31-32.
[3] Luke 12:10-12.
[4] Matthew 10:19-20.

Muslim-Christian Dialogue

Prophet Jesus (may Allah's peace be upon him) was in direct contact with the heavens from the cradle to the time of his ascension.

1. The good news brought by the Holy Spirit about his birth:

    And the angel said unto them, "Fear not: for, behold, I bring you good tidings of great joy, which shall be to all people. For unto you is born this day in the City of David a Savior, which is Christ the Lord."[1]

2. The descent of the Holy Spirit at Jesus's baptism.

    When all the people were baptized, it came to pass that Jesus also was baptized; and while He prayed, the Heaven was opened. And the Holy Spirit descended in bodily form like a dove upon Him, and a voice came from heaven which said, "You are My beloved Son; in You I am well pleased."[2]

3. Being led by the Holy Spirit to the wilderness during the temptation of the Devil:

    Then Jesus, being filled with the Holy Spirit, returned from the Jordan and was led by the Spirit into the wilderness.[3]

4. The Holy Spirit gave strength to Jesus during the prayers in the Garden of Gethsemane:

    And He was withdrawn from them about a stone's throw, and He knelt down and prayed, saying, "Father, if it is Your will, take this cup away from Me; nevertheless not My will, but Yours, be done." Then an angel appeared to Him from heaven, strengthening Him.[4]

---

[1] Luke 2:10-11.
[2] Luke 3: 21-22.
[3] Luke 4:1.
[4] Luke 22:43.

Jesus Prepares His Disciples to be Filled with the Holy Spirit on Thursday

> "But you shall receive power when the Holy Spirit has come upon you; and you shall be witnesses to Me in Jerusalem, and in all Judea and Samaria, and to the end of earth."[1]

The Holy Spirit calms the heart of a pious believer by endowing him with more peace and tranquility. For example, David, a prophet of Allah, implored Allah to leave the Holy Spirit in his heart, saying:

> Create in me a clean heart, O God, and renew a steadfast spirit within me. Do not cast me away from Your presence, and do not take Your Holy Spirit from me.[2]

Then there was Saul, who changed into another person because of being anointed and the coming of the Holy Spirit upon him:

> Then Samuel took a flask of oil and poured it on his head, and kissed him and said: "Is it not because the Lord has anointed you commander over His inheritance?"[3]

> So it was, When he had turned his back to go from Samuel, that God gave him another heart; and all those signs came to pass that day. When they came there to the hill, there was a group of prophets to meet him; then the Spirit of God came upon him, and he prophesied among them.[4]

Then the Holy Spirit left Saul because he disobeyed his Lord:

> But the Spirit of the Lord departed from Saul, and a distressing spirit from the Lord troubled him.[5]

From the above, it is clear that Prophet Jesus was a man and a servant of Allah. Moreover, the Holy Spirit is one of Allah's angels. Finally, there is nothing like Allah, Whose power is supreme. Allah has surely spoken the truth when He says:

---

[1] Acts 1:8.
[2] Psalms 51:10-11.
[3] I Samuel 10:1.
[4] I Samuel 10:9-10.
[5] I Samuel 16:14.

> It is not fitting for a man that Allah should speak to Him except by inspiration, or from behind a veil, or by the sending of a messenger to reveal, with Allah's permission, what Allah wills: for He is Most High, Most Wise.[1]

The Word of Allah

Someone asks why the Noble Qur'an uses the term "His Word" for Jesus, (may Allah's peace be upon him); what is meant by "Allah's Word" or "His Word" is the command "Be!" Allah uses the command when He creates things. Allah, Most Exalted, says, "Verily, when He intends a thing, His command is, 'Be!' and it is."[2]

Of course, there is no end to Allah's words, for He, Most Exalted, says:

> Say: If the oceans were ink (to write out) the words of my Lord, sooner would the ocean be exhausted than would the words of my Lord, even if We added another ocean like it, for its aid.[3]

Naturally, Allah refers to Jesus as "His Word" because Allah created him by saying "Be!" Allah, Most Exalted, says:

> Such (was) Jesus the son of Mary: (it is) a statement of truth, about which they (vainly) dispute. It is not befitting to (the majesty of) Allah that He should beget a son. Glory be to Him! When He determines a matter, He only says to it, "Be!" and it is.[4]

Elsewhere, when Mary is given the good news of the coming of Jesus, Allah, Most Exalted, says:

> She said: "My Lord! How shall I have a son when no man has touched me?" He said: "Even so: Allah creates what He

---

[1] Qur'an 42:51.
[2] Qur'an 36:82.
[3] Qur'an 18:109.
[4] Qur'an 19:34-35.

will: When He has decreed a Plan, He but says to it, 'Be!' and it is!"[1]

He also adds:

> The similitude of Jesus before God is as that of Adam; He created him from dust, then said to him: "Be!" And he was.[2]

Allah only conferred this name, i.e., His Word, upon Jesus, as compared to all other people, because the rest of humanity was created in the usual way. Every human being is created from a drop of sperm. This then advances to become a clot of congealed blood. Next, it becomes a fetus. Finally, the soul is breathed into the human body. In short, all other human beings (with the exception of Adam and Eve) were created from the fluids of parents, i.e., father and mother.

Jesus (may Allah's peace be upon him) was not created from male fluid. Instead, when the Holy Spirit (Gabriel) breathed into his mother by Allah's command, she became pregnant. Then Allah said "Be," and he was. No wonder Allah likens him to Adam, saying, "The similitude of Jesus before Allah is that of Adam; He created him from dust, then said to him: 'Be!' and he was."

The above is an account from the Noble Qur'an. The following are excerpts from the Old and New Testaments.

The Gospel of John says:

> In the beginning was the Word, and the Word was with God, and the Word was God.[3]

In the Epistle to the Hebrews, it says:

> By faith we understand that the worlds were framed by the word of God, so that the things which are seen were not made of things which are visible.[4]

In the second Epistle of Peter, the Bible states:

> For this they willfully forget: that by the word of God the heavens were of old, and the earth standing out of water and in water.[1]

---

[1] Qur'an 3:47.
[2] Qur'an 3:59.
[3] John 1:1.
[4] Hebrews 11:3.

Muslim-Christian Dialogue

In the Book of Psalms, it reads:

By the word of the Lord the heavens were made, and all the host of them by the breath of His mouth.[2]

In the above quotations the use of "word" clearly appears in four places. We know that the New Testament was originally written in Greek. The Greek for "word" is *logos*. This word has four meanings, i.e., a word, an order or command, a covenant, or news. Obviously, all the meanings apply to Allah's Will in that if He wills anything, all He does is say "Be!" and it is!

A Passage from the Gospel of John

This passage is one of the pillars upon which the Christian belief in incarnation was established. This was the primary foundation upon which the original proponents of incarnation based their formulation of the Christian creed, thus giving the creed a form which would be presentable to the people.

From the above passage (in the Gospel of John), the Christian missionaries understood that the Word is Allah, and Allah is the Word. They thought that the Word was that everything was created with Allah. They thought God had transformed into a human body and come down in the form of Jesus. This was the same Jesus whom people saw when he appeared in the land of the Jews, who conveyed a message in opposition to the Jews at that time, and who performed miracles for them. Due to these miracles, people differed in their understanding of the real nature of Jesus.

Such an understanding of this passage cannot be accepted unless one is extremely lax, i.e., to the point of defying reason and suspending one's intelligence. For example, consider the phrase, "In the beginning was the word." Which beginning does it mean? What is the time frame? If there is a defined time, does it pertain to Allah? Furthermore, is that consistent with Allah's absolute and perfect nature, which is not limited by anything,

---

[1] II Peter 3:5.
[2] Psalms 33:6.

Muslim-Christian Dialogue

even time and space? Certainly, Allah, may He be Glorified, is first, without a beginning.

Next, ponder the phrase, "...and the Word was with God." What exactly does "with" God mean here? How can the "word" be the "beginning", i.e., be first in an unlimited and absolute way, and then be "with God"?

Finally, think about the phrase, "...and the word was God." How can the "word" be with God and be God at the same time? This contradiction comes from this passage, as shown by its words and phrases. Does such an understanding come from a lax and inaccurate translation? Perhaps.

Correction of the passage by addition of edited parts, in order to realize the real message. The phrase "In the beginning was the Word," cannot be cited as meaning a decree or order. The divine decree or command, "'Be!' and it is," represents the phrase "...and the Word was with God." In other words, the divine order is eternal and forever and is one of the infinite attributes of Allah.

The phrase "...and the Word was God," is missing a word. It should read "...and the Lord of the Word was God." Surely, God is the One Who commands and prohibits absolutely.

Elsewhere, John says, "...and the Word was made flesh,"[1] This is also missing a word. The proper reading should be "...and the effect of the Word was made flesh." An example of this appears in the Book of Genesis regarding creation:

> And God said, "Let the earth bring forth the living creature according to its kind: cattle and creeping things and beasts of the earth, each according to its kind;" and it was so.[2]

> And God said, "Let there be light;" and there was light.[3]

Thus, the Word is only a divine decree in the phrases "let the earth bring forth..." and "...let there be light." This is further confirmed by the Epistle to the Hebrews: "By faith we understand that the worlds were framed by the words of God."[4] In other words, by faith we understand that the worlds were framed

---
[1] John 1:14.
[2] Genesis 1:24.
[3] Genesis 1:3.
[4] Hebrews 11:3.

by the command of God. In the Second Epistle of Peter, it says, "...by the Word of God the heavens were of old, and the earth..."[1] i.e., by the command of God the heavens were of old, and the earth. The Book of Psalms states, "By the word of the Lord the heavens were made."[2] Or restated, "By the command of the Lord, the heavens were made."

As such, the meaning is correct. The passage must be seen in this light. If we were to read the passage literally, it would read: "Surely the word is God." This is how it is stated. Now, if we add "...and the Word was made flesh"[3] to the previous phrase, the meaning becomes impossible if applied to Allah. Allah becoming flesh or a body or a shape or a form is impossible, for Allah is free of any change or alteration. Undoubtedly, any change means a new event or happening and that is impossible in regard to Allah.[4] As such the passage becomes defective in its structure and meaning. In fact, it does not really mean anything intelligible. If we were to read it according to its explanation, i.e., by substituting "God" for "Word", as they literally explain it, it would say, "In the beginning was God, and God was with God, and God was God."[5]

What does this mean? Regardless, the verse implies nothing about Prophet Jesus (may Allah's peace be upon him), directly or indirectly. So can we claim that this refers to Jesus?

It should be well known that the Gospel of John is unique in the sense that it is the only one of the four Gospels to be imbued with Greek ideas. It borrows a lot of philosophical statements of the Greeks.

But, someone may ask, then how did this theory of incarnation and sacrifice develop?

It was Paul who slipped in and inserted ideas propagating teachings of absolute disbelief and blasphemy. Barnabas testifies to this in the introduction to his gospel. He tried to infiltrate

---

[1] II Peter 3:5.
[2] Psalms 33:6.
[3] John 1:14.
[4] i.e., Allah was, is, and always will be; "new" or "old" does not apply to Allah.
[5] John 1:1.

Muslim-Christian Dialogue

very stealthily. Luke comments on the suspicion of Jesus' disciples about Paul:

> And when Saul had come to Jerusalem, he tried to join the disciples; but they were all afraid of him, and did not believe that he was a disciple.[1]

On another occasion, Paul tells his pupil, Timothy:

> And without controversy great is the mystery of godliness: God was manifested in the flesh, justified in the Spirit seen by angels, preaching among the Gentiles, believed in the world, received up in glory.[2]

In the Epistle to the Philippians, Paul says:

> Let this mind be in you which was also in Christ Jesus, who, being in the form of God, did not consider it robbery to be equal with God, but made Himself of no reputation, taking the form of a bondservant, and coming in the likeness of men. And being found in appearance as a man, He humbled Himself and became obedient to the point of death, even the death of the cross.[3]

In this way, Paul distorted the message of Jesus, a message of *tawhid* and a natural extension of the Law of Moses. Paul inserted the idea of the Trinity, which is a natural extension of the pagan religion of the Roman empire.

The Pagans and the *Masjid al-Haram* [4]

There is a question which reads: Why do the Saudi authorities prohibit Christians from entering the sacred places in the Kingdom of Saudi Arabia?

To begin with, the question needs correction. In the main, the Saudi authorities do not themselves prohibit entrance to Christians or others who associate anything with Allah. They are only enforcing Allah's commandment and complying with His

---

[1] Acts 9:26.
[2] I Timothy 3:16.
[3] Philippians 2:5-8.
[4] i.e., the Ka'bah and the mosque surrounding it, the Inviolable Mosque.

Muslim-Christian Dialogue

law. Regarding the prohibition of those who associate others with God from entering the premises of the Inviolable Mosque, Allah, Most Exalted, says:

> You who believe! Truly the Pagans are unclean; so let them not after this year of theirs approach the Sacred Mosque. And if you fear poverty, soon will Allah enrich you, if He wills, out of His bounty, for Allah is All-Knowing, All-Wise.[1]

Allah, Most Exalted, commands the believers who are pure in themselves and religiously pure to refuse entrance (to the *Masjid al-Haram*) to those who associate others with Him and are thus impure religiously. Moreover, they should not even come near it after this verse was revealed. It was revealed in the ninth year after the *Hijrah*.[2] Because of this, the Prophet of Allah (may Allah's peace and blessings be upon him) sent 'Ali to the delegation of Abu Bakr (may Allah be pleased with both of them) that year and ordered him to announce to the pagans that after that year no pagan could make the pilgrimage and no one nude could circle the Ka'bah. Thereafter, Allah made this happen and the rule went into effect.

Imam Abu 'Amr Al-Awza'i[3] said:

> 'Umar Ibn 'Abdul-'Aziz[4] (may Allah be pleased with him) wrote: "Stop the Jews and Christians from entering the mosques of the Muslims; obey the prohibition in His statement, 'The pagans are unclean.'"[5]

'Ata'[6] says, "What is forbidden is the entire mosque, for Allah, Most Exalted, says, '...let them not approach the Sacred Mosque after this year of theirs.'"[7]

Clearly, this verse points to the impurity of a pagan or anyone who associates anything with Allah. An authentic saying of

---

[1] Qur'an 9:28.
[2] Hijrah: the migration of the Prophet (pbuh) and the Muslims from Makkah to Madinah.
[3] Al-Awza'i— a famous Muslim jurist.
[4] 'Umar Ibn 'Abdul-'Aziz— a famous Umayyad caliph, sometimes called the fifth rightly guided caliph because of his piety.
[5] Qur'an 9:28.
[6] 'Ata'— a famous scholar from the first generation after the Prophet.
[7] Qur'an 9:28.

the Prophet (may Allah's peace and blessings be upon him) states, "...a believer does not become impure."[1] Concerning the impurity of a non-believer's body,[2] there is a general consensus among the scholars that his/her body or essence is not unclean, since Allah, Most Exalted, has made the food of the People of the Book[3] permissible.

When the Muslims were ordered to carry out the divine commandment, some people complained, relates Muhammad Ibn Ishaq,[4] saying, "...this will surely cut off our markets, destroy our businesses and sever all of our ensuing friendships." Accordingly, Allah revealed that, "...and if you fear poverty then soon Allah will enrich you out of His bounty if He wills."[5]

These are answers to some of the questions put forward. There were some questions which we did not answer directly, since they were answered in detail elsewhere in our discussions on other topics.

Conclusion

Before concluding this meeting, I'd like to say a few words to the Muslim general public about the gradual infiltration of the mannerisms, habits and practices of our predecessors among us.

Our Prophet (may Allah's peace and blessings be upon him) said, "You will surely follow the ways and customs of those before you."

I will try to enumerate in this conclusion some characteristics and practices which Allah and His Prophet cautioned us about. In fact, they forbade us to take on such ignoble traits. I won't comment much on the various Qur'anic verses or the prophetic sayings; surely, these verses and *hadiths* can fully express everything and really do not need any additional comments.

---

[1]Reported by Al-Bukhari.
[2]Or the body of anyone who associates anything with Allah.
[3]i.e., only the Jews and Christians.
[4]Muhammad Ibn Ishaq— a famous Muslim historian.
[5]Qur'an 9:28.

Muslim-Christian Dialogue

1. The Wisdom of the Noble Qur'an

A. Envy

Allah, Most Exalted, says:

> Quite a number of the People of the Book wish they could turn you (people) back to infidelity after you have believed, from selfish envy, after the Truth has become manifest unto them: But forgive and overlook, till Allah accomplishes His purpose; for Allah has power over all things.[1]

Allah criticizes the Jews for envying others. It ate them from within and made them sleepless at night. Why? Because Allah had endowed the Believers with useful knowledge (i.e., the true message of Islam) and strength to act righteously. Sometimes, those associated with knowledge and others may be tried by a tinge of envy for those whom Allah has made successful and guided to the proper knowledge and to righteous deeds

B. Stinginess

Allah, Most Exalted, says:

> Serve Allah, and join not any partners with Him; and do good—to parents, kinsfolk, orphans, those in need, neighbors who are near, neighbors who are strangers, the companion by your side, the wayfarer (you meet), and what your right hands possess: For Allah loves not the arrogant, the vainglorious; (nor) those who are niggardly or enjoin niggardliness on others, or hide the bounties which Allah has bestowed on them; for We have prepared, for those who resist Faith, a punishment that steeps them in contempt.[2]

Stinginess here includes withholding knowledge as well as wealth. As a matter of fact, the context clearly shows that being stingy with knowledge, i.e., withholding it, is the greater fault. Consequently, Allah characterizes them in more than one verse as those who conceal knowledge. For example, the Most Exalted says:

---

[1] Qur'an 2:109.
[2] Qur'an 4:36-37.

> And remember Allah took a covenant from the People of the Book, to make it known and clear to mankind, and not to hide it; but they threw it away behind their backs, and purchased with it some miserable gain! And vile was the bargain they made![1]

Similarly, Allah says:

> Those who conceal the clear (Signs) We have sent down, and the Guidance, after We have made it clear for the people in the Book, on them shall be Allah's curse, and the curse of those entitled to curse.[2]

Thus, Allah, Most Exalted, describes the People of the Book as concealing knowledge (i.e., of the true message of God). Sometimes they conceal their knowledge of the truth by withholding it; at other times they withhold knowledge because of its expediency in acquiring worldly possessions or positions. This sickness can easily afflict those associated with knowledge, for they at times conceal knowledge by withholding it from others or because they dislike for others to receive the same grace which they have received. At other times they do so to acquire something worldly. Also, at times, they hide what they know out of fear of people.

Sometimes the reason for withholding knowledge is when one scholar differs with others on some issue or aligns himself with some group which has also been opposed by others. In view of this, he conceals knowledge wherein is evidence for those who oppose his views, even if it was uncertain that his opponents were wrong.

Accordingly, 'Abdul-Rahman Ibn Madi says:

> The knowledgeable write what supports their views, as well as what opposes their position. In contrast, the heretics only write what supports their views.

C. Restricting truth-seeking to certain personalities

Allah, Most Exalted, says:

---

[1] Qur'an 3:187.
[2] Qur'an 2:159.

Muslim-Christian Dialogue

> When it is said to them, "Believe in what Allah has sent down," they say, "We believe in what was sent down to us," yet they reject all besides, even if it be Truth confirming what is with them. Say: Why then have you slain the prophets of Allah in times gone by, if you did indeed believe?[1]

That was after Allah had said:

> And when there comes to them a Book from Allah, confirming what is with them, although from of old they had prayed for victory against those without Faith, when there comes to them that which they (should) have recognized, they refuse to believe in it but the curse of Allah is on those without Faith.[2]

Allah, Most Exalted portrays them as having known the truth before the appearance of the Prophet (may Allah's peace and blessings be on him), who declared it openly and invited others to it. When the Prophet (may Allah's peace and blessings be on him) came to them they saw that he was a descendant of the Ishmaelites and not the Israelites, so they refused to obey and follow him and believe in him. In other words, they did not accept the truth from anyone unless he was one of their people or from their heritage. Needless to say, many people associated with certain sects and splinter groups suffer from this malady. They measure the truth by the personality associated with it, rather than measuring the personality by the truth.

D. Exceeding the proper bounds of worship

Allah, Most Exalted, says:

> People of the Book! Commit no excesses in your religion: Nor say of Allah aught but the truth. Christ Jesus the son of Mary was (no more than) a Messenger of Allah, and His Word, which He bestowed on Mary, and a Spirit proceeding from Him: so believe in Allah and His Messenger. Say not "Trinity": desist: It will be better for you: For Allah is One God: Glory be to Him: (far exalted is He) above having a

---

[1] Qur'an 2:91.
[2] Qur'an 2:89.

son. To Him belong all things in the heavens and on earth. And enough is Allah as a Disposer of affairs.[1]

In another place, Allah, Most Exalted, says:

> Recite to them the truth of the story of the two sons of Adam. Behold! They each presented a sacrifice (to Allah): it was accepted from one, but not from the other. Said the latter: "Be sure I will slay you." "Surely," said the former, "Allah accepts the sacrifice of those who are righteous."[2]

Exceeding the proper bounds defined by the Qur'an and the Sunnah, especially in relation to over-glorifying prophets and saints, has occurred in certain Muslim sects. Such unwarranted excessiveness led many of them to commit grave errors and heresies, such as the incarnation of God in man and physical union with God.

E. Monasticism

Allah, Most Exalted, says:

> Then, in their wake, We followed them up with (others of) Our messengers: We sent after them Jesus the son of Mary, and bestowed on him the Gospel; and We ordained in the hearts of those who followed him compassion and mercy. But the monasticism which they invented for themselves, We did not prescribe for them: (We commanded) only the seeking for the Good Pleasure of Allah; but that they did not foster as they should have done. Yet We bestowed, on those among them who believed, their (due) reward, but many of them are rebellious transgressors.[3]

This grave disease has afflicted many heretics. They thought themselves to be ascetic, devoted worshippers or poor. Yet they unnecessarily forbade themselves to partake of the permissible good things in life.

F. Assigning the right to legislate law to others besides Allah

Allah, Most Exalted, says:

---

[1] Qur'an 4:171.
[2] Qur'an 5:27.
[3] Qur'an 57:27.

Muslim-Christian Dialogue

> The Jews call Ezra the son of Allah, and the Christians call Christ the son of Allah. That is a saying from their mouths; (in this) they but imitate what the unbelievers of old used to say. Allah's curse be on them: how they are deluded away from the Truth! They take their priests and their anchorites to be their lords in derogation of Allah, and (they take as their Lord) Christ the son of Mary; yet they were commanded to worship but one God: There is no god but He. Praise and glory to Him: (Far is He) from having the partners they associate (with Him).[1]

The Prophet (may Allah's peace and blessings be upon him) explained the above verse to 'Adiy Ibn Hatim At-Ta'i[2] (may Allah be pleased with him). He said that this was because

> ...they made the prohibited things permissible for them, and they obeyed them. Likewise they prohibited what was permissible, and they followed them.[3]

This is also mentioned in their Scriptures:

> "And I say also unto you, that you are Peter, and upon this rock I will build my church; and the gates of hell shall not prevail against it. And I will give unto you the keys of the kingdom of heaven: and whatsoever you shall bind on earth shall be bound in heaven; and whatsoever you shall loose on earth shall be loosed in heaven."[4]

Even among the Muslims there are scholars, presidents and parents who give the right of legislating laws to others besides Allah. Accordingly, they readily accept whatever their scholars, leaders or parents tell them, without referring back to real knowledge or reading a book of guidance.

G. Rule of the majority

Allah, Most Exalted, says:

> Thus did We make their case known to the people, that they might know that the promise of Allah is true, and that there

---

[1] Qur'an 9:30-31.
[2] 'Adiy Ibn Hatim At-Ta'i: one of the Companions.
[3] Reported by Al-Bukhari.
[4] Matthew 16:18-19.

can be no doubt about the Hour of Judgment. Behold, they dispute among themselves as to their affair. (Some) said, "Construct a building over them." Their Lord knows best about them: those who prevailed over their affair said, "Let us surely build a place of worship over them."[1]

Because of rule by an ignorant majority which has no respect for Allah, the mosques of the Muslims today are filled with graves of prophets, saints and others. As a matter of fact, some mosques have been founded upon graves only presumed to be there.

H. Contempt for what our adversaries have

Allah, Most Exalted, says:

> The Jews say: "The Christians have naught (to stand) upon;" and the Christians say: "The Jews have naught (to stand) upon." Yet they (profess to) study the (same) Book. Like unto their word is what those say who know not; but Allah will judge between them in their quarrel on the Day of Judgment.[2]

Thus, the Jews accused the Christians of having nothing (concerning the true message) at all. Likewise, the Christians charged the Jews with having no knowledge at all! Undeniably, this is the style of every leader of a *tariqah*[3] or a sect. He claims that he and his followers have the unadulterated, real truth, while what others are following is nothing but falsehood having nothing to do with truth.

I. Differences of opinion due to insolent envy of each other

Allah, Most Exalted, says:

> We did aforetime grant to the Children of Israel the Book, the power of command, and prophethood; We gave them, for sustenance, things good and pure; and We favored them above the nations. And We granted them Clear Signs in affairs (of religion): it was only after knowledge had been

---

[1] Qur'an 2:113.
[2] Qur'an 18:21.
[3] *Tariqah*— a Sufi order that prescribes a certain way to conduct one's life.

granted to them that they fell into schisms, through insolent envy among themselves. Verily your Lord will judge between them on the Day of Judgment as to those matters in which they set up differences. Then We put you on the (Right) Way of Religion: so follow that (Way), and follow not the desires of those who know not. They will be of no use to you in the sight of Allah: it is only wrong-doers (who stand as) protectors, one to another: But Allah is the Protector of the Righteous.[1]

Such are the Children of Israel. Allah had blessed them with worldly things along with the true religion. Yet they divided into factions and sects. They condemned each other; in fact, they called each other disbelievers. Interestingly, this schism occurred after their having received true knowledge. It happened because of insolent envy of and wrongdoing to each other. Some thought they were above others; others transgressed all legal bounds.

So whoever imitates their way and follows in their footsteps by causing separation and division among the ranks of those who sincerely espouse and worship one God is one of them (i.e., those who cause division). Moreover, his end in the Hereafter will be the same as theirs.

J. Sectarianism

Allah, Most Exalted, says:

Be not like those who are divided among themselves and fall into disputations after receiving Clear Signs: For them is a dreadful penalty.[2]

This refers to the Jews and Christians. Each has divided into more than seventy sects. Muslims have been forbidden to follow them in this sectarianism. Regardless, the Prophet (may Allah's peace and blessings be upon him) informed us that his people would also divide into seventy sects. Every sect will end up in the Fire except one![3]

---

[1] Qur'an 45:16-19.
[2] Qur'an 3:105.
[3] i.e., every group except those following the Qur'an and the Sunnah as practised by the pious predecessors of the Muslims.

K. Distancing oneself from the way of the Believers

Allah, Most Exalted, says:

> If anyone contends with the Messenger, even after Guidance has been plainly conveyed to him, and follows a path other than that becoming to men of faith, We shall leave him in the path he has chosen, and land him in Hell—what an evil refuge![1]

Thus, the way of the Christians and Jews, and those who emulate them and follow in their footsteps, have nothing in common with the path of the Believers. It is only the path of immoral wrongdoers and those upon whom Allah's anger descends and the misguided.

L. Following vain desires[2]

Allah, Most Exalted, says:

> To you We sent the Scripture in truth, confirming the scripture that came before it, and guarding it in safety: so judge between them by what Allah has revealed, and follow not their vain desires, diverging from the Truth that has come to you. To each among you have We prescribed a law and an open way. If Allah had so willed, He would have made you a single people, but (His plan is) to test you in what He has given you: so strive as in a race in all virtues.

> The goal of you all is to Allah; it is He Who will show you the truth of the matters in which you dispute; and this (He commands): Judge between them by what Allah has revealed, and follow not their vain desires, but beware of them lest they beguile you from any of that (teaching) which Allah has sent down to you. And if they turn away, be assured that for some of their crime it is Allah's purpose to punish them. And truly most men are rebellious.[3]

---

[1] Qur'an 4:115.
[2] i.e., following or obeying someone or some system, or one's own opinions based on one's own inclinations, or what feels good and/or is lacking authentic proof.
[3] Qur'an 5:48-49.

Thus, whatever contradicts or differs from the Law of Allah, His Ruling or message (i.e., Islam) is vain. It is not true guidance. The slightest deviation from the straight path can lead one astray.

M. Hardened Hearts

Allah, Most Exalted, says:

> Has not the time arrived for the Believers that their hearts in all humility should engage in the remembrance of Allah and of the Truth which has been revealed (to them), and that they should not become like those to whom was given Revelation aforetime, but long ages passed over them and their hearts grew hard? For many among them are rebellious transgressors.[1]

Allah, Most Glorified, Most Exalted, forbids Believers to allow their hearts to become hard and indifferent to Islam. No doubt, indifference of the heart results from constant disobedience of Allah's message.

The above is only a little from a lot, or a drop from an ocean, in terms of what has been revealed in the Noble Qur'an concerning the behavior and habits of our Christian and Jewish predecessors, i.e., their attitudes and behavior towards the proper creed, righteous manners and use of knowledge.

In the above verses and others similar to them, there is a stern warning for us not to imitate their ways. This warning comes only to keep us from following into the abyss of worldly desires and from degenerating now and in the future.

The Wisdom of the Eminent Hadith

The Noble Qur'an has cautioned and warned us not to behave like the Jews and the Christians concerning beliefs, manners and practices. Likewise, prophetic *hadith* have expounded upon many such matters. These are issues which every Muslim must be fully aware of and comprehend.

---

[1] Qur'an 57:16.

A. Blind Following

Abu Hurayrah (may Allah be pleased with him) relates that the Prophet (may Allah's peace and blessings be upon him) once said:

> For sure, you will embrace the customs of those before you, much as they did with those that preceded them, so closely, i.e., inch by inch, foot by foot, yard by yard,[1] such that even if one of them enters the hole of a lizard, you will enter it as well.

Then Abu Hurayrah advised, "Read if you wish:

> And in the case of those before you, they were mightier than you in power, and more flourishing in wealth and children. They had their enjoyment of their portion: And you have of yours, as did those before you; and you indulge in idle talk as they did. Their works are fruitless in this world and in the Hereafter, and they will lose (all spiritual good).[2]

The Companions then said, "Prophet of Allah, (do you mean) like the Persians, Romans, Christians and Jews did?" And he answered, "Who else besides them."[3]

Ibn 'Abbas (may Allah be pleased with him) commented on this verse:

> Look how tonight is similar to last night. These (mentioned in the verse) are the Israelites; Allah likened us to them.[4]

In his explanation of this verse, Al-Baghawi[5] relates that Ibn Mas'ud[6] said:

> You people (i.e., Muslims) are most similar to the Israelites in manner and guidance. You will follow exactly what they

---

[1] The text literally says the distance of a handle length, and the distance between two widespread arms.
[2] Qur'an 9:69.
[3] Narrated by Ibn Jarir. Ibn Kathir says that it has a sister narration which is authentic.
[4] Narrated by Ibn Jarir.
[5] Al-Baghawi— a compiler of *hadith*.
[6] Ibn Mas'ud— a famous Companion of the Prophet.

are doing, though I don't know if you will worship the calf or not.[1]

In the authentic compilations of Al-Bukhari and Muslim, there is a *hadith* related by Abu Sa'id Al-Khudri (may Allah be pleased with him). He said that the Prophet (may Allah's peace and blessings be upon him) said:

> "You will certainly follow the ways of those before you so identically that even if they were to enter a lizard hole, you would also enter it." The Companions inquired (about "those before" them), "...Prophet of Allah, the Jews and the Christians?" The Prophet (may Allah's peace and blessings be upon him) responded, "Who else?"[2]

Additionally, Al-Bukhari narrates another *hadith* in his authentic compilation on the authority of Abu Hurayrah[3] (may Allah be pleased with him). He says that the Prophet (may Allah's peace and blessings be upon him) said:

> "The final Hour will only come when my people take on the ways of the previous cultures in every detail." He was asked, "Prophet of Allah, like (the ways of) the Persians and the Romans?" So, he said, "Who else besides them?"[4]

B. Competing for Worldly Things

'Amr Ibn 'Awf[5] relates that Allah's Prophet (may Allah's peace and blessings be upon him) sent Abu 'Ubaydah Ibn Al-Jarrah[6] to Bahrain to collect the *jizyah*. When the Prophet (may Allah's peace and blessings be upon him) signed a peace treaty with the people of Bahrain, he had deputed Al-'Ala Ibn Al-Hadhrami[7] to be its governor. Eventually Abu 'Ubaydah returned with money from Bahrain. The *Ansar* heard about Abu 'Ubaydah coming to town so they came to pray *Fajr*[8] with the

---

[1] i.e., if you will be reduced to worshipping idols like the golden calf of the Israelites.
[2] Reported by Al-Bukhari.
[3] Abu Hurayrah— a famous Companion of the Prophet.
[4] Reported by Muslim.
[5] 'Amr Ibn 'Awf— a Companion of the Prophet.
[6] Abu 'Ubaydah Ibn Al-Jarrah— a Companion of the Prophet.
[7] Al-Ala' Ibn Al-Hadhrami— a Companion of the Prophet.
[8] *Fajr*: the first (at dawn) of the five daily prayers.

Prophet (may Allah's peace and blessings be upon him). When Allah's Prophet (may Allah's peace and blessings be upon him) finished the prayer and began to leave they came to him, immediately surrounding him. The Prophet of Allah (may Allah's peace and blessings be upon him) smiled seeing all of them, and said, "I guess all of you have heard that Abu 'Ubaydah brought something back from Bahrain." They said, "Certainly, Prophet of Allah!"

Then he said, "Rejoice and hope for the best. Yet I swear by Allah that it is not poverty that I fear for you; rather I am afraid that worldly riches will become widely available to you as it was made available to those before you. I am afraid that you will compete with one another ruthlessly for worldly reasons, much as they vied with one another before. It will destroy you as it destroyed them."[1]

C. Being Seduced by Women

Abu Sa'id[2] (may Allah be pleased with him) says that the Prophet (may Allah's peace and blessings be upon him) said:

> The world is a sweet place and pleasing to look at. Remember, Allah has left you in charge of it (to establish Islam) to see how you are going to behave. So be wary of this world and protect yourselves (from its temptations). Likewise, be wary of women and protect yourselves (from their seduction). Remember, the first trial for the Israelites was women.[3]

D. Too Many Unnecessary Questions

Abu Hurayrah, may Allah be pleased with him, says that the Prophet (may Allah's peace and blessings be upon him) said:

> Be content with what I have left for you.[4] Remember, what destroyed those before you was their constant unnecessary questioning and then (turning around after being answered) opposing their prophets. So if I have prohibited something,

---

[1] *Sahih Al-Bukhari.*
[2] A Companion of the Prophet.
[3] *Sahih Muslim.*
[4] i.e., the Qur'an and the authentic Sunnah.

then stay away from it. Likewise, if I have commanded you to do something, then do it as much as you can.[1]

Thus he (may Allah's peace and blessings be upon him) commanded them (i.e., his Companions and all Muslims) to stop asking about things they were not commanded to do. He warned that the sole reason for the destruction of previous generations was their constant questioning and then opposing their prophets by disobeying them. Accordingly, Allah has informed us about the Children of Israel and their opposition to Moses' command to fight and struggle in the cause of Allah. On another occasion, they pestered Moses with a barrage of unnecessary questions concerning a heifer which they were commanded to slaughter.

E. Unnecessary Austerity

The Prophet of Allah (may Allah's peace and blessings be upon him) used to say:

> Don't be unnecessarily hard on yourselves such that hardship is imposed upon you. There have been people who were unnecessarily hard on themselves, so Allah was hard on them. Their survivors are found in cells and monasteries. "Monasticism—they invented it; we never prescribed it for them.[2]"[3]

F. Differences over the Divine Book

> Once there were some people sitting near the door (of the house) of the Prophet (may Allah's peace and blessings be upon him). Some of them asked the others, "Didn't Allah say such and such?" Others disputed, saying, "But didn't Allah say such and such?" The Prophet of Allah (may Allah's peace and blessings be upon him) overheard this, and he came out as one overwhelmed. Then he commented, "Is this

---

[1] Narrated in Al-Bukhari and Muslim on the authority of Abu Az-Ziyad, who related it on the authority of Al-A'rij, who heard from Abu Hurayrah.
[2] Qur'an 57:27.
[3] Cited by Abu Dawud in his *Sunan*. It is from the narration of Ibn Wahhab, who said that Sa'id Ibn 'Abdul-Rahman (Ibn Abu Al-Amya) informed him that Sahl Ibn Umamah told him that he and his father went to Anas Ibn Malik (governor) of Madinah. Anas then related what the Prophet said (hadith no. 4886).

what you were enjoined to do (i.e., to argue and dispute)? Is this what you were sent to do, to fling passages from the Book of Allah at each other? Previous generations went astray by doing so. None of you have said anything substantial. See what I have commanded you to do and do accordingly; and what I have prohibited stop doing at once."[1]

G. Believing that Certain Trees are Blessed

Abu Waqid Al-Laythi[2] relates:

We went out with the Prophet of Allah (may Allah's peace and blessings be upon him) to Hunayn. It was only recently that we had been non-believers. The pagans used to spend time (in devotion) at a certain lote tree. They would hang their weapons on it, so it was known as the Hanger. On the way, we also passed by a lote tree. So we asked, "Prophet of Allah, make a hanger for us just like the Hanger they have." So the Prophet of Allah (may Allah's peace and blessings be upon him) said, "*Allahu Akbar*, this is the customary practice (of people). I swear by the One in Whose hand is my soul that you are saying the same (thing) that the Children of Israel said to Moses, when he took the Children of Israel (with safety) across the sea. They came upon a people devoted entirely to the idols they had. They said: 'Moses, fashion for us a god like the gods they have.' He said: "Surely you are a people without knowledge."'[3] You will surely embrace the customs and ways of those before you."[4]

H. Division Along Ethnic Lines or Clan Distinction

'A'isha, may Allah be pleased with her, said:

When Usamah[5] spoke to the Prophet (may Allah's peace and blessings be upon him) concerning the Makhzumi[k] woman

---

[1] Narrated by Ahmad in his *Musnad* on the authority of 'Amr Ibn Shu'ayb, who heard it from his father, who heard it from his father.
[2] Abu Waqid Al-Laythi— a famous Muslim jurist.
[3] Qur'an 7:138.
[4] Narrated by Az-Zuhri on the authority of Sanan, who narrated it on the authority of Abu-Waqid Al-Laythi. This *hadith* appears in the *hadith* collections of Malik, An-Nisa'i and At-Tirmidhi.
[5] Usamah— a Companion of the Prophet.

Muslim-Christian Dialogue

who had stolen (something), he said, '"Usamah, are you interceding (on her behalf) against a legal punishment ordained by Allah, Most Exalted? This is what destroyed the Israelites. If someone from the upper class stole, they would let him go, whereas if someone from the lower class stole, they would carry out the punishment. I swear by the One in Whose hands is my soul, if Fatimah[2] bint Muhammad were to steal, I would cut off her hand."[3]

This is similar to what al-Barra' Ibn "Azib[4] related:

Once some Jews passed by the Prophet (may Allah's peace and blessings be upon him). They had with them a Jew whose face had been painted black and he had been whipped. So he called out to them, asking: "Is this the punishment for the adulterer found in your Book?" They said yes. So then he asked one of their scholars, "I ask in the name of Allah Who revealed the Torah to Moses, is this the punishment for adultery that you find in the Book?"

He said: No, and, had you not asked me in this way (i.e., in the name of Allah) I wouldn't have told you. We find it (i.e., the divine punishment) to be stoning. However, this (i.e., adultery) was widespread in our upper class. If we caught someone in the upper class (committing adultery) we would let him go. (On the other hand,) if we caught someone from the lower class we would carry out the punishment on him. So we said let us come together and decide on one punishment that we would carry out on the upper class and the lower class. Accordingly, we replaced stoning with blackening of the face and whipping (of the offender)."

(On this) he (may Allah's peace and blessings be upon him) commented (turning to Allah), "O Allah, I am the first one to revive Your command which they did away with," whereupon he ordered him (i.e., the offender) to be stoned to death. Thus, Allah, Most Exalted, revealed:

---

[1] Her name was Fatimah.
[2] The most beloved daughter of the Prophet.
[3] Narrated by both Al-Bukhari and Muslim.
[4] Al-Barra'— a Companion of the Prophet.

O Messenger! let not those grieve you, who race each other into unbelief: (whether it be) among those who say, "We believe" with their lips but whose hearts have no faith; or it be among the Jews—men who will listen to any lie—will listen even to others who have never so much as come to you. They change the words from their (right) times and places: they say, "If you are given this, take it, but if not, beware!" If anyone's trial is intended by Allah, you have no authority in the least for him against Allah. For such, it is not Allah's will to purify their hearts. For them there is disgrace in this world, and in the Hereafter a heavy punishment.[1]"[2]

I. Taking Gravesites as Places of Worship

Jundub Ibn 'Abdullah Al-Bajali[3] says:

Five days before he died, I heard the Prophet, may Allah's peace and blessings be upon him, say, "Before Allah, I clear myself of having a really close friend from among you. Allah has taken me as a very close friend, much like He took Abraham to be a very close friend. If I were to take a very close friend from my people, I would have taken Abu Bakr. I warn you that those who lived before you took the gravesites of their prophets and saints as places of worship and devotion. (Again) I warn you, do not take graves as places of worship; I certainly forbid you to do so."[4]

Similarly, 'A'isha and Ibn 'Abbas, may Allah be pleased with them, said:

During his death throes the Prophet, may Allah's peace and blessings be upon him, began to put a black *thawb*[5] on his face. Then he would remove it from his face after covering it. While in this state, he said, "May Allah's curse be on the Jews and Christians for taking the graves of their prophets as

---

[1] Qur'an 5:41.
[2] Narrated by Al-Bukhari and Muslim on the authority of Abdullah Ibn Murrah, who heard it from Al-Barrah Ibn 'Azib.
[3] Jundub Ibn 'Abdullah Al-Bajali— a Companion of the Prophet.
[4] Narrated by Muslim.
[5] the full-length garb worn by Arabs.

places of worship and devotion. (One should) be wary of what they did."[1]

On another occasion, 'A'isha, may Allah be pleased with her, relates that Umm Salamah and Umm Habibah,[2] may Allah be pleased with them, told the Prophet of Allah about a church called Maria, which they had seen in Abyssinia. They talked about its beauty in the pictures inside it. The Prophet of Allah (may Allah's peace and blessings be upon him) said:

> They were people who would build a place of worship over the grave of a pious worshipper or a righteous person who had died. They would put those pictures in it. These are the worst people in the eyes of Allah, Most Sublime and Exalted.[3]

Finally, Ibn 'Abbas, may Allah be pleased with him, says:

> The Prophet of Allah (may Allah's peace and blessings be upon him) cursed female visitors to the graves[4] and those who erect over them places of worship and lights.[5]

J. New, Unsubstantiated Holidays

Allah, Most Exalted, says:

> ...those who witness no falsehood and, if they pass by futility, they pass by it with honorable (avoidance)...[6]

Muhammad Ibn Sirin explains "those who witness no falsehood" as Palm Sunday[7].[8] Mujahid[9] comments that "falsehood" refers to pagan holidays. 'Umar[10] once said:

---

[1] Narrated by Muslim.
[2] Two wives of the Prophet.
[3] Narrated by Al-Bukhari and Muslim.
[4] This prohibition was during the early period, when women would wail and shriek, desecrating the graves. Later this ban was lifted, making it permissible for women to visit graves.
[5] I.e., made them sacred.
[6] Qur'an 25:72.
[7] The Sunday before Easter.
[8] Narrated by Abu Bakr Al-Khilal in *Al-Jami'* with a chain of narration linked to Muhammad Ibn Sirin.
[9] Mujahid— a famous scholar from the Successor generation.
[10] 'Umar Ibn Al-Khattab.

Avoid the small talk of those who don't know Arabic, and do not dare to join in with the pagans (i.e., those who associate others with God) on the day of their holiday in their churches.[1]

Thus, pagan holidays, or holidays made up by people, combine doubts (as to its authenticity), vain personal desires, falsehood and mere whim.

Once, Abu Hurayrah heard the Prophet of Allah (may Allah's peace and blessings be upon him) say:

We were the last ones (i.e., to come into this world as a religion), yet we will be ahead (of everyone) on the Day of Judgment, though they were given the Book before us, and we were given it after them. This is their day (Friday) that Allah mandated for them. But they differed and quarreled concerning it. Naturally, Allah guided us to it. Other people will follow us. The Jews tomorrow (Saturday) and the Christians, the day after tomorrow.[2]

On many occasions the Prophet (may Allah's peace and blessings be upon him) designated Friday as a holiday. In fact, he prohibited us from singling out Friday for fasting, since it is supposed to be a holiday.

K. Horns and Bells for Worship Services

Abu 'Umayr Ibn Anas relates that his *Ansari* uncle said:

The Prophet (peace be upon him) was concerned as to how to gather the people for prayer. The people suggested to him to hoist a flag at the time of prayer, so that when they saw it, they would inform one another, but he did not like it. Then someone mentioned to him the horn. Ziyad suggested the horn of the Jews.[3] He (the Prophet) did not like it. He said, "That is a matter for the Jews." Then they suggested to him the bell of the Christians. He said, "That is a matter for the Christians." 'Abdullah Ibn Zayd returned anxiously from there because of the anxiety of the Messenger of Allah (may

---

[1] Narrated by Abu Shaykh Al-Asfahani or 'Ata' Ibn Yassar.
[2] Narrated by Al-Bukhari and Muslim.
[3] i.e., the *shofar*, or ram's horn (ed.).

peace be upon him). He was then taught the call to prayer in his dream. The next day he came to the Messenger of Allah (peace be upon him) and informed him about it. He said: "Messenger of Allah, I was between sleep and wakefulness; all of a sudden a newcomer came (to me) and taught me the call to prayer."

'Umar Ibn Al-Khattab had also seen it in a dream before but had kept it hidden for twenty days. The Prophet (peace be upon him) said to me ('Umar), "What prevented you from telling me?" He said, "'Abdullah Ibn Zayd had already told you about it before me, so I was ashamed." Then the Messenger of Allah (peace be upon him) said, "Bilal, stand up, and see what 'Abdullah Ibn Zayd tells you and do it." Bilal then made the call to prayer.

[Abu Bishr reported on the authority of Abu 'Umayr that the *Ansar* thought that if 'Abdullah Ibn Zayd had not been ill on that day, the Messenger of Allah (peace be upon him) would have made him *mu'adhdhin*.[1]]

Thus, the Prophet of Allah (may Allah's peace and blessings be upon him) disliked the Jews' horn, blown into by mouth, or the Christian bells, struck by hand. This dislike also applies to (musical) sounds outside of prayer, since they are Jewish and Christian practices.[2]

The Building of a Muslim Personality

Since we have been prohibited from resembling them (non-Muslims) in their beliefs, morals, acts of worship, and any general or specific behavior, we have also been forbidden to resemble them, even in matters of outward appearance. Hence, any group of Muslims can safeguard their unique character from melting or dissolving into other personalities. Of course, this is an important point in building an independent entity, a cohesive unit and a strong society. In the following lines, we shall relate

---

[1] Narrated by Abu Dawud in *Sunan Abu Dawud*, "Kitab as-Salat," Hadith 498.
[2] Ibn Taymiyyah, *The Requirement of the Straight Path to Differ from the People of the Fire*.

some of what was narrated from the Prophet of Allah, may Allah's peace and blessings be upon him, in this context.

A. Dyeing Grey Hair

Abu Hurayrah relates that the Prophet of Allah (may Allah's peace and blessings be upon him) said:

> The Jews and the Christians do not dye (their grey hair) so be different from them.[1]

Abu 'Abdullah said:

> I would like everyone to change their grey hair and not be like the People of the Book. The Prophet (may Allah's peace and blessings be upon him) said, "Change (your) grey hair and don't look like the People of the Book."[2]

B. Longer Beards and Trimmed Moustaches

Ibn 'Umar[3] (may Allah be pleased with him) says that the Prophet of Allah (may Allah's peace and blessings be upon him) advised: "Be different from the pagans; trim your moustaches and lengthen your beards."[4] Abu Hurayrah (may Allah be pleased with him) says that the Prophet of Allah (may Allah's peace and blessings be upon him) said, "Trim your moustaches, grow your beards and be different from the fire-worshippers."[5]

C. Prayer in Sandals

Shaddad Ibn 'Aws (may Allah be pleased with him) says that the Prophet of Allah (may Allah's peace and blessings be upon him) said, "Be different from the Jews, for they don't pray in their sandals or their shoes."[6]

---

[1] Reported by Al-Bukhari and Muslim.
[2] Reported by At-Tirmidhi.
[3] Ibn 'Umar— a famous Companion of the Prophet.
[4] Reported by Al-Bukhari and Muslim.
[5] Reported by Muslim.
[6] Reported by Abu Dawud.

D. Pre-dawn Meal when Fasting

'Amr Ibn Al-'As[1] (may Allah be pleased with him) said that the Prophet of Allah (may Allah's peace and blessings be upon him) said, "The superiority of our fast, compared to the fast of the People of the Book, lies in taking a pre-dawn meal."[2]

E. Hastening to Break the Fast (at sunset)

Abu Hurayrah (may Allah be pleased with him) relates that the Prophet of Allah (may Allah's peace and blessings be upon him) said, "This way of life (Islam) will continue to prevail as long as people hasten to break the fast (at sunset), for the Jews and Christians delay it."[3]

F. Treatment of Menstruating Women

Anas[4] (may Allah be pleased with him) relates that when a woman was indisposed (during her menstrual period) among the Jews, they would not (even) eat with her in the house, (let alone) have sexual relations with her. So the Companions of the Prophet of Allah (may Allah's peace and blessings be upon him) asked the Prophet of Allah (may Allah's peace and blessings be upon him, about it). Thereafter, Allah, Most Exalted and Sublime, revealed the following verse:

> They ask you concerning women's courses. Say: They are a hurt and a pollution: so keep away from women in their courses, and do not approach them until they are clean. But when they have purified themselves, you may approach them in any manner, time, or place ordained for you by Allah. For Allah loves those who turn to Him constantly, and He loves those who keep themselves pure and clean.[5]

And the Prophet of Allah (may Allah's peace and blessings be upon him) said, "You may do everything with them except for having sex." When the Jews heard this, they remarked, "This

---

[1] A famous Companion of the Prophet.
[2] Reported by Muslim.
[3] Reported in *Sunan Abu Dawud*, "Kitab as-Siyam," p. 646, hadith 2346.
[4] Anas Ibn Malik— a famous Companion of the Prophet.
[5] Qur'an 2:222.

man does not want to leave a single one of our habits without being different from us."[1]

The prohibition against being like Jews or Christians and others from other sects and cults, which contradict what the Muslims have, is of such importance that the Prophet of Allah (may Allah's peace and blessings be upon him) generalized this commandment. 'Umar Ibn Al-Khattab (may Allah be pleased with him) said, "Whoever copies other people is one of them."[2] 'Abdullah Ibn 'Amr[3] said:

> Whoever builds on the land of the pagans, then celebrates their new year's day and their festivals, and copies them until he dies, will be raised among them on the Day of Judgment.[4]

Before concluding this meeting, I would like to state the following: Current Christian missionary efforts in full swing in Muslim lands are efforts which necessitate a serious and critical study. Their efforts attract attention. These concentrated and continuous efforts cast doubts and specious arguments in the way of those weak in their faith, thus deterring them from the way of Allah and His guidance.

Most surely these efforts have distorted, and are distorting, the message from its real context. Needless to say, changing and distorting Scriptures is old hat for the People of the Book. They have done it to their own Scriptures until they changed and altered it in word and meaning, in text and spirit. Today, some People of the Book, Jews and Christians, are trying to play this role regarding the Book of our Lord (i.e., the Qur'an). Even though they may have given up on changing the text, preserved in hearts and books, they are still hoping to succeed in creating doubts and misgivings concerning the meanings of the words, the impact of its expression and the fundamentals of the religion along with its details. This is what they are accustomed to doing. They write about Islam with this view only. They think that lies

---

[1] Reported by Muslim.
[2] Reported in *Sunan Abi Dawood*.
[3] 'Abdullah Ibn 'Amr Ibn Al-'As.
[4] i.e., he will be treated as a pagan.

and falsification are the best ways to attract Muslims and turn them away from the truth of their religion.

I must remind everyone: lies and falsehood do not live. Even if they live, they do not live long.

> Nay, We hurl the Truth against falsehood, and it knocks out its brain, and behold, falsehood does perish! Ah! Woe to you for the (false) things you ascribe (to Us).[1]

Indeed, Muslims should pay attention to this scheme and strategy. They must follow up on the lies of those Jews and Christians and remove them and put an end to them. They must confront and combat this onslaught.

Missionary work aims to destroy Islam in its own land among its adherents, such that the forthcoming generations of Muslims become Christians in name, appearance, language and essence. For this sinister purpose it takes advantage of a particular area which makes it easy for missionary work. That area would happen to be suffering from illiteracy, poverty or disease. Naturally it provides them with education, bread and the required medicines. This is one of the many forces of the Christian movement, or missionary movement, as they call it.

However, there are other faces and signs of this dubious movement. Namely, it is very bothersome to these people when they find that someone changes his name from Muhammad to Peter. Therefore, they thought of persuading Muhammad to keep his name—yes, his name only. Yet they will make sure to change his mind, his heart, his manners, his religion and his confidence in his faith. Thus he will become Christian in substance, even though he doesn't become Christian in name.

To achieve this end, they have taken advantage of the following factors:

A. Religious illiteracy

It is this illiteracy which has turned Islam into grave-worshipping, Sufism, superstition, deceit and trickery. Naturally, we find that missionary circles present their Islamic perspective by use of these above distortions. They present these distortions

---

[1] Qur'an 21:18.

to the people in books, pictures and films—only to tell the people that this is the Islam that they are fighting against and they want to get rid of.

We can only remind and warn everyone about this religious illiteracy. It is surely the most dangerous type of illiteracy. All educational facilities in Muslim countries, whether they educate directly or indirectly, must take notice of this by combating it and correcting the distortions.

B. Following the religion blindly

Missionary circles, assisted by the forces of colonial imperialism, in the past and at present, want to drown the Muslims completely in the blind following of their religion. Blind religiosity was never decreed in the Qur'an, nor did the Sunnah enjoin it. The moment the Muslims fall into the claws of this blind religiosity, it becomes very easy for their enemies to ensnare them and then poison their thinking.

Nothing can stop missionary work in all its forms and numerous organizations except Islam in its authentic form. This is a fact which we must realize as we prepare to enter battle, especially ideological warfare dealing with thought and beliefs, with any enemy.

C. Sinister sects

This is the third factor used by missionaries to destroy our world. They constantly stir up a set number of controversies. Then they repeat these issues again and again without the least bit of thought. When Muslim speakers respond to these issues, or issues raised by heretical sects, by giving clear and persuasive, well-documented answers, these people do not quit. No sooner are these issues put to rest by cogent reason than they stir up the same controversy anew.

Interestingly, I have noticed one thing in this gathering which we are in the midst of, namely that Allah, Most Glorified, Most Exalted, Who has promised to preserve His Book and make His Divine Way victorious over all other ways, uses these missionaries in the service of Islam. Amazingly, these missionary workers have no idea they have been used.

Muslim-Christian Dialogue

Thus, when they stir up these controversies and we respond, their own faults, errors and misguidance are clearly identified. Undoubtedly, Islam triumphs as the truth, whereas the religions which they follow are without doubt nothing but falsehood. I have conducted discussions with many of these people from the East and the West. Each time I end up with a positive result. This is not because of some special ability in me; rather it is the power and greatness of Islam. Moreover, it is not because of the opponents' weakness, lack of understanding or knowledge; rather, it is weakness in the message which they invite others to, and which they defend, and so on.

A poet once said:

> When Allah wants to publicize a good thing
> Kept hidden from others,
> He affords it an envious tongue.

In the end, we have said what we know. Surely Allah is the Most Knowledgeable. We have made every effort to present the truth to the best of our ability and as sincerely as possible. Yet, it is only Allah Who is responsible for opening eyes too blind to see the truth, ears too deaf to hear it, and hearts too closed to accept it.

Allah, Lord of Jibril, Mika'il, and Israfil,[1] Creator of the heavens and the earth, Knower of the Seen and the Unseen, You judge between Your servants in matters wherein they differ. With Your permission guide us in our differences to the truth. Surely You guide to the Straight Path whom You will. Allah, all thanks go to You and we praise You. You are the light of the heavens and the earth, Praise be to You. You are the Upholder of the heavens and the earth and whomsoever therein. You are the Truth. Your promise is true. Your statements are true. Our meeting You is true and certain. Paradise is true. The Fire is true. The Prophets are true. The Final Hour is true. Allah, to You I submit myself; in You I believe; upon You I depend; to You I repent; by Your power I struggle; and according to Your commandments I decide and I govern. Forgive me for what I have sent forth (to You, i.e., deeds) and for what I have failed to do;

---

[1] Jibril (Gabriel) is the angel of Revelation, Mika'il is the angel of death, Israfil is the angel who will blow the horn to signal the end of the world.

and for what I have done privately as well as publicly. You are my God. There is none to be worshipped besides You.

Lord of the Worlds, You do we worship and from You do we seek help. Guide us to the Straight Path, the Path of those on whom You have bestowed Your Grace. Those whose (portion) is not wrath and who go not astray. May Allah's peace and blessings be upon Muhammad, his family and his Companions.

FINAL SESSION

Concluding Remarks

A Word from Father James Bakheet Sulayman, Representing the Christian Side

[Father Sulayman will imminently announce his declaration of Islam]

Respected members of the Organization for the Revival of Islamic Activity in the Sudan; respected sir of the office of the Saudi Religious Attaché in Khartoum; respected and honored guests:

According to what was decided at the beginning of the first session, we were to give an opportunity to the scholars, Jamil Ghazi, Ahmad 'Abdul-Wahhab and Ibrahim Khalil, to respond to questions related to Islam and Christianity. We had forwarded these questions to Your Eminence, hoping to find explanations and clarifications which would remove pending doubts within ourselves. This was in the interest of knowing the truth from falsehood. Thereafter, we would give our opinion concerning the substance of the answers to the questions.

No doubt, all of you are expecting that we enter into a free discussion with you right now so we can respond to your answers and detailed explanations concerning the two faiths of Islam and Christianity.

Instead, we must say truthfully in front of Allah: we have no other response but to openly declare that Islam is *our* religion. We must adhere to all its values and standards because it is the truth. It is the light of the best people in this world and the Hereafter. Gentlemen, with this spiritual and objective beginning, we must announce that there are numerous responsibilities awaiting us, not just towards these brothers who have embraced Islam, but there are also many priests and men and women Christian leaders who need to know what we got out of this discourse between us.

Undoubtedly, this is part of our primary responsibility wherein we must cooperate. We must cooperate sincerely, not for any material benefit, but rather to let everyone know, whether Muslims or Christians, of the truths revealed by Allah, Most Glorified, Most Exalted, to the best of His creation, Muhammad, may Allah's peace and blessings be upon him.

Before I conclude, I would like especially to thank all those who participated with all the various means at their disposal to make this discourse a success, enabling us to emerge with positive results. This will be there for all future generations, not only in Sudan but for all peoples.

Wa as-salamu 'alaykum wa rahmatu Allahi wa barakatuh.

A Word from Shaykh Tahir Ahmad Talibi, Religious Attaché of the Embassy of Saudi Arabia (Khartoum)

In the name of Allah, Ever Beneficent, Ever Merciful.

All praise is due to Allah; we praise Him and seek His help and forgiveness. We seek refuge in Allah from the evil of our selves and our wrong deeds. Whomsoever Allah guides, none can misguide. Likewise, whomsoever Allah permits to be misguided, none can guide. I bear witness that there is no god except Allah, Who is free of any partners or associates. Furthermore, I bear witness that our leader, Muhammad (may Allah's peace and blessings be upon him) is His servant and prophet.

> You who believe! Fear Allah as He should be feared, and die not except in a state of Islam. And hold fast, all together, by the rope which Allah (stretches out for you), and be not divided among yourselves; and remember with gratitude Allah's favor on you; for you were enemies and He joined your hearts in love, so that by His Grace, you became brethren; and you were on the brink of the pit of Fire, and He

saved you from it. Thus does Allah make His Signs clear to you: that you may be guided.[1]

Mankind! Revere your Guardian-Lord, Who created you from a single person, created, of like nature, his mate, and from them twain scattered (like seeds) countless men and women; fear Allah, through Whom you demand your mutual (rights), and (revere) the wombs (that bore you): for Allah ever watches over you.[2]

You who believe! Fear Allah, and make your utterance straightforward, that He may make your conduct whole and sound and forgive you your sins: He who obeys Allah and His Messenger has already attained the great victory.[3]

Certainly the best discourse is the Book of Allah. The best form of guidance (after the Qur'an) is the guidance of Muhammad, may Allah's peace and blessings be upon him. The worst of matters are unwarranted innovations. Surely every unwarranted innovation is heresy. Heresy is nothing but straying from the truth. Any such deviation only leads to the Hellfire.

My honorable brothers, *as-salamu 'alaykum wa rahmatu Allahi wa barakatuh.*

Having attended this pleasant meeting and this blessed gathering, it gives me great pleasure and honor to address all of you at this meeting which we began with six consecutive sessions lasting more than twenty hours. It seems as if I should answer a question. It seems as if I see someone asking me how this meeting came about. What is the story behind organizing this gathering? As you all know, this gathering was for Muslims and Christians.

The story of this momentous gathering started with the evangelist priest, James Bakheet Sulayman. He had been very active in the various churches and was searching for the truth. Eventually, he came to my friend, the honorable Professor Juway'id An-Nufay'i of the office of the Educational Attaché of the Embassy of the Kingdom of Saudi Arabia. James informed

---
[1] Qur'an 3:102-103.
[2] Qur'an 4:1.
[3] Qur'an 33:70-71.

him that he was searching for the true religion and wanted to make some decision about it; moreover, he wanted to have a discussion on Islam so he might arrive at the real truth. Thereafter, he arranged a meeting between him and me. Here, Mr. James Bakheet Sulayman briefly told me about his life from the beginning up to that day. We then decided on a date for this meeting. We decided to meet on 23 Muharram 1401 A.H. (December 1, 1980 C.E.) at the Organization for the Revival of Islamic Activity in Omdurman.

After he requested this discussion, I met the Honorable Dr. Muhammad Jamil Ghazi, who had come to this area on a special invitation from some of his Muslim brothers to deliver some lectures on Islam in the Sudan. He, may Allah reward him handsomely, directed me to His Eminence, Shaykh Ibrahim Khalil Ahmad and added that he is a very good person who used to be a priest until Allah guided him to Islam, and he is very knowledgeable about such discussions. Then, there is also Brigadier General Ahmad 'Abdul-Wahhab, who is also the author of many books on Christianity and comparative studies between Islam and Christianity.

Subsequently, he himself, may Allah reward him handsomely, contacted both of them. They came immediately. The only thing that took them several days was the travel arrangements, reservations, and so on. All in all, they responded promptly and were present in Khartoum a few days before our meeting.

Our first meeting, as I have already mentioned, was last Monday. There, Father James gave us a number of questions pertaining to Christianity and Islam.

For example, some of the topics that he mentioned concerning Christianity dealt with the Trinity, the Crucifixion and the Sacrifice. Some of the topics concerning Islam dealt with the Qur'an, the truthfulness of the Prophet of Allah (may Allah's peace and blessings be upon him) and his being the last Prophet, jihad and war in Islam, alcohol, swine, and other questions, which you heard at that time last Monday. By the way, they have all been written down and recorded.

Muslim-Christian Dialogue

Their Eminences Dr. Muhammad Jamil Ghazi, Brigadier General Ahmad 'Abdul-Wahhab and Shaykh Ibrahim Khalil Ahmad, responded to these questions masterfully, one by one. They left no room for any doubt that Islam is the true way of Allah and any other way is absolutely false.

They answered all of their questions. In fact, they expounded upon them more than what the questions asked. They delivered many lectures over six days. Each day they met for three hours straight. Last night, at approximately ten o'clock, we concluded our sessions. Then we gave Father James an opportunity to reflect and consult with his colleagues after we had finished these sessions.

This morning, he came to me saying that he and his colleagues were all declaring that they want to enter the fold of Islam. Additionally, they frankly declared that it is definitely the true religion and anything else is falsehood. Moreover, they declare that the Qur'an is the truth and Muhammad, may Allah's peace and blessings be upon him, is right and true. They, if Allah Most Gracious wills, will announce this good news in front of you, one by one.

Respected brothers, I don't want to prolong my speech but I do want to say one last thing. I hope that Allah, Most Exalted and Sublime, will make this session the beginning of much more good to come for Islam and the Muslims.

Allah, Most Glorified and Exalted, says:

> It is He Who has sent His Messenger with Guidance and the Religion of Truth, to proclaim it over all religions: and enough is Allah for a Witness.[1]

The Prophet of Allah (may Allah's peace and blessings be upon him) says what means: "Surely this religion will shine on what the sun shines on (i.e., the entire earth)."[2]

Now I invite Rear Admiral Ibrahim Ahmad 'Umar, Secretary General of the Organization for the Revival of Islamic Activity in the Sudan, to come and present us with some concluding remarks. May Allah reward him handsomely.

---

[1] Qur'an 48:28.
[2] Sahih Muslim.

A Word from Rear Admiral Ibrahim Ahmad Umar, Secretary General, Organization for the Revival of Islamic Activity in Sudan

I seek refuge in Allah from the accursed Satan. I begin in the name of Allah, Ever Beneficent, Ever Merciful. May the peace and blessings of Allah be upon our leader, Muhammad, last of all prophets and messengers, and upon his family and his Companions.

Allah is the Greatest! Allah is the Greatest! Allah is the Greatest! "And say: Truth has (now) arrived, and Falsehood perished: bound to perish."[1]

On behalf of the Organization for the Revival of Islamic Activity, I greet you with the greeting of Islam: *As-salamu 'alaykum wa rahmatu Allahi wa barakatuh.*

The desire of the Christian participants to understand the differences between Islam and Christianity came from them. They wanted to determine after a thorough examination whether they should accept Islam based on its fundamental beliefs or reject it outright. For us as attendees this was an opportunity that perhaps would never come again.

To make this all possible, Allah graced us with the meritorious efforts of His Eminence Shaykh Tahir Ahmad Talibi of the office of the Religious Attaché of the Embassy of the Kingdom of Saudi Arabia in Sudan. He was the one who brought us and honored us and delighted us and told us about three great, revered and brilliant scholars. They are His Eminence Dr. Muhammad Jamil Ghazi, a scholar of the Noble Qur'an; the Honorable Brigadier General, a scholar of comparative religion specializing in Islam and Christianity on top of his vast military expertise, Brigadier General Ahmad 'Abdul-Wahhab. Along with both of them is a man who faithfully immersed himself in Christianity, becoming one of its greatest missionaries in the land of Egypt. He studied Christianity in depth and thoroughly understood the sacred Christian scriptures. He received top academic honors in Christian theology. Then a day came when the statement of Allah, Most Sublime Most Exalted, "...and surely

---

[1] Qur'an 17:81.

Allah guides whom He wills to the Straight Path..."[1] became consistent with the reverend. Accordingly, he walked the path of guidance and read the Noble Qur'an. He read it as a mature, cultured and well-enlightened scholar who understood exactly what he was reading. Soon he believed in it, having found in the Noble Qur'an—by which Allah guides those who follow it to paths of peace and security—what he had been looking for. He graduated from being a disbeliever in the message of Muhammad (may Allah's peace and blessings be upon him) to being one of the greatest believers in Allah and in the message of Muhammad, may Allah's peace and blessings be upon him. Indeed, Allah is the Greatest.

These three respected and eminent scholars spoke effectively, giving us an opportunity to savor their wisdom. But more importantly, they convinced all our friends who had questions with irrefutable proofs and decisive evidence. Indeed, Allah is the Greatest!

Here they are today before you as Muslims in truth and with sincere faith. After their accepting Islam, all of us must take care of them so that they learn and practice Islam correctly.

It is this true Islam which Ibn 'Umar, may Allah be pleased with him, relates:

> One day, while we were sitting with the Messenger of Allah (may the blessings and peace of Allah be upon him), there appeared before us a man whose clothes were exceedingly white and whose hair was exceedingly black; no signs of journeying were to be seen on him and none of us knew him.
>
> He walked up and sat down by the Prophet (may the blessings and peace of Allah be upon him). Resting his knees against his and placing the palms of his hands on his thighs, he said, "Muhammad, tell me about Islam." The Messenger of Allah (may the blessings and peace of Allah be upon him) said, "Islam is to testify that there is no god but Allah and Muhammad is the Messenger of Allah, to perform the

---

[1] Qur'an 2:213.

Muslim-Christian Dialogue

prayers, to pay *zakah*, to fast in Ramadan, and to make the pilgrimage to the House if you are able to do so."

He said, "You have spoken rightly," and we were amazed at him asking him and saying that he had spoken rightly. He then said, "Tell me about *iman*." He said, "It is to believe in Allah, His angels, His books, His messengers, and the Last Day, and to believe in divine destiny, both the good and the evil thereof."

He said, "You have spoken rightly. Now tell me about *ihsan*." He said, "It is to worship Allah as though you see Him, and while you see Him not, yet truly He sees you." He said, "Now tell me about the Hour." He said, "The one questioned about it knows no better than the questioner."

He said, "Then tell me about its signs." He said, "That the slave-girl will give birth to her mistress, and that you will see barefooted, naked, destitute herdsmen competing in constructing lofty buildings." Then he went away, and I stayed for a time. Then he said, "'Umar, do you know who the questioner was?" I said, "Allah and His Messenger know best." He said, "It was Gabriel, who came to you to teach you your religion."[1]

Dear brothers, this is our message to our people and to our brothers who have entered the fold of Islam. It involves teaching them their Islam, and we will, with Allah's permission. In fact, we will encourage them to be people who propagate Islam among their families and relatives. We will help them to make a decent living through respectable professions, if Allah wills.

All that has happened is true enlightenment. Surely Allah guides to His Light whom He wills. So I welcome our brothers in Islam, the religion of truth. Thanks, especially, to our respected, eminent scholars.

In conclusion, I would like to give you the good news that everything occurring in these sessions in the past few days, Allah willing, will be published and distributed—in Arabic, English and French. By the will of Allah, we hope that this will be

---

[1] Narrated by Muslim.

translated into all the languages of the world. Truly, only Allah grants success.

Wa as-salamu 'alaykum wa rahmatu Allahi wa barakatuh.

A Word from Shaykh Muhammad Hashim Al-Hadiyyah, President, Association of Supporters of the Prophetic Way (Sudan)

In the name of Allah, Ever Beneficent, Ever Merciful. All praise is due to Allah, Lord of the Worlds. May Allah's peace and blessings be upon the Trustworthy Prophet, his family and his well-guided Companions, who guided others.

As-salamu 'alaykum wa rahmatu Allahi wa barakatuh.

This gathering was a total surprise to me. We had agreed—after disagreeing about it yesterday—to meet at six o'clock this evening for something else. I had no idea about this celebration and this pleasant finale until only a half hour ago. Nevertheless, I am extremely elated. Nothing can beat this.

My only request of those who have accepted Islam today is that they exert all their efforts to learn their religion. But I have a special request of Dr. Muhammad Jamil Ghazi. I would like to ask him to take special care of these brothers so that they learn Islam with the creed of our pious predecessors. We should remember that the Muslims divided into sects, factions and heretic splinter groups only when they split their unified creed into different, unsubstantiated views; consequently, their unity was destroyed and they began to fight with each other. If only they had been satisfied with what the Qur'an recommends when it says:

> You who believe! Obey Allah, and obey the Messenger and those charged with authority among you. If you differ in anything among yourselves, refer it to Allah and His Messenger, if you believe in Allah and the Last Day: That is best, and most suitable for final determination.[1]

Allah has made this Qur'an easy. He has stated clearly that it is easy for one who sincerely wants to understand and comprehend it. Yet, the Devil comes and whispers to some people

---

[1] Qur'an 4:59.

who claim to be Islamic scholars and who claim to be inviting others to Islam. Accordingly they begin to claim that the Qur'an has both obvious meanings (i.e., for the common people) and hidden meanings (privy only to certain people like themselves). This certainly is the first nail in the coffin of the Muslim brotherhood.

Dr. Jamil holds a high rank of trust and honor among us. I don't really want to praise him while he is sitting here, though he is worthy of much praise. In view of this, I would like him to watch over these young men and take special care of them by confining them to the Book of Allah, their Lord, and the Sunnah of their Prophet (may Allah's peace and blessings be upon him) and concentrating on their clear meanings in Arabic.

I would like to relate a statement made by someone who is a non-Arab. He is a man from southern Sudan. He accepted Islam and is proud of it. Someone once asked him, "Which sect do you belong to?" He said, "We don't accept the Sufi way in the South for it divides the Muslims; we only teach the Qur'an, because this is what unites them and makes them one nation, one people."

Therefore, I hope that Mr. James Bakheet Sulayman and his colleagues will prepare to go to Egypt, if Allah wills. There, I hope you will live in the school of *tawhid* and study Islam. You will see what they gave to the world regarding the basics which elevated the weak and made them strong; which made the poor rich, and turned the ignorant into scholars. Their program of action was this Qur'an, with its clear message explained by the great Prophet, who was blessed with a unique eloquence.

Also, I would like Dr. Jamil to confine their remembrance of Allah to the way of the Prophet of Allah, may Allah's peace and blessings be upon him.

I congratulate them for their Islam, first of all. I wish them success in their future life. Surely, all of us, with Allah's help support and care, will provide strong support and make their new life a life of comfort and happiness.

Perhaps you already met our mature and erudite Muslim brother, Shaykh Ibrahim Khalil when he was talking about his previous life and then his new life: After all this, he attributes all the grace to Allah, Lord of the Worlds, for filling his path with true faith.

Allah, Most Sublime Most Exalted, tells our great Prophet (may Allah's peace and blessings be upon him):

> And thus have We, by Our command, sent inspiration to you: You knew not (before) what was Revelation, and what was Faith; but We have made the (Qur'an) a Light, wherewith We guide such of Our servants as We will; and verily you guide (men) to the Straight Way...[1]

> It is true you will not be able to guide everyone whom you love; but Allah guides those whom He will and He knows best those who receive guidance.[2]

Once again I thank everyone, and I fully support what the Honorable Rear Admiral Ibrahim Ahmad 'Umar said about Brigadier General Ahmad 'Abdul-Wahhab, brother Jamil, and Professor Ibrahim Khalil. There is no doubt that they have added knowledge to our library which we did not have before. May Allah reward all of them handsomely and may Allah bless them with more of His knowledge.

I have said all I have to say, and I ask Allah's forgiveness for myself, for all of you and for all Muslims from every sin. Please seek His forgiveness, for He is Ever-Forgiving Ever-Merciful.

Wa as-salamu 'alaykum wa rahmatu Allahi wa barakatuh.

Concluding Comments by Professor Ibrahim Khalil Ahmad, on Behalf of His Colleagues

In the name of Allah, Ever Beneficent, Ever Merciful. All praise is due to Allah, Lord of the Worlds. May Allah's peace and blessings be upon our leader, Muhammad, his family and his Companions.

This is actually the place for my beloved brother, Dr. Muhammad Jamil Ghazi, to speak. He is the one who has stayed away from his children for five consecutive months, inviting

---
[1] Qur'an 42:52.
[2] Qur'an 28:56.

people to Islam. He has spared no effort to convey the truth to others; thus this podium really belongs to him. However, he prefers that I speak on his behalf. I thank him for his confidence and trust.

Your Excellency of the office of the Religious Attaché of the Saudi Embassy, Your Eminence, Rear Admiral Ibrahim Ahmad 'Umar, representing the Democratic Republic of Sudan:

I would like to talk about two issues only, not three: first, about the danger from missionary organizations in Muslim countries, and second, about the strength of Islam, which is growing in spite of the obstacles and schemes hatched by the missionaries.

Perhaps the presence of the number of people before us and those who have embraced Islam is conclusive proof that these young people had fallen under some heavy influence that made them forget their way of life, their Islam, their country. Then they went astray, not knowing the right way for themselves, until they were guided to come here. We came here, yet we never said that we can guide people or do something to them. Certainly the only one who can guide is Allah, Most Glorified, Most Exalted. We are like the farmer who sows seeds; the development of these seeds and their fruition is in Allah's hands.

You have already seen some of these blossoming flowers. But through them I see thousands and thousands of Sudanese who have fallen prey to colonialism. All these people must come back to Islam with much strength and happiness.

Missionary work is conducted in five centers: schools and educational institutions, hospitals, homes, sports clubs, and open areas such as streets and various crowds, where the missionary worker goes from street to street, from town to town and from house to house.

What Jesus once said to the Jews is also true of these missionary workers. He said, "Woe to you, scribes and Pharisees who show off because you travel on land and sea to win one person. When you catch him you make him a candidate for Hell much more than yourselves."

People, the mission of calling others to Islam must be recognized and reassessed. There has to be a plan instituted to do

Muslim-Christian Dialogue

away with this danger embodied in the missionary delegations present in our Islamic lands. I say this from experience. I was in the University of Asyut in 1976 C.E., where I gave a lecture to the students of the University. The first lecture was about Prophet Muhammad (Allah's peace and blessings be upon him) in the Torah and the Injil. The second lecture was about Jesus (may Allah's peace be upon him) in the New Testament and the Noble Qur'an.

I proved irrefutably that Jesus (may Allah's peace be upon him) was not crucified or killed. The evidence for this came from the Gospels themselves. Based on this, any concept or belief founded on the Crucifixion could only be false. Naturally, anything based on falsehood likewise could only be false. After all, Allah Himself is capable of forgiving people! Besides, which requires more ability or power, creation of the heavens and the earth or forgiving a human being? Many Qur'anic verses confirm that Allah, Most Glorified, is Ever Forgiving, Ever Merciful.

In the Gospel, Jesus (may Allah's peace be upon him) invites to the concept of the Oneness of God. He never claimed that he was the son of God, god incarnate, or anything like it. Jesus (may Allah's peace be upon him) only confirmed that the Holy Spirit was one of Allah's angels. Jesus never said that this Holy Spirit was the third person in a Trinity, such that it is a third part of God or Allah, Most Glorified, Most Exalted.

Any intelligent person, when he/she thinks with his/her mind, can only conclude that the concept of the Trinity completely contradicts all reason, knowledge, and the pure Unity of Allah.

Congratulations to our brothers for entering the fold of Islam.

When I spoke in Asyut—I can confirm everything true in your presence—seventeen young people of the University of Asyut immediately and boldly declared their entrance into the fold of Islam.

The second statement I want to make is, dear brothers, Allah, Most Glorified, Most Exalted, has guided you to Islam. When Dr. Jamil Ghazi requested me to speak to you it was so I could appear as an example for you. When I embraced Islam, I did not do so accidentally or abruptly; rather I began studying Islam, its creed, its laws, and its code of morals. I studied it from the beginning of 1955 C.E. to the end of 1959 C.E., i.e., for five consecutive years. I did that until I was sure and then I declared my Islam. I immediately felt that Islam obligated me to one crucial responsibility, which was to convey this message to all and invite people to the message that there is none worthy of worship except Allah, and Muhammad is the Prophet of Allah.

For this gathering, I would like to go back in time to before 1955 C.E. Back then I was one of the major leaders of disbelief. I used to misguide Muslim youth. Perhaps today, Allah, Most Glorified, wants to reassure me, when I see these young people embracing Islam, that He truly has forgiven my past sins. I say to you, beloved young people, you must develop a comprehensive understanding of Islam. Whoever among you has a certain amount of knowledge and understanding should put forth all his efforts to help his Muslim brothers.

I wish you all the best, and much success and happiness in the shade of Islam, the religion of truth, righteousness and certainty.

Wa as-salamu 'alaykum wa rahmatu Allahi wa barakatuh.

Muslim-Christian Dialogue

References

Muslim References

1. Al-Bukhari, Muhammad Ibn Isma'il (d. 256 AH). *Al-Jami' Sahih Al-Bukhari*.
2. Ghazi, Dr. Muhammad Jamil. *Dumu'un Qadimah* (Ancient Tears).
3. Al-Hindi, 'Ala ad-Din 'Ali Ibn Husam ad-Din. *Kanz al-'Umal fi as-Sunan wa al-Aqwal* (Treasure of the Workers in the Sunan and Statements).
4. Al-Hindi, Shaykh Rahmatullah. *Izhar al-Haqq* (Bringing out the Truth).
5. Ibn Kathir, Abu Al-Fida' Isma'il Ibn 'Umar Ad-Dimishqi, 'Imad ad-Din (d. 774 AH). *Tafsir Ibn Kathir* (Commentaries of Ibn Kathir).
6. Ibn Al-Qayyim, Shams ad-Din. Muhammad Ibn Abu Bakr Shams ad-Din. *Hidayat al-Hayara* (Guidance for the Perplexed).
7. Ibn al-Qayyim, Shams ad-Din Al-Jawziyyah. *Zad al-Ma'ad fi Hadyi Khayr al-'Ibad* (Provision for the Hereafter from the Guidance of the Best Worshipper).
8. Ibn Taymiyyah, Ahmad Ibn Abdul-Halim (d. 728 AH). *Al-Furqan bayna Awliya' Ar-Rahman wa Awliya' Ash-Shaytan* (The Criterion Between the Allies of the Merciful and the Allies of Satan).
9. Ibn Taymiyyah, Shaykh al-Islam Ibn Taymiyyah Ahmad b. Abdul-Halim Ibn Abdus-Salam (d. 727 AH). *Al-Jawwab as-Sahih liman Badalla Din al-Masih* (A Reliable Answer to Those Who Changed the Religion of Christ).
10. Al-Khatib, 'Abdul-Karim. *Al-Masih fi at-Tawrah wa al-Injil wa al-Qur'an* (Christ in the Torah, the Gospel, and the Qur'an).
11. Muslim Ibn Hajjaj Al-Qushayri (d. 279 AH). *Sahih Muslim Ibn Hajjaj*.
12. An-Nasa'i, Ahmad Ibn Shu'ayb (d. 303 AH). *Sunan An-Nasa'i*.
13. Al-Qurtubi. *Tafsir Al-Qurtubi*.

14. At-Tirmidhi, Abu 'Isa Muhammad Ibn 'Isa. *Sunan At-Tirmidhi.*
15. Shalibi, Mutawalli Yusuf. *Adwa'un 'ala al-Masihiyyah* (Rays of Light on Christianity). Ad-Dar Al-Kuwaitiyyah.
16. .... *Tarikh al-'Aqidah.*

Non-Muslim References

1. Caird, George. *Saint Luke.* Penguin Books. London, 1963.
2. Dodd, C.H. *The Parables of the Kingdom.* Fontana Books. London, 1964.
3. *Encyclopedia Americana*, 1959 C.E.
4. *Encyclopedia Britannica*, 1960 C.E.
5. Fenton, John. Dean, College of Divinity of England. *Saint Matthew.* Penguin Books. London, 1963.
6. Grant, F.C. Professor of Divinity, United Institute of Divinity, N.Y. *The Gospels: Their Origin and Their Growth.* Faber and Faber. London, 1957.
7. Harnack, Adolph. Professor of Church History, University of Berlin. *The History of Dogma.* Constable and Co. London. 1961.
8. Lanczkowski, Guntar. Lecturer in History of Religions, University of Heidlberg. *Sacred Writings.* Fontana Books. London, 1963.
9. MacKinnon, D. M., et al. *Objections to Christian Belief.* Constable and Co. London. 1963.
10. Marsh, John. Dean, Mansfield College Oxford, Member, Central Committee, World Council of Churches. *Saint John.* Penguin Books. London, 1963.
11. Muir, Sir William. *The Life of Muhammad.*
12. Nineham, Dennis. D.D. London University, Chief Editor of the Penguin Series. *Saint Mark.* Penguin Books. London, 1963.
13. (author unkn.). *The Lost Books of the Bible.* World Publishing Co. N.Y. 1926.